R.H. Ture

D1144766

THE OLD TIME STARS'
Book of
MONOLOGUES

All rights reserved. No part of this publication may be reproduced, stored in a retrieval system or transmitted in any form or by any means, electronic, mechanical, photocopying, recording, or otherwise, without the prior permission of the Copyright owner, Reynolds Music.

THE OLD TIME STARS'
Book of
MONOLOGUES

300 monologues written or performed by CHESNEY ALLEN ☐ ARTHUR ASKEY ☐ H. M. BURNABY ☐ ALBERT CHEVALIER
GRACIE FIELDS ☐ CYRIL FLETCHER ☐ WILL FYFFE ☐ GEORGE GROSSMITH ☐ MILTON HAYES ☐ HARRY HEMSLEY
STANLEY HOLLOWAY ☐ NOSMO KING ☐ NORMAN LONG ☐ ERNEST LONGSTAFFE ☐ ELLA RETFORD ☐ SAX ROHMER
SUZETTE TARRI ☐ JACK WATSON ☐ ALBERT WHELAN ☐ BRANSBY WILLIAMS and many others

WOLFE PUBLISHING LIMITED
10 EARLHAM STREET LONDON WC2

The monologues contained in this volume
are published singly, with music, by Reynolds Music, who will supply a catalogue and
price list on request.
    Write to: Reynolds Music, c/o Keith
Prowse Music Publishing Co. Ltd., 28/42
Banner Street, London EC2.

ISBN 72340440 2
© Reynolds Music 1971
Reprinted 1972

Typesetting by Print Origination Liverpool

Printed in Great Britain by
Redwood Press Limited, Trowbridge, Wiltshire

CONTENTS

5

7

8

9

10

INTRODUCTION

The Monologue—the self-contained, stand-up recitation as distinct from a soliloquy incorporated in a longer dramatic work—was shaped by the music hall.

Though its ancestry lay in the broadsheets and street recitations of the 18th and early 19th century, its form, content and presentation were moulded by the music hall as positively as were the popular songs of Victorian and Edwardian England.

Like the music hall song, the monologue has earned a special place in the folk art of Britain's urban industrial society. It was the poetry of the working class. It reflected their attitudes, affirmed their values—or, rather, the values their betters had conditioned them into accepting. It acted sometimes, through laughter or tears as a safety valve and at others, through fatalism or bathos, as a sop or an opiate.

The monologue thrived on adversity, domestic or international. The harder the times, the nearer the threat or actuality of war, the greater the output of monologues and the more receptive the audiences.

The main appeal of the serious monologue was to the emotions, emotions aroused by patriotism, jingoism or sentimentality—the repressed sentimentality of the strong, silent man doing the things he had to do, or the blatant appeal of a man bereft of wife, sweetheart, child, horse or dog.

There is an element of xeonophobia in some of the monologues. There appear never to have been any Chinese, Negroes or Spaniards, only Chinks, Niggers and Dagoes. And there appear never to have been any clean specimens of these gentlemen.

Take, for instance, the uncompromising start to *The Whitest Man I know:*

> *He's a-cruisin' in a pearler with a dirty nigger crew,*
> *A' buying pearls and copra for a stingy Spanish Jew.*

Charming . . .

To have deleted such references, however, or to have omitted the monologue altogether, would have been to detract from a collection which has a good deal of intrinsic social and historical interest. To anyone offended by the references, our apologies, and the consolation that the times they are a-changing.

How much times *have* changed can be gauged by looking at some of the attitudes expressed.

The jingoism of *The Answer of the Anzacs*, for example. There is old mother lion on Dover cliffs having nasty things done to her by the German eagle. Suddenly a hundred thousand cubs come sailing 12,000 miles to her defence. Sounds as if Winnie the Pooh should have been in charge of the fleet.

13

There is the dated cockney whine of *Castles In The Air:*

> *'I'm just a simple scull'ry maid. I'm wot they calls no class.'*

and of *The Char's Lament:*

> *'Life ain't much catch for the likes of me.*
> *It's just a matter of scrubbing.'*

If ever there was a case for Women's Lib., sentiments like these provide it.

Another fatalistic attitude is that of the down-and-out in *'Arf a Cigar:*

> *'You can 'ave your cigars but I wouldn't change places*
> *Wiv the chap as threw this one away.'*

Not 'arf, he wouldn't.

The strong-silent-man-in-the-Great-Outdoors syndrome is illustrated quite chillingly in *By The Yukon Trail:*

> *'There are dead men's bones;*
> *And the cold wind moans;*
> *And the howl of the wolf in counter-tones*
> *And God's hand over all.'*

It gets near to self-parody in Robert Service's *The Shooting of Dan McGrew:*

> *'Back of the bar, in a solo game, sat Dangerous Dan McGrew,*
> *And watching his luck was his light o' love, the lady that's known as Lou.'*

With *The Green Eye of the Little Yellow God,* the swift appearance of a thousand parodies was inevitable. Mad Carew's combination of infatuation, exhibitionism, sacrilege, larceny and pure stupidity makes him the perfect target. He must have turned enough times in his grave by now to have shoved the little marble cross halfway up Annapurna.

For all of this, however, the monologue still appeals, still survives. Though it has disappeared from the mass entertainment scene, it is still heard nightly in clubs, pubs and knees-ups.

It survives because it is simple, uncomplicated, unsophisticated and peculiarly honest. It strikes an attitude, tells a story. The teller stands up, says his piece, and gets off, leaving behind him laughter, tears, or breasts swelling with noble sentiment.

Let's hope we never get too clever for it.

Cliff Parker

ADMIRAL'S ORDERS

BY GEORGE ELLIS and HERBERT TOWNSEND 1926

The Admiral gave the order,
 "Fleet will sail at three",
The Flag-lieutenant scrawled a chit,
 The Signal-yeoman jumped to it,
And answering pennants did their bit:
 "Fleet will sail at three",
On battleship and cruiser
 Far flung across the sea,
Bugles rang and whistles blew,
 Orders filtered down and through,
Seamen cursed—as seamen do—
 "Off agin at three!"
The Cap'en read the order:
 "Just my luck," said he,
"Does my round of golf *right* in,
 Feel like driving on the pin,
Every putt would hit the tin,
 Now we're off at three."
The Engineer-Commander,
 A wily bird was he,
"Hang it, my repairs, you know,
 But take your knitting down below,
And make the demned old scrapheap go,
 Full steam up for three."
The Senior Sub. was furious,
 "Filthy luck," said he,
"Have to wire my fancy gear,
 Sorry cannot lunch, old dear,
Can't desert, should get thick ear,
 Think of me at three."
Leading-stoker 'Awkins,
 A mirthful man was 'e,

He mustered all his watch below,
    And said "I suppose you matlows know
This blinkin' clankin' rattlin' wall-eyed
    Bilge-tank sails at three?"
Able-seaman Murphy,
    Slapped his thigh with glee:
"Faith 'tis Bridget that will bawl,
    For when tonight I go to call,
'Tis me that won't be there at all!
    Indade we're off at three!"
The Admiral gave the order,
    "Fleet will sail at three".
Dead to time in smooth progression.
    Moved the long grey grim procession,
Silent duty's swift confession:
    "Fleet had sailed at three".

THE AERONAUTS

BY EDWIN JOHN   *1936*

Young Arty, owd Bill's nephew, won a prize in t'
        football sweep
    And thought he'd buy an aeroplane, and got one
        on the cheap.
He called on Bill t' next Sunday, his ideas were
        romantic
    He said "Hop in t' plane Uncle, let's fly across
        Atlantic!"
Bill said "All right, that suits me lad, Atlantic, how
        far's that?"
    Art said "About four thousand miles." Says Bill "I'll
        fetch me hat."
Young Art took off in gradely style, tho' only a
        beginner,
    Bill's missus saw them off and shouted "Don't be
        late for dinner!"

16

They'd been aloft for several hours when owd Bill
    gave a sigh,
"What's up Uncle?" says Arty. Bill replies, "Eh, lad!
    I'm dry!"
"Could do' a sup?" grins Art, "O.K. we'll have
    one wi'out fail,"
    And out he fetched some bread and cheese and
        onions and bottled ale.
It didn't take them long to finish food, and put
    back drinks..
    Then Arty waggled joy stick while owd Bill had
        forty winks.
T' next day Bill were gettin' bored; "Still nowt
    but sea!" he cried,
    "What are we crossin' this 'ere for, and what's
        on t' other side?"
"America's not far," says Art. Bill grunts "I'm
    very glad,
    For I'm gettin' that there dry again, so just step
        on it, lad!"
That afternoon they sighted land. "By gum!" says Bill,
      "That's queer!
    Who's yon big lass in t' nightgown on t' water over theer?"
'"That's Liberty, we're near New York," young Art
    had got it pat;
    "She's a buxom wench," grinned Bill and politely raised
        his hat!
They flew above the skyscrapers, the city were
    a big un,
    Bill weren't very impressed wi' it, he'd sooner live
        i' Wigan.
They landed in a field near town, said Arty, "There!
    we've done it!"
    They'd just climb'd out, when up there roared a car
        wi' armour on it!
Some sour lookin' chaps jumped out, and each one
    had a gun;
    T' leader shouts, "Hands up! I'm Public Enemy Number
        One!
Fork out your dough, you suckers, and make it good
    and snappy!"

Bill handed over one and three while looking
    far from happy.

Young Arty had no brass at all, he'd spent all his on t'
    plane,
    So gangsters cussed and swore a bit, and then
        drove off again.

Bill cussed an' all, and swore of U.S.A. he'd
    have his whack;
    "Young Art," he said, "turn plane round, lad, and let's
        be flyin' back!"

And so they started on their way, and Bill heard
    Arty yell
    "T' engine's missin'!" "What" cried Bill, "have they
        pinched that as well?"

That night up sprung a hurricane and Bill got quite
    a fright,
    A lightnin' flash sing'd his moustache, it was a
        ruddy night!

It blew and blew for hours on end, they rocked and
    pitched and tossed;
    Young Art though he said nowt to Bill, thought them
        as good as lost.

T' climax came next afternoon, they could see nowt for rain
    When suddenly gust of wind hits 'em and blows
        both wings off plane!

"Jump out, Uncle" roars Arty, "and use thy parachute!"
    Bill looked a bit askance at this, but nodded
        remainin' mute.

He jumped and Arty jumped an' all and everything
    went well;
    "I wonder where we'll land?" shouts Art. " 'Appen,"
        says Bill, "in 'ell."

They both descended graceful like, they didn't land
    too hard,
    Bill blinked around and said "Blow me this 'ere's
        me own back yard!"

Bill's missus then comes out and shouts in voice that
    rattles winders
    "D'you call this bein' home to time? Thy dinner's
        burnt to cinders!"

18

"But Aunty," said young Art, when they'd come inside
    out o' t'draught,
"We've flown to U.S.A. and back!" She said, "Don't
    talk so daft!"
At pub that night they stood pints round and told their
    tale of glory
But them as heard just shouted "Liar" or "Tell me the
    old, old story!"
And though they often tell this yarn, and ne'er a
    detail miss
They've never convinced nobody, not from that day to this!

AFTERWARDS

BY LEONARD POUNDS and CUTHBERT CLARK   *1919*

Now the God of War has ceased to rule,
    And I'm back at my desk again.
The saddle gives place to a well-worn stool,
    And the rifle makes way for the pen.
The tick of the clock on the office wall
    Displaces the big guns' roar,
The 'phone-bell has ousted the trumpet-call,
    A soldier am I no more.
The past few years now appear a dream;
    An illusion vast and grand,
The maxims' rattle and shrapnel's scream
    Just echoes of Slumberland.
As I lie abed in the early morn
    I wake from sleep profound,
As without on the wind, most clearly borne,
    I imagine I hear this sound:-
Even that call, which I used to hate
    The command to get out of bed
Inspires regret, and a yearning great

For the life that is past and dead.
I turn with a sigh to resume my sleep,
    But as soon as I doze once more,
My heart gives a throb, and from bed I leap
    At the sound of this call of yore:
"All you who are able, come off to the stable,
    And water your horses and give them some corn."
I return to bed for an hour or so,
    And at eight I rise at last,
Then again, as I down to breakfast go,
    Comes that phantom trumpet blast:—
"Come to the cook-house door, boys, Come to the
        cook-house door."
    When I reach the office so grim and bare,
And a start at work have made,
    I long to "slope arms" with a ruler there,
And the paste-pot's a hand grenade.
    Inside the ledger I next will look,
But no figures I seem to see,
    The only entry inside the book
Reads "Kit inspection at 3."
    And the almanac, I do declare,
Reveals itself to me
    As a charge-sheet shewing just why I'm there
"Awarded life-long C. B."
    As the charwoman passes the manager's lair,
With a slov'nly gait,
    I'm impelled to shout "March to attention there!"
Or "Keep that back up straight!"
    I collect my thoughts with a weary smile,
And endeavour to settle down
    To examining bills on a rusty file,
And I conjure a "business" frown.
    Here, 'mid the City traffic's row,
How I miss my dear old "gee!"
    I wonder who grooms and rides him now
Does he wonder what's happened to me?
    My body is here, but my soul's afar;
It exists in the stormy past.
    The faces of comrades remain with me
And will do until the last.
    When discharge from the Army of Life comes round
20

And Death stands guard at the door,
　　I shall hear "Lights out" distinctly sound,
As it did in the world-wide war.

AIN'T IT FAIR

BY H. M. BURNABY and HAROLD ARPTHORP　　　　　*1935*

This Country's goin' to the dawgs, bin goin' years
　　and more,
　And so is this 'ere pipe o' mine, the blinkin' thing
　　won't draw.
'Ere's yer 'umble blowin' dahn it, suckin' of it,
　　is it right?
　Struth I bought it *noo* at Woolwich for a tanner,
　　Toosday night.
Money wasted—daylight robb'ry—A regular de-loosion
　　and a snare,
　It's a crime ter tempt the pocket of a honest workin'
　　bloke,
So 'e's got to blow 'is brains aht every time 'e wants
　　a smoke.
　Yet somebody's responsible—'oo is it? 'oo can tell?
Wot's that, get an 'airpin? Yerss! 'oo orf of my
　　old gel?
　Ow can I when she's shingled? There's times when Life
　　is 'ell.
Oh, Lor limme, Lizer, Ain't it fair?
　Yerss! when a feller's dyin' fer a smoke, its
　　pretty rough,
'Ere's me 'bacca—'ere's me lighter, full o' this
　　'ere petrol stuff.
　A bran noo flint and wick an' all all ready
　　nice an' pat.
Nah! if I could fix me pipe up—Blimey! nah wot's
　　wrong with that?

Done it on me—Blinkin' myst'ry—
Driving anybody to despair.
There—that's got it, Nah me little pipe's all right
And I'll fix this blinkin' lighter if I stops 'ere
'arf the night.
I tell yer when it comes ter troubles I can find a few,
Whas-say? Take a mahthful of me 'bacco for a chew.
Wiv teeth like mine? I don't fink, blimey, this
ain't arf a do,
Oh Lor lumme, Lizer, Ain't it fair?
Wot I sez no matter where yer goes there's suffink wrong.
I put some matches in me pocket when I come along
Yerss! 'ere they are now p'raps I'll get a blinkin'
smoke at last.
Good matches these blarst!
Well! I arsks yer Can yer beat it? Ain't that enough
to make a hangel swear?
I've been messin'with this pipe an' lighter, till I'm
in a sweat,
And that's wot's made me trahsis damp an' got the matches
wet.
Blow pipes aht? I've got strength enough to blow
a 'urricane.
These matches, *AND* this lighter I could chuck 'em
dahn the drain.
'Ullo! nah what abaht it? Struth! me pipe's blocked up
again!
Oh Lor lumme, Lizer, Ain't it fair?

ANSWERED

BY ELLA WHEELER WILCOX and GEORGE HAY   *1914*

Good-bye—yes, I am going.
   Sudden? Well, you are right.
But a startling truth came home to me
   With sudden force last night
What is it? Shall I tell you?—
   Nay, that is why I go.
I am running away from the battlefield,
   Turning my back on the foe.
Riddles? You think me cruel!
   Have you not been most kind?
Why, when you question me like that,
   What answer can I find?
You fear you failed to amuse me,
   Your husband's friend and guest,
Whom he bade you entertain and please—
   Well, you have done your best,
Then why, you ask, am I going!
   A friend of mine abroad,
Whose theories I have been acting upon,
   Has proven himself a fraud.
You have heard me quote from Plato
   A thousand times, no doubt;
Well, I have discovered he did not know
   What he was talking about.
You think I am speaking strangely?
   You cannot understand?
Well, let me look down into your eyes,
   And let me take your hand.
I am running away from danger—
   I am flying before I fall;
I am going because with heart and soul
   I love you—That is all.
There, now, you are white with anger.
   I knew it would be so.
You should not question a man too close
   When he tells you he must go.

THE ANSWER OF THE ANZACS

BY LAWRENCE EASTWOOD and EDGAR ROOKSBY   1916

There was once a mother Lion,
   And she stood on Dover cliffs,
Where the water wags and washes,
   Where the salt the Sea-Horse sniffs.
And she growled: "The clouds look angry,
   They'll burst in storm today—
And all my cubs are distant,
   Twelve thousand miles away."
And mother stood there all alone,
   And mother *meant* to stay,
Though all her cubs were distant,
   Twelve thousand miles away.
Then rose a mighty eagle,
   And it screeched at Dover cliffs,
Where the water wags and washes,
   Where the salt the Sea-Horse sniffs.
"I'll break you, mother lion,
   Though you're mighty proud today,
Don't count upon your cubs, my dear,
   Kids don't turn out that way."
Still mother faced the storm alone,
   For *that* was mother's way.
But her cubs were calling to her—
   Twelve thousand miles away.
Then hove in sight a mighty fleet,
   That made for Dover cliffs—
Where the water wags and washes,
   Where the salt the Sea-Horse sniffs.
And from that mighty fleet there sprang
   The "Anzacs" in array—
A hundred thousand cubs
   From twelve thousand miles away.
And mother locked them to her breast,
   Then thundered 'cross the bay—
"My cubs are all around me,
   They're by my side today;

24

You've blundered, master eagle,
And your blunder's deep and vast;
For mother England's mighty cubs
Will bring you down—*at last!*

AREN'T MEN FUNNY?

BY DION LANE and HILDA BERTRAM   *1924*

When I was quite a little girl my mother used to say:—
    "Aren't men funny?"
Now I'm grown up I say the same thing twenty times a day,
    "Aren't men funny?"
They're as full of contradictions as an egg is full of meat.
    They're shy, they're hot, they're cold, they're sour and yet
        they're sweet;
They're one big great conundrum; and so I'll just repeat
    "Aren't men funny?"
They'll gaze into their sweetheart's eyes, (not knowing
        love is blind,)
    Aren't men funny?
And use up all the words of love in "Nuttall's" they
        can find,
    Aren't men funny?
They'll kiss her sixteen times an hour; her lips,
        her eyes, her cheek,
    But, when they're wed, she, feeling "down," one little
        kiss would seek,
He'll say, "But, dear old girl, you know, I kissed you twice
        last week".
    Aren't men funny? STINGY!
He'll rule the land with iron hand, and yet his baby's "boss,"
    Aren't men funny?
He'll *die* for *his* opinions, if his wife gives hers, he's cross,
    Aren't men funny?

25

He says "I love the girl who's made of real sterling stuff,
   With commonsense and brains; if she's got those, well,
      that's enough."
And yet he'll go and marry some young giggling bit of fluff;–
   Aren't men funny? THEY'RE ALL ALIKE!
They say it's man's prerogative to grumble and to grouse,
   Aren't men funny?
The dinner's cold; a button's off; all's wrong about the house,–
   Aren't men funny?
They'll storm and tear, (p'reps even *swear*,) declare
      they will not stay.
   They'll dash off to the "Pictures," or perhaps go to a play,
Bring home a box of chocolates, and kiss our tears away,–
   Aren't men funny? THEY ALL DO IT!
They're woman's greatest blessing, tho' they cause *most* of her
      troubles,
   Aren't men funny?
They don't like "soft soap" yet you'll find them always
      "blowing bubbles,"
   Aren't men funny?
They'll shed their blood like water to defend their native soil;
   Wounds they simply glory in, from nothing they recoil,–
At *home* they have a fit if on their neck they have a boil,
   Aren't men funny? LOOK OUT FOR SQUALLS!
But still, with all their little ways, and though we still must ask
   Aren't men funny?
We cannot do without them, tho' often they're "a task,"
   Aren't men funny?
We women do our level best, at all times, to impress them,
   Tease them, scold them, flatter them, and sometimes
      caress them:-
Deep in our heart of hearts we say, (and mean it too,–) God
      bless them, BUT
   Aren't men funny? I ASK YOU

ARF A CIGAR

BY MARTYN HERBERT and HERBERTE JORDAN   *1925*

Performed by Will Deller

I've found a cigar, leastways, 'arf a cigar,
 Well it's only a stump, still it's there.
Not a bad sort o' find when you're down on your luck;
 It'll last twenty minutes, wiv care.
Things 'as bin pretty bad, an' I'm very near broke,
 I've not 'ad a smoke all the day.
It don't run to cigars, so 'ere's jolly good luck
 To the chap as threw this one away.
I shan't 'arf cause a stir as I stroll in the Park,
 (I shall probably sleep there tonight,)
Obnobbin' wiv some o' the swells as I know,
 Well, that is, I know 'em by sight.
It gives you ideas when you're smokin' cigars,
 I shan't lunch at Lockhart's to-day
I shall dine with Duke 'Umphrey, an' kid I'm a torf,
 Like the chap as threw this one away.
Very likely the feller as threw this away
 'As troubles enough of his own;
A position to keep up, a 'alf dozen kids,
 An' a wife as won't let 'im alone.
So I dare say I'm 'appier, when all's said an' done,
 Wiv me shag an' me dirty ole clay.
You can 'ave your cigars, but I wouldn't changes places
 Wiv the chap as threw this one away.

ATOMS

BY E. A. SEARSON and CUTHBERT CLARKE   *1923*

When you've looked up in the heavens on a cold
  and frosty night,
With its myriads of stars that give their scintillating light,

27

And have realized another world is centred in each star,
  Have you thought at times, with awe, how insignificant
      we are?
If you've moved in vastly places where all nature's
      stern and wild,
  Seen the Alps or Himalayas with their miles of mountain
      piled,
Watched the torrents of Niagara or the sands of the Sudan,
  What an atom in the universe appears the puny man.
For the space the psalmist gives us still we strut upon our
      stage,
  And we play our little dramas, and we fuss and fume and
      rage,
Playing comedy or tragedy throughout our little hour,
  While nature, all majestic, is unchanging in its power.
Yes, we feel our insignificance, it's proper that we should
  And with troubled hearts we're apt, at times, to wonder
      what's the good.
Wonder what's the good of anything, why struggle on and fuss?
  Where's the value, in this mighty scheme, of microbes
      such as us?
There's an answer, though, good people, if you've reached
      this train of thought,
  Rest assured that you *are* wanted, you are not put here
      for naught:
You are links in this creation, you've a mission, it is clear,
  Any shirking, I feel certain, puts some detail out of gear.
It is not in all we mortals to achieve the thing
      that's great,
  To win battles, found religions, build an Empire, rule
      a state,
We can do good, though, in little things, help others, play
      the game,
  Try and leave this old world happier than it was before
      we came.
You may underrate this gospel, think it scarcely worth
      the while,
  Doubt the value of the hand-squeeze, of the cheery word
      or smile,
But the little kindness passes on, with tendency to grow,
  Drop a pebble in the water, watch how far the ripples go.

Never mind about our littleness, there's no need to be cowed,
   We are put here in God's image, and that ought to make us
     proud,
So in our little pilgrimage, until we journey west,
   Let us trust the mighty Architect, just that, and do our best.

AUCTION OF LIFE

BY GEORGE ARTHURS and GIL ROY   *1928*

Performed by Fred Lewis

Life is like a game of Auction Bridge,
   You shuffle and you deal!
But whether you happen to cut high or low,
   You soon will discover, as through life you go,
Some men do the calling, while others say "No!"
   And pass!
You meet a young lady whose features are fair,
   And you think, as partners, you'll make a fine pair,
So you fall in love and you quickly declare
   "Two Hearts!"
Then you press your suit, oh, life's simply grand,
   She leads—to a jeweller's shop in the Strand,
And then every time she exposes her hand,
   "Diamonds!"
You quickly get married, 'mid cheering and grins,
   And you feel like Dummy when that phase begins.
But eighteen months after the doctor says "Twins!"
   You're doubled!
But soon the love game gets a bit slow,
   You miss your nights out with the boys, don't you know.
Your partner declares you've revoked when you go
   TO CLUBS!
Then somebody else trumps your trick on the sly,
   He plays his cards well and she bids you good-bye.
Then, full of remorse, you go to her and cry
   "Fresh deal!"
But all will come right and the rubber you'll gain
   If you will play fair. Have no fear of chicane,

29

When you kiss and make up, then you obtain
  "Grand Slam!"
So scorn all conventions and never play small,
  When you keep the score and the game is Love all,
And honours you'll gain when you die, and the call
  Is a *SPADE!*

"BABY"

BY GREATREX NEWMAN and ALICE PARDOE   *1926*

A handful of nothing, dropped down from the skies,
  A wee turned-up nose, two questioning eyes;
Two chubby hands, and the quaintest of grins,
  Some silks and some satins, two BIG safety pins.
A life to be lived, with its laughter and tears,
  A mother's fond hopes, and a mother's dread fears;
A mother's sweet thoughts, and a mother's soft prayers—
To send all the sunshine, and banish the cares.
A little pink dot, in a cosy wee cot;—
  A warm little fire to undress him;—
A tip-toe to peep, at his smile when asleep;—
  His Majesty BABY— God Bless Him!

A BACK-WOOD PENANCE

BY HARRY KENNETH WYNNE and CUTHBERT CLARKE   1915
Performed by Bransby Williams

He's away across the Prairie,
   Growing lean and lank and hairy,
Slinging booze across a counter in some hole that God's
      forsook;
   But the Angel who's recording
Knows the secret that he's hoarding,
   And he's got a credit balance in the Lord Almighty's Book
They had followed him from Dover,
   Half the length of Europe over,
Till they thought they had him corner'd near to Barcelona
      Town,
   Then they drew their meshes tighter,
But they found he was a fighter,
   And he slipp'd between their fingers, tho' they nearly
      ran him down.
He had laid his plans so neatly
   That he disappear'd completely,
And they couldn't spot his hiding, tho' they followed ev'ry
      clue,
   Till, at last, tho' ceaseless working,
They'd a hint that he was lurking
   Somewhere round the River Niger, not so far from
      Timbuctoo.
Then they thought that they could find him,
   For a trail he'd left behind him,
And they traced him back to Turkey, and from there to
      Aden Bay,
   But he dar'd not cut it finer,
So he slunk aboard a liner,
   And I found him, sick and helpless, in the streets of
      Mandalay.
Then I fed him from my table,
   And as well as I was able
I nurs'd him thro' a fever, hiding him the while from sight;
   Why he came remain'd a myst'ry,
Till I chanc'd to learn his hist'ry

31

As I watch'd beside his pillow thro' the silent, tropic night.
He spoke in rambling phrases when the fever touch'd his brain
   Of a girl he'd lov'd in England; and his suit was not
      in vain.
But her brother, high in office, had been brib'd, and
       gave away
   A diplomatic secret it was treason to betray.
The girl, of course, knew nothing, so to save her from
      disgrace
   Her lover took the onus in her guilty brother's place;
He fled away from justice, and an outcast he became,
   A hunted, homeless wand'rer, with a slur upon his name.
I saw, as he grew stronger,
   That I could not keep him longer,
Though I begg'd him not to leave me his brave spirit knew
      no rest;
   A handgrip, and we parted,
Then, silently, he started
   To seek a safer hiding in the Backwoods of the West.
So he's far across the Prairie,
   Growing lean and lank and hairy,
Slinging booze across a counter in some hole that God's
      forsook;
   But the Angel who's recording
Knows the secret that he's hoarding,
   And he's got a credit balance in the Lord Almighty's Book.

BEACHCOMBER

BY GERALD MORRISON, TED STEELS and JOE CAREY   *1944*

Somewhere west of Lagos, beneath the blazing sun,
   Shunned by all the decent folk, I'll drink with anyone;
Beachcomber people call me, well, that's just what I am,
   Yet only just a while ago I thought I was a MAN!
Just waiting for the mailboat now, that brings my measly dole,
   So I can buy the golden 'rye' that rots away my soul.

Curse the heat, the sand, the flies, the coolies' awful din,
    Will the mailboat never come?
For God's sake, where's the gin?
    Visions pass before my eyes of what I might have been.
Instead I'm like a leper here, shunn'd as a thing unclean.
    Bah! what does it matter now? What are my affairs,
If I sink down, right down to hell, no one ever cares.
    No tender hand to hold me back, no love, no sympathy;
The only friends that I have got are outcasts, just like me.
    Yet sometimes looking thro' the mist, I seem to see a face,
Golden hair and laughing eyes, in some sweet country place.
    She, whose face I sometimes see was once my promised wife,
Who should have led me onwards to a long successful life.
    God knows how I loved that girl, 'twas heaven for a while,
For I was her devoted slave, I loved her every smile,
    I used to lay awake and build my castles in the air,
And in my dreams then I would kiss her laughing eyes, her hair.
    How she led me on and on, and how I paid the price,
For now I know that I was just a fool in Paradise.
    She made me lose what faith I had in all the human race,
What pettiness and meanness lay behind that angel face!
    'Twas just another shattered dream, then come the
            aftermath;
Her's was the hand that sent me on this God-forsaken path;
    So now I curse where once I blessed, and know I was a fool,
To let a woman wreck my life, and use me as a tool.
    So here I lay to curse and rot, a wastrel, nothing else,
Waiting for the boat that brings me sweet forgetfulness,
    Curse the heat, the sand, the flies, blast the coolies' din,
Will the mailboat ever come?
    For God's sake, where's the gin?

BE A MAN

BY FRANK A. TERRY and HAROLD ARPTHORP   *1935*

Be a man if you can,
   A man's man too.
Have a plan—if you can,
   To pull you through.
Don't walk about with no ambition,
   Don't live on foolish superstition.
Don't trust to luck,
   Get there by pluck,
Be a man—if you can—with a plan.
   You won't get a job if you wait till it comes.
You'll never win battles by beating drums.
   Go into the fight, and fight for your right,
With a plan—like a man—if you can.
   Have you ever watched those big ships go by,
In to the horizon and fade in the sky?
   Do they trust to luck to get there if they can?
Do they heck!
   On the deck—
Is a man with a plan.
   When you feel whacked and there's three rounds to go,
Don't chuck it up—it's easy I know
   The other chap possibly feels just as blue,
Let HIM do the quitting—it mustn't be you.
   Throw out your chest
Make the next round your best,
   And get into your man—with a plan—if you can.
Make life your servant, don't be its slave,
   Fortune you'll find will come to the brave;
Straight from the goalmouth,—make that your aim,
   With an Englishman's motto—"Playing the game;"
BE A MAN—WITH A PLAN—IF YOU CAN!

BIG BELLEW AND THE CHINEE MAID

BY MILTON HAYES and CUTHBERT CLARKE   *1920*

A man was found—stiff, cold and bound,
   On the steps of a 'Frisco pier,
His dead eyes glared, as if Hell had bared
   The nethermost pits of fear;
And this is the story of Big Bellew,
   And a maid—and the Mandarin Hi-Chen-Foo.
Big Bellew ran a risk or two
   In the freights of his leaky scow,
And many a load transhipped, and stowed,
   From the hold to some Chinee dhow,
For the Yellowmen dream, and pay their fee,
   And the trail of the Poppy gets lost at sea.
On one of his jaunts he struck the haunts
   Of the Mandarin—Hi-Chen-Foo—
A venomous Chink, with a lust for drink,
   And the traffic of Big Bellew;
And the Mandarin traded, and paid the toll,
   And the price of his dream was his daughter's soul.
Big Bellew was no beauty, and he wasn't improved that night,
   There was some roughhouse, and a knife was flashed,
And Skipper Bellew got badly gashed,
   And his face showed a fresco the Chinks had done,
But he carried his deal and the maid he'd won,
   And he stuck to his bargain tight.
Then dope went out of favour,
   And running it ceased to pay,
So Big Bellew took a poker joint,
   On the waterfront 'Frisco way,
And a little pale face would oft be seen
   To peep from the door of Bellew's shebeen,
As tho' the tides' eternal roll,
   Had secrets to tell to her heathen soul,
And the zephyrs that soughed thro' the Golden Gate
   Would whisper, "The Gods of the Poppies can wait."
One night, when stakes were mounting high
   And drinks were off the shelf,

A Yellowman came, and watched awhile,
　Then took a hand himself;
And when a Chinee gambles, and at "pay up" hasn't gained,
　There's a jigsaw plot, and a chowchow scheme that a wise
　　man wants explained.
But Big Bellew saw gold to win,
　And the spell of the Poppy was closing in.
The Yellowman came again to play, then brought his friends
　　along,
　And 'twas certain soon that class saloon
Would end as a pigtail jamboroon—
　Chinks upstairs, and chinks below,
Till hardly a white man cared to go,
　And the eyes of the Chinee Maid were bright,
For the Spell of the Poppy was closing tight.
　It came at last—a fake half done—
A curse— and Bellew with a loaded gun,
　But the soul of the big man failed his head,
His brain was drugged with a nameless dread.
　His eyes were fixed on a baleful face
That leered from the door of that Godless place,
　And vengeance from Poppyland faced Bellew,
In the eyes of the Mandrin Hi-Chen-Foo;
　And China makes certain when vengeance is loosed,
And the Curse of the Poppy came home to roost.
　A sudden crash—out goes the light,
A pigtail deftly twisted—tight,
　Then silence thro' the brooding night,
And the Poppy has worked her spell.
　A man was found—stiff, cold and bound,
On the steps of a 'Frisco pier;
　His dead eyes glared, as if Hell had bared
The nethermost pits of fear;
　And this is the story of Big Bellew,
And a maid and the Mandarin Hi-Chen-Foo.

BILL

BY F. CHATTERTON HENNEQUIN and BLANCHE GASTON-MURRAY 1911

He was always big and clumsy and his voice is deep and gruff,
But he has got the kindest heart, although his coat is rough—
He isn't much to look upon, except may be his eyes,
And they are just the softest brown and more than human
wise.
Oh they sold me a pup when I bought my pal,
With a dozen lines or so of pedigree,
But the friendly little hail of your sympathetic tail,
Shows your breeding and your true gentility.
You were not exactly steady—no, your youth was very wild,
Though I nursed you thro' distemper, your behaviour made
me wild.
Your ways were not respectable, your habits they were sad—
Your morals,—don't you wink at me, were most uncommon
bad.
But in every kind of weather, both in sunshine and in rain,
He was content to stick by me in common loss or gain.
I've tramped along this road of life until I couldn't stand,
I've woke to find him close beside, and felt him lick my
hand.
There were women said they loved me, so they did a little
while,
There are friends who when they met me have forgotten
how to smile.
I never let it worry me although they pass me by,
For Bill's a friend, whose love will end, when he lies down
to die.
Don't tell me that you're growing old, for all your muzzle's
grey,
I couldn't do without my pal, to cheer me on the way.
So just you take it easy Bill, there's only you and me—
When one is gone the other will be lonely, don't you see.
Most all the parson taught me I've forgotten but I know,
There was something 'bout a mansion, where the tired
people go,
A place of rest for such as us, away from grief and sin—

37

But if they don't admit you Bill, well I'm not going in—
Oh they sold me a pup when I bought you my pal,
With a dozen lines or so of pedigree,
But the friendly little hail of your sympathetic tail,
Shows your breeding and your gentility.

BILL'S TROMBONE

BY EDWIN JOHN   *1938*

When Bill were late from work one night he hadn't come
            to harm
    But when he did arrive he carried parcel under th' arm.
"What's that?" said owd Bill's missus in a somewhat doubtful
            tone,"
    "I bought it secondhand," said Bill wi' pride, "its
            a trombone!"
That properly set missus off, but Bill didn't dispute her,
    He just ate tea and went upstairs and took his trombone
            tutor.
First blast he gave cracked window pane and it were
            such a row
    T' neighbours thought as somebody were torturin' a cow!
And policeman on his beat outside turned pale and phoned up
            station,
    And streets away folk bunged up ears, there was some
            consternation!
As weeks went by his tone improved and neighbours got
            immune,
    And now and then they even thought they recognised a tune.
A circus come to town one day wi' band trombonist ill,
    And manager were in a sweat until he heard of Bill.
He found him in the "Dog and Duck" and offered him a job,
    Wi' loan of fancy uniform as well as fee five bob
That night in tent Bill looked a treat and music sounded
            grand,
    Especially when Bill were playin' same tune as the band!

38

All Wigan folks was there enn block, Bill's missus were that
        proud,
    She said "Bah Gum! I never knew our Bill could blow that
        loud!"
The star turn of the show were then a furrin' looking chap
    Climbed into cage o' roarin' lions and didn't care
        a rap!
At least he didn't care until the biggest lion made
        bold
    To sock him one in t' lug wi' paw and laid the beggar
        cold!
Then this ferocious animile walked straightway out of cage
    And glared around the circus ring lashin' his tail wi' rage.
There weren't no rush for doors or owt, and all was
        still as still,
    For t' folks was petrified wi' fear, all exceptin' owd Bill.
He climbed down from his seat in t' band and walked
        into the ring,
    And putting trombone next lion's ear, he blew like
        anything!
At this the creature gave a roar, but owd Bill didn't flinch,
    He blew another mighty blast and never gave an inch.
This made the lion blink a bit, he thought as Bill were spoofin',
    And then he let off such a roar as nearly fetched the
        roof in!
Bill looked the lion up and down and said "All right,
        you gump,"
    Then took trombone and blew a noise resemblin t' last
        trump!
He blew trombone clean inside-out, and spellbound folks all
        saw
    T' lion put tail betwixt his legs and touch forelock
        wi' paw.
He gave a coo like little dove, his face were drawn and sad,
    As owd Bill shoved him back in t' cage, and people
        cheered like mad!
And as he stood in t' circus ring before the cheerin' masses,
    He found himself kissed on both cheeks by buxom circus
        lasses!
"Look here, me lad," said missus, when she got Bill home
        that night.
    "Dunna thee play wi' lions no more thee gave me such a
39

fright!
"I'll tell thee what," she added, "I've ne'er heard of such
      a thing
  As kissin' them there hussies in a public circus ring!"
Bill said he wouldn't play no more as his trombone were burst,
    The runnin' cost were far too high in keepin' down
        his thirst!

BLACK ROGER

BY CAROLUS REX   *1922*

Performed by Bransby Williams

Watchin' the tide go out,
  Over the shiny sand,
Leavin' it there, as smooth an' as bare,
  As the back of a baby's 'and!
Only a quarter to twelve.
  Fifteen minutes from now
Afore I can dip my bow sprit
  In a pint at the Bull an' Cow.
After the life I've led.
  Perils by land and sea,
Nobody knows wot a dog I've been,—
  Nobody—not even me!
Think o' the wrecks I've seen,
  Through my spy-glass standin' 'ere.
Think o' the gallant lifeboat lads,
  Wot I've watched from the end o' the pier!
It's a pretty spot—Dozey Bay—
  As any I've been to or seen,
Tho' as I've stood just 'ere for the past forty year
  I don't know *when* I've been!
I knows ev'ry winkle an' crab,
  Wot lives in this part o' the sea.
First thing I says is' "Good mornin', crabs,"
  An the crabs all wink at me!
The pirate of Dozey Bay—

That's wot they calls me down 'ere.
They asks me to pitch yarns of bloodshed an' sich,
    An' they stands me pints o' beer.
I'm the fisherman's sailin' mark,
    Which 'as earned me many a swipe.
Comin' in they all steer in a line with the pier
    An' the end o' my old clay pipe!
Old ladies they offers me tracts—
    An' I makes little children cry
When I leans on the rail an' I pitches my tale
    Of the 'orrible days gone by.
Yes! I was a pirate once—
    That's wot I used to be!
Scuttlin' a boat or cuttin' a throat
    Was all alike to me!
Now that my whiskers is grey,
    It sounds a queer remark
To tell you once I was known I was
    As Black Roger the Ocean Shark!
From Clyde to Vigo Bay—
    Wherever that may be!
You only 'ad to whisper the words
    In pidgin or Portugee.
"Black Roger the Ocean Shark"—
    Lor' lummy, you'd 'ave seen
Strong men feel queer, upset their beer,
    An' ev'ry face turn green!
Mine was a name o' dread.
    Wot a black 'eart I'd got—
Black as my whiskers used to be,
    An' as 'ard as a galleypot.
I owned 'alf the Spanish Main,
    No cat's 'ad so many lives,
I'd a couple o' score of a crew or more,
    An' I 'ad about ninety wives!
There was white 'uns an' brown 'uns too—
    An' some just as black as my boot,
Two dozen was fair, with long golden 'air,
    An' one was as bald as a coot!
Ho! I didn't *know* she was bald.
    I might never 'ave tumbled the game,

Only one night she left 'er thingummyjig
   On top of the wot's-is-name!
There was one 'ad a wooden leg!
   Ah! she was a lucky wife!
I reckon I owe to that timber toe
   As I didn't lose my life.
We was cast away in a boat,
   We'd been wrecked in a dreadful gale.
'Alf barmy with thirst, our 'eads fit to burst,
   When "A sail!" I ollers—"A sail!"
'Ow to attract their heye?
   We was crazy with despair
When I ties my shirt to 'er timber toe
   An' she waves 'er leg in the air!
Watchin' the tide go out
   Good mornin' mum, thanks! Tails win! Tails!—
Ho! the door's open now at the old Bull an' Cow.
   It's time that the tide come in!

BREF

BY LIONEL KING and DORIS PRIME   *1928*

We've got a big window what'd fixed in our house,
   It's as big as, well, I don't know what.
I breathed on it and drawed an old man,
   And my nanny she smacked me a lot.
She picked up a duster and wiped it all off—
   I fink it was nasty of her.
So I pulled back the curatins and shut both my eyes,
   And took a big bref and went "Huh"
'Cos that makes the window all foggy,
   You can write your whole name in a "Huh."
Of course if you draw an awful fat man,
   You must do an awful big "Huh."
And once in the winter the frost came one night,
   And our window got ever so froze,

It looks just like hundreds and fousands of trees,
  They'd growed in the night, I suppose.
I fought they looked pretty and sparkled so bright,
  But I knew they would melt with a "Huh,"
So I crept to the window as nanny came in,
  But before she could catch me, I went "Huh."
And that made the window all foggy,
  Nanny smacked me because I went "Huh"
But when I'm alone, and there's no one about,
  I just please myself and go "Huh"
My daddy is learning to breathe on the glass,
  But he can't get his breath, he's so fat,
He gets out of bed when he finks I'm asleep,
  And he frows up the window—like that.
He shuts up his eyes, and breathes frough his nose,
  Like this:
        (Inhale through nostrils and
        exhale through mouth, as if
        deep breathing at an open window)
But he always forgets that the window's not there,
  So whatever's the good of the Huh?
It can't make the window all foggy,
  If it's up at the top when you Huh,
But my daddy he tries, and he puffs, and he blows,
  But he's not got enough bref to go Huh
So now when they leave me alone in the room,
  They fink I am good, I believe,
I draw lots of horses and funny old men,
  And I wipe 'em all off with my sleeve.
And if they come in, well, I get on the floor,
  And hark to our pussy-cat's purr.
And I play with my toys 'til I hear them go out,
  Then I go to the window and "Huh."
'Cos that makes the window all foggy,
  You can write lots of things in a "Huh"
You try when your nanny's not looking at you.
  It's easy—that's all I do—"Huh."

THE BRIDEGROOM OF ST PIERRE

BY J. MILTON HAYES and R. FENTON GOWER   *1915*

From the side of his bride, in her wedding array,
  To his corps at the front he was ordered away,
And the woman knelt down in an anguish of prayer
  That the saints in their mercy might guard him with care,
And the grim voice of war, booming far thro' the air,
  Mock'd the crucifix watching her pray.
At Liége he did his bit, with his bay'net brawn and wit,
  Ever risking life and limb for Belgium's sake,
But one night the Huns, in hiding, caught him unawares
    whilst riding
  With despatches he had volunteered to take:
Then the news that he was dead reached the bride, who
    bowed her head
  'Neath the figure of the Crucifix, in prayer,
And the patient Lord of Sorrows shared her vigil,
    till the morrow's
  Sun had made a golden halo of her hair.
That self-same night the one she mourned had planned
    his hope forlorn,
  Had freed his bonds and watched his chance—exhausted
    weak and worn,
His fingers round the sentry's throat— a rough and tumble
    fight—
  A stealthy snake-like crawl—a dash for freedom thro'
    the night—
A bullet in his shoulder, breathing hard, with lips set tight,
  He was picked up by his countrymen at dawn.
He was taken to the base, where those God-sent women face
  All the horrors that attend the cross of red,
And he sent his bride a letter, as his wounds were growing
    better,
  But it never reached the wife who thought him dead;
For the Uhlans had swept down on that peaceful Belgian town,
  Yet his nurses hid the truth with news they made,
But, when comrade's gossip told him, neither plea nor threat
    could hold him,
  And *he started on a personal crusade.*

44

His uniform he left, and donned a priestly garb instead:
  He passed the Belgian sentries with the cowl drawn o'er
      his head.
A "Dominus Vobiscum" here, a mumbled blessing there,
  By strategy and patience he achieved what few would dare,
And stood at last, beside his home at St. Pierre,
  Near the ruins of the church where he'd been wed.
From an open window near, gutt'ral accents he could hear—
  Drunken swine whose calls for wine befouled the air.
Came a woman's voice that pleaded, then the bestial jest
      that speeded
  Base desire—the woman's cry of dark despair!
Thro' the window open wide he who waited there outside
  Sped to save her, like an angered God of storm.
There he saw his bride defenceless—in a stupor—lying senseless,
  At the mercy of those fiends in human form.
His blood afire with hatred attacked with Beserk might,
  But odds were all against him, and they pinned and bound
      him tight.
Their vengeance meant the woman's shame, he overheard their
      plan,
  And suffered all the anguish that can sear the soul of man:
A prayer, from out his spirit, to the Gates of Heaven ran,
  And the wrath of God sped swiftly thro' the night.
From outside comes the song of hoof and the gun:
  The relief, swift and sudden—defeat of the Hun!
'Midst the clangour of battle and clashing of steel
  The bridegroom and bride 'neath the crucifix kneel,
And the Lord hears the prayer that their hearts would
      reveal:
  Our Father Thine own will be done."

A BRITON'S DREAM

BY V. F. STEVENS and ERNEST LONGSTAFFE   1943

I came home from my work last night as tired as I
    could be.
  You see there's plenty doing now for working chaps like me
I slumped down in my fav'rite chair, no need for counting sheep;
    And weary from the workshop's din I soon was fast asleep:
And whilst asleep I dreamt the vellum of the hate drums broke
    I lived in Britain freed once more from wartimes' heavy yoke.
And once again I saw the land, the land that gave me birth
    The Britain that I know so well the finest place on earth.
I saw the friendly 'bobbie' so unlike the bull necked Hun.
    I saw him move on scores of folk, and he didn't have
    a gun.
I saw the British people tending gardens green and fair.
    I saw the street lamps light again and watched the
    kiddies stare.
I saw the looms of Lancashire and Yorkshire in full swing
    I saw the Norfolk and the Suffolk lads a harvesting,
I saw the southern fishermen attending to their floats
    I saw the men of Tyne and Tees busy making boats
I saw the Scottish uplands, so rugged, bold and free
    The regal home of Kings and Queens, the Clyde and
    'bonny Dee'
I saw the slopes of Snowdon, the castles, hills and dales
    From whence came men of Harlech, the land of song—
    "Welsh Wales!"
I saw the green and shamrock'd sweeps of Erin's lovely isle
    Where Irish hearts *were* happy and Irish eyes *did* smile,
I saw the rolling Devon hills I saw the Cornish coast
    I saw things that Britons know so well, and love
    the most.
The 'Public Bar' on Saturday night; a drink and a game of darts,—
    Church on Sunday morning—Sunday's joint, and apple tarts
I saw the school kids when at play, did not look up in dread
    Their eyes were on a cricket ball, and not a hail of lead.
I saw good workers houses, saw these workers were content,
    Saw their busy hours well used and their leisure times well
    spent,

I saw them read the morning news the same as me and you
   They read about a "Better World" and smiled because 'twas
      true
The tears and sweat and blood they'd shed, had not been all
      in vain
   For God had blessed their Britain, and she was *Great* again.
I woke refreshed and realised the need in which we stand
   Of the great and splendid energies possessed throughout
      the land,
And if we use them as we should I know one day we'll find
   That God will make that dream come true, for US and all
      mankind.

BROOM AN' CO.

BY GREATREX NEWMAN and FRED CECIL   *1915*

Performed by Bransby Williams

This meetin' of the partners in the firm of Broom an' Co.,
   Is 'eld because the cash in 'and 'as run exceedin' low,—
In fact the firm is stoney broke, they've neither crumb
      not crust,
   They've tried to raise the wind—but found they've only
      raised the dust.
Ten years ago a crossin' sweeper easy earned 'is keep,
   But now—wi' naught but motor cars—there's only *smells*
      to sweep.
Besides, it's no use me an' you abreakin' of our 'earts,
   We can't compete against them swagger Corporation carts.
The truth is mate, we're past it,—yes, we'll 'ave to
      shut up shop,
   We're growin' old,—why both of us is nearly bald on top.
When you was young, an' trim, an' smart, why then you'd
      almost brains,—
   You was a marvel then at fetchin' fag-ends out o' drains,
An' if a stray cigar stump should be chucked down
      by a gent,
   You dashed off with your 'ead down like a blood 'ound
      on the scent.

I'll bet you ain't forgot the day you found that shillin'?
   No—The share 'olders got dividends that night from
      Broom an' Co.
Sometimes our luck 'as bin right in, an' sometimes—well,—it
   ain't,
   But you've kep' always cheerful though—no grousin', nor
      complaint.
An' when at times I've 'ad the 'ump, an' felt fed-up or ill,
   You've seemed to kind o' smile at me, an' whisper "stick
      it Bill."
For years you've swep' that crossin'—rain or sunshine—every
   day,
   You've never wanted over-time nor struck for 'igher pay;
While ev'ry *Sunday* mornin' you was always to be found,
   In a churchyard, gently sweepin', round a little raised up
      mound;
An' while you've quietly swept about, I've sent to 'Eaven
      a prayer—
   That *we* might pass them Golden Gates—an' sweep a crossin'
      there.

THE BUS CONDUCTOR

BY GRAHAM SQUIERS and FRED CECIL   1922

Some people think conductors have a bloomin' easy life,
   Wot *I* say is, they want another think,
I'm always on the go, *I* am, unless I'm comin' back—
   Crikey! and I *could* do with a drink.
From 'ere to there—and there to 'ere—for hours at a stretch,
   An' often late at night—and yet I stick it,
Folks thinks I've nothin' else to do but wander up an' down,
   An' ring my bell and 'and 'em out a ticket.
And as for 'andin' tickets, I suppose *you* think it's jam,
   It ain't—it's only *bread,* an' stale at that,
The passengers I get at times—I'd like ter shove 'em orf,

I'd one to-day—the 'aughty swank-faced cat!
She says "This note is all I have, I want the change correct,
    And not all silver either—" Can yer lick it?
So I gives 'er nine and ninepence—all in pennies—one by one,
    An' rang my bell—and 'anded *'er* a ticket.
An' Johnnies—Mashers—you know—toffs, I'd one o' them
        tonight,
    'E stops my 'bus an' says "Aw haw, aw haw."
I says "The same to you with ribbons on" an'—'e replies,
    "Where might this jolly bus be making for?"
I says "It might be Egypt or Kamschatka, but it ain't,
    It's the Oval—where we tries to play at cricket,"
'E says, "Aw haw aw haw", again, so I says—" 'E—he he",
    An' rang my bell and 'anded *'im* is ticket.
There's them well fed old gents at times—you know with
        frontispiece,
    The sort wot beams an' corls me "My good man"—
Wot 'as an eye for flappers—if the missis ain't about,—I've
        seen 'em an' I know—san fairy ann.
    I 'ad a Russian bloke to-day—a Bolshie-bloomin'-vik,
All matted 'air, Lord knows 'ow 'e can stick it,
    Calls me "Comrade"—I says—"Cheero—Tarzan of the apes,"
And rang my bell—and 'anded *'im* is ticket.
    My old gal's in the 'orspital, that's why I'm 'ere alone,
That's why the last nine weeks 'ave seemed so long.
    She's comin' out next Friday—some blokes *might* say that's
        bad luck,
But jokes apart—she ain't no longer strong.
    She's got a kind of sense of humour too, the same as me,
An' if she 'adn't, Gawd knows 'ow we'd stick it,
    But still we'll smile until the chief Conductor comes along,
And rings *'is* bell—and 'ands us *both* a ticket.

BUT HE DIDN'T

BY CUTHBERT ROSE and WINIFRED FAIRLIE   1923

A maid and a subaltern sat 'neath a tree,
 The shimmering sunshine revealed them to me,
I was walking near by, so I couldn't but see,
 I ought to have fled, but I didn't.
The amorous South wind came whispering love,
 Their lips met in kisses, the soft cooing dove,
Caressed his fond mate, in the branches above,
 I heard her say "Stop!" but he didn't!
The youth in his wooing was dashing and bold;
 The maid was fair, yielding, not prudish or cold,
When strained to her heart in a rapturous fold,
 She ought to have screamed, but she didn't!
But why proceed further with this tale of woe,
 The maid was a maid, as these modern maids go,
An' action is promised she now wants to know,
 If he meant what he said, but he didn't.

BUT I DUNNO

BY HICKMAN SMITH and IVOR DENNIS   1942

I sometimes think I'd rather be
 A crow up in a big elm tree,
Than be a rooster in a pen
 Who gives a crow just now and then.
But I dunno.
 You see, it seems a crow can't crow
At least I'm told that this is so,
 But roosters crow the whole day long
And seem to think their crow's a song.
 But I dunno.
But crows up in the big elm tree
 Are safer far it seems to me,

Than roosters wandering in a pen,
  At the beck and call of men.
But I dunno.
  A crow's a crow, oh right enough,
'Tis sad they're old and very tough,
  But a rooster's worth more by a peck,
Especially if you wring its neck.
  But I dunno.
A rooster can't roost in a tree
  Like crows can, so it seems to me,
But if you kill him oh dear oh,
  You'll have no Rooster with a crow.
But I dunno.
  So why not let the rooster roost,
And let the crows crow just as they use't.
  It doesn't matter much to me
As I ain't either don't you see.
  But I dunno.

BY THE YUKON TRAIL

BY J. MILTON HAYES and R. FENTON GOWER   *1942*

By an old wood shack on a northern track,
  Where the snows of Alaska fall,
There are dead men's bones;
  And the cold wind moans:
With the howl of the wolf in counter-tones,
  And God's hand over all.
A lonely man staked out a claim
  That never seemed to pay,
And late one night a stranger came
  Who'd chanced to lose his way.
They supped and smoked and talked awhile,
  And then a silence fell,
And each man dreamt of a woman's smile,
  And a woman's fond farewell.

51

That silence touched the hearts of both,
    And each man told his tale,
How he'd longed and pined for a lucky find,
    For the sake of a girl he'd left behind
In a far-off English vale.
    Then each one showed a photograph,
Each signed with a loved one's name,
    And they looked on there, by the candle flare,
To discover the perfect pair,
    And the signatures the same.
Black hate flashed out from both men's eyes:
    They fought—and one man failed to rise.
For Death had come to claim a prize,
    By the lonely Yukon trail.
One man dug deep and deeper still
    To hide the dead thing there;
The fearsome words "Thou shalt not kill,"
    Seemed thundered thro' the air.
At last, in frenzied haste and dread,
    He crossed the cabin floor,
And thrust the dead outside the shed,
    Then locked and barred the door.
He toiled and toiled with spade and pick
    In the light the candle gave;
When the sudden gleam of mighty seam
    Showed gold that came like a hell-sent dream
From the heart of the dead man's grave.
    He heard the howl of wolves outside,
And shook in every limb,
    As they fought and tore by the cabin door
At the thing that breathed but a while before;
    The madness came to him.
A loaded gun—a broken prayer.
    A shot that rent the startled air.
Then dawn came up and peeped in there.
    By the lonely Yukon trail.
There are dead men's bones where the cold wind moans
    By that shack on the Yukon trail;
There are two lives paid for the love betrayed,
    For the broken vows that a woman made
In a far-off English vale.

THE CABMAN'S RAILWAY YARN

BY E. A. SEARSON and HERBERT TOWNSEND   *1920*

A hint to those performing this monologue at places other than in the London District.

To sustain the interest among local audiences it will be advisable for the performer to substitute names of places fairly within the immediate neighbourhood for those printed "Bexhill," "Willesden," "Ilford," etc.

> Here, keb, sir, d'you want a four-wheeler?
>> You don't? No, exactly of course,
> No one does, they never want me sir,
>> And they don't want the keb or the 'orse.
> Take you down the Strand for a bob sir?
>> Patronise the old firm Billy Webb,
> Here make it half a thick 'un guv'nor!
>> And I'll give you the 'orse and the keb.
> Nothing doing? Orl right keep your 'air on,
>> Yer needn't get ratty and shout,
> Don't slang an unfortunate bounder
>> Who's down, and who's very near out.
> Time was when I wasn't a cabby.
>> I was once on the railway, a fact,
> And I might have been general manager,
>> If it hadn't have been I got sacked.
> It was back in the time of the strike sir,
>> My line was 'it 'ard sir, you see,
> And men were so scarce in those times sir,
>> Why, they even thought something of me.
> And day after day they got shorter
>> And shorter of workers, and so
> They bunged me on the train sir, one evening,
>> To take her to Bexhill you know.
> Well, it wasn't for me to make trouble,
>> Though it didn't seem right I must say,
> I'd never before *been* to Bexhill,
>> And I 'ad no idea of the way.
> Still I got a shove-off at eight-thirty,
>> And things for a time went on fine,

53

Till they pulled me up sudden at Willesden,
 And said I was on the wrong line.
So I was, it was no good to argue,
 But it wasn't my fault you'll admit,
Still I went back and looked for my line, sir,
 And discovered it after a bit.
To a porter I says. "I want Bexhill!
 Which way do I take this 'ere train?"
He says "Straight on until you reach Clapham,
 Then if you're in doubt ask again."
I cheered up and pushed on a bit further,
 But I somehow seemed all of a maze,
For in front I could see the lines parted
 And branched off in different ways.
My stoker, Bill Jones, hollers quickly,
 "The left hand for Clapham, hold tight!"
But I knew what a liar Bill Jones was,
 So I pulled her head round to the right.
Bill *'ad* spoke the truth for a wonder,
 As I found out before very long,
For an hour after, when I reached Ilford,
 I knew very well something was wrong.
It's a mystery to me how I got there,
 But the night was as dark as could be,
And you couldn't 'ave blamed any driver,
 Let alone a poor novice like me.
Well we turned round the train and went back, sir,
 The Inspector he showed us a light,
He said, "Straight on until you reach Stratford.
 And then bear a bit to the right.
Keep off the down line if you can mate,
 I'm telling you plainly, because
I hope with good luck by twelve thirty,
 You'll get back to wherever you was."
Well I carefully followed directions,
 Got through London without any slip,
And glad enough too, for the passengers
 By now were beginning to chip.
I felt a bit doubtful at Barnet,
 But I ran through the station quite fast,
And I felt very proud two hours after,
 When I saw Clapham Junction at last.

Then I give 'er 'er 'ead, and we moved some,
   Bill stoked up the furnace with care,
And I said, "If we keep on the metals
   By seven we ought to be there."
And the men in each signal box shouted,
   And waved some red flags at us too,
I 'ollers back "Are we down-hearted?"
   And Bill 'e calls out "Toodle oo!"
At last there looms out a big station,
   And lights on the water I saw,
I says, "Bill, I believe we 'ave got there."
   But Bill only murmurs, "O lor!"
We ran to the end of the station,
   Where the book-stall man's busy at work;
We came up with a bump on the buffers,
   Which brought the train up with a jerk.
You'd have thought there'd been a mishap, sir,
   The passengers swarmed out in a group,
Was it Bexhill? No, matey, Victoria!
   We'd been bloomin' well looping the loop.

CAMOUFLAGE

BY C. W. CUNDY and PAULINE WILTON   *1918*

I'm unhappy, so I am, I can't enjoy me beef nor jam, And I'm
   grumpy and as 'umpy as a camel,
   Bin an' stopped my leave, Oh ho! what were fixed up long
      ago
The trouble is I've got it and I feel afeared to go,
   And its all along a tin o' green enamel.
Now fancy spendin' New Year's Eve when you ought to be on
   leave,
   In a dug-out where the damp is slowly tricklin',
All along a tin o' green and a sniper lank and lean

'Oo was swearin' and a straffin' and a snippin' in between
Till the sergeant told me off to stop 'is ticklin'.
So I trimmed myself in straw, with a grass and 'ay couffure
And I clothed myself in faggots wot a pal 'ad,
And the sergeant took a brush and some green and sticky
slush
And 'e painted me all over till I couldn't raise a blush
And I looked just like a vegetable salad.
So I crep't out in the night and I waited for the light,
But the sniper saw me fust and scored an inner;
I 'eard the twigs divide but I signalled 'im a wide
And I squinted down me barrel and I let me finger slide,
And I pipped 'im where 'e used to keep 'is dinner.
Yus, I busted up the Bosh but I found out at the wash,
That enamel' was a fast and lastin' colour,
And the soap I used to clean made me shine a brighter
green,
I'm a cabbage, I'm a lettuce, I'm a walkin' kidney-bean,
And I ain't a leavin' Flanders till its duller.

THE CANE BOTTOM'D CHAIR

BY W. M. THACKERAY   1910

In tattered old slippers that toast at the bars,
    And a ragged old jacket perfumed with cigars,
Away from the world, and its toils and its cares,
    I've a snug little kingdom up four pair of stairs.
To mount this realm is a toil, to be sure,
    But the fire is bright, and the air rather pure;
And the view I behold on a sun shiny day,
    Is grand through the chimney-pots over the way.
This snug little chamber is cramm'd in all nooks
    With worthless old knicknacks and silly old books,
And foolish old odds, and foolish old ends,
    Crack'd bargains from brokers, cheap keepsakes
        from friends.

Old armour, prints, pictures, pipes, china, all cracked,
　Old rickety tables, and chairs broken-backed;
A two-penny treasury, wondrous to see,
　What matter? 'tis pleasant to you, friend, and me.
No better divan need the Sultan require
　Than the creaking old sofa that basks by the fire;
And 'tis wonderful, surely, what music you get
　From the rickety, ramshackle, wheezy spinet.
That praying-rug came from a Turcoman's camp,
　By Tiber once twinkled that brazen old lamp;
A Mameluke fierce yonder dagger has drawn,
　'Tis a murderous knife to toast muffins upon.
Long, long through the hours, and the night, and its chimes,
　Here we talk of old books, and old friends, and old times,
As we sit in a fog made of rich Latakie,
　This chamber is pleasant to you, friend, and me.
But of all the cheap treasures that garnish my nest,
　There's one that I love and I cherish the best;
For the finest of couches that's padded with hair
　I never would change thee, my cane-bottom'd chair.
'Tis a bandy-legg'd high shoulder'd worm-eaten seat.
　With a creaking old back and twisted old feet,
But, since the fair morning when Fanny sat there,
　I bless thee, and love thee, my cane-bottom'd chair.
If chairs have but feeling in holding such charms,
　A thrill must have passed through your withered old arms;
I looked, and I longed, and I wished in despair;
　I wished myself turned to a cane-bottom'd chair.
It was but a moment she sat in this place;
　She'd a scarf on her neck and a smile on her face;
A smile on her face, and a rose in her hair,
　And she sat there and bloom'd in my cane-bottom'd chair.
And so I have valued my chair ever since,
　Like the shrine of a saint, or the throne of a prince;
Saint Fanny, my patroness, sweet I declare,
　The Queen of my heart and my cane-bottom'd chair.
When the candles burn low and the company's gone,
　In the silence of night as I sit here alone—
I sit here alone, but we yet are a pair,
　My Fanny I see in my cane-bottom'd chair.
She comes from the past and revisits my room;
　She looks as she then did, all beauty and bloom;

So smiling and tender, so fresh and so fair,
And yonder she sits in my cane-bottom'd chair.

THE CAPTAIN'S WHISKERS

BY KENNETH BLAIN   *1947*

Performed by Arthur Askey

It was Christmas day last Easter,
  On a Friday night in June,
I shall not forget that day until I die.
  We were in the Bay of Biscay
Just a mile from Barking Creek,
  When the Captain hung his whiskers out to dry.
He was known as Mad Carew,
  And he lived on Irish stew,
And the space around his tongue was always dry.
  He would drink for hours you bet,
And to save them getting wet,
  We used to hang his whiskers out to dry.
He was only ninety-four,
  Maybe less or maybe more.
And he grew a beard to save his buying a tie.
  But one night the silly goop,
Let his beard dip in the soup,
  So we had to hang his whiskers out to dry.
He was gentle as a child,
  That's except when he was wild,
And he was always wild 'tween you and I.
  And as he'd got a sloping jib,
He used to dribble down his bib,
  So we had to hang his whiskers out to dry.
His beard was flaming red,
  He was born with it he said.
When his mother used to shave him he would cry.
  So they let it grow apace,

58

And when they washed his face,
  They used to hang his whiskers out to dry.
Once he spoke about his ma,
  Who lived out in Zanzibar,
And the poor old fool just started out to cry.
  And he cried about his mummy,
Till the tears ran down his waistcoat,
  So we had to hang his whiskers out to dry.
Then one day he caught a chill,
  He was very, very ill,
And he died and went to glory in the sky,
  Now after show'rs blown to and fro,
Hanging on a bright rain-bow,
  I can see his whiskers hanging out to dry.

CARDS

BY J. A. McLAREN   *1910*

Life is like a game of cards.
  Want of luck success retards.
If you've got a hand you play it.
  If you lose you're wild and say it.
Commerce, business, stock exchange,
  All come under chance's range.
So I'll point out, if I may,
  The games of cards in life we play.
A sweating-den—Englishmen
  Starved by foreign labour;
It's the same bad old game—BEGGAR MY NEIGHBOUR.
  Ev'ry day in married life,
Cards are played by man and wife.
  If the game goes all the way
There's the very deuce to pay.
  Take the married man who might
But won't, and stays out all night.

Wife resolves to end the game
So sits and waits by candleflame.
Hears his key—down goes she,
(Darkness serves to cloak her);
He says *(hic)* "M'dear." She says "Here." POKER
Matrimonial games for two
If played by three will never do,
If the odd man gets too chummy
Law steps in and acts as dummy.
Nearly every day you see
Bad revokes by Mr. Three,
Someone cries "Mis-deal" and then
They cut for partners all again.
Man of course gets divorce,
To Law Courts takes a stroll-oh!
His duet is all upset SOLO
To maintain our country's sway
Taxes cheerfully(?) we pay.
Yet one quite inclined to scoff is
When one thinks of our war office.
Lazy limbs and sleepy heads,
They've got sofas, why not *Beds?*
Yet I won't in fairness shirk
Saying "They've been *known* to work."
All red tape, yawn and gape,
Sense, well just a scrap;
One game they play, ev'ry day *(yawn)* NAP.
Games, like dogs, each have their day,
Become the rage then fade away,
And it seems that woman's views
Chop and change like fashion's hues.
Once she sought domestic life,
Hooked a man, became a wife,
Now she yells, with strident throat,
"Don't want a home—I want a vote."
But woman still her bitter pill
Will be, I'm much afraid,
When tired of strike—no-one's wife, OLD MAID.

THE CARETAKER

BY CHARLES J. WINTER   *1912*

Performed by Bransby Williams

We've had a fine time and no kid, puss,
    We've been 'ere two year come next week.
Still the 'ouse isn't let, and not likely,
    Although we've oft 'ad a near squeak.
But the yarn that I pitch is so creepy,
    Not a soul cares the 'orrers to face,
So we can rest easy and sing, puss,
    There's no place like 'ome.
You want to look over the 'ouse sir?
    Why certainly, step this way.
It's a 'ouse anyone might be proud of,
    So the 'undreds that's seen it say.
Don't mind the cat jumping about sir:
    Maybe she is after a rat,
She's at it from morning to night sir,
    But there's swarms of them still for all that,
'Ow they get 'ere I'm sure is a marvel,
    Leastways *'twas* a marvel to me,
Till one morning I spots on the reason,
    When a hextra big fat one I see.
I figgers it out like this 'ere sir,
    Their numbers would not always swell
If they didn't come out from the sewer,
    And besides that accounts for the smell.
Is the smell very bad? well not always,
    Why *sometimes* the air is quite clear.
And I've only 'ad three bouts of typhoid
    In the two years I 'ave been 'ere.
No, the smell's not so bad as the damp sir,
    For that fairly gets into your bones,
And you'll never be free from rheumatics
    While the damp rises off of them stones.
But there—what's the good of complaining,
    There's even some blessing in that,
For the fungus and moss on the 'earthstone
    Makes a lovely soft bed for the cat.

61

And if I don't sweep over the floors, sir,
    For a day or two after some rain,
The mildoo's that white and that pure, sir,
    It's as pretty as snow in a lane.
Any sounds? well not doorin' day sir,
    But at midnight there's moans and there's groans,
And a 'orrible smell of blue brimstone,
    With shrieks and the rattlin' of bones.
As a fact that's the one serious drawback,
    And I'm sorry I let an 'int drop,
(Don't give me away to the owner,
    Or he'll 'ave me kicked out neck and crop.)
But the sounds that we get 'ere at midnight
    Forget them, well I never shall.
I'm sure I'd go stark, staring balmy,
    If I 'adn't the cat for a pal.
It comes of that there Jack the Ripper,
    What once used to live 'ere they say,
'E made this a kind of 'eadquarters
    When putting his victims away,
And now all their ghosts come to 'aunt 'im.
    A shrieking and dragging great chains.
Well, I'm sure I'm a pretty tough 'andful,
    But that there beats the rats and the drains.
What! you *like* the house from my description?
    And you wish that you'd come 'ere before?
Well, I'm 'anged if that don't take the biscuit!
    Then I shan't be wanted no more!!
I suppose you're some newspaper feller
    That wants in a ghost house to hide?
Or a chap that's been chucked by 'is sweetheart,
    And wants to commit suicide?
Or perhaps you are studying "hefluvias,"
    If so you've a chance that is prime!
Beg pardon? *What! You are the landlord!!*
    O hang it! I've done it this time!

CASTLES IN THE AIR

BY STANLEY C. WEST and MARJORIE BROUGHTON　　　*1923*

I'm just a simple scull'ry maid, I'm wot they calls
　　　no class
　　And beauty ain't my portion if yer trusts a lookin' glass.
But thanks to what the missus calls a strong imagination,
　　I kids meself I'm 'eavenly, and 'eaps above me station.
And often on a winter's night, when I 'ave done me job,
　　I sits and builds my castles up before the kitchen 'ob;
Sometimes I am a countess or a princess tall and sweet,
　　And quite forgits the beetles 'formin' fours' around me feet.
I close me h'eyes and see's meself wif lovely orbin 'air,
　　And vi'lit h'eyes and pearly teeth, and diamonds ev'rywhere.
I rides in Rotten Row sometimes and knocks the
　　　Johnnies silly,—
　　I once 'ad ten lootenants round me car in Piccadilly.
I 'as me yacht out sometimes and I sails the seas afar,
　　Me fav'rit guest on them occasions is a movie star.
My hero was proposing once, "Oh Yes, my dear," I said,
　　Then cook bursts in the Kitchen, and cries "Emma!—'orf
　　　to bed!"
I dreams a bit when I'm at work, and then it ain't no joke,
　　You'd be surprised if you could see the plates and things
　　　I've broke.
It's 'ard to think your lover is a colonel in the Navy,—
　　While splashing to your armpits in cold tea and last
　　　night's gravy;—
Sometimes at the theayter in the gallery I gets,
　　And kids meself I'm in a box, with diamond lorganets.
I tries to think it's dukes and dukesses as round me sit,
　　It spoils it tho' to see your duke spit pips into the pit.
'Ere shall I tell yer? Yus! I will, when nursè 'ad got
　　　a cold,
　　She give me once our missus's new baby for to 'old.
I rocked it till it slep' and then I sit as still as death,
　　I reckon for an 'alf an hour I never drawed a breath,
And Gawd knows wot me dreams was while I 'ad that child
　　　to 'old,

'E knows it wasn't motorcars, nor coronets o' gold.—
And when nurse took that baby off—wot wasn't mine to keep,
   I give up kiddin' for that night, and 'owled meself ter sleep.

CHANCE IT

BY H. M. BURNABY and CUTHBERT CLARKE   *1922*

A schoolboy once decided he would like to jump a stream,
   But doubted his ability to carry out the scheme.
He tried his luck and landed just as fit as any fiddle,
   And the precept that prevented him from landing in
         the middle,
Was—Chance it!
   The streams we have to jump in life are many, some
         are wide.
At times it seems impossible to gain the other side.
   But mud and weeds are holding out a cordial invitation
To those who shiver on the brink—beware of hesitation—
   Why not Chance it?
You're standing on the kerbstone and you're feeling very sour,
   Been held up by the traffic for a quarter of an hour,
Now why not make a dash and should a motor disconcert you,
   Just pray that it's a Ford and shove it over it won't
         hurt you,
Go on—Chance it!
   While on your walks abroad a comely damsel you espy,
And you're not exactly certain if she's given the glad eye.
   You're thinking if I were to speak, she'd deem my
         conduct shady,
Remember what the poet said re faint heart and fair lady.
   I think so, Chance it!
A friend of yours arrives in town from Boston U.S.A.
   You take him to the club to while an hour or two away,
Of the prohibition movement may be he's a keen supporter,
   Then you wonder if his poison's "Black and White", or
         barley water—
Gee! Chance it!

64

You've been celebrating something in the good old
    fashioned style,
And you've reached home at last altho' it's taken quite
    a while.
Two doors stand closely side by side—you don't know which
    to enter,
    Shove your key into the keyhole of the one that's in
        the *centre*—
Schanse it!
    No matter what your walk in life no matter what your creed,
No matter what your business if you're aiming to succeed.
    Be you tinker, tailor, soldier, sailor, beggar, thief
        or so on,
Simply take this as your motto it is pretty safe to go on
    What I've said, Chance it!

CHARGE OF THE NIGHT BRIGADE

BY ELPHINSTONE THORPE and WOLSELEY CHARLES   *1911*

    Down the steps, down the steps,
        Down the steps blundered—
    Right down the area steps, policeman 600
        "Come down; don't be afraid,
    Missus is out," cook said.
        Right down the area steps
    Strode six hundred.
        "There now, try that," she said,
    Was he all dismayed?
        No! though the bobby knew
    Someone was plundered.
        His not to make reply
    "I can't eat rabbit-pie,"
        His but to have a try,
    Down at the table sat, policeman 600.

Rabbit to *right* of him,
Cold beef to *left* of him,
  Pork pie in *front* of him, (all of it plundered.)
What is there left to tell
  Beef, pork and rabbit fell
Into the jaws of,—into the mouth of—well—,
  Policeman 600.
Flashed his good weapon bare,
  Flashed as it turned in air,
Sabr'ing the pork-pie there,
  Slicing the cold beef,
While cook stood and wondered.
  Never a word he spoke,
Right thro' the crust he broke,
  Pie-crust and rabbit reeled from his master stroke,
Shattered and sundered.
  Then he sat up again,
Sat up, and pondered.
  Pocket to right of him—
Pocket to left of him—
  Pocket behind him—
All were nigh sundered.
  Stuffed like a shrapnel shell
Why? Well they heard the bell,
  · Then he who fed so well
Crept off with bated breath
  Carrying, sad to tell,
All that was left of it,
  Left by six hundred.
When can the memory fade
  Of the grand meal he made,
While the cook wondered?
  Honour the kitchen jade!
Honour the meal he made!
  Noble six hundred.

CHARM

Written, Composed and Performed by LAWRENCE VANE   *1922*

Patter can be performed in character of a Dame, with bonnet and shawl.
Here we go! Oh, dear. You know it isn't all sunshine being a widow. I've been a widow these 5 years come Michaelmas Tuesday. I have to go about so much alone. Nasty dark lanes, too! And it doesn't do for us girls to wander about unprotected. You never know! You never know when you may get the glad eye or the postman's knock!
I'm looking for a little unfurnished cottage and—a man. A little nest for two.

That's the aim of all us girls—a little nest for two.
But how do we get it? How do we get it?
By charm!
They say we have two million girls too many,
Quite the wildest thing I ever read.
For, when we speak of girls, we separate the pearls
From the plain unlucky ones who never wed.
And when we've got the pearl and plain divided,
Well may you knit your eyebrows in alarm,
Take a chance with any, but you'll find we've not too
      many
Girls that have that quality of charm.
What is it that holds men like a magnet?
What makes you play the devil with us girls?
What is that net that few of you escape from?
Tinker, tailor, soldier, sailor, dukes and earls—
What is it makes some little child attractive?
Awake or when asleep in perfect calm—
I ask you all who love just such a youngster,
It's charm, just charm.
Now I don't like to talk about myself, girls,
The fact remains I do attract the boys!
True my figure's vile, but the men do stare, and smile
Students speak of me as "some big noise."
If I sit between some pretty girls at dinner,

67

The men, you'd be surprised, are such a tease!
   My face is not my label, no, but underneath the table
It's *my* hand, girls, that always gets the squeeze!
   What is it that holds men like a magnet?
What makes you play the devil with us girls?
   What is that net that few of you escape from?
Tinker, tailor, viscounts, dukes and earls—
   Love? 'tis often mere infatuation,
Pretty looks alone may do much harm.
   What made my husband leave me for another?
Charm, just charm!

THE CHAR'S LAMENT

BY HAROLD SIMPSON and SYDNEY LENTON   *1944*

(Char enters with bucket and mop. She wears an old
fashioned bonnet, glasses and overall)

Life ain't much catch for the likes of me,
   It's just a matter of scrubbing,
When I thinks of the woman I meant to be
   Well, it fairly starts me blubbing,
Why can't I be like other gals?
   (And some of them ain't no beauty!)
With lots of good looking boys for pals
   And one who will call me cutey?
Why do I never have a date?
   Becos I ain't got glamour!
Why 'ave I never found a mate?
   Becos I ain't got glamour!
Why do the boys all pass me by?
   Why do they never wink their eye?
They prefers their pint of wollop, that's why!
   Becos I ain't got glamour!
There are lots of women in 'istory
   Who couldn't 'ave been without it,

They may 'ave 'ad better looks than me,
    Tho' some-'ow I seems to doubt it;
Cleopatra now, she was Egypt's Queen,
    She 'ad glamour enough for twenty,
And 'Elen of Troy who I've never seen,
    She must 'ave 'ad "it" in plenty.
Why do I never 'ave a date?
    Becos I ain't got glamour!
Why 'ave I never found a mate?
    Becos I ain't got glamour!
Why when with love my 'eart is stirred
    Must all me fondest 'opes get blurred?
Why do I get the blinking bird?
    Becos I ain't got glamour!
While scrubbin' I 'ad a dream one day,
    It made me go all goofy,
A fairy godmother came my way
    With a lot of spoofy spoofy;
She waved a wand about me 'ead
    Till I nearly started squeallin'
I couldn't 'ave told you the words she said
    But they gave me a creepy feelin'.
Ermyntrude! you shall have a date.
    I'll give you lots of glamour,
Give you a handsome Prince for mate,
    Make you better than Dorothy Lamour!
(The lights go up and reveal her as a young and pretty girl in
      a dainty frock)
    Now will you boys all pass me by?
Now will you never wink your eye?
    No! you'll just leave your beer and cry: *(Whistle)*
Ain't she got glamour!

CHEERFUL CHARLIE

BY F. CHATTERTON HENNEQUIN and
PHYLLIS NORMAN PARKER   1916

AUTHOR'S NOTE Mr. Hennequin acknowledges with pleasure that the idea for this Monologue was personally suggest-
ed to him by a fellow author Mr. Bertram Burleigh who had
already written and published a story entitled "The Pessi-
mist."

We called him Cheerful Charlie, a pessimistic chap,
   Who never saw no good in life, but only black mishap.
On sunny days he shook his head and said it smelt like rain,
   He'd eat and drink enough for two, then say it caused
      him pain.
He looked just like a funeral, the day that he was wed
   And whispered in his best man's ear "I might as well
      be dead."
When war broke out he gave a sigh and said "They'll soon
      get here
   And we shall live on sauerkraut and dirty lager beer;
And if they fail, well what's the odds them Russians,
      mark my word,
   Will turn on us and scoop the lot; we can't win, it's absurd.
If I enlist it won't help things I know that ALL IS LOST;
   Most likely we'll be submarined before we get acrost."
But when we fell back, give him his due, he didn't say a word,
   And all the time when things went wrong his voice was
      never heard.
He took his whack and did his bit and always helped a pal,
   And oftentimes he's closed their eyes as tender as
      a gal.
But when we got the upper hand and things were going strong
   I'm blest if he don't start afresh and say "it can't last long."
He grumbled through three victories and cursed at 60 Hill.
   Because he said he came away from home and never made
      no will.
He says."Each hour may be your last and mine too, don't
      forget it!"

Then someone hit him with a spade and said "Lor Lumme!
    let it!"
We had to take some big Redoubt, we knew the day before,
    And Charlie says "It's suicide, the regiment is no more!"
But he was first inside their trench and laying Germans out,
    When in we tumbled after him, just as he got his clout.
They carried him to hospital and took away one arm;
    And pinned a medal on his breast to keep the beggar calm.
The Colonel says "Cheer up my man, we've got them fairly
    beat!"
    Then Charlie gives a mournful smile, and says "Ho yes!
    but where's the Fleet?"
So he's gone back home to Blighty but he's left a blank
    behind,
    For we took no stock of his poison gas when we knew his
    heart was kind.
But in his favorite little pub he' turned the beer all sour
    With the dismal tales of 'orrors that he tells them
        by the hour
The potman's gone and drowned himself, the barmaid's off
    her chump,
    And ever blessed soul he knows has got the blooming
    hump!

CHRISTMAS BELLS

BY W. W. MAYNE and LESLIE HARRIS   *1906*

INTRODUCTION—Ladies and Gentlemen, For the purpose
of this recital, I want you to be kind enough to picture to
yourselves, two little ragged, homeless urchins standing in the
street on Christmas Eve, listening to the Christmas Bells—the
elder child speaking to the younger.

'Ear the bells a-ringin' Bill? That's 'cos it's Chris'mus-eve:
    But it ain't for you an' me as they's a-ringin'.

71

W'en we is cold an' 'ungry, Bill, it's 'ard to make believe
　　As we kin 'ear the 'appy angels singin'
If we'd a bed ter sleep in, an' could git enough ter eat,
　　Them bells of hangels' voices might remind us:
But not w'en we've ter doss, Bill, in the cold and cruel street,
　　W'ere the bobby's nearly allus sure to find us.
No, Bill, to me an' you them bells means only grief an' pain.
　　For they tells of weeks an' weeks of winter wevver,
An', p'raps Bill, we may never see the summer sun again,
　　But die of cold an' 'unger, Bill, togever.
It's drefful 'ard on you, Bill, 'cos you're sich a little kid,
　　Wot didn't oughter know a bit o' sorrer
An' wouldn't if them Christchun folks 'ud do as they was bid
　　By 'Im 'oos birfday's goin' ter be ter morrer.
But it was 'Im wot said—"Let little children come to me!"
　　A meanin' jes' sich little coves as you Bill,
But I ain't got no chance, becuz I'm neely ten yer see,
　　An' I tell yer as I knows a thing or two Bill.
Yer can't sell hevenin' papers, so's ter git yer bit ter heat—
　　Like I done since the time as I were seven
Wivaht a-pickin' up enough o' badness in the street
　　Ter leave no earfly chance ter git ter 'eaven.
Them coves, wot comes ararnd wiv tracks, 'as summ'd me up
　　　　a treat:
　　I'm a houtcast, little 'eevun, pore lost sinner—
P'r'aps they'd a bin the same if they'd bin brought up in
　　　　the street
　　An' 'ardly ever 'ad no proper dinner.
But Bill, w'en you an' me is dead. I'll come along o' you
　　An' you shall hinterdooce me as your bruvver,
An' 'Im as knowed wot sorrer wos is sure to let me froo.
　　'Cos w'y? We've bin sich pals to one anuvver,
Ain't we, Bill?

CIGARETTE CARDS

BY MARGARET HOWE and CYRIL BAKER　　　　　　*1939*

If you should smoke a cigarette, in train or tram or bus,
　And total strangers that you meet start talking, please don't
　　　fuss.
Though it's not strictly British and you hate it from
　　　the start,
　Don't get the answer ready, "I'm a stranger in this part".
For they haven't murky motives like the blokes in novelettes,
　They only want the cards you've got inside your cigarettes.
Now if knitting is a mystery and your wife's two purl
　　　one plain,
　Keeps on driving you quite crazy, very soon they can explain.
Both the double clove-hitched reef stitch and the Shark tooth
　　　cable twine.
　If you'll only take the trouble to read series number nine.
Though you've followed Mr. Middleton, your rose trees have
　　　got blight,
　And your hollyhocks insist on shrinking quite two feet per
　　　night.
Quickly number three will settle that, or turn to number four,
　If you want to know the way to get back tools you've
　　　lent next door.
They've the stones unturned in Parliament since Julius
　　　Caesar came,
　And each single "avenue explored" you'll find them all by
　　　name,
Also pictures of that famous "fence" each member sits with glee.
　You can find them all, with footnotes, done in series
　　　thirty three.
Your pet goldfish may have typhoid and it sadly flaps its
　　　fins,
　And you've looked for help in Whitaker and asked for
　　　Godfrey Winn's,
But if you want really sound advice on how to treat your pets,
　You just simply can't get better than from cards in
　　　cigarettes.

If you're keeping ducks or chickens, they will tell you how
    to spot
Any green-eared red minorca from a pink-eyed wyandotte
They've got staggers, and they're starving—Heavens knows just what
    they need
But the only other card you've got's about canary seed.
Golf by self-tuition's easy, that's if you complete your set.
The old Colonel's badly bunkered and I think he's still
    there yet
He's cursed the course, the Cabinet, and giv'n the caddy hell,
    'Cause the poor kid said, "Gosh! Guv'ner, you need
    number eight as well".
For the total annual sneezes brought on by the common cold
    Or how to find a train that runs to Potash-on-the-Wold,
How to tell high tide in Leap Year or to play Tom-Tom
    Duets,
    You'll find all with diagrams on the cards in cigarettes.

THE CIVILIANS

BY NOSMO KING, PERCY NASH and ERNEST LONGSTAFFE   *1941*

The British fighting forces are a pattern to the world,
    They command respect and honour where 'ere our flag's
    unfurl'd,
Their courage and tenacity, they've proved in countless ways,
    And never more heroically than in these stirring days.
But courage isn't only found beneath a uniform,
    Our wonderful civilians too have stood up to the storm.
These civilian men and women who have reached the
    very height,
    Of loyalty and courage in the front line of the fight.
Cheerfully and bravely they have answered to the call.
    Their fame will live for evermore for God has blessed
    them all.
And when the devastation and the smoke has cleared away,

There'll remain a figure standing in the glory of the day.
On its brow a crown of laurels, and a smile upon its face
   'Tis the emblem of the people, of a never beaten race
The people of a country who have stood up unafraid
   To face the fearful carnage and the terror of the raid,
So let us all with grateful hearts each night and ev'ry morn,
   Fall on our knees and thank our God, that we are
   British born.

A CLEAN SWEEP

BY GREATREX NEWMAN and FRED CECIL   *1913*

Performed by Bransby Williams

I've 'ad lots o' jobs,—some was good, some was bad,—
   But the one as I counts the most strange,
Was once when I went to a millionaire's 'ouse
   To sweep out the chimneys an' range.
They wanted it doin' at night, rather late,
   When the fires weren't in use, arter tea,—
So I goes ter the place, an' I strolls up the drive,
   About eight o'clock it 'ud be.
When I gets ter the hentrance I sees two fat blokes
   Dressed in gold, an' I 'ears one say:
" 'Er Ladyship 'as bin hexpectin' Yer Grace,
   Will Yer Grace kindly foller this way?"
Well I looks round ter see who 'e means by "Yer Grace,"
   But there weren't no one there, 'ceptin' me,—
So I think p'r'aps "Yer Grace" is the *French* word
      fer "sweep,"
   So I follers the bloke just ter see.
Then a lady, all larfin', comes out of a room,
   An' ses:—as she looks at me clothes,—
"Why really, I shouldn't 'a' knowed yer Yer Grace,
   If it weren't fer that wart on yer nose!"

75

Then she opens a door, an' I sees a big room
  Full o' folks all dressed up in strange things,—
Some was soldiers, some nurses, some sailors, some cooks,
  An' sev'ral was hangels wi' wings.
Well, then the band stopped, an' the dancers sat down,
  An' a fat gent comes up on me right,
An' 'e puts sev'ral coins in me fist, as 'e ses:
  "There's the ten pounds I borrowed last night."
Then a lady comes up, an' ses: "Really Yer Grace
  I've larfed till me sides are quite sore,"—
So I ses: "Get some Zam Buk, an' rub 'em wi' that!"
  An' everyone near, give a roar.
Then one ses: "Why weren't you at the hopera last night?
  'Ad yer bin playin' polo or goff?"
I ses: "No I'd bin playin' at *bathin' the kids,*
  'Cause the missus 'ad took a night off!"
Well then us 'ad supper,—it weren't arf a spread,—
  The best feed I've 'ad in me life!—
An' everyone larfed, an' sed: "Isn't 'e fine!"
  When the *blankmange* slipped orf o' me knife.
An' they didn't arf roar when I upset me glass
  Down a girl who was dressed all in white,—
But it didn't show much, fer I dusted 'er frock
  Wi' me sleeve, an' me serviorite.
Then the lady as I 'ad fust met in the 'all,
  Who the others all called "The Dookess,"
She 'ands me a lovely gold watch, an' she ses:
  "That's the prize for the best fancy dress,"
Arter supper us went ter the ballroom,
  An' I tried a dance as they called *"Pass-de-Quart,"*—
But I soon chucked it up, 'cause me old 'ob-nail boots
  In the ladies' frocks kep' gettin' caught.
Then the Dookess, 'er ses: "Your *finance* 'as just come,"
  An' a young gal in low hevenin' dress.
Comes straight up ter me,—an' starts larfin', and ses:
  "Well Percy, you do look a mess!"
Then she ses: "I 'ave just got that ten thousand pounds
  That was lef' me last year by me aunt,—
So now we'll get married next month, shall we dear?"
  I ses: "No *love,*—hus bloomin' well *shan't"*
So she ses: "Why what *reason* is there for delay?
  The pater no longer forbids,"—

I ses: "There's *ten* reasons!"–"What are they?" she hasks,
   I hanswers: *"One* wife an' *nine* kids!"
Then she ses: "What a bounder you are for a joke,
   And you always so serious keep;–
Now come Percy love–" I ses: "Eh! Look 'ere miss,
   I *ain't* 'Percy love,'–*I'm the sweep!"*

THE COCKNEY TRIMMER

BY A. D. RIVER and HERBERT TOWNSEND   *1941*

I'm a trimmer in a merchant boat, wot tramps around
     the ocean,
  A-fetchin' grub and other things wot keeps the world
     in motion.
(Yus!) We goes away for munfs on end, don't often see the
     misses,
  (Nah!) We mostly sees a lot o' coal, and the sea wots
     filled wiv fishes.
I got a mate named Basil Cross, but I just calls 'im
     Jumper,
  And 'im and me's been lots of trips a-trimming down
     the bunker.
He's always got a cheery smile upon 'is cheery, fizog
  And as I'm long, and 'e is short, they call us Gog
     and Magog.
(Yus!) We shovels coals, and then more coal, for 'ours and
     'ours and 'ours,
  You'd never think there was so much in all this world
     of ours.
(Nah!) 'An no sooner do we get it down, and cleans the
     bunker empty,
  Than the skipper takes us into port, and finds out where
     there's plenty.
('Eartbreakin' I calls it.)

You'll maybe see our rusty sides, when next you're
    on a liner,
A-cruisin' round the Seven Seas, or on a trip to China.
    She's not a bloomin' "Cutty Shark" (Nah!) bluff lines a
    cargo lumper, (Yus!)
And down below, still shovellin' coal, 'll be me and my
    pal Jumper.
    They calls our ship the Gertie Lee, some calls 'er
    Dirty Gerty.
(Yus!) Well it's all the bloomin' coal she eats, that makes
    poor Gertie dirty.
    But for all 'er grime, 'er rusty sides, and the way we
    grouse about 'er.
She does 'er job, we earn a bob, and them's the things that
    matter.
    So when you see one of these craft, a-crawling round the
    briny. (an they do crawl)
Or comin' up the River Thames, don't turn and say
    "Cor blimey!"
    For even tho' you thinks she looks a blot upon the
    landscape,
Without 'er aid, to Britain's trade, you'd 'ave a bloomin'
    'eartache.
You'll never 'ear about 'er likes, except when there's a
    war on,
    And then they wonder wot they'll do, about their food
    and iron.
Well our old tub, 'll bring your grub, and carry on undaunted,
    Unless a mine or tin-fish hot, hits us where it's not wanted.
And even then you needn't fear, there's plenty more and
    finer,
    To carry on and bring the fings, from Egypt and from
    China.
And wiv the help of Air Force boys, and our bruvers in
    the Navy
    You'll get your meat, (yus) and lots to eat, while Fritz won't
    sniff the gravy.

COFFEE CUP'S RACE

BY CLIFFORD GREY & GREATREX NEWMAN and
WOLSELEY CHARLES 1925

Performed by Bransby Williams

You've heard about a Coffee Cup's Derby?
   Well, I trained that horse for the race,—
I've trained over ten thousand winners,
   And five thousand more for a place.
The Coffee Cup looked like a Shetland,
   Her tiny black mane shone like silk,
Her mouth was so small that to feed her
   We had to condense all the milk.
We stabled her out in a greenhouse,
   In the hope that she'd grow, under glass,
But Coffee Cup never got bigger,
   She still remained just *demi-tasse.*
The first big event that she ran in,
   I felt scared to death I must own,
She raced for a bride and a fortune,—
   To win me the Derby,— and Joan.
The bookmakers all tried to dope her,
   They knew that the horse couldn't fail.
They tried to put glue in her porridge,
   They tried to put salt on her tail.
On the way to the race I got anxious.
   I'd heard of the crooks in the town,
So I took Coffee Cup in a taxi,
   In case she got pinched going down.
We got to the race-course in safety.
   But Hawkins, the jockey, then struck,
He objected to ride on a Friday,
   In case it should bring him bad luck.
I rang up the Labour Exchanges,
   But they got all mixed up on the 'phone—
And sent round a heavyweight boxer,
   A giant of thirtyfour stone.
There wasn't time now to replace him,
   So off he was sent on the course,
The mob gave a yell when they saw him,

He was *three times* the size of the horse.
As soon as he sat in the saddle
    Poor Coffee Cup started to cough,
He just put his knees in the stirrups,—
    The flag fell—Hurray!—they were off!
The first quartermile was a whirlwind,
    But gamely away there she pegged,
The weight I could see must be telling,
    For the horse was becoming bow-legged.
But Coffee Cup still plodded onward,
    The corner she somehow got round,
The jockey had hard work to ride her,—
    His feet kept on touching the ground.
The others were gaining upon her,
    She gave a low pitiful whine,
I saw the poor horse had got hiccoughs,
    As well as a kink in her spine.
I knew now she'd not stay the distance,
    She seemed to have cramp in her legs,
She staggered—she fell—she lay helpless,—
    Poor Coffee Cup,—drained to the dregs.
Then up jumped that stout-hearted jockey,—
    Tho' I had quite given up the ghost,—
He stooped, and he picked up the horse in his arms,
    And ran with her—*first past the post!*

COMMON SENSE

BY A. HICKMAN-SMITH & NOSMO KING and
                                    ERNEST LONGSTAFFE   1938

When trouble looms around you and danger lies ahead;
    When your faith is almost shattered and your hopes are
        nearly dead,
There is always something left you—and its not a mere pretence,
    View your difficulties calmly—and use your common
        sense.

When there's talk of strife and danger and rumours fill
	the air.
When the facts are so distorted, that your views
	become unfair,
When mere trifles get so magnified until they seem
	immense,
Just forget your party politics—and use your common sense.
Other folks have got their troubles and they've got their
	point of view;
And its not in human nature—, all to think the same as you.
Try to see things from *their* angle,—listen in to their defence,
	And you'll come to agreement,—if you use your common
	sense.
Though we're given brains and judgment—quite a few of us
	I guess;
Let others do our thinking—and with borrowed views
	impress
Many other thoughtless people—who as a consequence,
	Believe the things they wouldn't—if they'd used their
	common sense.
Life is far from easy, tempers frayed and feelings sore;
	Because the world is suffering from an aftermath of war.
Rationing, controls and queues have grown to be immense!
	When they surely could be lessened—if we used our common
	sense.
Now the clouds have all departed—and there's brightness in
	the air,
And once again instead of strife—there's gladness everywhere,
Now the gloom of yesterday has gone—the feeling of suspense,
	It is because when things looked hopeless—SOMEONE USED
	HIS COMMON SENSE!

CONFIDENCE

BY HICKMAN SMITH and ERNEST LONGSTAFFE   *1939*

Confidence is what we need throughout the world today,
  Confidence in what we do and in the things we say,
Confidence, so great and sure, that nations trust each other,
  And all the races of mankind will treat each other
    as a brother.
There's plenty of everything upon this good old earth
  To supply the needs of every one, no matter what his worth.
Food for every living thing, by nature is provided
  If only we could see that is was equally divided.
No need for any living thing to hunger or to thirst:
  No need to quarrel who should be the last or be the first:
A just consideration for the rights of every one,
  Would make this world a Paradise for all to live upon.
Help for all the weaker ones, if given by the strong,
  Would add a greater zest to life, and help the world along:
And faith in justice and the right, once more would be fulfilled
  And sweet content would be our lot as the Great Creator
    willed.
The Creator of the Universe had nobler things to view
  When He gave the sun, the moon, the stars, and life to
    me and you.
The woods and streams, the mountains high, the sea and golden
    shore,
  Were never meant to be the cause of senseless, bloody war.
Oh would we had the will and power to insist on nature's plan,
  And build a world of Peace upon the Brotherhood of man,
No race for powerful armaments and the sacrifice of youth,
  But a world of true contentment built on Faith and Trust
    and Truth.
Oh men and women of the world, whatever be your creed
  Consider well your every thought your every act and deed
So that your children's children, and theirs, till time doth cease;
  Will live in perfect happiness, in unity and Peace.

CONSCIENTIOUS ALF

BY F. CHATTERTON·HENNEQUIN and PHYLLIS NORMAN
PARKER   1916

He's a little pale-faced skinny cove that doesn't weigh ten stone,
    And he used to have a conscience, now his fist is full
        of bone.
He's got a punch like Jimmy Wilde and Billy Wells in one,
    You just say "How's your conscience Alf?" and then you'll
        see some fun.
He used to preach against all wars, and violence and such,
    Outside the pubs on Saturdays but no one listened much,
Till one fine day he fell in love, then war broke out on top,
    And his life was not worth living, for his girl says "Shut
        up shop!
You go and put on khaki quick and give your tongue a rest"
    And Alf, whose mind was artful, says "Eliza, I'll attest!"
And so he did in Group sixteen, without a single squeal,
    Then spat upon his two and nine, "What ho! when I appeal!"
When Group sixteen was cited, oh! he went up like a bird,
    And laid his case before them, such a case was never heard.
He told them how he loved them all, his heart was soft and kind,
    Until the blessed chairman's eyes, with tears was nearly
        blind.
Mousetraps he says was sinful, flypapers made him squirm,
    And he'd never fished for tiddlers, 'cause he couldn't
        hurt a worm.
The whole tribunal sat and sobbed, the sitting was dissolved,
    And from Military service, Alf was then and there absolved.
So home he went to Liza, full of joy, but not for long,
    For he found her with a Naval chap, and going very strong!
Then Alf felt something go off Pop! He barked just like a dog,
    He fell upon that sailor bloke and downed him like a log.
The air was full of hymns of hate, they made Eliza cough,
    And six coppers and a fireman had to pull young Alfred off.
They strapped Jack on an ambulance, and as they bore him past,
    I heard him say "God bless old Tirps, the fleet's
        come out at last!"
Then Alf's Eliza grabbed his ear, her face was one broad grin,

"Now where's that blessed conscience Alf? You've done
    the old thing in
You join the London Scottish, say you're Mac, and wear
    a kilt,
    And if you find your knees are cold, I'll lend you
      mother's quilt!"
So Alf goes back and tells 'em straight, "I thought my
    'eart was kind,
    But now it ain't, you sign me on! I've changed my blooming
      mind!"

A CONTRAIRY BREEZE

BY W. SAPTE Jnr.   1904
    'Twas in the brig, the Nancy Trig,
      We were sailin' on the main,
    First as I guess'd nor-east by west,
      And then right back again—
    For the wind was cruel contrairy.
      We'd a first-rate crew and the skipper too
    Was an easy one to please,
      There was none aboard as we could afford
    To blame for that there breeze—
      But it sartinly was contrairy.
    From day to day we made no way,
      Which at first we didn't mind.
    For with quoits and skittles and grog and vittles
      Amusement we could find—
    Till the wind left being contrairy.
      But after a twelve-months' standing still, when we was
        tired o' play,
    The cap'n come, a lookin' glum, and thusly he did say—
      "This 'ere wind's cruel contrairy."
    And then he spat, and look'd around, and then he says,
        says he
      "For more nor a year we've lain about here, wherever
        it may be—

Where the wind's so durned contrairy.
Our owners o' course'll think we're a loss,
Which'll give 'em a deal o' pain.
Our wives'll shed a tear for the dead
And then they'll marry again—
For women's so durned contrairy.
But tho' that's bad it ain't the wust,
Which is, if you want to know,
We've very little more in the vittle store
And the grog's a gettin low—
Oh! cuss this wind contrairy.
Now ain't there a man as can hit on a plan
For makin' a bit o' way,
And any reward as I can afford
I'll very gladly pay
To cheat this breeze contrairy."
And then the skipper went below
And we knew as things were queer.
And we left off skittles and eked out the vittles
And felt as life was drear—
With the wind so cruel contrairy.
Well that day week we was pretty nigh dead,
And longed for a drop o' drink,
And overcome by famine, we was all of us dammin'
And swearin' like anythink—
For the wind still kep' contrairy.
Then up the vessel's poop I climbs
And looks around the main,
And over the side a thing I spied
As gave me hope again—
Tho' the breeze was so contrairy,
What gave me hope was a length of rope
As stiff as a maintopmast,
And I see clear as day why we made no way,
For we was a-hanchored fast—
Which made the wind *seem* contrairy.
Then up I leapt and I almost wept
As I sung out "Boys, yeo ho,"
And as soon as we was able we cut that cable,
And homeward we did go—
With the wind no more contrairy.
And the skipper he come and he said "It's rum

As we never noticed it afore—
   But never once again do I sail upon the main
If you Bill, stays ashore—
   Lest the wind should turn contrairy."

THE COQUETTE

BY ARTHUR COLES ARMSTRONG and SURTEES CORNE   *1910*

The man was a fool,—as some men are;
   And the woman—well, she belonged to her sex.
To the man, 'twas a matter of life, or death;
   To the woman—well, she belonged to her sex.
She stroked his chin, and she smoothed his hair,
   As he closed his eyes in delirious bliss.
"I love you! I love you! I love you!" he cried,
   Then he bartered his soul for the sake of a kiss.
The woman drew back, for there's something good—
   Yes, e'en in the heart of a vain coquette.
She had captured his soul, his life was hers,
   But she didn't want it,—at least, not yet!
"You must leave me now—you must try to forget!"
   Her heart was stone, yet her eyes were wet.
Then the world grew dark with a throb of pain,
   For the man no sun would shine again
He was good, he was staunch, he was honest and pure,
   But there's something a man cannot always endure.
He was not the first man that from Paradise fell,
   Yet he plunged into viciousness, plunged into hell.
It was brandy, and horses, and women, and dice—
   Deep in the depths of unspeakable vice.
She was false, she was fickle,—a vain coquette,
   And he drank—for hang it! he couldn't forget!
Three short weeks are three long years,
   When spent in bitterness, sorrow and tears,

But at last came a voice from the midnight sky,
  That was sweet as the song of the lark on high;
For it murmured of peace, of the blessings of sleep
  And it promised to dry the eyes that weep:
But his soul drew back, he held his breath;
  For the voice he heard was the voice of Death.
A ballroom—brilliant with light and good cheer—
  And the woman she says to her cavalier,
With a musical laugh, "Oh! he'll never fret,
  Like all the rest he'll soon forget."
But the moon shines down on a different place,—
  On a bloodstained throat and a ghastly face,
Where nothing is heard save the tick of the clock,
  And the door is locked and they knock and knock.
There's a moral in this; don't play with fire
  And don't, on your sleeve, wear your heart's desire
And remember this—a woman will fret
  For the things she thinks she never will get.
And it's certainly true, as sure as fate,
  We can get all we want if we work and wait—
So next to your heart this maxim keep;
  It's better to laugh than to weep.

THE COWARD

BY F. CHATTERTON HENNEQUIN and HARRY MAY HEMSLEY 1913

Performed by Bransby Williams

It was muttered in his club-room, it was whispered
    in the mess,
  As the rumour grew with telling, men believed it
    more or less.
Over cards they say it happened, grew to earnest from
    a joke,
  And tho' twenty heard the insult, yet the coward
    never spoke.

He had friends of course who waited, said his reasons
    must be good,
    But he did not give his reasons, and they never
        understood.
One by one they drifted from him, till the tale of friends
    was done,
    Tho' they shunned him like a leper, yet the coward
        spoke to none.
So the poison quickly spreading, reached at length his
    lady's ear,
    And she proudly said "I trust him," Tho' her heart was
        chill with fear,
All in vain she waited, hoping, till her faith in him
    grew weak,
    Then she gave him back his freedom, yet the coward would
        not speak.
Next his grim old Colonel heard it, and his brow grew
    black as night.
    "By the love I bore your father, By the God of truth
    and right,
They are liars all who say it"—then the man's heart
    nearly broke,
    "Tell your father's friend the truth boy," yet the coward
        never spoke.
So his Colonel sorely puzzled, got him transferred
    to the front,
    Where the snarling Hills-men squabble, and our Tommies
        bear the brunt,
They were ambushed in a donga, with all hope
    of rescue past,
    Came a whisper of surrender, then the coward spoke
    at last.
"We were sent here for a purpose, to uphold our Country's
    fame,
    If these dogs shall take us living, they will spit upon
    our name,
We must take the fighting chances, till our paltry lives
    are sped,
    Ere I give the word surrender you shall see me damned
    and dead."
On the Afghan border lying with his secret unconfessed

Is the coward with his story, locked for ever in
    his breast.
Were the reasons for his silence, such as you or I
    might guess?
Should he speak a friend's dishonour,
or a woman's shame confess?.
    More than this we may not question, for the truth is
    with the dead,
Till our secrets are discovered when the lives of men
    are read.
    But the Judgment Book will show it, clear of blame, free
    from disgrace,
When the coward gives his reasons, to his Maker face to face.

THE CUP

BY CHAS. W. ANSON and HAROLD ARPTHORP   *1927*

The great day dawned at last sir, so I tidied up the hearth,
    I kissed our pet canary and I filled its little bath.
I took down from the parlour wall the motto "Bless
    our Home",
    And in it wrapped my toothbrush, my pyjamas and
    a comb.
The wife is soundly sleeping, so outside the bedroom
    door
    I left for her a saucerful of milk upon the floor.
I shook the front-door mat sir, and I wound the "eight-day"
    up—
    Then took a third return sir, to do battle for the
    Cup.
The whole town saw us off sir, ev'ryone was there
    that day,
    If anyone was absent, well, they must have stayed
    away
And when we got to London the whole team embraced
    the guard,
    A gentle undertaker kindly gave us each his card.

At last we reached the stadium! I still can hear
    the roars
  That greeted my appearance in a breastplate
    and plusfours.
My rival spun the coin sir, and the umpire shouted "Wide!"
  I tried a mashie shot sir, and I chose the Surrey side.
The game began at once sir, as we had to wait until
  The referee was ready— he was drawing up his will.
And when he blew his whistle, all the p'lice for
    miles around,
  Made for the various exits and went home by
    Underground.
We won the first three sets sir, but I'm sorry to relate
  We'd six men out at half-time—and No Trumps upon
    the slate.
Our fellows passed like clockwork—they had passed
    exams at school,
  And every time they passed I put a penny in the pool.
Their forwards got the ball sir, and our fellows
    got the hump,
  But every man among them came down at the water-jump.
I sprang into the saddle and I freely used the whip,
  And then oh glorious sound sir, came a long and
    loud "Hip! Hip!"
The crowd rose as one man sir, as right through their
    ranks I broke,
  And made straight for their goal sir, with my famous
    trudgeon stroke.
I broke the halfmile record sir, and I might be
    going yet
  If I had not miscued sir, and nosedived into the net.
They gave me a free kick sir, and I kicked both hard
    and true,
  The ball went through a glasshouse in the Gardens
    down at Kew.
A boy scout brought the ball back—his good deed
    nobly done,
  And told the gladsome tidings—how I had holed
    in one.
And then the King sent for me—proudest moment of
    the day!—
  But, as I stood before him—ah! he faded right away!

My wife stood in his place sir, in her hand she
   held a cup
And saucer, and she said these words—"It's six o'clock.
   Get up!"

DAWN PATROL

BY WARREN HASTINGS and HERBERTE JORDAN   *1942*

I had a brother dressed in blue,
   An airman young and fine.
At dawn beside his Hurricane
   I took his hand in mine.
He said with a smile I knew so well,
   "Just off for a spot of fun."
I placed his hand in the Hand of God,
   And he flew toward the sun.

THE DEAR CHILDREN

BY F. RAYMOND COULSON and BELLAMY STEPHENS   *1913*

I love the sunny presence of a child.
   Dear children's happy influence has grown
Around my heart. (That boy will drive me wild
   Confound you, *will* you let the cat alone!)
How sweet it is to see the winsome grace,
   To hear the merry shouts of girls and boys;
Their voices seem like music in the place;
   (You squalling imp! Stop that infernal noise!)
It makes me feel a child myself again

To watch their playful gambols; and I think
Of days when—(Oh, it's driving me insane—
  You little wretch! You've upset all the ink!)
How fondly doth the happy parent gaze
  On infant forms that know not yet the shock.
Of life's hard toil. How innocent their ways
  (Great Jupiter! Young Tom has smashed the clock!)
I sit and watch them 'neath my lattice play,
  And though the window of my room is shut,
Me thinks I hear their little voices say—
  ("Jemima's tumbled in the water-butt!")
How joyous are the lads! Affection's tear
  Wells to my eyes; I feel my heart beat quick
With pride parental. (Eh? What's that I hear?
  "Your boy has smashed my winder with a brick!")
Ah, happy childhood! Soon 'twil pass a-lack!
  So let them laugh while we old folks admire.
(Oh, this last straw has broke the camel's back—
  They've gone and set the summerhouse on fire!)

DEVIL MAY CARE

BY CHAS. H. TAYLOR and CUTHBERT CLARK   *1905*

Performed by Bransby Williams

Fly, if you see me in the street
  Leave me to drift—to drift.
Turning aside if by chance we meet,
  Pray that the end come swift.
Once I was spick and span like you,
  Had money and all to spare:
Do you remember me? Yes you do!
  Dear old Devil-may-Care
Devil-may-Care who paid your debts
  When you'd gone the pace too fast;
Devil-may-Care whom the world forgets,
  But Devil-may-Care to the last.

Some of you tell today with pride,
　　Aye! brag of it here and there.
How you scattered the Pathans side by side
　　With Dashing Devil-may-Care.
You were plucky enough in days gone by
　　But you haven't the saving grace,
To look at me boldly in the eye
　　When you meet me face to face.
Not that I want it, Heaven knows;
　　Shabby with wear and tear,
Little remains now I suppose,
　　Of what once was Devil-may-Care.
How do I live? Well—never mind,
　　That's a secret I can keep;
I manage a sort of meal to find
　　And a place where I crawl to sleep.
To sleep, and see in a fitful dream
　　The wraith of a face once fair,
And a woman's eyes, whose tender gleam
　　Once dazzled old Devil-may-Care.
To wake, and wonder what might have been
　　Had the game been fairly played;
To wearily fumble the tangled skein
　　That a woman's fingers made.
We waltzed together the night we met—
　　'Twas an Indian summer night
And I gazed my fill in her eyes deep set
　　And her soul seemed pure and white.
Every one told me she was false,
　　And by Heaven! I proved it well;
And I danced the Devil's eternal waltz
　　That spins on the brink of Hell;
Till I reeled from the verge with a heart that broke,
　　And with pockets with nothing in.
And the world took the first for a lively joke,
　　But the last was a deadly sin.
What does it matter? It soon will end
　　With the sentinel's "Who goes there?"
And to Death I shall cheerfully cry—"A friend!"
　　And he'll say "Pass, Devil-may-Care."

93

A DICKENS' MONOLOGUE

BY *GEORGE PHILLIPS and W. R. SIMMONS* 1910

On a winter's night when wind and rain rage with a
    sullen roar,
With a pipe, a book, a blazing fire,— what does
    a man want more?
The firelight gleams on rows of books. What shall I read
    to-night?
Shall fancy roam in musty tome or a modern novel light?
Books well known, books unknown, books of immortal fame,
    Books whose fame is Empire-wide, bearing an honoured
    name.
Novels, poets, classics, modern wits and ancient sages—
    But I take one lettered "Copperfield" and turn its
    well loved pages.
Through Canterbury's sleepy streets in fancy now I roam
    To an ivy-covered, gabled house, 'tis Agnes Wickfield's
    home.
I climb the wide oak staircase and opening wide a door,
    There a pale faced, red haired clerk I see, stroking
    his lantern jaw.
Then from his seat at the high oak desk the slimy creature
    slides,
And rubbing his hands with vicious glee, towards me
    slowly glides.
    He greets me with effusion, but his handshake makes
    me creep.
He's a very 'umble person—his name Uriah Heep.

IMPERSONATION OF URIAH HEEP. "David Copperfield".

"Yes, Master Copperfield, I am working late, but I'm
    not doing office work.
Oh no, Master Copperfield, I'm improving my legal knowledge
    by reading through 'Tidd's Practice.'
    Oh! what a writer Mr. Tidd is, Master Copperfield. I'm
    a very 'umble person, Master Copperfield,

And I learnt my 'umility in a very 'umble school.
Father and me was brought up at a Foundation School for
boys,
And they taught us to eat 'umble pie with an appetite.
Where's my father now? At present he's a partaker
of glory, Master Copperfield,
But only in a very 'umble way, you know.
Must you be going now? You don't know'ow grateful I am
To you for 'onouring our 'umble roof. Goodbye, Master
Copperfield. Good-bye.

Curse him, the puppy!
Little does he know that I've got old Wickfield under my thumb,
And when I've crushed him I'll marry Agnes in spite of you,
David Copperfield— Curse you!

Oh! you've come back—for your gloves and stick.
Here they are. Good-bye once more and may Gawd bless you.

The firelight fades from the sad, sad page of a book we all know
well,
Where the master's pen has written the tale of Little Nell.
A storm-torn sky, a night-bird's cry, a glimpse of a struggling
moon—
In a churchyard still, on a lonely hill, I walk in the gathering
gloom
On a new-made grave, 'neath a yew-tree's shade, a poor old man
is kneeling.
He came at dawn, he was there at noon, now night is on him
stealing,
A gentle madness holds his brain, he knows not care or sorrow
With child-like faith? he murmurs "She'll come a-gain to-
morrow."

IMPERSONATION OF GRANDFATHER "Old Curiosity Shop."

Sh! softly—she's asleep in there my Nelly. Sh! We must not
wake her,
Though I should be glad to see her eyes a-gain— To see her
smile—
There's a smile on her face now, but it's fixed and changeless.

95

I would have it come and go, but that will be in God's good
time.
See here, her little shoes—she kept them to remind her of our
last long journey together.
Her little feet were bare upon the ground;
They told me afterwards how the rough stones had cut and bruised
them—
But she never told me that, no, God bless her! and I've
remembered since,
She walked behind that I might not see how lame she was.
She's sleeping soundly, and no wonder. Angel hands have
strewn the ground deep with snow,
That the lightest footstep may seem lighter yet,
And the very birds are dead, that may not wake her.
She used to feed them, sir. They never flew away from her.
How is it that the shutters are all up, and the folk are nearly
all in black today?
They say my Nelly's dead, but, no! She'll come a-gain tomorrow.
In the destroyer's steps there rise up new creations, which defy
his power,
And his dark path becomes a way of light to heav'n
She'll—come—again—to morrow."

And once again the scene is changed, in Paris now I stand,
While shrieks of hate and blood lust rings thro' the desolated
land.
A-long the death-cart rumbles, with its load of living dead,
To where Madame La Guillotine up-rears her ghastly head.
There Carton gladly gives his life for the freedom of his friend,
And thus his wasted, ill spent days, haste to a noble end.
A little world of love he sees in England fair and free,
And the knitting women, counting, murmur softly, "Twenty
Three."

IMPERSONATION OF SYDNEY CARTON "A Tale of Two Cities."

Goodbye, Lucie, goodbye, Life. Lead on, my gaoler!
Few are so weary of life's load as I am.
The world in which I have done so little, and wasted so much,
fades fast from me,
And in its stead I see the lives of those for whom I lay down
my life,

Peaceful, useful, prosperous and happy in that England which
    I shall behold
I see that child who lay upon her bosom, and who bore my name,
A man, winning his way up the path of life which once was mine.
    I see him winning it so well that my name is made illustrious
        by the light of his.
I see the blots I threw upon it faded a-way.
    I see him foremost of just judges and honoured men, bringing
        a boy of my name.
With a forehead that I know, and golden hair to this place,
    Then fair to look up-on, and I hear him tell the child my story
        in a tender and a faltering voice.
It is a far, far better thing that I do, than I have ever done,
    It is a far, far better rest that I go to than I have ever known.

A DORG'S LIFE

BY MARTYN HERBERT and HERBERTE JORDAN   *1925*

Life 'asn't been no blinkin' bed o' roses
    Since my missus came in-to a bit o' brass,
She's all for getting in-to 'igh Soci'ty,
    An' she's down on anything wot isn't class.
Our ole pals isn't good enough.
    We've 'ad to tick 'em off.
An' she's got 'er work well cut out,
    Turnin' me into a torf.
I've got to wear a collar now on week-days,
    I mustn't wear no 'orsey lookin' suits,
I mustn't wear my albert wiv the football medals on,
    I mustn't wear my saucy yeller boots.
I mustn't wear white spats wiv flannel trousers,
    Or, if I do, there's trouble an' there's strife,
I mustn't wear my carpet slippers wiv my dinner jacket,
    Oh, I tell you it's a fair dorg's life.
You wouldn't credit 'ow my wife 'as altered,
    She used to be a reg'lar modest sort

But now she's fairly potty over dancing,
　　She says as 'ow she's goin' to 'ave me taught.
We use-ter 'ave a good name once, respectable, though poor,
　　Well, you couldn't call us poor, nor yet respectable
　　　　no more.
I use-ter 'ave to fasten all 'er dresses,
　　Right up the back,—a fine old time it took.
Well 'er new evenin' dresses now, they save me all the trouble,
　　'Cos they 'aven't any blessed back to hook.
If I say I don't approve of shimmy-shakin'.
　　She simply shuts me up just like a knife.
Now she's goin' to a fancy ball as Eve—wiv me as Adam!
　　Oh I tell you, it's a fair dorg's life.
We use-ter 'ave sixpennorth at the pictures,
　　Or else go in the gall'ry at the "Brit,"
Of course, if it was special, like the pantomime at Christmas,
　　Then we use-ter queue up for the early pit.
But all that's far too vulgar for my missus nowadays
　　It's Covent Garden Op'ra now, or else these 'igh-brow plays.
You can't 'ave any monkey nuts or winkles,
　　You can't suck oranges, it ain't the fing
You must'nt sing the choruses, they'd tell you that was rowdy,
　　'Sides, there isn't any choruses to sing.
Between ourselves I'm fair fed up wiv Op'ra,
　　But it's classy, an' it seems to suit the wife
So she's goin' to take me wiv'er to another one next Tuesday,
　　Oh, I tell you it's a fair dorg's life.
Of course you 'aven't moved in 'igh-class circles,
　　But if you'ad you'd know just 'ow it feels.
It's my 'ead wot does the circles, I can tell you,
　　I worries till at times it fairly reels.
I've to study 'ow to eat, an' 'ow to dress, an' 'ow to walk
　　I've got to study every word I'm usin' when I talk.
I mustn't talk 'orse-racin' to the curate,
　　I mustn't tell the ladies saucy jokes,
I'm not allowed to swear before the servants, if you please,
　　Life's pretty 'ard for really swagger folks.
I've got to leave off sayin' 'My old woman',
　　Though everybody knows as she's my wife,
I mustn't say "Gor Blimey" when I'm talking to the Bishop,
　　Oh I tell you it's a fair dorg's life!

DREAMIN' OF THEE

BY EDGAR WALLACE and ERNEST LONGSTAFFE   *1938*

Performed by Cyril Fletcher

Dreamin' of thee! Dreamin' of thee! Sittin' with my elbow on
    my knee,
    I orter be a polishin' the meat dish an' the can—I orter
    draw the groceries—for I'm an ord'ly man,
But wot are bloomin' rations, an' wots a pot or pan,
    When I'm dreamin' O my darlin' love of thee.
Dreamin' of thee! Dreamin' of thee! Firin' at the rifle range
    I be.
    I've missed a fust class targit—an' I've missed the 'ill behind,
I nearly shot a marker once! (which wasn't very kind)
    The orficer he swears at me—but really I don't mind,
I am dreamin' O my darlin' one of thee.
    Dreamin' of thee! Dreamin' of thee!   Me, as was smart as
    smart I cud be!
My kit is all untidy—an' its inches thick in dust,
    An' my rifle's fouled an' filthy, an' my baynit's red with rust,
They've tried to find a reason but I've seen 'em further fust,
    An' they never guess I'm dreamin' dear of thee.
Dreamin' of thee! Dreamin' of thee! They can't make out
    wot's comin' over me
    The fellows think I'm barmy, an' the Major thinks it's drink,
The Sergeant thought it laziness, so shoved me in the clink!
    The Colonel called it thoughtlessness, so gave me time to think,
An' to dream again my darlin' one of thee.
    Dreamin' of thee! Dreamin'of thee! Wot's two hours sentry go
    to me.
A sittin' in a sentry box a thinkin' of your eyes,
    The ord'ly orficer come along an' took me by surprise
'E said as I was sleepin' an' the usual orfice lies,
    When I was only dreamin' love of thee.
Dreamin' of thee! Dreamin' of thee! Wond'rin' what they're
    goin' ter do ter me—
    Oh when I'm in the Ord'ly Room I know I'll cop it 'ot,
I'll be 'auled before the C.O. p'raps git sentenced to be shot
    But whether I git punishment, or whether I do not,
They can't prevent me dreamin' love of thee.

THE DREAM RING OF THE DESERT

BY J. MILTON HAYES and R. FENTON GOWER   1912

The Merchant Abu Khan shunned the customs of his race,
  And sought the cultured wisdom of the West.
His daughter—fair Leola—had the desert's supple grace,
  With an English education of the best.
The suitors for her hand were as grains of desert sand,
  But the merchant bade the Arab swarm begone:
And he swore a mighty oath, she should only make her troth
  With an Englishman—an Englishman or none!
The chieftain Ben Kamir, tho' rejected, stayed to plead,
  But Abu Khan replied, "Thy suit is vain.
I cast aside my kinsmen and I scorn the prophet's creed;
  So get thee to thy tents—across the plain."
"Enough," the Chief replied, "Thine eyes are blind
    with pride,
  But Allah hears my prayers and guides my star.
With patience I shall wait till I am called by Fate,
  And then I shall return to Akabar."
The right man came at last in the month of Ramadhan,
  An Englishman who learned to love her soon.
His suit was proudly sanctioned by the merchant Abu Khan,
  And the wedding was to be at the full moon.
The merchant, in his pride, thought the news too good to hide,
  And it circled round the desert near and far:
Circled round and caught the ear of the chieftain
    Ben Khamir,
  And he turned his camel's head to Akabar.
The chieftan wore his robe of green, an emblem of
    his rank.
  And many bowed in honour of the man.
But heedless of their reverence he beat his camel's
    flank,
  And rode on to the house of Abu Khan.
The merchant, from his roof, saw the chief, but held aloof,
  A suitor twice dismissed was one to shun—
But Kamir declared his ride was in homage to the bride,
  And the merchant's fears vanished one by one.

100

"Leola," said the Arab, as she came to greet the
    guests,
"Thy praises are beyond what I can sing,
But let this little token bring the fortune of the best."
    And he placed upon her hand an opal ring.
"Tis more than what it seems, and its spell shall
    gild thy dreams,
For 'twas carried by Mohamet, Allah's Priest."
Then the chieftain said goodbye, and she watched him
    with a sigh,
    As he rode across the desert to the East.
Leola dreamt a dream most strange, and nightly 'twas
    the same,
    And love within her breast began to peep.
A voice from out the burning sandhills called and called
    her name,
    And waking she would long again for sleep.
The wedding eve's bright moon saw her rise as from
    a swoon,
    With the dream voice ringing still within her ear,
Saw her glide toward the sand, where the stately
    palm-trees stand,
    To the desert, and the arms of Ben Kamir.
The chieftain pointed Eastward to the plains he
    loved so well,
    And told her of his plans for hasty flight.
The dream-ring on her finger held her soul within
    its spell,
    And they rode across the desert thro' the night.
On the morrow, lined with care, at the Maghrib
    sunset prayer,
    The merchant joined the worshippers unshod.
And he cried with spirit broken, as the Meuddin's
    chant was spoken,
    "Mahomet *is* the prophet—God *is* God"

THE DUET

BY *ELLA WHEELER WILCOX* and *GEORGE HAY*   1920

I was smoking a cigarette; Maud, my wife, and the
    tenor McKey
Were singing together a blithe duet.
And days it were better I should forget came suddenly
    back to me.
Days when life seemed a gay masque ball,
And to love and be loved as the sum of it all.
    As they sang together the whole scene fled,
The room's rich hangings, the sweet home air,
    Stately Maud, with her proud blonde head,
And I seemed to see in her place instead
    A wealth of blue-black hair,
And a face, ah! your face,—yours, Lisette,
    A face it were wiser I should forget.
We were back—well, no matter when or where,
    But you remember, I know, Lisette,
I saw you, dainty and débonaire,
    With the very same look that you used to wear
In the days I should forget.
    And your lips, as red as the vintage we quaffed,
Were pearl-edged bumpers of wine when you laughed.
    Two small slippers with big rosettes
Peeped out under your kilt-skirt there,
    While we sat smoking our cigarettes.
(Oh, I shall be dust when my heart forgets!).
    And singing that self-same air;
And between the verses for interlude
    I kissed your throat, and your shoulders nude.
You were so full of a subtle fire,
    You were so warm and so sweet, Lisette;
You were everything men admire,
    And there were no fetters to make us tire;
For you were—a pretty grisette.
    But you loved, as only such natures can,
With a love that makes heaven or hell for a man.
    They have ceased singing that old duet,

Stately Maud and the tenor McKey.
  "You are burning your coat with your cigarette,
And *qu'avez vous,* dearest, your lids are wet,"
  Maud says, as she leans o'er me.
And I smile, and lie to her, husband-wise,
  "Oh, it is nothing but smoke in my eyes." ·

AN EAST-END SATURDAY NIGHT

BY F. RAYMOND COULSON and ROBERT M. ANGUS   *1914*

Saterday nite in Bethnal Green,
  Naptha lamps a-flarin'
Along the gutters for nearly a mile,
  And men and wimmen blarin'.
Men and wimmen with kippers and whelks,
  Taters, an' beans an' marrers,
Nearly a mile in Bethnal Green
  Nothin' but costers' barrers.
Saterday crowds in Bethnal Green
  Sunday dinners a-buyin',
Some without the money to buy,
  Lookin', an' longin', an' sighin'.
Kids wot 'aven't bin washed for years
  Moppin' up 'a 'penny ices,
Mothers o' famerlies gittin' their meat,
  An' batin the butcher's prices.
Pub's an fried fish shops all full,
  Wives in blazin' rages,
'Usbands up to the same old game,
  Blewin' the whole week's wages.
Fat old wimmen o' sixteen stone,
  Simperin', drunk and leery,
Little gals leadin' their fathers 'ome,
  Staggerin', boozed, and bleary.
Pickpockets, blokes on the kinchin' lay,
  Fellers and gals amashin',

Twig young 'Arry acrost the way
  Givin' his tart a thrashin'.
An' twig that pale little barefooted kid—
  Looks as ef she was dyin'—
Sobbin' as ef she'd break 'er 'art.—
  Wonder wot set her cryin'?
Foller that barefooted kid of eight
  Into a lonely turnin'.
Foller 'er up to a fust-floor back,
  Where a taller candle's burnin'.
Father's awaitin' there for 'er,
  An' don't 'e welcome 'er?—Rather!
That little kid's bin out ter beg
  For money—for drink—for father!
"Only tuppence? Wy, dash yer eyes,"
  (There's a look on' is mug like killin'),
"I told yer not to show yer face
  Until you'd copp'd a shillin'."
Father ups with 'is 'eavy fist,
  Swears as 'e'll smash and blind 'er.
An' out she dashes, that terrified kid,
  With that 'orrible face behind 'er.
Out she dashes, an' runs, an' runs,
  Pantin', with tears a-flowin',
Out throo the crowd in Bethnal Green—
  Too frightened to look where she's goin'.
There's a roar in 'er ears like the roar of the sea,
  There's a buzzin', an' whirlin', an' hummin',—
Ere's the larst bus comin' up Bethnal Green;
  But that kid don't see it comin'!
Yells, an' shrieks, an' a surgin' crowd,
  Larst bus stops in a hurry.
—"Lift 'er on to the stretcher, Jim,
  Orl rite, mum, don't you worry;
A doctor won't be no good to 'er,
  Gord bless yer, she's gorn to clover!"—
Saterday nite in Bethnal Green, An' another kid
      run over,

EIGHTY AND THREE

BY LESLIE JAMES   *1948*

directions   most   the staff

I'm known to the king and the best of nobility,
   I'm Jenkins, the butler—in service, you see,
And mine is a job that needs mental agility,
   A happy possession, I'm sure you'll agree.
When announcing the gentry, I've just the right touch,
   I remember their names and their titles and such.
And though I'm no chicken, I still have ability.
   I've worked all my life, and I'm eighty and three!
I've always been one to appreciate quality,
   A sense of good humour is vital to me;
I often join in with the innocent jollity
   When ladies are taking their afternoon tea;
But the time I like best is when they start to dine,
   For it's then I can get a good sniff of the wine!
Though the *smell* of a cork won't induce much frivolity—
   I still reach the cellar at eighty and three!
I've lived several years more than three score and ten.
   And mingled and mixed with the wealthier men.
But the rich have their troubles, like you and like me,
   When a friend is more comfort than wealth, don't you see?
So if I am spared, I shall be to the end,
   None other than Jenkins—the butler—the friend.
My motto in life is the one word—'civility,'
   My humble success still depends on that key.
I've served with a joy never touched by humility.
   And serving, I've known what true friendship can be.
In the problems of life I've been helped from the start,
   Now I know you won't mind if I open my heart—
But there's one Lord far greater than all the nobility,
   And I'm still in *His* service at eighty and three.

EMPTY GLASSES

BY HAROLD SIMPSON and DAISY HILL   *1945*

I stands be'ind the blinkin' bar as closing time comes round
    And 'opes the stroke of ten ain't far before I 'ears it sound,
The room is full of noise and 'um just like a lot of bees,
    I 'as to shout like kingdom come, "Time gents, time
        if you please".
Then when the last of 'em is gone I locks up for the night.
    Then looks around and gazes on a most depressing sight.
Just empty glasses by the score and empty bottles too,
    Those empty glasses make me sore; there's washing-up to do.
I ups and 'eaves a 'earty sigh and starts upon me job,
    Then starts to dream of days gone by, I does, so 'elp me bob.
I dreams of gents in fancy dress I've somewhere read about
    Who'd drink three bottles, nothing less, before they passes out.
    I dreams that I can see them now, the good old-fashioned
        sort,
With 'and in air and lordly bow they drinks a toast in port.
    Then when they've tippled all they can, that's more than
        I'd be able.
Each fine old English gentleman slides underneath the table.
    Yuss, empty glasses that's my theme as I've 'eard
        speakers say,
Just empty glasses made me dream, one dream 'as come to stay.
    A supper table laid each night, one empty glass is there,
"God send our boy back home alright," is me and
        mother's prayer.
    And then I sort of trims my sails, starts washing-up like 'ell,
But can't 'elp thinking of what tales an empty glass can tell.
    Oh, blast. I've broke one, what a shame, the boss'll think
        I'm canned
I'll 'ave to tell 'im that it came to pieces in my 'and.
    Did I say empty glasses, why here's one with sumthin in,
I never lets a drink go by, so cheerio, chin, chin.

'ERBERT, A.B.

BY F. C. HENNEQUIN and PERCY WATSON   1915

Now I ain't proud I never 'old wiv lookin' down on folks
  'Ose education ain't first class like some more
    favored blokes.
I pity's them for what they miss they wasn't brought up
  right
  To never 'ave no savvy fair nor mix wiv the Helite.
But one thing hiritates me and drives me horff my chump
  A chap wot drops 'is Haitches gives me the bloomin' ump.
But once I had a shipmate not so very long ago,
  A finer man was never shipp'd from Portsmouth to the 'Oe,
'Is manner wiv the ladies was a thing to dream about,
  Tho' when it came to Haspirates 'e always left 'em out.
Once we was with two nice young girls, real 'igh
    class extra jam,
  When in the midst of supper 'e says " 'Orace 'ave some
    'am."
On one occasion off Spithead a princess come on board,
  Wiv duchesses and h'admirals and 'is nibs the First
    Sea Lord.
She patted guns and looked at things as pleased as she
    could be,
  Till a gust of wind took hoff 'er 'at and blew it out
    to sea.
Then 'Erbert put 'is spoke in and 'e put the lid on fair,
  'E says "Never mind yer 'at miss, you just 'old on
    to yer 'air."
But soon we 'ad our 'ands full with something diffcrent quite,
  When we caught the Deutchers napping and they 'ad to
    stand and fight.
We sank one blessed cruiser and the sea was black around,
  Wiv struggling 'uman creatures wiv the wounded and
    the drowned.
When we launched our boats and 'Erbert went to save them
    from their fate
  'E says "Now then 'Orace 'urry never mind their 'ymn
    of 'ate."

And then from their 'ead quarters some German h'airships
  came
  To drop their bombs on friend and foe—a dirty
    wicked game—.
Poor 'Erbert's boat went under but we launched another
    quick
  And pulled away like demons, till I thought my back
    would rick.
And when we got quite close to them my word I give a yelp,
  For I knew that it was 'Erbert when some-one shouted
    "'Elp."
'E'd saved a German 'ambone who was pretty nearly drown'd,
  And 'Erbert 'e was wounded as we very quickly found.
We got 'im to the sick bay but the doctor shook is 'ead,
  And I 'eard 'im say beneath 'is breath "It's a marvel
    'e ain't dead."
When the chaplain asks 'im gently "Is there 'ope?" 'E
    answers "none"
  Then 'Erbert gives a sort of smile and whispers " 'Ow's
    the 'Un?"
We said the 'Un was mending and 'e whispers "That's
    all right,"
  And so low we 'ardly 'eard 'im it was something like
    a fright,
"If I've killed a lot of 'umans, well I saved one life
    to-day
  Will they know it where I'm going sir, is it 'Ell or
    'Eaven, eh?"
Then the Chaplain says "It's 'Eaven man" and turned 'is 'ead
    aside,
  But the Haitch he dropp'd on purpose went with 'Erbert
    when 'e died.

FALLEN HALO

BY HARRY WYNNE and CUTHBERT CLARKE   *1919*

Performed by Bransby Williams

You ask what it means, the painting there
  Of the white-robed girl in the old oak seat,
With the saintly face, and the golden hair,
  And the broken Halo at her feet.
She sat just there in the old oak chair,
  In the radiant sun of a summer noon.
And we pledg'd our troth not with mighty oath,
  But with hearts that beat to the self-same tune.
Then I took my brush as she linger'd there,
  She was all my world, and I seem'd to see
A golden halo round her hair,
  So I painted her as a saint might be.
I felt so sure she was good and pure,
  That in dreams by night, and in thoughts by day,
I built her shrine in this heart of mine,
  Till I woke to find that her feet were clay.
It's the same old story—a strong man's love,
  And the power that lies in a woman's spell,
To raise his soul to the heights above,
  Or cast it down to the deepest hell.
Then I set may face and I went the pace,
  And I curs'd my God and I long'd to die.
And I sometimes think that I touch'd the brink
  Of the Great Unknown, where our futures lie.
I awoke at last when my cash was spent
  And my credit stretch't to its utmost span,
And I sat and thought what the future meant.
  But I vowed, thank God, "I will be a *man*."
I came back here, tho' it cost me dear,
  For the painting stood on the easel there,
And the great flood-tide of my love and pride
  Surged thro' my soul with a black despair.
Then I took a brush in my shaking hand,
  I could almost hear my own heart beat,
And I painted out the golden band
  And I placed it, broken, at her feet.

Tho' the halo's fallen and rent apart,
  It's a band of gold and it shineth yet;
And I know, deep down in my broken heart.
  That I love her still, and I can't forget.

A FALLEN STAR

BY ALBERT CHEVALIER and ALFRED H. WEST   *1898*

Thirty years ago I was a fav'rite at the "Vic."
  A finished actor, not a Cuff and Collar shooting stick.
I roused the house to laughter, or called forth the silent tear,
  And made enthusiastic gods vociferously cheer
Those were the days, the palmy days, of historic art,
  Without a moment's notice I'd go on for any part.
I do not wish to gas, I merely state in self-defence,
  The denizens of New Cut thought my Hamlet was
      immense.
Thirty years ago! I can hear them shout "Bravo,"
  When after fighting armies I could never show a scar,
That time, alas! is gone, and the light that erstwhile shone
  Was the light of a falling star.
From patrons of the circle too, I had my meed of praise,
  The ladies all admired me in those happy halcyon days.
My charm of manner, easy grace, and courtly old-world air,
  Heroic bursts of eloquence, or villain's dark despair.
I thrilled my audience thrilled 'em as they never had
      been thrilled
And filled the theatre nightly as it never had been filled!
Right through the mighty gamut of emotions I could range
  From classic Julius Ceasar to the "Idiot of the Grange."
Thirty years ago! I was someone in the show,
  And now I pass unrecognised in crowded street or bar!
The firmament of fame holds no record of my name,
  The name of a fallen star!
The dramas that I played in were not all up on the stage.
  Not did I in an hour become the petted of the age.

110

Oft in my youthful days I've sung "Hot Codlins" as the
    clown,
And turned my face away to hide the tear-drops rolling
    down.
And when the pit and gallery saw I'd wiped the paint away,
    They shouted "Go it, Joey. Ain't 'e funny? Hip hooray!"
My triumphs, and my failures, my rise, and then my fall!
    They've rung the bell, the curtain's down, I'm waiting
        for my call!
Bills—not those I owe—But old play-bills of the show!
    My name is Hamlet, Lear, Virginius, Shylock, Ingomar!
The laurel on my brow—a favourite—and now—
    Forgotten! a fallen star!

THE FAMOUS NAME OF "SMALL"

BY V. F. STEVENS and LAURI BOWEN   *1935*

There are names as written down in Britain's history,
    Sooch as Drake and Nelson, Iron Dook an' all.
But coom to work it out, bloomin' names like them are nowt,
    When reckoned wi' the name of Samuel Small.
From the day that Conquering Bill came here in One-o-
    sixty-six,
    The name of Small 'as always 'eld its spell.
It were a Small as plucked the posies, for the "Battle
    of the Roses",
    There were a Small at Waterloo tha knows as well.
One Small coom down from Lancashire to join wi' Robin
    Hood,
    'E 'ad a saucy posh green suit and curly locks,
'E were one o't Smalls from Wigan, but, By Gum, 'e were
    a big 'un,
    'E must a' stood nigh seven foot in socks.
Underneath the greenwood tree, they gave Sam a long oak
    staff,

A kind o' scaffold pole cut fresh from glen.
An' they told 'im there at once, it were for crackin' folk
      on't bonce,
  'Cos they hadn't 'eard of ruddy muskets then.
Sam very soon got doughty wi' is scaffold-pole of oak,
  As an archer, 'is skill won all their hearts.
At 'undred yards 'e'd kill a sparrow, 'e were 'ot wi' bow
      and arrow.
  Well, the Smalls today are champion at darts.
But alas! it were 'is fondness for stringing bows at birds,
  That eventually brought owd Sam to grief.
'Cos 'e weren't content wi' potting 'em, in't forest
      outside Nottingham,
  'E draws a bow at bird belonging t' Chief.
It happened in this way, one day Robin were on scrounge,
  And he chanced to roam a longish way from camp;
So Sam thought he'd try to carry on wi' the pretty wench
      Maid Marion
  And 'e tried 'is luck and slung 'er the glad lamp.
Now this pretty wench Maid Marion
      she were a comely dame,
No 'igh'eeled shoes nor swanking wi' bobbed 'air,
  She'd not gone in for slimmin', like your bloomin'
      modern wimmin',
A gradely lump o' lass she were, so there!
  "Good morrow, fairest damsel," said Sam, all gushing like,
"Gad-zooks! I'd like to walk with thee I trow."
  But when Marion got a sight o' this great Wigan blighter,
Said she, "If Robin comes there'll be a row."
  "Don't fill your pretty head with thoughts like that," said
      Sam,
"Besides 'e rode away at early dawn."
  And Sam started into doing a reet champion o' wooing,
But just then they heard a blast on Robin's horn.
  Now that single plaintive note which rang through
      Sherwood's glade,
Were a sign that Robin wanted 'elp and such.
  So his men soon gathered round, Robin counted them
      and found
One short, but did he worry? Ho! not much.
  'E soon tumbled it were Sam, and guessed what 'e were 'at,
And tha knows 'e never even clenched a fist;

'E just turned to Friar Tuck and said, "I wish that
    blighter luck,
I'm glad because that dame's on't transfer list.
But we mustn't let 'im get away wi' such a trick as that,
We must make a pris'ner of 'im," Robin said,
    "And according to our creed 'e'll consider 'imself freed,
The moment 'e and Marion are wed."
    Now remember what I said at first about our famous names,
And about theer always being one called Small,
    Well, Sam and Marion went great guns, for she bore him
    Seven Sons,
And every one a Sam! She did an' all!

FILTHY LUCRE

BY WISH WYNNE and BERNARD KITCHEN   *1932*

I'd go and drown me bloomin' self for two pins.
    I'd run away if I knew where to go.
Father's uncle, him abroad, has died and left us all his money,
    Why he didn't take it with 'im, I don't know.
Now we don't live down in Barker's Court no longer,
    We're living in a place they call "Park View,"
We've got five rooms on our own, and there's only fourteen
    of us,
    We lose our bloomin' selves in 'em, we do.
I wish we'd never had the rotten money.
    We're all as mis'rable as we can be.
We don't know nobody and nobody knows us,
    And no-one wants to as far as I can see.
We don't get any fun, not like we used to.
    Father's doing things he never did before.
Mother 'asn't 'ad a black eye now for weeks and weeks
    and weeks,
    And we were so happy when we were poor.
I always thought me mother's name was 'Liza.
    It's the only name I ever knew she had;

Now father calls her Elizabeth, ain't it a rotten name?
   And she calls 'im Herbert—'Erbert's just as bad.
If yer want to know something, we've got a slavery.
   But yesterday I punched her on the nose.
So she's going 'ome on Saturday, a jolly good job too.
   Still me mother'll get another one I suppose.
I wish the bloomin' bank would bust or something,
   And let us be just like we used to be.
We mustn't fight, we mustn't pinch, we mustn't swear,
      it's awful.
   If anyone is sick of it, it's me.
The girls at Park View College they all hate me.
   Barker's Court girls they won't speak to me no more.
And now me mother says we've got to go to Sunday School,
   And we were so happy when we were poor.
I want to go where we know all the people,
   It's rotten, straight, where we're a-living now.
Yer never sees a fight unless the sparrers start a-sparrin',
   Then the neighbours all complain about the row.
We're all respectable in Park View Terrace.
   Well, a parson lives at number twenty-two.
We've all got handles on our doors, and blinds up at the
      winders,
   And the copper comes down by hisself, he do.
Oh, I want to see Bill Johnson slosh his missus,
   The same he used to ev'ry Saturday night.
And throw his mother down the stairs and fling things at the
      copper,
   And see Ginger Bill and Hoppy have a fight.
Now I've go to comb me hair out ev'ry morning,
   And me face it ain't 'arf getting awful sore,
'Cause every time I get it dirty now I've got to wash it,
   And we were so happy when we were poor.

THE FLYING BOATMAN

BY CHARLES J. WINTER   *1916*

Performed by Bransby Williams

Stick to your trade is the motter for me,
   And a wonderful good motter too,
The cobbler should stick to 'is wax so I say,
   And the joiner should stick to 'is glue.
I've follered the sea for forty odd year,
   But I once by mistake broke away,
And I follered the air just by way of a change,
   For the whole of one perishing day.
It 'appened like this some aeronaut chap
   To the village 'ad brought a balloon,
And 'e anchors it down in a field, for next day
   'E was giving a show about noon.
Well I leant on some rails looking seaward,
   And dreamed of the bar at the Magpie and Stump,
When my pipe was sent flying right out of my mouth,
   And I gets an almighty great thump.
The wind 'ad sprung up, the balloon 'ad broke loose,
   I was lifted right clean off my feet,
For in passing, the anchor 'ad dragged on the ground
   And then stuck in my trousers' seat!
I often 'ave 'eard of a rise in the world,
   But *this* rise would be 'ard to match,
And I blessed my old woman who'd done such good work
   When she sewed on my trousers that patch.
Up went the balloon, and I dangled beneath
   Like a worm on a fisherman's line.
Down below were my boats all let out by the hour
   Not a penny of which would be mine.
I 'ollered and screamed till my voice got quite hoarse
   And my throat got uncommonly dry,
But all I could 'ear was some kids who cried out
   "Look, old Ben's going up to the sky!"
I travelled all day with the 'ot sun above
   And the blue rolling waters beneath,
When I 'ears a loud hiss, the balloon sprung a leak
   And the gas rushes out of the sheath.

Then I 'ad an idea, I'd been often blown out
  By the drinking of bottles of Bass.
So I climbed up and placed my mouth over the hole
  And sucked in the Hydrogen gas!
I started to swell and my buttons flew off
  With the sound of a crackling spark,
And as the balloon 'ad quite shrunk, why I
  Chopped it away with a cutting remark.
Relieved of its weight I bobbed up so 'igh
  I thought I'd bash into the stars.
Then I gently and gracefully fluttered to earth
  Like the man in the "Message from Mars."
Down below was the land I'd crossed over the sea
  So I knew I should come down in France,
But the Frenchies it seems didn't quite like the look
  Of me doing my aerial dance.
They started off firing their pistols and guns
  Till the shots flew about me like rain,
So I kicked off me boots, rose, and caught some fresh wind
  And then sailed back to England again.
But when I touched ground why I bobbed up again
  Till I'd covered a furlong or two,
And so I proceeded with bounds and with 'ops
  Like a terrible great kangaroo.
In the village the news of my going 'ad spread
  And the people were running about,
They'd rung all the bells, they 'ad let the dogs loose
  And old Jack the Towncrier was out
Announcing they'd give a reward of ten bob
  Which the Mayor 'ad made up to eleven
To the one who would bring them back old Boatman Ben
  Who 'ad taken a trip up to heaven.
But up to the evening they'd not heard a word.
  They were all of them getting the pip,
When they see me come bounding and bouncing along
  Like springheeled Jack out on the rip.
They threw me a line which I caught in the air
  And 'eld firmly grasped in my 'and.
Then they 'auled me to earth to the toon of the
  "Conquerin' Hero" played by the Town Band.
They thought I'd float off so they sat on my 'ead
  Till I couldn't see out of my eyes,

But the gas I got rid of cussing and swearing
   Redooced me about half the size.
I ain't got well yet, but I'm getting along
   With the 'elp of some Guiness and Bass,
But still you can tell by the way that I talk
   I have still got a good deal of gas!

FOR A WOMAN'S SAKE

BY LORNA FANE and CUTHBERT CLARKE   *1908*

Performed by Bransby Williams

He fought for his country as brave men will,
   Who *die* for their country's sake,
But there was a mightier motive still
   And a higher prize at stake.
He fought for the fame where glory lies;
   To win a smile from a woman's eyes.
He spurred on his horse to its utmost speed,
   And thick in the fight rode he,
And many a noble heroic deed
   Was done in his bravery.
But the one reward he craved was this,
   To feel the touch of a woman's kiss.
He lived in the saddle from dawn till night,
   And often till dawn again.
And the sun rose red on a ghastly sight,
   Of wounded amidst the slain:
But thro' the horror of time and place,
   His thoughts were full of a woman's face.
He stuck to his colours until the last,
   Then sailed for his native land,
For his heart was hungry to feel the clasp
   Of a woman's tender hand.
But life had something to teach him yet,—
   That women of fashion soon forget.

He had staked his all on the woman's vow,
  His life on a woman's kiss,
And nothing that mattered could happen now,
  Since what had happened was this;
That he, who fearless had faced the foe,
  Passed from her presence with head bowed low.
He went to the dogs at a quicker rate
  Than many a man grown grey,
For it's very easy to find Hell's gate
  When the Devil leads the way.
And one more soul was damned in despair;
  For the sake of a woman false and fair.

THE FOREIGN LEGION

BY J. MILTON HAYES and HARRY WYNNE   *1912*

From the town of Ainsefra, looking eastward, 'neath your
  hand,
  You will see the great Sahara thro' it's veil of shimm'ring
  heat.
You will see the rising cloud of dust that moves across
  the plain;
  You will catch the glint of bayonet and the flash of
  snaffle chain.
You will hear the distant whisper of the drum taps
  measur'd beat,
  As the Foreign Legion marches o'er the sand.
Ainsefra; its grove of palmtrees and the cafe in the
  shade,
  The everlasting drill and barrack square,
Moorish merchants—Arab traders—Foreign Legion on parade,
  Moslem Temple, and the droning of a prayer.
Robes of scarlet—yellow turbans—here and there the Jewish
  brand,
  The bugle call, the Mueddin chanting low,

118

The heavy scent of spices, and the breath of sunbak'd sand
  From the great Sahara sleeping down below.
In the Legion there are Uhlans, there are Yankee engineers,
  There are Russians who are wanted by the Czar,
There are merry little Irishmen who once were fusiliers,
  There are snappers from Vienna, there are English
    bombadiers,
For they don't ask awkward questions when recruiting, in
    Algiers,
  For the Foreign Legion out in Ainsefra.
To the cafe by the palmgrove once a little dancer came,
  With her twinkling feet and roguish laughing face.
She would nurse them thro' a fever, she would join in
    ev'ry game,
  And her presence made their world a sweeter place.
If there chanc'd to be a quarrel she would thrust herself
    between,
  She insisted that her friends should all agree.
From the drummer to the Colonel they ador'd her as a queen,
  And there ne'er was such a queen as Blanche Marie.
When the news came of rebellion they were lin'd up in the
    square
  With the order to proceed to Ouargla.
Blanche Marie was there to cheer them, and to offer up
    a prayer,
  As she waved the yellow scarf that used to grace her
    pretty hair,
And the colour sergeant snatch'd it as he pass'd her standing
    there.
  Then the Foreign Legion march'd from Ainsefra.
Then the sandstorms and the fever and the endless burning
    plain,
  The chill of night to claim its toll of dead,
The salty marsh, the mirage, bleaching bones to mark their
    train,
  And the vultures ever waiting overhead.
By the dunes of Birelmida came the sudden night attack,
  The song of steel, the cries of man and beast,
The Touaregs pressing forward, and the Legion falling back,
  As the streaks of crimson ting'd the distant East.
'Twas then the colour sergeant wav'd a flag that all
    might see,

And they rallied round the flag with loud "Hurrah"—
For they saw it was the yellow scarf of pretty Blanche
 Marie,
And they seemed to hear a little voice that whispered
 "Fight for me!"
Then they fought, like laughing devils, till the road in front
 lay free,
And they march'd on to the gates of Ouargla.
To the town of Ainsefra, from the distant desert land,
 Comes the remnant of the Legion with the vultures
 flying near.
Gaunt and wasted, like the skeletons of what they used to be,
 Yet they conjure up a smile and raise a cheer for Blanche
 Marie.
Half the legion hears the rollcall, half the legion
 answers "Here!"
While the other half lies bleaching on the sand.

FRISCO SAM - BAD MAN

BY WARREN HASTINGS and HERBERTE JORDAN   *1938*

Say! Folks, you ever seen a rip-snortin', gun-totin' rattlesnake
with boots on? Wall, Strangers, you're lookin' at one here
right now. Yes Sir! You're a' lookin' at pizen dynamite an'
fork lightenin' what's liable to blow-up at any split second.
Wow! *(Suddenly draws gun from belt, jumps in air and lands
with feet wide apart, head thrust forward in menacing
attitude, scowling face, guns levelled. After keeping this
posture for a few seconds slowly relaxes, and returns guns to
belt).*
Say! Folks, you wanter know who I am? I'll tell you who I
am. I'll say I'm Frisco Sam—Bad Man.

Why, Strangers, you know me,
Frisco Sam from Sanfransee,
120

Alabam or Tennessee—
    That's me!
I'll say I'm goldarn tough.
    I'll say I'm all-fired rough.
No guy can't call my bluff— 'S'enough!
    Say, when I'm on the spree.
Hell's gates jest *yearn* for me.
    There's sure some jubilee—Believe me!
When I get riled an' sore,
    Jest watch me snort, an' roar,
An' shoot strangers by the score—or more
    When Sheriffs see me—Say!
You watch 'em fade away,
    Or kneel right down 'an pray—Hey!
I've shot so many men,
    Eighteen-hundred an' ten.
I stopped a' countin' then Amen.
    I runs my own graveyard,
Epitaphs by the yard.
    Grave-diggers working hard, sure, pard.

*Wall, folks, I allus believes in givin' a corpse a real
comfortable, elegant, slap-up funeral. So I bin a' writin' a few
obituary epitaphs fer them bone-headed critters what had a
slight misunderstandin' with me, and in consequence has
passed away sudden—with their boots on. I allow I ain't no
high-falutin', fancy, pen-pushin' poet, but I done my best, an'
I reckon I've pre-dooced one or two epitaphs such as any
reglar corpse oughter be proud of. Jest get this one fer a
start—(Produces small book from hip pocket)*

The bones what's buried here below, belonged to Silas Carr.
    If he hadn't a' drunk Frisco's drink by mistake, he
        wouldn't be where 'e are.
Herc's another
    Reposin' here in this cold clay, lies all what's mortal
        of Reuben Gray.
He put so much whisky an' rum away, that his pickled
        remains won't ever decay.
    I'm mighty proud of that there effort, Strangers.

Here's another—
Here lies the body of One-Eyed Pete. He died while
standin' on his feet,
He was took sudden while on the bust. Ashes to ashes an'
dust to dust.
And another—
Under this sod lies "Killer" Dan, who died thro' ignorance
He might a' bin chawin' terbaccer yet, but his gun got
caught in his pants.
*Dan was sure hot on the draw—but he was unlucky. There's
only two kinds of people where I come from—the Quick an'
the Dead.*
*Here's the last one, an' I guess William K. Shakespeare
couldn't a' done no better—*

Here lies the karkis of Two-Gun Jake. Shed no salt
tears mother.
He sure was a four-flushing low down snake an' so was
his goldarn brother.

*The burg where I hail from is known as Paradise City. The
place ain't very big. The population is allus bein' redooced so
rapid that it ain't never had time to grow. There's only 18
buildings in Paradise City—17 saloons an' one undertaker's.
The undertaker is the richest man in the country. Strangers,
believe me, that place is so allfired tough that rattlesnakes
eat outer yer hand in the street. Shootin' is continuous day
an' night, an' the noise is such that you can't hear yerself
speak. The boys allus talks to each other in the deaf an'
dumb language. An' when I've said that I guess I've sure said
a mouthful.*
Now, Folks, you all know who I am here below.

I ain't no fancy movie star
I ain't no cowboy lar-de-dar
But when I'm down at Casey's Bar,
I guess I'm the whole darn show—an' I oughter know!

THE GAME OF LIFE

BY BOND ANDREWS   *1897*

This life is like a game of cards which mortals have to learn,
   Each shuffles, deals and cuts the pack, and each
      a trump doth turn.
Some bring a higher card to the top some will
      bring a low,
   Some hold a hand quite full of trumps, whilst others
     few can show.
In playing some throw out their trumps their winning
     cards to save.
   Some play the king, some play the deuce, but many
     play the knave.
Some play for money, some for love, and some for
     worldly fame,
   But not until the hand's play'd out, can they count
     up their game.
When hearts are trumps we play for love, and pleasure
     rules the hour,
   No thought of sorrow checks our joy in beauty's rosy bow'r.
We laugh, we sing, sweet verses write, our cards
     at random play.
   And whilst the heart remains on top our life's a holiday.
When diamonds chance to rule the pack, then players
     stake their gold,
   And heavy sums are lost and won by players young
     and old.
Each one, intent upon the game, doth watch with
     eager eye,
   That he may see his neighbour's cards and cheat him
     on the sly.
When clubs are trumps, look out for war on ocean
     or on land,
   For awful deeds of blood are done when clubs are
     held in hand.
Then lives are staked instead of gold, the dogs of war
     are freed,

And sad it is for any land where clubs once
    get the lead.
Last game of all is when the spade is turned by the
    hand of Time.
He waits for the end of the players' game, in ev'ry
    age and clime.
No matter how much each one wins or how much each
    one saves,
The spade will finish up the game, and dig the
    players' graves.

THE GARDENER'S STORY

BY E. A. SEARSON and HERBERT TOWNSEND   *1916*

A small lemon please, thank you kindly.
    Nothing in it? no thank you, not me.
I'm a tote, though I wasn't, not always.
    I used to drink frequent and free.
I don't say it boastful, that's silly,
    But I did use to do the job brown.
And when I at last gave up the tiddley,
    There was more than one pub that shut down.
My job? I'm a Gardener when working,
    I'm resting just now, so to speak,
But if the missus ain't better by Monday,
    Someone must do something next week.
I took a dislike to the Gardening
    Thro' a 'orrid experience I 'ad,
Which came as a shock to the system
    And was very near driving me mad.
I'd been taking my lotion too freely
    Yes, matters were getting quite warm.
And as I'd run thro' the whole of my ready,
    I made up my mind to reform.
So I drank what was left in the bottle
    And the gentleman's garden I seeks,

Where my odd job of digging and 'oeing
    'Ad been waiting for three or four weeks.
I'd been digging for several minutes,
    And was taking a rest for a term.
When casting my eyes on the ground sir
    I suddenly spotted a worm.
I've seen a few worms sir, while gardening
    And digging and 'oeing the beds
But this one it fair took the biscuit,
    And I'm blowed if it hadn't two 'eads.
If I catch that I thought it's a fortune
    'E'd fetch goodness knows what at a sale
So I let go the fork I was 'olding
    And made a quick grab at his tail.
As I grasped it, it seemed to grow bigger
    It was thick as my fore-arm I found.
Then before I 'ad time for much thinking
    The worm went 'eads first in the ground.
I clung like grim death to the reptile,
    With my fingers I took a firm 'old,
But its strength, it was simply enormous,
    It pulled me right down in the mould.
But I wouldn't let go, that's my spirit,
    I 'eld on for all as I was worth
So we started to go down together
    Right into the bowels of the earth.
There were many more worms I kept seeing
    All colours, blue, yellow and pink.
Yes, talk about back to the land sir,
    It was all right for me, I don't think.
And the worst of it was that the climate
    As our way we continue to force
Got warmer and warmer and warmer
    As it naturally would do of course.
We got lower and still it got 'otter
    In my fright I thought suddenly well,
By the temperature and the direction
    We're going to, there I couldn't tell
I'd 'ave given my 'and to get back sir,
    As I thought of my 'ome with a tear
I was almost releasing my 'old sir,
    When I struck on a brilliant idea.

125

For a saying I'd many times 'eard of,
    In my brain began sudden to burn
A true and a simple old proverb,
    If you tread on a worm it'll turn.
And at once I resolved I'd tread on 'im,
    And I prayed that my nerve mightn't fail,
It worn't easy to tread on 'im gov'ner,
    And me 'anging on to 'is tail
Still I swung my feet over my shoulders,
    While I still kept a grip on 'is nibs,
And I poised my 'ob-nails for a moment
    Then dropped 'em bang on to 'is ribs.
And the trick worked as right as a trivet
    'E suddenly slackened 'is pace,
And to my great relief, the next minute
    Completely went right about face.
And 'e made for the surface like lightning
    Through the same path we'd made the descent,
And the sweat, it poured off me like rain, sir,
    At the terrible rate that we went.
I shrieked in my terror, I did, sir,
    Though of sense I was nearly bereft,
And I soon recognised the direction
    We made straight for the garden we'd left.
We burst thro' the old garden border
    Made a blooming great 'ole in the 'edge,
Smash'd the cucumber frame all to pieces,
    And the same evening I signed the pledge.

THE GIRL AT THE BALL

BY GEO. LOGAN and WYN GLADWYN   *1926*

There are old-fashioned fogies who talk about "Cupid",
  And "love at first sight", it's ridiculous, stupid!
Yet, while memory lasts, I shall always recall
  Just a girl whom I met—quite by chance—at a ball.
The purest of accidents brought us together,
  We talked about commonplace things—and the weather;
But somehow she—well—she was different, that's all!
  Oh! the wonderful eyes of that girl at the ball.
Such a shy little maid, neither pert nor designing,
  But oh! she had eyes that just couldn't help shining!
They say there were other girls, beautiful—tall,
  But they passed me unnoticed, that night at the ball.
'Twas many years later I learnt the full story,
  My heart holds her image and crowns it with glory,
For she'd made a sacrifice some might think small,
  Oh! the sad, wistful eyes of that girl at the ball!
First a father hardpressed, then a rash speculation,
  A whisper of scandal that spelt ruination,
The creditor off'ring to settle it all
  For the hand of the girl whom I met at the ball.
I knew that she loved me, though no word was spoken,
  'Twas there in her eyes; but her poor heart was broken.
We parted—a banal "Good-night!" that was all!—
  And I dreamt of the eyes of that girl at the ball!
Ah, that night was the first and the last time I met her,
  I light my cigar and I say "I'll forget her!"
But each ring of smoke, be it ever so small,
  Frames the face of the girl whom I met at the ball.
Sometimes by the fireside I watch the flames leaping,
  And out of each flame I see two brown eyes peeping;
I know it's all nonsense, and yet—after all—
  How they haunt me, those eyes of that girl at the ball!

127

THE GIRL AT THE STATION

BY DOROTHY SCULL and ALFRED H. WEST   *1911*

I can't believe you're goin'
  When I see you standin' there
To think this time tomorrow Bill—
  You'll be miles away from here,
Well, I ain't the one to stop yer,
  But you must bear in mind,
There's another sort of courage, Bill
  In us wot stays be'ind!
Oh! no! I ain't cryin',
  I got a 'orrid cold.
It's yer old Gawblimy uniform
  Makes you look so strong and bold.
Why! I can see you killin' Germans,
  Jest you give it to 'em 'ot.
Yes Bill! It's a 'orrid cold, a 'orrid cold I got.
  In fact a perfect noosance!
An' now the train's agoin' to start,
  An' though I loves yer dearly Bill,
Don't you think I'll break my 'eart.
  No! good-bye old boy,
Gawd bless you!
  Yes! I'll write and you'll write too.
Good-bye—Lor! Yes! I loves yer.
  Gawd! 'e's gone. Wot shall I do?

GIRLS! (according to a 14-year-old-boy)

BY DOROTHY TURNER and ERNEST LONGSTAFFE   *1922*

Ugh! Don't ask *me* what I think about girls—
  I'm fed up with the whole blinkin' crowd.
Sisters and cousins and aunts and such things
  Ought never have been allowed.

128

I've got some of each, an' I give you my word
    There's not one in the whole blinkin' lot
That can talk to a chap for a minute on end
    Without spoutin' some silly rot.
The niff of face powder all over the house,
    Is enough to turn anyone sick.
But when they expect me to kiss 'em Good-night
    I guess it's a trifle too thick.
An' look at the rum sort of clothes that they wear—
    All neenong, and gores, and that stuff
Called crepe-de-thingummy, that falls into bits
    If you handle 'em just a bit rough.
I'm hustled and ordered from pillar to post
    I can't call my soul my own,
It's "Freddie do this" or the other old thing
    Wish they'd jolly well leave me alone,
But if ever I'm wanting a button sewn on
    Or the school badge put on me straw hat,
They've gone to a cooking or ambulance class
    Or some new fangled piffle like that.
They'll yell like the deuce at a beetle or mouse
    And to see a dead cat makes 'em faint,
But it licks me completely the nerve that they've got
    To make a chap feel what he ain't.
Why they'll talk to a fellow who's won the V.C.
    As if he'd done nothing at all,
And a chap who can run up his century, sure,
    Must answer to *their* beck and call.
And crumbs—as for honour, they haven't a spark,
    For if ever I do nick a fag,
Or get in the pantry to sample the tuck,
    It's odds on that someone'll lag.
The conceit of them, too—why they reckon sure thing,
    They'll be marrying heroes and earls
But it ain't much good grousing about 'em I s'pose
    They couldn't help being born girls.
There's only one blessing as far as I know
    For a chap who's got sisters like me,
When ever some Johnny comes foolin' around
    And wants to spoon on the Q. T.
He'll tip me a bob to keep out of the way,
    Ugh, as if I should bother my head
129

To look through a keyhole, I'm only too glad
   To be off to the pictures instead.
I must keep me eyes open, if they spot me here now
   They're sure to start making a song
'Bout being untidy, or washing me neck,
   So I think p'r'aps I'll hop it—so long!

THE GLUTTON

BY L. E. BAGGALEY and HERBERT TOWNSEND   *1940*

Seven hundred years odd come next August,
   Skegness had a bit of a shock,
When a great crowd of fellers on horses
   Were seen gathered under the clock.
At first it were thought t'were an outing,
   Till somebody spotted King John,
Who were hiding away from the barons,
   On account of a row that were on.
In those days there weren't any pierrots,
   At least they weren't properly known,
So if visitors wanted enjoyment
   It had to be fun of their own.
Now the King, he were one for a frolic,
   So after a gallon of beer
He announced he were going mixed bathing,
   Wi' a lass he'd got off with on t' pier.
He borrowed a tandem from t'garage,
   And Mabel said "Let's be off, Jack."
So they started, and she took the front half,
   While King took it easy at back.
In less than an hour sea were sighted,
   Tide weren't as far out as they'd thought,
And Mabel soon popped on her costume,
   While John donn'd an old crown he'd brought.
They splashed and cut all sorts of capers,
   Not taking much notice of tide,
Till King, who were getting a thirst on,

Commenced out of t'water to stride.
When he came to look round for his raiment,
    T'were a most tragic moment for John,
For t'were all washed away—save his trousers.
    Aye, even his scout belt were gone!
"Well, ain't that annoying," said Monarch,
    "I'm sure I can't walk thro' the town
And appear before crowds of me subjects
    In a pair of grey flannels and crown!
We mun walk along sands to some village,
    I'm certain 'twould be more discreet,
And then, when it's dark, we'll go inland
    And happen get summat to eat!"
So off they trudged, maid in wet costume—
    And King in his flannels much smirched—
He were feeling annoyed, c'os a seagull
    Had lit on his crown and sat perched.
At last when a pub were reached safely
    And a nice fire were warming their feet,
The King asked "Hast got any lampreys?—
    Then bring us two surfeits—toot sweet."
Now John, he were partial to lampreys
    And had soon finished his little pile
And were helping the lass wi' her plateful
    A' laughing and chatting the while.
He'd forgot for a time that his armour
    Were every bit swep' out to sea,
And the piece round his middle—like corsets
    Had it's use when he'd had a big tea!
And lampreys are prone to expansion,
    (Which means when they're eaten—they swell.)
And John muttered "Ich dien"—or summat like that,
    Which meant he weren't feeling too well.
Landlord were just saying to swineherd,
    "Nay lad, that's no fly, it's a hop!"
When there came from direction of t'parlour,
    The sound of a very loud "POP."
The host took one look round the portal,
    Then shut it wi' never a word.
In fact he said nowt till he'd drunk half a pint
    To the health of KING HENRY THE THIRD!

131

GOOD-BYE AND GOD BLESS YOU

BY NOSMO KING and ERNEST LONGSTAFFE   *1939*

I love the Anglo Saxon speech
   With its direct appeal:
It takes a hold, and seems somehow
   To sound so very real.
I don't object that men should air
   The Gallic they have paid for
With "Au revoir," "Bon soir Cherie,"
   For that's what French was made for.
But when a crony takes your hand
   In parting to address you,
He drops all foreign words and says
   "Good-bye, old chap God bless you."
It seems to me a sacred phrase
   With reverence impassioned,
Handed down from righteous days
   Quaintly—yet nobly fashioned.
Into the porches of the ear
   It steals with subtle unction,
And in your heart of hearts appears
   To work its gracious function.
And all day long with pleasing song
   It lingers to caress you,
I'm sure no human heart goes wrong
   That's told "Good-bye—God bless you."
I love the words—perhaps because
   When I was leaving mother,
To join the others over there
   We looked at one another,
I saw then in her dear old eyes
   The love she couldn't tell me,
A love eternal as the skies
   What ever fate befell me.
She put her arms around my neck
   To soothe the pain of leaving,
And though her heart was nigh to break
   She spoke no word of grieving—
She said "I will not cry my dear

For fear it should distress you,"
And with her parting kiss she smiled
And said, "Good-bye—God bless you."

GOOD NIGHT, DAD, SEE YOU IN THE MORNIN'

BY MARTYN HERBERT and HERBERTE JORDAN   *1947*

It's funny wot a difference a kid makes in your life,
   I only 'ad the one,—young Alf,—you see, I lost the wife.
An' so I 'ad to bring 'im up; o' course I done my best,
   An' 'e grew up clean 'an decent, an' I reckon that's the test.
I mind when 'e was just a kid, an' busy wiv 'is play,
   I'd say, " 'ere, time for bed, ol' son," an' 'e'd pack up,
     an' say,—
"Good night, Dad, see you in the mornin'."
   That was all, an' off 'e went to bed.
An' when I went up later on—we'd just one room, you see,—
   I didn't want to wake 'im, so I'd sneak in quietly,
But 'e'd always wake up just enough to snuggle up to me,
   An' say, "Night Dad, God bless, see you in the mornin'."
We 'ad some good ol' times together, little Alf an' me,
   'E'd do the shoppin' for me, an' 'e used to get my tea.
Then I'd 'elp 'im wiv 'is 'ome work, 'e was proper clever, mind,
   It wasn't very long before 'e'd left me well behind.
On Saturday 'twas football, an' the pictures, p'raps, at night,
   An' I enjoyed it same as 'im, yes, we was pals all right.
"Good night, Dad, see you in the mornin'."
   Now an' then we'd 'ave a special treat.
I remember one bank 'oliday I took 'im to the Zoo,
   At night I says, "Enjoyed it, son?" 'e says, "Not 'arf,
     dad, coo!
That monkey in the end cage there, 'e wasn't 'arf like you.
   Good night, an' thanks, Dad, see you in the mornin'."
Sometimes of course, 'e'd play me up; well 'e was just a lad,
   An' 'e was full of spirit—mind you, nothing mean or bad—

'E'd get a bit excited when 'e got wiv other boys,
   An' maybe I'd get mad when I was fed up wiv their noise.
I remember once I leathered 'im, an' when 'e went to bed,
   We both felt kind o' quiet when 'e come to me an' said.
"Good night, Dad, see you in the mornin'.
   Sorry dad, I didn't mean no 'arm."
I says, "Now that's all right, ol' son; we'll just forget it, eh?
   'Cos there's tomorrow comin'; see, an' that's another day."
You should 'ave seen 'is grin an' 'eard the little blighter say,
"Good night Dad, friends Dad? see you in the mornin'."
An' then o' course 'e grew up, same as youngsters 'ave to do.
'E 'ad 'is job, an' 'e'd 'is girl, but 'e 'ad 'is ol' dad too.
An' then 'is call-up papers come along, an' off 'e went,
   I'd 'eard them talk of loneliness; now I knew wot it meant.
'E always come 'ome for 'is leaves, an we'd forget the war
   Until it come the last one, an' I 'eard 'im say once more—
"Good night Dad, see you in the mornin'"
   'E went across on D-Day, 'n' that was that
So out there on the beaches there's a part of me wot lies,
   But somewhere down inside me there's another part wot tries
To live up to that kid o' mine, an' there's a voice wot cries,
   "Good night son, see you in the mornin'."

GRANDAD'S SPECTACLES

BY GEORGE WICK   *1927*

Performed by Bransby Williams

A child as she sat on her grandad's knee,
   Looked up in his face, and said,
"You've always your glasses on, grandad dear,
   Can't you let me wear them instead?
I'm longing to look through them, do let me try,
   I'm wondering what I shall see."
The old man as he looked on the child, with a sigh,
   Said "you couldn't see through them like me.
When I was a child" the old man went on,

"I had bright eyes just like you;
A world I could see, full of joys, all for me,
  And all that I heard seemed quite true;
No glasses could alter, no spectacles change,
  That vision I saw in my youth,
Only eyes that are aged, though to you it seems strange,
  Can see through the glasses of Truth.
If you could see through grandad's spectacles,
  How different it all would seem,
Life would then be stern reality,
  Though to you it is one sweet dream;
And friend from foe, child, you would know,
  It would alter your whole life's plan,
If you could see through grandad's spectacles,
  Like grandad can.

GRAND OLD GIRLS OF BRITAIN

BY DAVID JENKINS   *1944*

Performed by Suzette Tarri

You can talk about your monuments,
  Your bits of ancient Rome;
But there's a sight more stirring
  You can see right here at home.
It's the grand old girls of Britain
  Who are somewhat past their prime,
They'll never get their medals
  Tho' they earn them all the time.
The grand old girls of Britain—
  They're marching every day
With shopping bag equipment,
  They tread the pavement way;
With footsteps rather weary
  And shoulders rather bowed,

135

They toddle down the Broadway
    To join the queueing crowd.
The tired old girls of Britain;
    They're wearing out their legs,
Through trudging back and forward
    So as not to miss the eggs;
They scorn your five-bob peaches,
    Your posh ten guinea hats,
But they'll climb up half a mountain
    For a bit of cooking fat.
The cute old girls of Britain;
    They're mighty hard to beat,
They're smart as Mister Sherlock Holmes
    At finding stuff to eat;
They gaze behind the counter,
    Their eyes are old but keen,
They know that what they're looking for
    Is very seldom seen.
The great old girls of Britain,
    When the war is really won,
Will get their compensations
    And their little bit of fun.
When the tradesmen call for orders,
    She'll say: "Blimey so it's you!
Well, try the tradesmen's entrance
    And form a blinking queue!"
The tired Old Girls of Britain,
    With rheumatics in their joints;
Through tramping round from shop to shop,
    Getting value for their points;
They spurn your fancy pine-apples,
    Your peaches and all that;
But they'll climb up half-a-mountain
    For a bit of cooking fat.
So when you youngsters of today
    Are in the prime of life;
And feeling fit and fine
    In spite of all the years of strife;
You'll owe it to the mothers
    Who stood there in the queue;
They didn't get things for themselves,
    They got them just for you.

GRANNIE'S RINGS

BY ARTHUR CHAPMAN and M. HELLER　　　　　　　　*1935*

You are tired of your play, little woman,
　　As tired as tired can be;
So put all your dollies to bed, dear,
　　And sit by your old grannie's knee;
You would look at my watch would you, darling,
　　And play with the bright glitt'ring things;
And try on your dear chubby fingers
　　Each one of your old grannie's rings.
You may take all but one off, my darling,
　　That one never goes from my hand;
You wonder, my pet, why I value
　　So mighty, that simple old band.
But, dear, there's a woman's life story
　　Enclasped in that circlet of gold;
For it tells, child, of love won and treasured,
　　This ring worn so thin and so old!
Such a ring may be yours, little woman,
　　In the days that are coming to you;
And Oh! may the hand that will give it,
　　Be loving and honest and true;
And when, like your grannie, my darling,
　　You've grown, oh so grey and so old,
May you still have your greatest of treasures
　　A plain simple worn ring of gold,
May you still have your greatest of treasures
　　A plain simple worn ring of gold!

THE GRAVEDIGGER'S WEDDING

BY KEVIN PAUL and HAROLD ARPTHORP   *1926*

'Twas the day of the gravedigger's wedding,
   The churchyard was shrouded in gloom,
And the lads of the village sat silent,
   As they played tiddley winks on a tomb.
The villagers trooped up the High Street,
   Trying their best not to grieve,
They were losing their jolly young sexton,
   And alas there could be no reprieve,
Mr. Coffin, the star undertaker,
   Was giving his daughter away,
And despite his morose occupation,
   Was doing his best to look gay.
He had finished the final arrangements,
   And had measured both bridegroom and bride,
He had ordered the finest brass fittings,
   And the hearse in which homeward they'd ride.
The villagers all were invited,
   Invitations sent out to each guest,
Said "Be in the churchyard at mid-day,"
   And ended "No flowers by request."
The bride wore a gown of black muslin,
   And everyone said she looked grand,
A veil of black *crêpe* o'er her shoulders,
   And she carried a wreath in her hand.
The bridegroom had laid down his shovel,
   In order to take up a wife,
And he whispered aloud to the verger,
   "It's the sorriest day of my life!"
He arrived an hour late for the wedding,
   And the crowd were all getting alarmed,
He had been in the old "Crown and Anchor"
   Getting completely embalmed.
The parson was solemnly waiting,
   The bride and the groom at the rails,
Her train was held up by two pages,
   His pants were held up by two nails,

And when the parson had joined them and blessed 'em,
   They were sentenced for better or worse,
And the organ played "Rescue the Perishing,"
   As they hurried away in the hearse.
The guests followed on to the breakfast,
   The bridesmaids were sent in a cab,
The feast was laid out in the parlour,
   The best man laid out on a slab.
The verger had charge of the breakfast,
   The most popular toast that he gave,
Was "Health and long life to the bridegroom,—
   May he live to dig many a grave."
The breakfast was very near over,
   The guests were half screwed in their chairs,
The husband was asked where the bride was,
   He answered "The body's upstairs."

THE GREEN EYE OF THE LITTLE YELLOW GOD

BY MILTON HAYES and CUTHBERT CLARKE   *1911*

There's a one-eyed yellow idol to the north of Khatmandu;
   There's a little marble cross below the town;
And a brokenhearted woman tends the grave of 'Mad' Carew,
   While the yellow god for ever gazes down.
He was known as 'Mad' Carew by the subs at Khatmandu,
   He was hotter than they felt inclined to tell,
But, for all his foolish pranks,
   He was worshipped in the ranks,
And the Colonel's daughter smiled on him as well.
   He had loved her all along,
With the passion of the strong,
   And that she returned his love was plain to all.
She was nearly twentyone,
   And arrangements were begun
To celebrate her birthday with a ball.
   He wrote to ask what present she would like from
      'Mad' Carew:
They met next day as he dismissed a squad:

And jestingly she made pretence that nothing else
would do . . .
But the green eye of the little yellow god.
On the night before the dance
'Mad' Carew seemed in a trance,
And they chaffed him as they puffed at their cigars,
But for once he failed to smile,
And he sat alone awhile,
Then went out into the night.... beneath the stars.
He returned, before the dawn,
With his shirt and tunic torn,
And a gash across his temples.. . . . dripping red
He was patched up right away,
And he slept all through the day,
While the Colonel's daughter watched beside his bed.
He woke at last and asked her if she'd send his tunic
through.
She brought it and he thanked her with a nod.
He bade her search the pocket, saying, "That's from
'Mad' Carew,"
And she found.... *the little green eye of the god.*
She upbraided poor Carew,
In the way that women do,
Although her eyes were strangely hot and wet;
But she would not take the stone,
And Carew was left alone
With the jewel that he'd chanced his life to get.
When the ball was at its height
On that still and tropic night,
She thought of him.... and hastened to his room.
As she crossed the barrack square
She could hear the dreamy air
Of a waltz tune softly stealing thro' the gloom.
His door was open wide, with silver moonlight shining through;
The place was wet and slippery where she trod;
An ugly knife lay buried in the heart of 'Mad' Carew . . .
'Twas the vengeance of the little yellow god'.
There's a one eyed yellow idol to the north of Khatmandu;
There's a little marble cross below the town;
And a brokenhearted woman tends the grave of 'Mad' Carew,
While the yellow god for ever gazes down.

GREENFINGERS

BY H. M. BURNABY and HARRY STOGDEN   *1953*

Country garden—April morn—
  Round about the crack o' dawn
Old Greenfingers stamps along,
  In his heart—a happy song.
What he's doing—isn't much—
  Got a sort o' magic touch,
Charms the seeds and makes 'em grow—
  Old Greenfingers—seems to know!
Back view of his corduroys—
  Stirs the mirth of wayward boys,
It appears—his roomy pants—
  Makes them think of—elephants!
But the ancient doesn't care—
  Sowing here—preparing there—
Swiftly flies each fragrant hour
  While Greenfingers wields his power.
April turns—to May—to June
  Songbirds sing a merry tune—
Old Greenfingers stands aside—
  Views his work with glowing pride—
"All comed out jest loike I sed—
  Could you beat that flower-bed?
Foinest show round here for moiles!"
  Old Greenfingers nods and smiles.
July— August— Autumn near,
  Comes the fading of the year;
God's green children—one-by-one
  Shed their seeds, a duty done.
Nature rings her passing bell—
  Garden waits on Winter's spell,
Evening breezes—softly sigh,
  Old Greenfingers—says—"Good-bye!"

HABITS

BY MAB DAVIS   *1946*

Habits are the things you do,
   That mother tells you NOT to!
Yet you keep on doing 'em
   Becos, somehow, you've got to,
There's bitin' nails, and sniffing,
   And standing on one leg—
And leavin' all the white stuff
   You find inside your egg.
There's fidgettin', and whistling,
   And shufflin' with your feet,
Talking with your mouth full,
   And "noisin' " when you eat.
There's suckin' your lead pencil,
   Tiltin' up your chair,
Elbows on the table,
   And messing up your hair.
There's frowin' stones, and gruntin',
   And kickin' things about,
Puttin' hands in pockets
   When you ought to keep 'em out.
There's making funny faces,
   And always saying "eh"?
Forgettin' you've a hanky,
   And getting in the way.
There's lots of other things as well,
   (I'm *always* being told!)
I don't suppose I'll ever learn,
   Not even when I'm old,
Becos, I'll tell you sometin',
   (Honest! it's quite true!)
Half the things that I do, Well!
   Daddy does 'em too!

THE HARTIST'S MODEL

BY ROBERT RUTHERFORD and HAROLD ARPTHORP   1924

To look at me you wouldn't think that I'd been *everything!*
 I've been a crossing-sweeper, and I've likewise been a king!
I've been a ruddy pirate, though I never went to sea;
 I've been a bloomin' belted h'earl—without a pedigree;
A bishop and a murderer, a scrapper and a saint;
 And *anything* that anybody ever tried to paint.
A h'artist's model's what I am a queer perfession too;
 Though h'gnorhamuses may think you've nothing else to do
Except to sit upon a "throne" until your feet get tired;
 But take my word, to do it right, you 'ave to be *h'inspired.*
"Cos why?" you say Why 'cos the model plays the
        part
 Creating all the masterpieces of the painter's h'art!

The h'artist simply gets 'is brush and paints what 'e can *see;*
 But the model 'as to *live* the thing—or else where
        would 'e be?
We've got to get what's called, in stoodio talk, "h'atmosphere,"
 And let me tell you that's a thing that takes you many
        a year.
"Ow do I do it?" Well, you see, the characters I pose,
 I thinks their thoughts, and speaks their words, as well
        as wears their clothes.
Suppose I'm bein' painted as an Arab in the sand—
 I wraps my turbine round me 'ead and then I takes my stand;
I thinks about the camels, and the palm trees, and the 'eat,
 Till I raise a twenty gallon thirst and blisters
        on my feet.
I sings about the shieks until I gives myself catarrh
 And then I eats the blinkin' dates from off the calendar.
Sometimes the work is very 'ard, as well as very queer,
 Like when I'm as a chimpanzee 'ung on the chandelier.
And when I stand for Samson, why! to get the pose all right
 I 'ave to 'old a sack of coal to keep my muscles tight.
O' course I sometimes gets it soft; one job I likes a treat
 Is bein' painted as a copper standin on his beat;

And as an "unemployed" I once laid on my back all day,
  And got into the part so well forgot to draw my pay.
You should 'ave seen me yesterday—you would have done a
    stare—
Supposed to be a Scotchman, with a kilt and knees all bare.
I kep' on shoutin' "D'ye ken!" "Hoots! Toots!" and "Hecks
    the noo!"
And fancied—only fancied—I drank Scotch till I was "foo;"
And with my loaded bagpipe shot an 'aggis on the rocks;
  And then I danced a Highland Fling until I split my socks.
Historic characters is where I always makes my mark:
  I posed last week as Noah—'im that married Joan of Arc.
I seemed to see my animals come marching two by two,
  The lions roarin' savage, like you 'ears 'em at the Zoo.
And when the h'artist said he'd done, and told me I could scoot,
  I shouted quite unconscious like, "All change for
    Arrowroot".
The job I likes the best of all is when I'm Santa Claus,
  Although the great long beaver's rather tirin' to the jaws.
I always get the chilblains, and my nose it fairly shines,
  And I hears the sound of kids asingin' Christmas
    carolines
The other day I 'ad a pose that seemed to suit me prime,
  A dandy—now, we calls 'em knuts—of Queen Victoria's
    time,
With clothes like I was married in—I felt a reg'lar don,
  So just to give the wife a treat I goes home with 'em on.
The missus smiles at first, then what she did you'll never
    guess,
  She goes and finds—from Lord-knows-where—'er faded
    weddin' dress;
And standin' there, in that old gown, an' lookin' like
    a saint,
  She made the sort o' picture then that nobody can
    paint.
And the job that I enjoys the wurst—no matter what
    the pay—
  Is posin' as a soldier, like I did the other day.
I thought about the war, and all them lads and our young
    Bert,
  The only kid we ever had—and that's what made it 'urt:
144

And when I got back 'ome that night the missus seemed to
    see,
Although I never said a word, just what was wrong with me.
And as we sat there 'and in 'and, 'er lookin' like a saint,
    I guess we made a picture no one on earth could paint.

HEDGING

BY COURTNEY HOPE and BASIL HEMPSEED   *1951*

I've worked for you people for most of my life,
    I'm a hedger and ditcher by trade,
And I've know'd the odd roads and byways,—
    'Fore most of the hedges were made,
Oh yes, I'm official, I'm paid by you folks
    For doing a job as I love;
For drinking in air that's as sweet and as clear
    As them clouds you see sailing above.
Me father was hedger before me, you see;
    He taught me the lore and the care,
How to cut 'em and splay 'em and lay 'em all trim,
    When they grows out of bounds, as it were.
I'm now eighty two, and you'd never believe,
    The tales I could tell of these roads,
And the 'umans as use and misuse 'em all day,
    'Cos they don't know no better, pore toads!
They dash by so fast in the dust as they make,
    You can't see the whites of their eyes,
And if some of 'em guess'd what they miss'd ev'ry day,
    They wouldn't half get a surprise!
They don't know the feel of the sun on your back,
    And the smell of the hawthorn in May!
They don't hear the rabbits all whispering small,
    Or listen what hedge-sparrows say.
They don't have no time to stand still and breathe,
    They've never seen lichen in spring,
Or held in their hands a titmouse's nest,

Or heard a young nightingale sing.
Sometimes the rich 'uns'll stop their big cars
    And unpack their hampers and eat,
And gobble and chatter and talk silly talk,
    And never see what's at their feet.
I've gathered white violets as early as March,
    And in the hedge bottom I've found
Little wild strawberries, sharpish to taste,
    And hidden by leaves on the ground.
The days don't seem long when you're under the sky,
    With the west wind all sweet on your face,
And I reckon I know, as I've know'd all these years,
    That for me there is no other place.
I've time to think thoughts as no dollars can buy,
    Sort of talk to my Maker you see,
And I'm certain sure, through the birds and the flowers,
    Sometimes He talks back to me.

"HE DID"

BY GREATREX NEWMAN and ALICE PARDOE   *1926*

Cupid sat upon a sunbeam
    Looking very deep in thought.
With his little bow and arrow
    He was out in search of sport.
Soon he spied a youth and a maiden,
    By a rose-bush partly hid,
And although he hated hurting
    Those who might be merely flirting,
Though he knew 'twas disconcerting,
    Still,—HE DID
To that youth and that maiden
    All the world became so fair,
And the birds all started singing
    In the lilac-scented air.
And he asked her—might he kiss her?
    He would do as she should bid;—

146

And although she said she couldn't
   Ever let him, and she wouldn't,—
Most improper, and she shouldn't—
   Still—SHE DID.
Then he told her that he loved her,
   In a voice of joy and pride,
And he asked her would she wed him?
   Would she be his blushing bride?
And the maiden cast her eyes down,
   And remained in silence long;—
Do you think the story ended
   In the way that fate intended?
And that Cupid murmured "Splendid!"
   No,—YOU'RE WRONG.
For the maiden then admitted
   One small fact that she had hid,—
That her HUSBAND might not let her,—
   And she told the youth he'd better
Go away and soon forget her,—
   And HE DID.

HIDDEN GOLD

BY PEGGY GILPIN and NOSMO KING   *1951*

A steel grey sky with scurrying black clouds
   A wind that drives and bends the leafless trees,
A lashing rain that beats relentlessly
   Falling in little murky pools to freeze.
But as this chill day dies, a patch of gold,
   Radiant and pure sweeps o'er the lowering skies,
Transforming all things in its heart'ning glow
   Uncov'ring a new beauty to our eyes.
For though the clouds seem'd gloomy and unkind
   The sun was shining all the while behind.
And there are folk just like that wint'ry day,
   Their words are bitter and a frown they wear.
They are so dreary have no time for joy,
   Their youth seems swallowed up in gloom and care.
And we who know not what its cause may be,

Rail at their sorrow do not try to find,
If we can help to lift it, and may be, reveal
    The qualities that lie behind.
Because in ev'ry heart however cold,
    Seekers will find a vein of hidden gold.
If as we go about our daily lives,
    Working and playing, we can yet find time
To smile a little, to diffuse
    The radiance of that humanity, gift so sublime,
If we can help the bitter ones among us,
    Weighed down maybe, with misery and pain.
Their smiles will answer ours, their coldness vanish
    Only sweet understanding will remain.
And we shall know happiness untold,
    Because we hoped to find that Hidden Gold.
And in these days of war and strife and anguish,
    With danger near and hard times p'raps ahead.
With lies and calumny and threats of horror
    Seeking to fill our hearts with fear and dread.
We must be confident, our will unbending,
    Fighting for liberty until that day,
When in a brave new world of right triumphant
    Reason and laughter shall again hold sway.
Finding when pain and sacrifice shall cease,
    The Hidden Gold of honourable peace.

THE HINGLISHMAN

BY F. RAYMOND COULSON and LESLIE HARRIS   *1913*

The Hinglishman jumped hout of bed one morn,
    An 'e ses to 'iself ses 'e—
"Thank Gord, I'm a Hinglishman bred an' born,
    An' there's no foreign make abart me.
There's the same British blood in my 'art an' my 'ead
    Wot in Nelson an' Wellington ran."
A picter of Nelson 'ung over 'is bed,

An' 'e looked at it (printed in Sweden) an' said,
"Thank Gord I'm a Hinglishman."
So 'e combed 'is 'air wiv 'is comb, (made in France),
An' 'e put on 'is French silk scarf;
In the glarss (made in Austria) takin' a glance,
Saw 'is physog an' gave a loud larf.
"Har! Har!" 'e ses to 'iself, "ole cock—
You was built on the werry best plan."
('Ere 'e looked at the time by the German clock,)
"Thank Gord I'm a Hinglishman."
So 'e put on 'is watch (it was Swiss) an' 'is chain
(German silver) "I feels quite a treat"
'E ses to 'iself—"But I'm gettin' a pain
In my innards for somethin' to eat."
So 'e went darn to brekfust, an' sat in 'is chair
(A chair wot was made in Japan)
An 'e ses to 'is missis "Selina my dear,
I'm starved; but, har, har! a fine spread you've got 'ere,
Thank Gord I'm a Hinglishman."
On the toast (which was made of American wheat)
An' the butter (prime Dutch) 'e begun,
Then 'e tackled a slice of Australian meat
An' two h'eggs (laid in France) nicely done,
Wiv a rasher (American) all of 'em fried
In a werry bright German made pan;
Then some tea (grown in China) 'e soon stowed inside,
Wiv Austrian sugar, an' said, full of pride,
'Thank Gord I'm a Hinglishman!"
Yus, the Hinglishman's blood is all foreign made
An' so is 'is muscle an' bone—
If the parts wot was genuine Hinglish was weighed,
Wy, there's scarcely a harnce of 'is own!
Dutch, French, American, German, Chinee
On a real cosmopolitan plan 'E's built.
If a man's wot 'e eats, don't yer see?
We're furriners! that's wot we are— you an' me—
An' I larfs wen a cove to 'iself, ses 'e—
"Thank Gord I'm a Hinglishman."

THE HINDOO'S PARADISE

BY HERBERT HARRADEN   1907

Performed by Bransby Williams

A Hindoo died.
  A happy thing to do
When twenty years united to a shrew.
  Released, he hopefully for entrance cries
Outside the gates of Brahma's Paradise.
"Hast been through Purgatory?" Brahma said.
"No I've been married, I have been married,"
  And he hung his head.
"Come in! Come in! And welcome, too, my son,
  For marriage and Purgatory are as one."
With joy supreme he entered Brahma's door,
  And knew *that* bliss he ne'er had known before.
He scarce had entered in the garden fair,
  Ere another Hindoo craved admission there.
The selfsame question Brahma asked again.
  "Hast been through Purgatory?" "No! What then?"
"Thou canst not enter," did the God reply.
  "But he who went in had been no more than I."
"All that is true, but he has married been.
  And so on earth *he* suffered for his sin."
"Married! 'Tis well! For I've been married *twice.*"
  "Begone! Begone! We want no fools in Paradise!"

HIS FIRST LONG TROUSERS

BY EDGAR A. GUEST and KATHLEEN SHAW MAYER   1913

Say young fellow, just a minute,
  They're your first long trousers, Eh?
And your little grey knee breeches
  Are for ever put away,
And your blouses and your stockings

150

And your little caps are gone,
For the shirts and cuffs of manhood,
And you've got a derby on.
Yes—you look well in them sonny,
Why I can't believe my eyes!
For it doesn't seem a year ago
Since you were just this size,
And a little pink cheeked youngster.
Why you toddled more than ran
Every night to meet your daddy,
And today you are a man!
Oh I don't know how to tell you.
But I want to—yes I do.
That your mother and your daddy,
Both are mighty proud of you,
And we're going to miss the baby
That from us today has gone,
And that baby we'll remember
Though he has long trousers on.
We are banking on you sonny
And we'll help you all we can,
But it's up to you remember,
Now to prove you are a man.
You can make us mighty happy.
You can make us mighty sad,
Just remember it's not manly
To do things you know are bad.
I'm not going to preach a sermon,
Mother's put your blouse away,
And your breeches, and I saw her
Crying over them today.
And I thought perhaps I'd give you
Just a thought to dwell upon.
Please remember you're her baby
Though you've got long trousers on.

HOW WE SAVED THE BARGE

BY ARTHUR HELLIAR and CUTHBERT CLARKE   1908

Performed by Bransby Williams

I'm a Captain, that's what I am, sir, a nautical man
    by trade,
    Though I ain't tricked out in a uniform with buttons of gold
      and braid.
I ain't the Captain it's true of one of these floating
    grand hotels,—
    It's true as I ain't the skipper of one of these Clacton or
      Yarmouth Belles.
I'm the Captain of this 'ere barge, sir, wot's known as
    the "Slimy Sal,"
    And a faster boat there ain't on the length or breadth of
      the whole canal.
Though I'll own so far as the breadths concerned that ain't
    much praise o' course,
    And the number of knots an hour she makes has summat to do
      with a horse.
Have I ever had any adventures, the same as one meets
    at sea?
    I should rather just think I 'ave, sir, not *one* but a dozen
      may be.
If it wasn't as 'ow my throat's so dry as to almost stop
    my breath,
    I'd tell yer the way as the missis and me was snatched from
      the jaws of death.—
Her courage it was too as saved us, 'er courage what pulled
    us through,
    Or I wouldn't be standing here thirsty—well thank'ee,
      don't mind if I do.
One morning some two or three weeks ago, our cargo had all
    been stowed,
    We'd 80 odd tons of coal aboard which o' course was a
      fairish load,—
We'd got a new 'orse that day, sir, too good for the job
    a lot,
    He'd once been a Derby winner, though 'is name I've
      clean forgot.
He was standing harnessed on to the barge, the missis and I
    was aboard,

When all of a sudden we feels a jerk and he starts of his
    own accord.
Something or other had startled him, what it was I never
    could think,
Though I fancy he'd 'eard some gent like you wot 'ad offered to
    stand me a drink.
I flew like a flash to the rudder, and I pushes it 'ard
    alee,
And the missis 'ad 'oisted a flag of distress to the chimbly,
    I could see.
We 'adn't a fog'orn or whistle aboard but the missis she yells
    like two,
But the louder she screamed out "Clear the course" the faster
    the old 'orse flew.
He thought he was back in the days gone by, a-winning some
    famous race,
'Twas a race with death for the missis and me at that
    awful 'cadlong pace.
'Ouses and trees went flying by—a mighty splash and
    a shock—
And we'd passed bang through, without paying too, the closed
    up gates of a lock.
Just then when we'd whizzed through a tunnel she yells from
    the lower deck
And says "If that 'orse ain't pulled up pretty quick, I can
    see as we're in for a wreck."
We only got thirty or forty miles till we gets to the end
    of the course,
It's a case of which 'olds out the longest the bloomin' canal
    or the 'orse.
But before I tells 'ow we was saved, sir, there's one thing
    I'd like yer to know,
My missis was once in a circus as a h'artist I mean,
    years ago.
She used to perform on the tightrope and wonderful tricks
    too she done,
But of course, that's all finished and over, her weight being
    seventeen stun.
Then she stood on the deck where I stood sir, and
    I sees a gleam come in her eye,
She says "It's a chance in a thousand, but it's one
    as I'm willing to try.

The 'eadlong career of the 'orse must be stopped, it's our
   last and our only hope.
There's only one way to get at 'im, I must walk to his back
   on the rope."
She gives me one farewell 'ug sir, takes an oar for a pole
   in 'er hands,
Then smiling, as tho' in a circus, on the tow-rope a second
   she stands.
I closed both my eyes after that sir, for the sight would a
   made me unnerved,
For a 'orrible death 'twould 'ave meant for 'er if the
   barge for a moment had swerved.
But I opens 'em wide in a moment, for I 'ears a loud kind of
   a crack,
And I sees that theer 'orse all collapse in a 'eap, for
   the missis 'ad broken 'is back.
As soon as the crisis was over, on the deck in a swoon
   sir I dropped,
But the barge went on for a mile and a 'arf on its
   lonesome afore it was stopped.
Why didn't we cut thro' the rope, sir, and 'ave let the
   'orse loose instead?
Just fancy you thinking o' that now why it never
   came into my 'ead!!

THE HUMAN TOUCH

BY E. J.GARGERY, NOSMO KING and ERNEST LONGSTAFFE 1939

In this wonder-world of progress in which we live today.
   We find what intellect can do with lifeless earth and clay.
We see how man can utilize, from Nature's mystic store,
   The forces lying dormant there and never used before.
And when inventions multiply, and science does so much,
   We rather tend to minimise the vital *Human Touch*.
We've attained the age of iron, of machinery, of force.
   We've reached the point where *Robots* do the work of man
   and horse.

We've found the means of harnessing the ingredients of
    our sphere,
And made them do the jobs *men* did, before machines
    were here
For in our workmanship today in music, art and such,
    The medium of a soulless tool oft kills the *Human Touch.*
We had our lesson in the war, of where it all might lead,
    When scientist and chemist worked to meet the nation's
    need.
The slaughter of a million men, by gas, by steel, by gun.
    Taught the awe-struck sons of earth what mind and brains
    had done;
But midst the welter and the blood, with faltering hands,
    we'd clutch
    That clear, white, shining, radiant touch, the heroic
    Human Touch.
There's surely something very wrong when Christian men
    employ
    Their brains and power and knowledge, merely to destroy:
One day these great inventions that benefit so few,
    May claim Poetic Justice by destroying me and you.
And should that day come, be assured we couldn't hope
    for much,
    For we lose our very birthright, when we lose the
    Human Touch.
So in this age of progress in which we have our place,
    If we would seek the mainspring of the glory of our race.
Then it's deeper than the working and the probing of the
    mind,
    And it's loftier than the products of the genius of
    our kind!
The *Human Touch* the touch Divine upon the earthy clod
    That takes the vileness out of man and brings him
    nearer God.

THE HURDY GURDY MAN

BY MARTYN HERBERT AND HERBERTE JORDAN   *1921*

I'm a shabby, pathetic old figure, I know,
    An echo of bygone days;
And people make fun of my old box of tunes,
    And the old-fashioned airs that it plays.
I can't give them ragtime or up to date music,
    Or Jazz with its clatter and bang;
All mine are tunes of a quieter age,
    The songs that our grandmothers sang.
Songs that bring with them the fragrance of lavender,
    Songs that were tuneful and gay;
Songs that our mothers would croon by our beds,
    Till the dream-man had led us away.
Off to the land where all cares are forgotten,
    Away down the starlit track;
And now when we've wandered and lost our way,
    The old tunes will lead us back.
We're wheezy and old now, the organ and I,
    But still we keep pegging away.
And the folks still go by with a nod and a smile,
    For the quaint old-world tunes that we play.
And I just like to fancy, old friend, bye and bye,
    They'll miss us a bit when we're gone.
And all round the streets where we used to be known
    The old tunes will still longer on.
And maybe they'll hear just an echo at times
    When they're worried a bit and upset.
They'll think of the old hurdy-gurdy and smile,
    And the memory will help them forget.

I AIN'T 'ARF A LUCKY KID

BY CHARLES and BILLIE HAYES   *1924*

I ain't arf a lucky youngster!
   I ain't arf a lucky kid!
Fink I got the duddest job now
   Wot a youngster ever did!
Both the marster an' the missis
   'As religion bad, yer see;
Not as I minds wot *they* do
   But they tries convertin' me.
Lookin' 'appy 'ere is sinful,
   Singin' songs leads straight ter woe,
Give the glad ter the butcher-lad An'
   I'll be booked fer dahn below!
Marster maikes me kneel at prayer time,
   Sez as that's the 'oly way;
Wonder 'ow 'e'd fancy kneelin'
   If 'e'd scrubbed at floors orl day!
Can't do wot I want to; no 'ow!
   'Ave ter do jis' wot I'm bid,
I ain't 'arf a lucky youngster!
   I ain't 'arf a lucky kid!
Went away wiv 'em lars Haugust,
   Summer 'olidays, yer know;
   Packs up orl our bits an' pieces,
Sez a prayer and' orf we go!
   Stays at some ole mucky farm'ouse
'Stead o' decent seaside digs;
   No boys rahn fer twenty mierls,
Nothin' ceptin' cows an' pigs.
   Spends me time in dissipation
Pickin' daisies an' the like.
   Let me sit up till nine firty,
Oh I gits the proper spike!
   But even there I lands in trouble
(It's a happy life is mine!)
   One day missi sez ter me,
"'Ere! Taike these bits aht ter the pig."

So I taikes 'em ter the marster,
Thort she meant 'im, straight I did!
I ain't 'arf a lucky youngster!
I ain't 'arf a lucky kid!
Orlways meets me boy mos' reg'lar
Of a Thursday arternoon,
John 'e taikes me to the pichers
('Andy sort o' place ter spoon).
Thursday lars' we meets my sister,
"Taike me wiv yer, please", she wept,
"I'm so lonely!" I sez, "Cheese it!"
"Pig!" she sez, an 'orf she swept.
Then I finks o' marster's sermons
Swollers 'ard an' sez "Come on!"
So she tacks on like a glue-pot,
Sits right dahn 'long side o' John.
Yesterday she comes ter see me,
Tryin' 'ard to 'ide 'er glee,
Sez, "I got some nice news for yer,
News concernin' John an' me.
Will yer be our little brides-maid?
Fixed it yesterday, we did!"
I ain't 'arf a lucky youngster!
I ain't 'arf a lucky kid!

IF I'D MY WAY

BY J. MILTON HAYES and H. NEIL VERNON   *1911*

If I could only have my way
I'd renovate this jaded earth,
And poverty would cease to be,
For labour would be paid its worth.
Human brotherhood would thrive,
No drones *then* would haunt the hive;
Honest work alone would pay
If I could only have my way.

If I could only have my way
  I'd stimulate all noble thought,
For ev'ry mind can be refined
  And class distinction set at nought.
Human souls would cease to doubt,
  Narrow views would broaden out,
Men would see the light of day,
  If I could only have my way.
If I could only have my way
  I'd soothe the sorrow-laden heart,
And cleansed of guile the world would smile,
  For joy would reign in every part.
Pain and sorrow I'd prevent,
  And in their place cause merriment.
Love for all our thoughts should sway
  If I could only have my way.
If I could only have my way
  I'd like to live my life again,
To make amends, to make true friends
  Of all my suffering fellowmen.
Mean desires and jealous hate
  Oft warp our souls until too late;
But *Peace on Earth would come to stay*
  If I could only have my way.

IF WE ONLY KNEW

BY MEL. B. SPURR and BOND ANDREWS   *1897*

It's a curious thing to reflect sometimes
  On the various incidents passing around.
To think of the number of horrible crimes
  Whose authors have never as yet been found.
A murderer's hand may be clasped in ours,
  In the grasp of friendship, warm and true.
Should we love it the less or cease to caress,
  If we only knew?

If we only knew?
How many a tie that once was sweet
Has been cruelly snapped by a slanderer's tongue!
How many a friend whom we used to greet
With welcoming words, and to whom we clung
In joy or in sorrow, in pleasure or pain,
Has suddenly seemed to be false and untrue:
How oft should we find that our doubts were unkind,
If we only knew!
If we only knew!
There are some will sigh and whisper low
Of a love that is changeless, and deep, and pure:
And we think—do we not? when they tell us so,
That of *somebody's* heart, at least, we are sure.
But fancy is apt to wander about,
And to sip from a hundred flowers the dew:
Would our love be as deep, would our jealousy sleep,
If we only knew? If we only knew?
Then comes the time when "the knot" is tied:
Surely of life its most charming scene!
The bridegroom looks on his beautiful bride,
And dreams of a future all bright and serene.
Let the lad dream on: shall his hopes be fulfilled?
One turns out a slattern? Another a shrew?
How many would pause at the very church doors?
If they only knew! If they only knew!
This world is composed of rich and poor,
And each sees life in a different way:
Whilst Lazarus begs door to door,
Dives fares sumptuously every day.
But, which is the happier, peasant or lord?
That is a problem solved by few:
For the rich man may sigh, as the peasant goes by
If we only knew! If we only knew!
A tradesman fails, and his credit is gone!
He has hardly a shilling to call his own.
He may have been patiently struggling on,
But his prospects are blighted, prosperity flown.
The world, in its wisdom (?) no doubt, will condemn,
But don't let *us* treat him as heedless men do:
Tho' he failed so ignobly, he may have fought nobly.
If we only knew—If we only knew!

160

We are ever too apt to be hard on a man
　Who doesn't appear to have success:
Instead of helping him all we can
　We strive to render his chances less.
A kindly word, or a friendly hand,
　May help him—who knows?—to pull easily thro:
It may give him fresh life to renew the strife.
　If we only knew—If we only knew!
It's each for himself, and the weak to the wall!
　So runs the world for ever and aye.
The stout hearts advance—whilst the feeble ones fall.
　To perish alone, on the world's highway.
Let us succour the frail ones, bearing in mind
　That though in this world we meet not our due,
For a kind act done, a crown may be won
　In the world to come— If we only knew!

IF YOU'LL PARDON MY SAYING SO

BY WARREN HASTINGS and HERBERTE JORDAN　　　　　*1941*

Spoken. "Watkins, the perfect family butler, addresses the young
　　　　master who is still abed"

A lady to see you Mr. Archibald, sir.
　The matter appears to be pressing.
Luncheon was served quite an hour ago,
　I did not awaken you, sir, as you know.
There are times, sir, when sleep is a blessing.
　I have here some ice, sir, to place on your head,
And also a whisky and "polly."
　I don't know what time you retired to bed,
But the party sir, must have been jolly,
　If you'll pardon my saying so.
The lady in question a waiting below,
　Is accompanied, sir, by her mother,
And also a prize-fighting gentleman, sir,
　A pugnacious character one might infer,

161

Whom the lady describes as her brother.
    The elderly female is quite commonplace,
A most vulgar person, I fear, sir,
    Who shouts in a nerve wracking falsetto voice,
And her language is painful to hear, sir,
    If you'll pardon my saying so.
The prize-fighter person is burning with hate.
    He refers to you, sir, as a "twister."
He threatens to alter the shape of your "clock,"
    To break you in half, sir, and knock off your "block,"
Unless you do right by his sister.
    The young lady says, sir, with trembling lips,
That you made her a promise of marriage.
    She wants to know why she should eat fish and chips,
While you, sir, ride by in your carriage,
    If you'll pardon my saying so.
Sir John has a dreadful attack of the gout,
    He is fuming to beat all creation.
My lady, your mother, is up in the air.
    She is having hysterics, and tearing her hair,
And borders on nervous prostration.
    Would you wish me to pack your portmanteau at once,
And look up the times of the trains, sir?
    Or perhaps you would rather I brought you a drink,
And a pistol to blow out your brains, sir.
    If you'll pardon my saying so.

I'M A LITTLE BIT OLD FASHIONED
IN MY WAYS

BY H. M. BURNABY and CUTHBERT CLARKE   *1931*

People call me an old 'has been', out of date—perhaps I am.
    I've lived just long enough to know the real thing
        from the sham.
I've *had* my time I'm on the shelf quite harmless
        now it's true.
    A fossil I admit it for I don't mind telling you
I'm a little bit old fashioned in my ways, that's what
        it is.

It's many years since first I went to school
Then small boys would take a pride in
    Standing *up* to any *hidin'*.
Why we *used* to grin and bear it, and keep *cool!*
    But give a boy a belting now his master gets the sack!
It's wonderful the racket folks can raise
    Did ye hear such twaddle nincompoops and molly-coodles
I'm a little bit old-fashioned in my ways!
    In *my* young time a man would never try to ape
        the gent.
He'd always face the music and he *would* say what
        he meant.
    He'd drink an honest glass of beer he'd swear an honest curse,
He'd always call a spade a spade, and sometimes something
        worse!
    I'm a little bit old-fashioned in my ways. I am, no doubt.
These night-clubs now they're *not* just in my line
    Drinking up to early morning till the P'lice without
        a warning
Fetch you up before the Beak to pay a fine.
    There may be those that fancy it as far as I'm
        concerned
They charge too much for drinking now-a-days.
    When I used to wet my throttle Scotch cost
        three-and-six a bottle!
I'm a little bit old-fashioned in my ways!
    The papers seem to be chock full of burglary and crime
While poor Divorce Court Judges must be working overtime.
    And I glance up at my Jennie busy knitting in her
        chair,
With her cheeks like rosy apples and the silver in her hair.
    I'm a little bit old fashioned in my ways. It must be so.
Well there it's not so easy to explain.
    In derision p'r'aps I'm chaffed at and I'm left
        behind and laughed at
By the modernist but still I can't complain.
    I've possibly forgotten more than some folks ever knew
And yet I've no regret for manhood's days.
    Jennie's seventytwo God bless her, still I kiss her
        and caress her
I'm a little bit old-fashioned in my ways!

INASMUCH

BY JOHN WARREN and REX BURCHELL　　　　　*1924*

As I gave a few pence to a man in the street
　　Who told me a pitiful tale,
A friend said to me "You are a fool,
　　Well, you've bought him a quart of ale.
There's only one in a hundred
　　Of these beggars' stories true,
It's my belief that most of them
　　Are far better off than you".
I replied "My friend you are probably right
　　But this motto read, mark and learn.
Better be "had" by ninety nine,
　　Than miss doing one good turn."
If you won't spare a beggar a copper
　　For fear of being caught
Give what costs nothing, a friendly word,
　　A smile, and a kindly thought.
If you send a man *one* hundred pounds
　　He doesn't receive eleven
But a kindly thought gains a thousandfold
　　On its passage from Earth to Heaven.
If you seek an excuse to your conscience
　　For the coppers you often grudge.
"He brought it on himself", you say,
　　But who are you to judge?
If it's a woman who's down and out,
　　Don't rake up her doubtful past.
Is there one of you here today dare say
　　"I the first stone can cast."
Ninety-and-nine may be wrong un's,
　　But, one may deserve your tears
I'm not what you'd call religious,
　　And I've not read the Bible for years.
But I always remember those wonderful words
　　That I learnt at my mother's knee
"In-as-much as ye did it to the least of these
　　Ye did it unto Me".

THE INDIA RUBBER MAN

BY WARREN HASTINGS and HERBERTE JORDAN   *1943*

This is the story of Senor Poloney,
    The India Rubber Man,
Who worked in a side-show attached to a circus,
    And lived in an old caravan.
In manner most charming, if somewhat alarming
    He'd knot both his legs round his middle,
Then tie his big toes to the end of his nose,
    And play "The Lost Chord" on a fiddle.
This genteel performance was greatly admired,
    By people who came in their dozens;
Some bringing their gals, their wives, or their pals,
    Their uncles, their aunts and their cousins.
Now Senor Poloney was madly in love
    With a young lady known as "La Swallow"
Whose breathless performance upon the trapeze
    Was a dangerous calling to follow.
Alas! Though Poloney "La Swallow" adored,
    She did not return his affection.
There can be no doubt she was never without
    Of boy-friends a goodly collection.
Whenever Poloney could wrangle the time,
    He'd wander inside the arena.
To gaze on "La Swallow" with love-stricken eyes
    Feeling better because he had seen her.
One day when "La Swallow" was doing her stuff,
    She suddenly missed her connection.
From high in the air, with a wail of despair,
    She fell in a downward direction.
The welkin then rang with the horrified cries
    Of the crowd; thereby causing a ruction.
As frantic with awe, the young lady they saw
    Being hurtled to death and destruction.
Then just like a ferret who'd sat on a tack,
    Poloney, his eyes fairly popping,
Dashed out with a shout and threw himself down
    On the spot where "La Swallow" was dropping.

The smack was the same as wet fish on a slab
  As on poor Poloney she landed.
Then bounced up again to the top of the tent
  And caught the trapeze single handed.
So Poloney the hero and lovely "La Swallow"
  Were wed, and there's little to add.
But two bouncing babies are learning the fiddle,
  To play "The Lost Chord" like their dad.

I OFTEN WONDERED IF MY MOTHER KNEW

BY ARTHUR MATZ, FRED ELTON and ALF. J. LAWRENCE   1920

I often wondered if my mother knew, when as a lad,
  From the straight and narrow path I often strayed.
I stole the jam, told gentle fibs, made faces at my dad,
  And sometimes with some wicked boys I played.
But at nighttime when I went to her to bid the fond
    goodnight,
  Her sweet grey eyes would search me through and through,
And my guilty conscience troubled me until far in the
    night,
  Ah! I often wondered if my mother ever knew.
I often wondered if my mother knew, when as a youth,
  The different girls who set their caps at me.
And well, I was not backward, I admit it, 'tis the
    truth,
  I loved them all yet still kept fancy free.
I started smoking dreadful weeds, and drinks well two
    or three.
  I thought it quite the proper thing to do.
A headache in the morning, well, I put that down to
    tea.
  Ah! I often wondered if my mother ever knew.
I often wondered if my mother knew, when as a man,
  With the good old latchkey in my grasp at last,
The times I had, the hours I kept, the so-called fun
    began,

I went the pace, and Jove! the pace was fast.
How sometimes in the early hours,
    I'd come home with the milk,
Creep past the mater's room, oh! feeling blue,
    The next day turn my pockets out, the usual lace and
        silk.
Ah! I often wondered if my mother ever knew.
    I'm older now, much older, and I've children of my
        own,
My eldest son is just turned twenty-three,
    And it seems poetic justice that Inventions that
        I've had,
Are now being tried upon the wife and me.
    So in solemn retrospection, for at my age this begins,
And I think of my old mother kind and true;
    She loved me dearly all the time—in spite of all
        my sins—
GOD REST HER SOUL Of course— of course she knew.

I THINK I'LL HAVE ANOTHER THINK

By STEPHEN RUSSELL and CHARLES PRENTICE   *1933*

I often sit and meditate and wonder,
    And think and turn over in my mind.
Then p'r'aps I'll think again in case I blunder,
    And second thoughts are best, I sometimes find
Now in the village pub I started thinking,
    And thought and thought and thought but nothing
        came.
So finishing the liquor I'd been drinking
    I asked the Boss to deal me out the same.
And when a third I'd put away
    I seemed to think as clear as day.
So as my brain was in the pink,
    Thinks I, I'll have another think.
I thought of Darwin's evolution theory,

And wondered if from monkeys we're derived,
If before that from some prehistoric oyster
    To our present day perfection we've arrived.
The fishes in the sea may be our cousins,
    Some men look just like codfish in their types.
What relation to a zebra is a mack'rel
    He must be some because they've both got stripes.
A million years hence we shall be—
    Ah that's a bit too deep for me.
It's all about as clear as ink.
    I think I'll have another drink.
The dreams I dream require some explanation,
    The other night in slumber's soft caress.
I dreamt I'd got to head a deputation,
    To fit the goddess Venus with a dress.
They bound my eyes and gave me a tape measure,
    The goddess said "Don't trouble over me."
I answered "It's no trouble, it's a pleasure".
    And groped my way to where I thought she'd be.
I'd just got my tape measure out,
    And then I heard the missus shout,
"It's nine o'clock, Get up, you gink".
    A happy ending—I don't think!

'IS PIPE

BY CHAS H. TAYLOR and CUTHBERT CLARKE   *1905*

Performed by Bransby Williams

You're not as 'andsome as you was,
    Old pipe, if truth be told,
But we ain't parting just becos
    You're black, and worn, and old.
I'm not in many many ways
    The cove I used to be;
And ain't a flattering when I says
    You're stronger now than me.
You cost a bob at first, may be;

You ain't no fancy touch,
But there, you're worth as much as me,
And that, Gawd knows, ain't much.
We draw'd together from the fust;
We knows each other's ways;
And you're a pal as I can trust—
That's somethink nowadays.
She give yer to me, my old gal—
My gal wot used to be;
Wot 'appy times we 'ad ol pal,
Eh? 'er and you and me!
Times lightly passed, like 'arf a ounce
Of 'bacca, keerless drawn
An' blown away, they all amounts
To somethink when they're gone.
She says: "Yer won't forgit me Bill!
I knows yer, I can tell;
But sometimes of a evening, will,
You act I'm there as well?
An' when you're smoking quiet,
Will you talk to me? becos
I might be very near you, Bill."
Supposin' now she was!
She's gone to heaven, and that's the place
Where all the past's forgot.
So some religious covey says—
Who knows a blooming lot!
Lord! if I thought she could forgit
Them days wot used to be—
Well it 'ud 'urt above a bit,
Old pal, eh? you, and me.
Let's wait a while—what must be must,
The time ain't far off when
You'll be ashes, an' I'll be dust,
For ever, an' ever, Amen.

IT'S A FUNNY OLD WORLD WE LIVE IN

BY ALEC KENDAL and HERBERT TOWNSEND   *1921*

It's a funny old world we live in;
   Well, the world's not exactly to blame,
It's the folk you've to greet, that you meet in the
      street,
   Makes you think what a life, what a game.
When you're doing all right, you're on velvet,
   They'll shake hands, "Delighted, you know."
But when down and out, there isn't a doubt,
   It's a rather anaemic "Hullo!"
When you strive to get on you're not noticed,
   And when you get on the right track,
They'll remark as they stare,
   "I knew that chap there,
When he hadn't a rag to his back."
   If you're clever and climb up the ladder,
And keep piling the quids away,
   They'll smile and they'll sneer and murmur "Dear,
      dear
Ain't he a lucky dog Eh?"
   If you haven't a brain, and get rich quick,
How does he do it they think.
   If you never do good you're a stick in the mud.
And some one is sure to say "Drink!"
   If you save up your money, you're selfish,
If you squander or give it away
   They'll say as a rule, "Fancy the fool.
There'll come a time some day."
   If you do a good turn and help someone,
"It's an advert' for you," they'll reply,
   But there's one consolation 'midst all this sensation
We get a good name when we die.
   It's a funny old world we live in,
Nothing but Bluff and Swank.
   And there's only four Pals—your Health, Wife and Kid,
And the BIT you might have in the bank.

IT'S NOTHING TO DO WITH YOU

BY ARTHUR KLEIN 1930

Performed by Gracie Fields

You wonder why I live this life of misery,
    Don't try to offer me your sympathy.
The past– do I regret it?
    I try so hard to forget it.
What's the use,
    I've no excuse,
I suppose.
    If I'm found hanging around,
What's it got to do with you?
    Day after day, just wasting away,
What's it got to do with you?
    The world is just a sham.
I'm fed up with life And I don't care a hang.
    What is my name? And from where I came?
What's it got to do with you?
    I haven't a friend,
Where will I end?
    What's it got to do with you?
Just down and out– knocked about,
    I'm not going to squeal, And you'll not hear me
        shout.
For I've had my own way,
    And the price that I pay
Has nothing to do with you.
    They say that life, that life is what you make it,
Yet strange the tricks that fate on you will play.
    Every tale has a beginning,
I'm more sinned against than sinning,
    I know I'm wrong,
But one must live,
    I suppose.
If I'm found hanging around,
    What's it got to do with you?
Day after day, just wasting away,
    What's it got to do with you?
The world is just a sham,
    I'm fed up with life And I don't care a hang.

171

What is my name and from where I came?
    What's it got to do with you?
I haven't a friend;
    Where will I end?
What's it got to do with you?
    Just down and out—
Knocked about,
    If I lay dead there,
Who would care?
    I've had my day,
And the price that I pay
    Has nothing to do with you.

I WOR AFRAID

BY WISH WYNNE and G. FORBES RUSSELL   *1933*

Down on the farm where I be working now,
    There's a lad as comes courting I;
And as I were milking my cowses one day,
    He says, says he, as he were going by:
"I'm thinking hard of getting wedded, lass.
    I've never been wed afore,
How would you like to eh?"
    But I says "Eh Garge, oh lor!"
He says, "Aye you, you'd be alright."
    But eh! I wor afraid.
Then at last I says "Well, I don't know quite."
    But eh, I wor afraid!
Then just as I were going away,
    He caught me hands and he made me stay,
Kissed I and said, "You'll be my wife one day."
    But eh! I wor afraid.
One Eastertide Garge took I to a fair,
    I'd never seen a fair till then.
Eh! lights, and music, and people it wor grand,

Shouldn't I just love to go again.
We saw all the sights and went to a theatre,
   A dancing girl to see,
Garge said he'd heard a lot of talk of her,
   And he were wondering what like she'd be?
When I saw that girl! "Oh dear!" I said.
   Eh, I wor afraid!
And I felt all my face go a burny red.
   Eh, I wor afraid!
With folks all looking at her how she dare,
   Dancing with her legs and feet all bare,
And there were Garge a sitting just beside me there.
   Eh, I wor afraid!
One summer morning round about July,
   Garge says to I, says he,
"Meg, we've been a courting now for nigh on a year,
   And I'd like to know when wedding's going to be?"
So last Sunday morning us two went to church,
   I never felt so queer afore,
And when the time came for I to say "I will!"
   Eh, I nearly sunk into the floor.
Then Garge, the big daft silly thing,
   Eh, I wor afraid!
On my thumb he put the ring,
   Eh, I wor afraid!
Then my old grand-mother she shook her head,
   "All yer troubles will start from today," she
      said,
"I know what I am saying, I be three times wed!"
   Eh, I wor afraid!

JACK

BY FRED ROME and ADA TUNKS   1910

Performed by Bransby Williams

'Tis ten long years since first we met,
   He came not from a famous set,
A tiny pup, a precious pet
   My little Jack.
He was not born of high degree,
   He had no lengthy pedigree,
But he was all the world to me
   My little Jack.
Folk may think my ways absurd,
   For I told him all that had occurred,
He understood most every word
   My little Jack.
Once the victim of a heartless theft
   Of home and all I was bereft,
I was happy for I'd one thing left,
   My little Jack.
And when the funds and food were low,
   The same affection he'd bestow,
How different from the world we know,
   Was little Jack.
And when I once was taken ill,
   He lingered by my bedside still,
The only one my heart to thrill
   Was little Jack.
Each morn upon my humble bed,
   He'd greet me with a drooping head,
What sorrow on his face I read,
   My little Jack.
And when our hardship days had flown,
   And many hardships we have known,
Still he ate his humble bone,
   My little Jack.
One night I lost him on his way,
   Some friend had led my Jack astray,
I watched and waited day by day,
   For little Jack.

And when a weary week passed by,
　　One night I heard a piteous cry,
My Jack returned to me to die,
　　Poor little Jack.
My only friend in pain and play,
　　My life's sunshine had passed away,
My only pal in stillness lay,
　　My little Jack.
He was but a dog, a beast I know,
　　I'm a fool perhaps to worry so,
But my only friend on earth below
　　Was little Jack.
His tiny life is at an end,
　　But Heaven never more can send,
A stauncher pal, a truer friend
　　Than little Jack.

JIM BLUDSO

BY COLONEL JOHN HAY and ERIC MARÈO　　　　　*1913*

Performed by Bransby Williams

Well no! I can't tell where he lives because he don't
　　live, you see!
　　Least ways, he's got out of the habit of livin'
　　　like you and me.
Where have you been for the last three years, that you
　　haven't heard folks tell,
　　How Jimmy Bludso passed in his checks the night
　　　of the Prairie Belle?
He weren't no saint them engineers is all pretty much
　　alike;
　　One wife in Natchez-under-the-Hill and another
　　　one here in Pike.
A keerless man in his talk, was Jim, and an awkward
　　man in a row,
　　But he never funked and never lied, I reckon he
　　　never knowed how;

175

And this was all the religion he had to treat his engines
    well;
    Never be passed on the river: to mind the Pilot's
        bell:
And if ever the Prairie Belle took fire a thousand
    times he swore,
    He'd hold her nozzle agin the bank till the last
        soul got ashore.
All boats has their day on the Missisip and her day
    came at last.
    The Movastor was a better boat, but the Belle
        she wouldn't be passed.
And so come tearin' along that night the oldest craft
    on the line
    With a nigger squat on her safety valve, and her
        furnace crammed, resin and pine.
The fire burst out as she cleared the bar and burnt
    a hole in the night,
    But quick as a flash she turned and made for that
        willowbank on the right
There was runnin' and cursin', but Jim yelled out
    over all the infernal roar.
    "I'll hold her nozzle agin the bank till the last
        galoot's ashore!"
Throught the hot black breath of the burning boat,
    Jim Bludso's voice was heard
    And they all had faith in his cussedness, and
        knowed he would keep his word.
Sure as you're born they all got off, afore the
    smokestack fell.
    And Bludso's ghost went up alone in the smoke of
        the Prairie Belle.
He weren't no saint, but at judgment I'd run my chance
    with Jim:
    Longside of some pious gentlemen, that wouldn't
        shook hands with him
He'd seen his duty a deadsure thing and went for it
    there and then:
    And Christ ain't goin' to be too hard, on a man that
        died for men.

JIMMY JOHNSON

BY H. M. BURNABY   *1922*

He was Mr. Jimmy Johnson, and he earned a weekly wage,
And his life was eventful as a squirrel's in a cage.
He was only one of many, who've forgotten how to feel,
   He was something in the City, and he helped to turn
      a wheel.
He possessed a wife and kiddies, living somewhere
      Brixton way,
   And he drew his humble pittance, weekly, every
      Saturday,
And the bit of grub on Sundays that it managed to
      contrive,
   Provided the incentive to go on— to keep alive.
And that was why he added rows of figures nice and neat,
   He was Mr.Jimmy Johnson—life was sweet.
Then somewhere a bugle sounded, and he kissed his pen
      good-bye.
   His stool he kicked from under him— no time to wonder
      why,
He embraced his wife and kiddies, and he told 'em not
      to pine,
   He was Private Jimmy Johnson, number 12129.
He liked it when they asked him if he minded forming
      fours,
   He presented arms "by numbers" to the sergeant's
      loud applause.
He bought a little toothbrush—and a tin of "Soldiers
      friend",
   They said with luck he might become a soldier in
      the end.
He didn't quite appreciate the stuff he'd got to eat,
   But he was Private Johnson—Life was Sweet.
Then Jimmy Johnson found himself up in the firing line,
   Where he learned the art of warfare—number 12129.
The sergeant came and told him they were going to attack,
   Then he got that sinking feeling, but he bravely
      kept it back.

They reinforced his courage with the regulation rum,
    And he trusted to the Fates, to steer him clear
        of "Kingdom Come."
Stranger figures loomed about him, minds with but one
        single thought,
    So he dealt with the obstruction, in the way that
        he'd been taught.
'Twas in self-defence he did it—quite an ordinary feat,
    But he was Private Johnson—Life was Sweet.
He is Mr. Jimmy Johnson, and he's got an empty sleeve,
    And he's smiling very bravely—while he's trying
        to believe
He was something in the Army, now he's broken on
        the wheel,
    Once again he's one of many who've forgotten how to
        feel,
Forgotten by the stay-at-homes—who not so long ago,
    Said they didn't want to lose him, but they thought
        he ought to go.
And he's holding on tenaciously, and hoping p'raps
        some day,
    He will find the silver lining, when the clouds
        have rolled away.
You can see them all around you, some sell matches
        in the street,
    There are many Jimmy Johnsons—*Is* life sweet?

JOE'S LUCK

BY L. WALDRON and CUTHBERT CLARKE   *1913*
Performed by Bransby Williams

Dear old Joe he was one of the best
    And everyone's pal without doubt
The sort of chap that would give you his boots
    And swear he walked better without.
Why I've known him to give his last dollar away
    To some other fellow in need,
And explain that he fasted from choice don't you know,
    He was seedy and gone off his feed.

He told us they called him a waster at home,
  We knew that he'd both grit and pluck,
Yet somehow things never went rosy with him,
  But we chaps put it down to Joe's luck.
A gentleman's son we all knew him to be,
  And the breed in him showed plain enough,
But he never let on to the boys who he was
  And he chummed in with sundry and rough.
The life of a cowboy is not very soft,
  But he stuck it quite well for all that,
And though he rode reckless and faster than most
  Like a toff in the saddle he sat.
Jack and I were his pals right away from the first
  And we showed him the ropes all we could,
Tho' mind you his pride would prevent us sometimes
  From doing as much as we would
He told us the story of how he left home,
  How he'd got in the hands of a Jew,
And the guv'nor—the name that he gave to his dad—
  Faced ruin to pay what was due.
How he bid his own people good-bye in remorse
  And swore to repay all the debt.
But fortunes he found even out in the West
  Were not quite so easy to get.
He liked nothing better—a pipe, and a chat
  Round the fire of a night just we three
Then he'd talk of old England and how he'd return
  With the money—when wealthy was he.
One evening we sat in our usual way
  When the mail brought a letter for Joe,
A solicitor's name was embossed on the flap,
  He showed it with face all aglow.
"Maybe it's the money boys—coming at last,"
  He said with a shake in his voice.
We gave him a thump on the back for good luck,
  Just to show him how we should rejoice,
He opened the letter with quivering hands
  His face turning white as he read—
"It's come boys"—he shouted, "I knew luck would
      change",
  Then he gasped—just fell back— and was dead.

JOHNNIE! ME AND YOU

BY CORNEY BRAIN   *1907*

Oh! Johnnie! 'ere's a dinner party
  Look at all them things!
Oh! look at all them dishes
  Wot that powder'd footman brings!
Well if they eat all that there food
  'Ow poorly they will be!
'Ere jump upon my back Johnnie!
  Now then you can see!
Oh! Johnnie! look at that ole gent,
  They've took 'is plate away!
Afore 'e's finished 'arf 'is food,
  That is a game to play!
No! that ain't beer they're drinkin' of
  Not likely, why that's fizz!
Oh! look at that great pink thing there,
  That's salmon fish, that is!
I think there's some mistake 'ere Johnnie!
  We ain't arst tonight!
We could a-pick'd a bit eh! Johnnie?
  We've got the appetite!
Seein' all that food there
  Makes yer 'ungry, that it do!
We ain't 'ad no dinner-parties lately!
  Johnnie! me and you!
Oh! Johnnie! look at that old gal,
  With only 'arf a gown,
The h'ice she's swaller'd must 'ave cost,
  Ah! well nigh 'arf a crown.
She's 'avin 'arf a quartern now,
  And wants it, that she do,
When I've eaten too much h'ice myself,
  I've 'ad that feelin' too!
Oh! Johnnie! they've pulled down the blind,
  I call it nasty mean.
They're all ashamed that's wot they is,
  Ashamed o' bein' seen.

A-eatin' all that food like that,
'Tain't decent, that it 'ain't!
We wouldn't pull no blinds down
If we'd 'arf o' their complaint!
So come along, let's orf it, Johnnie,
Orf it to the Strand,
Now don't yer go a cryin' Johnnie,
'Ere give me your 'and.
'Ungry, Johnnie, so am I. We'll get a brown or two
A-callin' "Keb or Kerridge, Captin'!"
Johnnie! me and you!

A "JOLLY GOOD SORT"

BY LEONARD POUNDS and CUTHBERT CLARKE   *1919*

Now you'll oft hear a man called "a decent old sport,"
Or, equally often, "a jolly good sort."
To obtain such distinction have e'er you enquired
Just what are the qualifications required?
Have ever you pondered? Have ever you thought
What consititues, really, "A jolly good sort?"
Is it he who is known to his cronies as "free,"
Thro' his loud repetitions of "have one with me?"
Who is known round about for the money he spends,
And thus gains a wide nightly circle of *"friends?"*
Who ogles the fluffy-haired girl at the bar,
And who smirks when he's told "What a terror you are!"
Whose newspaper every day may be seen
With the "Racing" page thumb-marked, and all the
rest clean?
Who spends each whole ev'ning at one of those haunts
Where a man who leaves early does so amid taunts?
Come, all of you fellows whose friendship he's bought
Do *these* qualities make up "a jolly good sort?"
Have you never reflected that he you extol
May in some other place play a far diff'rent role?

181

That although among you he's "Hail fellow, well met!"
   His best humour's reserved just for your special set?
That those hours which are spent with you folk ev'ry
     night
   May be stolen from those whose they should be by
     right?
That his company, given so freely to you,
   Would be also esteemed in that place where it's due?
Of his life you've one side been permitted to see,
   Now observe the reverse of the picture with me.
There's a tired little woman who's darning a sock,
   With a wistful glance now and again at the clock.
The youngster is hours ago tucked up in bed;
   "When will Daddy be home?" were the last words
     he said.
He arrives home at last, though quite sober he's not;
   That today's his wife's birthday he cares not a jot,
And she sighs as she notes that no present he's brought.
   Does he still fill your bill as "a jolly good sort?"
Now we'd not have a fellow a prig or a prude,
   Nor with fierce puritanical notions imbued.
But cannot one follow a line that's between?—
   A path 'twixt the waster and humbug, I mean?
Yes, the man, who, when after day's work is done,
   May feel like a drink, and he *has* it—just *one*
He's sufficient will-power, when he's loudly besought,
   "Come on, have another one, do!—something short!"
To insist that he *won't,* and eludes all their snares,
   They may call him hen-pecked, but it's little *he*
     cares.
He'll finish his drink up, and bid all "good-night,"
   For his fireside with him's a prospective delight.
And mean he is not, for he'll give or he'll lend
   When a comrade's resources have come to an end.
He prefers the quiet bliss of his own little home
   To the gaily lit bar, or a nocturnal roam.
His four year old laddie is *his* something short,
   That man's *rightly* labelled *A jolly good sort!"*

JUST A SITTER-IN

BY MARGARET MUIRHEAD and DAVID JENKINS   1950
Performed by Suzette Tarri

I'm not a shorthand typist—I was never one for speed—
   Or a snappy shop-assistant—askin. "Wot does modom need?"
I fancied bein' a "clippie." but my chances were thin,
   I missed the bus—and now my job is
Just a "Sitter-In!"
   My dancin' days are over, an' those *were* the days, no doubt!
But I never seemed to get the chance to be a "Sitter-Out!"
   The game of Love's a gamble—and I couldn't play to win . . .
So fate decreed that I should always be a "Sittin'-In."
   When the baby's sleepin' peaceful, and 'is folk are at
      the "flicks."
I sit and do me jumper while the clock just ticks and ticks;
   An' sometimes there's a tear or two rolls down a knittin'
      pin . . .
It's funny what you think of when you're just a
      "Sitter-In."
   With me ears pinned back to listen for the slightest
      little cry,
Me fancies keep me busy and the moments seem to fly
   They can keep their film stars wiv their shiny air
      an' sloppy grin
A bit of make-believe is free to
   Just a "Sitter-In!"
I kid myself 'e's mine for keeps, that little chap
   in there,
   I build 'im castles in the sand, and kingdoms in the
      air.
I give 'im lots of 'ints and tips for keepin' up
      'is chin—
   That's *one* thing that I'm expert at, tho'
I'm just a "Sitter-In!"
   Too soon my dreams are shattered, an' I know the time
      'as come,
To say—"Ah, well, you've 'ad it—There's 'is daddy
      and 'is mum!"
   But I feel me job's got SOMETHING when 'is daddy,
      with a grin,

Says to me, "May 'Eaven bless you—for bein'
Just a Sitter-In!"

JUST LIKE I SAID

BY V. F. STEVENS and CUTHBERT CLARKE   *1938*

Some blokes give me the willies— they're so cocksure
    of themselves,
    Allus finks as wot they say of must be right;
I got a pal just like it, 'e gets on my nerves
    'e do—
    'E'll argue white is black, and black is white.
But getting over me aint quite so easy as 'e finks,
    And I proved it to 'im too, the other day,
'E backed Ole Spikey Collins to beat Joe Briggs at
    darts.
    And when Joe Briggs won I 'ad to turn and say,
'Ere yar! what'd I tell yer!
    Trying to kid yerself you're blinkin' smart.
I told yer Spikey Collins was a duffer at the game,
    The way 'e *'olds* a flight ud break yer 'eart.
You've lorst us all a drink all round a-backin' of
    that cove.
    I told yer *too* 'e wasn't any good.
I told yer at the *very—very* first 'e wouldn't win it.
    And 'e didn't too, just like I said 'e would.
We 'ad our annual dinner, a little while ago,
    And that's a fing wot caused a proper bust;
My pal said that the soup is always served before
    'hore-duves'
    But I said "No! hore-duves is always fust."

184

We entered in an argument and nearly came to blows,
　　But at last I got it *my* way, never fear,
'Cos when the show was over with 'hore-duves' fust
　　　　on the bill,
　　I 'ad great pride in shoutin' in 'is ear.
'Ere yar! What'd I tell yer!
　　Trying to kid yerself you're blinkin' smart.
If *you* 'ad to serve a dinner it is very plain to
　　　　see,
　　You'd land yerself right in the bloomin' cart,
Soup before hore-duves!!! I never 'eard o' such a fing,
　　I spose you fink Sauterne's a kind of stew.
I knew they didn't serve the soup before hore-duves,
　　　　so what!
　　No more they don't, just like I said they do!
I was at the snack and snaffle in the "Crown" the
　　　　other night,
　　A-talkin with some blokes on modern art,
One of 'em said a Whistler was a bloke wot sucked a
　　　　flute!
　　Such higgerance yer know gave me a start.
But anyway, from that we got to arguing the point.
　　On the colour of the street-lamps round the park,
I said "Grey" and 'e said "Green", so when we went
　　　　to look,
　　I couldn't 'elp but say just for a lark,
'Ere yar! what'd I tell yer!
　　Trying to kid yerself you're blinkin' smart!
You must be bloomin' colour-blind if you say that's
　　　　a green,
　　If an Irishman wore that-'e'd break 'is 'eart.
Field Grey! that's wot yer calls it, 'cos *ME*, I
　　　　ought to know.
　　A bloke wot earns 'is livin' sloshin' paint,
You said "Green", I said "It wasn't" so take
　　　　another look,
　　And there it is, just like I said it aint!

THE KID

WRITTEN, COMPOSED and PERFORMED BY TOM KILFOY   *1914*

There's a battleship, that's swinging to her anchors
    somewhere North,
There's a sailor's "kit" at auction. You'll agree.
They'll fetch *ten times their value,* just for memory
    of the "Kid,"
    Who was working out his penance, in that ship upon
      the sea.
He was ragged, he was dirty, and he'd not been overfed,
    But he didn't fear the judge nor yet the cop.
He'd been pinched for playing banker with some others
    of his tribe,
    And his legs were just too short to beat the "slop."
The judge gave him the option. *He* hadn't much to
      lose.
    "The Prison or the Navy? you can choose."
So the Kid, he chose the Navy. Jail was not for such
      as he,
    And he went to work his penance, in a ship upon
      the sea.
He was washed and fed, and clobbered, and they made the
      beggar work,
    But he slogged and worried through it, with a smile.
With the hose the jaunty froze him, and he was kicked from
      here to there,
    And his life was simply hell just for a while.
Yet he stuck it like a good 'un; he was never known
      to grouse,
    And he learned to fence, and fight, and wash his neck;
And he kept his record cleaner than the sturdiest
      A. B.
    He was working out his penance in that ship upon the
      sea.
They sent him out to China, where he studied Pagan
      ways,
    And he learned a lot of things he didn't know.
Still he always had a feeling of respect for woman-kind,
    And he rung down' in their presence to dead slow.

He slugged a crowd of Dagos once for bullying a girl.
They knifed him till his soul was all but free.
In the sick bay he was mended, th'o he's not the man
  he was;
  But, he's working out his penance, in that ship
    upon the sea.
When, one night, the storm was raging, all the hatches
  battened down.
Above the crash of waves, and winds that roared,
Rang the Bosun's "pipe" and order, rapped out, just
  like a knife
Hands! Man the Whaler! Quick! Man overboard!!
We'd scarce obeyed the order, when The Kid shot o'er
  the side.
He'd a line around his waist, his arms were free.
He meant to save that jaunty, tho' 'twas one he
  hated most.
He was working out his penance, in that ship upon
  the sea.
The lifebelt flared, we watched it and we paid the line
  out slow.
The searchlights found him, fighting inch by inch;
And we cheered and yelled, like blazes, when we saw
  he'd got his man,
And we rove a stronger line on to the winch.
The whaler fought towards them. He was very nearly
  done.
The boys all grabbed to save him, just as he
Pushed the jaunty to our gun'nle; then he chucked it
  up, Poor Kid.
He'd worked out *all* his penance in that ship
  upon the sea.
"There's a battleship that's swinging to her anchors
  somewhere North.
There's a sailor's kit at auction. You'll agree.
They'll fetch *twenty times their value* just for
  memory of The Kid
Who was working out his penance in that ship upon
  the sea.

THE KILLJOY

BY NOSMO KING and ERNEST LONGSTAFFE 1937

The Killjoy died and passed along
 To that peaceful happy State:
He'd often pictured in his dreams
 And stood before the gate.
He tried to pass the portals,
 When a quiet voice said "Stay!
What did you do on earth my friend
 And who are you anyway?"
The Killjoy in astonishment
 Said, "Surely you know me
And all the splendid things I've done
 To help humanity?
To administer the law
 I did my duty in a way,
That made me feared by every
 Common sinner in my day.
I did my very best to ban
 All Sunday games, and then
I closed the public houses
 To the working man at ten.
Music Halls and Theatres
 I abhorred, and in "Revue"
The shameful human female form
 I hid from public view.
Lovers in the open parks
 A pretty price they paid—
They were most severely dealt with
 By the Purity Brigade—
And should a good man fall from grace
 And dare to misbehave,
Relentlessly I'd hound him down:
 Aye even to the grave."
The voice cried "Stop: I've heard enough:
 It's very plain to see
You haven't judged your fellow men
 By standards set by me—

188

But by your own small, narrow soul
    Oh, how could you succeed?
Self righteousness your watchword,
    Intolerance your creed!
You've been sadly misinformed
    That fact is very clear,
Only those who've radiated joy
    Can ever enter here.
But you have lived to kill that joy,
    You must reap just what you sow
Besides the laughter here would shock you,
    You'll be happier *below*
The Killjoy trembled like a leaf
    And said "Am I awake?
I cannot dwell with murderers
    There must be some mistake"
"There's no mistake" the voice replied
    "It's just your point of view—
Perhaps you've never stopped to think
    They might object to you!
You've quite a lot in common
    Though you both play different roles,
They only kill men's bodies,
    But *you* destroy their souls."
And so the Killjoy joined his friends,
    Who'd kept for him a seat
With all the other Killjoys—
    Just to make their Hell complete.

THE LADY WITHOUT THE LAMP

BY G. B. LAWRENCE, NOSMO KING and HERBERT TOWNSEND1948

He was telling his class of the Crimean War,
    Of the soldiers who fought and who died,
And of how Florence Nightingale, bearing a lamp
    Could be seen at the wounded men's side.

189

"That woman," said he, "is a lesson for all
  Of steadfastness, courage and love,
Just one fine example of what can be done
  With the power that comes from above"—
Then a boy's hand shot up,
  And a voice said "But Sir—she wasn't the only one!
There must have been others out there at the front
  Or the work never could have been done."
"Why yes," said the teacher, "some forty or more
  Were helping to nurse at the camp,
But hers was the name that won honour and fame
  As 'The Lady who carried the Lamp' "
So today in the world, there are some who find fame
  For the wonderful things they have done
Some deed of courage, some generous act
  And they soon find a place in the sun.
While others just carry on with their jobs
  And the world never makes any fuss,
They just struggle along, even when things go wrong
  Like the Browns—or the Smiths or like Us.
No limelight for them—no newspaper headlines.
  No Royalty claim them as friends.
They just play their parts in the drama of life
  And then quietly slip out at the end.
Yet—this old world could never keep going
  On its long and its difficult tramp,
If it weren't for the fellow without a name
  And "The Lady without a Lamp."

LASCA

BY FRANK DESPREZ and CUTHBERT CLARKE   *1916*

It's all very well to write reviews,
  And carry umbrellas, and keep dry shoes,
And say what everyone's saying here,
  And wear what everyone else must wear;

But to-night I'm sick of the whole affair,
  I want free life and I want fresh air;
And I sigh for the canter after the cattle,
  The crack of the whips like shots in a battle,
The mêlée of horns and hoofs and heads
  That wars and wrangles and scatters and spreads;
The green beneath, and the blue above;
  And dash and danger, and life and love.
        And Lasca!
Lasca used to ride
  On a mouse-grey mustang
Close to my side,
  With blue serape and bright-belled spur:
I laughed with joy as I looked at her!
  Little knew she of books or creeds.
An Ave Maria sufficed her needs;
  Little she cared, save to be by my side
To ride with me and ever to ride.
  She was bold as the billows that beat,
She was wild as the breezes that blow,
  From her little head to her little feet
She was swayed in her suppleness to and fro
  By each gust of passion.
She would hunger that I might eat,
  Would take the bitter and leave me the sweet
But once, when I made her jealous for fun,
  At something I'd whispered or looked, or done,
One Sunday, in San Antonio,
  To a glorious girl on the Alamo:
She drew from her garter a dear little dagger
  And, sting of a wasp it made me stagger!
An inch to the left, or an inch to the right,
  And I shouldn't be maundering here to-night!
But she sobbed, and sobbing so swiftly bound
  Her torn reboso about the wound,
That I quite forgave her.
  Scratches don't count in Texas.
Why did I leave the fresh and free
  That suited her and suited me?
Listen awhile and you will see,
  But this be sure—in earth or air—
God and God's laws are everywhere.

And Nemesis comes with a foot as fleet
On the Texas trail as in Regent Street.
 The air was heavy the night was hot,
I sat by her side and forgot, forgot;
 Forgot the herd that were taking their rest,
Forgot that the air was close opprest,
 That the Texas norther comes sudden and soon,
In the dead of night or the blaze of noon,
 That once let the herd at its breath take fright,
Nothing on earth can stop their flight,
 And woe to the rider, and woe to the steed
Who falls in front of their mad stampede!
 Was that thunder? No, by the Lord!
I sprung to my saddle without a word.
 One foot on mine and she clung behind.
Away on a hot chase down the wind!
 But never was foxhunt half so hard,
And never was steed so little spared
 For we rode for our lives.
You shall hear how we fared in Texas.
 The mustang flew and we urged him on;
There was one chance left, and you have but one.
 Halt! jump to the ground, and shoot your horse;
Crouch under his carcase and take your chance;
 And if the steers in their frantic course
Don't batter you both to pieces at once
 You may thank your stars;
The cattle gained on us, and, just as I felt
 For my old six-shooter behind in my belt,
Down came the mustang and down came we
 Clinging to-gether and—what was the rest?
A body that spread itself on my breast.
 Two arms that shielded my dizzy head,
Two lips that hard on my lips were prest;
 Then came thunder in my ears
As over us surged the sea of steers.
 Blows that beat blood into my eyes
And when I could rise,—Lasca was dead!
 I gouged out a grave a few feet deep,
And there in Earth's arms I laid her to sleep.
 And there she is lying and no one knows:
And the summer shines and the winter snows.

For many a day the flowers have spread
A pall of petals over her head;
And I wonder why I do not care
For things that are like the things that were.
Does half my heart lie buried there
In Texas, down by the Rio Grande?

THE LAST BOTTLE

BY PETER CHEYNEY and HAROLD ARPTHORP   1925
Performed by Bransby Williams

Good night good Toby—old servant, faithful friend,
    As sound as this old wine throughout the years,
And faithful still—Good night!
    So you are the end of many dozens of a famous blend
That links these days up to the olden time,
    When men could ride and drink, and drank like men,
And loved good horses as they loved good wine.
    Gad! I remember—It seems but yesterday,
When shouts and laughter made the rafters ring,
    When from the table top, proudly I'd give the toast:
Friends! charge your glasses! Gentlemen—the King!
    For we were all King's men in those old merry days,
Loyal to the land we tilled—the land we trod.
    Men who were proud to count their Country and their
        King
Second to none other—save their God.
    And when they laid my father to his rest
In that quiet country churchyard on the hill,
    We drank a silent toast.
Deep in each breast
    The thought that he had loved you as I love you still.
Old wine, companion of our bygone days
    In time of trouble, happiness and stress,
You bound each friend to us with splendid faith,
    And drove dull care away with your caress.

193

Tonight across the silence comes a whisper,
    My Father's voice from outside earthly bounds.
The words sound clearly on my listening ear,
    The words he spoke when first I rode to hounds:
"Ride straight my son, and teach your son the same,
    Choose carefully your horses and your wife,
Remember that you bear an ancient name,
    And guard your honour as you guard your life".
And I remembered and my heart I steeled
    To play the game as he would have me play.
And then I met her on the hunting-field.
    'Twas golden sunset at the close of day,
In fancy I can see her dear eyes shine,
    And hear her murmured word of soft consent.
That night I drank to her in this old wine,
    Before I knew what life or true love meant.
I can remember the birthday of our boy,
    How bon-fires flared, and life was full of joy
Because of him.
    He would have been a man of thirty years—
Full-voiced and courage fine,
    If he were here, together we would sit,
And laugh o'er this last bottle of good wine.
    But he, my son, sleeps soundly on the hill, with my
        fore-fathers.
Boy, I drink to you!
    To all you might have been and might have done
If you had stayed the course. But you were gone,
    Ere your first race of life was yet begun.
I see your young face smiling through the years,
    Your eyes a-flashing with the joy of youth,
Just as your mother's eyes smiled through her tears,
    And she has left me too.
My dear, she waits for me, sending her love
    In many a happy thought, until I join her.
For, like this old port, my drops of life are running low.
    And I await, with patient happiness
The call to walk the way we all must go.
    Sweetheart, in fancy I can see you smile
So sweetly, as you nod your snow-white head.
    I shall be with you in a little while,
And when I go our ancient race is dead.

194

My dear, I drink to you.
To all the bygone days,
 To all our times of happiness and cheer.
 To all our ventures on life's pleasant ways.
 To our next meeting. My love! My dear!

THE LAST TOAST

BY W. OGILVIE and KATHLEEN SHAW MAYER   1913

They were our little play-mates
 In the far-away cradle days,
With their toddling gait and their lisping speech,
 And their wonderful baby ways;
And the daisies grew for their dimpled hands
 And the sunbeams shone for their curls,
And they were our little playmates,
 Let us drink to them now—"The Girls."
And the days went by and we found them fair,
 And we found them, oh, so sweet,
And we fell in love with their rippling hair,
 And the trip of their dainty feet,
And the beauty the good gods gave them,
 They doubled with silk and pearls,
And the days went by and we found them fair,
 Let us pledge them to-night—"The Girls."
Now, some of those wayward misses
 Have grown to be widow or wife,
Some are only a dream of kisses
 To mock at a lone man's life.
But whether they played for pastime,
 Or whether they fought us fair,
Let us pledge them once in the ruby wine
 For the sake of the days that were.
Now fill to the brim with hemlock!
 And lips that are tired of wine
195

Shall drink to the hearts that were broken
In days of the dear lang syne.
Shall drink to the buried laughter,
Shall drink to the old loves dead;
For the world has stolen our playmates
And the girl of our heart is wed.

THE LAST TOKEN

BY W. A. EATON and BOND ANDREWS   *1898*

A holiday in Rome—the azure sky
Was all unflecked by the clouds as if the eye
Of the Eternal looked from Heaven's high dome
On the great city, proud, Imperial Rome!
The Coliseum was crowded, row on row
A sea of human faces all aglow
With mad excitement for the day would be
A rare occasion of wild revelry.
For there were gladiator fights and shows
Of manly strength and as a fitting close
To the diversions of that joyous time
A band of Christians, whose most heinous crime
Was preaching a new doctrine, were to be
Thrown to the lions that all the crowd might see
How little the strange God, to whom they prayed,
Cared if his followers were stoned or flayed.
The sports are over and the setting sun
Is hurrying towards the West as if to shun
The sickening sight. A sudden hush upon the people
      fell,
And then uprose a fierce and savage yell.
See where they come, that faithful little band,
Chanting a hymn about their Fatherland:
The Heaven of which they speak with so much joy,
That home of happiness without alloy!
See yonder maiden with the saint-like face

196

And form of beauty, full of fire and grace,
She lifts her head as if she were a queen.
No trace of fear in her actions seen.
Now come the lions growling with rage,
   Hungry and glad to leave their tight-barred cage.
See yonder royal beast with flowing mane
   Lashing his side and roaring with disdain,
Gazing around upon the yelling crowd,
   Answering their shouts by growlings long and loud.
The maiden stands as statue-like as death,
   The crowd in terror gaze with bated breath.
While as she stands, there falls just by her feet
   A lovely rose, still filled with perfume sweet.
Upward she gazes with wide-open eyes,
   Ah well she knows who flung the dainty prize.
'Tis he, her lover, who had vainly tried
   To win her from the faith for which she died.
He worshipped Venus, Bacchus, and the train
   Of heathen gods who do their votaries chain
To sinful pleasures, making virtue nought.
   She was a Christian, and had often sought
To stir his heart with love of Him who died,
   But he had laughed at her most earnest prayer,
And tossed a goblet in the sunny air,
   And said "We live and die, then take our fill
Of pleasure now, and let them groan that will.
   Why should we waste our youth in solemn fast,
If we are buried just like dogs at last?
   Nay, drive this Christian nonsense from your head
And be my own, and then when we are wed
   We will worship Venus and the God of Love.
Give me your hand, say Yes, my gentle dove."
   And as she told him she must confess
Her faith in Christ through martyrdom no less
   Was the reward of all who worshipped Him,
Of all who dared to chant their holy hymn.
   And now she was to prove her faith by death.
The lions were close, she almost felt their breath
   Upon her cheek. She stood with anguish dumb,
And strained her eyes to see if he had come
   To watch her die. The rose had fallen there,
She stooped and placed it in her raven hair.

Then looked again and saw her lover's face,
And arms held down as if he would embrace
Her even now. A moment, and she turned
From her set purpose. Then new ardour burned
Within her breast and she stood proud and calm,
As if she knew the lions could do no harm.
And then uprose the Christians' holy hymn.
The sickening sight now makes the senses swim.
And we will draw a veil o'er the sad scene.
Night in the Coliseum—the crowd has gone—
One being wanders in that scene forlorn.
He stands upon the place where she had died.
And breathes the name of Christ the crucified.
And stooping down, among the martyred dead,
He finds a rose now dyed a deeper red.
Some fragments of a dress he knew was hers,
He places in his breast and new life stirs
Within his heart, and as he leaves the place
With head bowed low, with slow and solemn pace.
He softly murmurs as he homeward goes:
"Jesus, be Thou my guide till life shall close."
But was he coward? Did he hide away?
Not many weeks, on a great festal day,
Another band of Christians stood to die,
Lifting their glorious hymn of triumph high.
Where she had stood he boldly takes his stand,
A withered rose clasped in his strong right hand.

LAUGH AND THE WORLD LAUGHS WITH YOU

BY ELLA WHEELER WILLCOX and D'AUVERGNE BARNARD 1904

Laugh and the world laughs with you.
Weep, and you weep alone:
For this stolid old earth
Has need of your mirth,

It has troubles enough of its own.
   Sing, and the hills will echo it:
Sigh, and it's lost on the air;
   For they want full measure
Of all your pleasure,
   But nobody wants your care,
Feast, and your halls are crowded,
   Fast, and they'll pass you by;
Succeed and give,
   And they'll let you live,
But fail—and they'll let you die:

THE LAY OF THE FOUNTAIN PEN

BY LYELL JOHNSTON   *1914*

No one would quite imagine such an oddity as I,
   Could ever be accredited to think;
Yet as a Mabie Toddity, some funny things I spy
   In my "scrawl" of life, that's spreading writing
      ink;
I'm not a fancy toy.
   Just a present from her boy,
To the daintiest miss you ever struck, or ever walked
      or ran;
   But altho' of neuter gender,
I was jealous when my sender
   Got a spanking kiss and called a *Duck* for giving
      her a *Swan*
I'm just a fountain pen,
   But I'm sure that many men
Must be envious of the luck with which I'm blest;
   For I'm couched in swagger case,
When I'm in my resting place,
   And lie at ease reclining on her breast;
Can you grasp what someone misses
   As I get the real kisses,

When lovingly we scribble "billet douxs?"
  I close my nib and wink,
For ev'ry time she stops to think,
  She puts me to her lips and gently chews.
When some fancy whim has got her,
  Then she sketches on the blotter,
Till with thirst I'm running down and feeling ill;
  So then just out of spite,
I refuse to mark or write,
  Till she wets my feed by giving me a fill;
The only time she swears
  Is when perchance she'll unawares
Lay me down and rush to send a telegram;
  Then those scratchy pens and pencils,
Like the Post Office utensils,
  Learn what *they* are and the faithful friend
    I *am.*
I have a recollection,
  Once she wasted her affection,
Altho' just at the time it wasn't fun;
  On a stupid stylograph,
But at length I had the laugh,
  For she had to knock him down to make him run;
Now of late I'm in the dumps,
  For a thing that clicks and jumps,
Called a typemachine has put my speed to shame;
  Still I hold a proud position,
For whate're the missive's mission,
  I'm the chap that's requisitioned,
Just to sign the *Darling's name.*

LEGS

BY WARREN HASTINGS   *1945*

LEGS–LEGS–LEGS.
   See 'em on the tables, see 'em on the chairs,
See 'em on the parlour maid walking up the stairs,
   See 'em on the horses, see 'em on the dogs,
See 'em on the pussy-cats, see 'em on the frogs.
   See 'em when they're mutton, see 'em when
      they're pork,
See 'em when they're wooden, see 'em when they're cork,
   See 'em on the elephant, see 'em on the flea,
And on lovely people same as you and me.
   See 'em on a camel, see 'em on a crow,
See 'em at the theatre dancing in a row.
   See 'em on the soldiers as they march in step,
See 'em on the jitter-bugs full of gin-and-pep,
   See 'em on a Scotsman, see 'em on a Greek,
See 'em in silk stockings, beautiful and sleek.
   No matter what you call 'em pins, or props,
      or pegs,
Limbs, or shanks, or spindles–they're Legs–Legs–Legs!

THE LESSON OF THE WATERMILL

BY SARAH DOUDNEY and BOND ANDREWS   *1897*

     Listen to the watermill,
       All the livelong day,
     How the creaking of the wheel
       Wears the hours away.
     Languidly the water glides,
       Useless on and still,
     Never coming back again
       To that watermill.

And the proverb haunts my mind,
  Like a spell that's cast
The mill will never grind
  With the water that has passed.
Take the lesson to yourselves,
  Loving hearts and true.
Golden years are fleeting by.
  Youth is fleeting too.
Try to make the most of life,
  Lose no honest way,
Time will never bring again
  Chances passed away.
Leave no tender word unsaid.
  Love while life shall last,
The mill will never grind
  With the water that has passed.
Work while yet the daylight shines,
  Man of strength and will,
Never does the streamlet glide
  Useless by the mill.
Wait not till tomorrow's sun
  Beams upon your way,
All that you can call your own
  Lies in this to-day.
Power, intellect and strength,
  May not, cannot last,
The mill will never grind
  With the water that has passed.
Oh! the wasted hours of life.
  That have drifted by
Oh! the good we might have done,
  Lost without a sigh.
Love that we might once have saved
  With but a single word,
Thoughts conceived, but never penned,
  Perishing unheard.
Take this lesson to your heart,
  Take, oh hold it fast,
The mill will never grind
  With the water that has passed.

THE LIE

BY TED LYMBERY and HERBERT TOWNSEND   *1923*

The bachelor spake to his Benedict pal
  He met in the street one day,
Of the girl he intended to make his wife—
  The one he had waited for all his life—
Who had stolen his heart away.
  He raved of her beauty, her charm, and her grace,
(As lovers religiously do).
  And talked of the glorious years in store,
With happiness reigning for evermore,
  And the Benedict smiled—He knew!!
The Benedict spake to his Benedict pal,
  When nearly a year had flown,
Of his capable wife and his excellent flat.
  (You'll observe that from "charm" it had come to
      that),
And his smile rather sickly had grown.
  He hadn't much time, now, to visit the club,
At home finding plenty to do.
  Still he'd marry if he had his time again—
An obvious lie—(it was perfectly plain).
  And both of the Benedicts knew!!

LIFE IS LIKE A GAME OF FOOTBALL

BY ALEC KENDAL and A. W. PARRY   *1938*

Life is a game of football,
  We each have a place in the team,
Whether amateur or professional,
  For points we plot and scheme.
We're born just like a wee ball,
  And soon we're taught the pace,

Right from the day we enter the fray
    We're kicked all over the place.
We all begin as amateurs
    From then on it's ding dong,
Through penalties, fouls and scrimmages,
    We dribble our way along,
We get in many tight corners,
    And emerge with many a scar,
To find ourselves offside, maybe,
    In the net or over the bar.
Oft-times we get reverses
    Go half-back and full-back too,
Though at half-time we may be losing
    We charge forward to win our way thro'.
The going at times may be heavy
    But the goal for which we aim,
Is well worth all the tackling,
    So we keep on playing the game.
We have our last kick in the Final
    The season draws to a close,
The game is done, have we lost or won?
    When the referee's whistle blows?
Into which league shall we enter?
    How's the score with you and I?
Will it be relegation? Or the play-ground in the sky?

LIFE'S PATHWAY

BY CHAS. J. MOORE and WILLIE ROUSE   *1925*

Fair maid, it is an ancient truth,
    That to the sparkling eyes of youth,
The wine of life is red.
    Quaff on! Laugh on!
But when, with heart weighed down with care
    With sorrow silvering your hair,
The bitter days and nights creep on,
    Weep on!

Aye, weep, for tears will bring relief,
　And help to soften ev'ry grief,
Then lift your eyes that you may see
　Some others' keener agony.
Seek then to soothe them in their pain,
　And so find joy in life again.
Give sympathy and still give on.
　For in the giving you will find
Rare happiness and peace of mind,
　Choose then this path and go right on
Fight on!
　So when the fight is o'er at last,
And shadows close around you fast.
　You gaze along the path you trod,
That brought you daily nearer God,
　When sick and sad you still pressed on,
Rest on! Rest on!

THE LIGHTHOUSE KEEPER'S STORY

BY ARTHUR HELLIAR and CUTHBERT CLARKE   *1909*

You want to hear of the bravest deed ever done on the
　　land or sea?
I rather think I can tell yer *that* for it appears
　　'twas done by *me*.
It was when I was lighthouse keeper a year or two back,
　　not more.
The lighthouse was built on a rock, sir, arf a mile
　　pretty near from the shore.
A storm for a month had been raging, no boat could
　　approach as we knew,
And the steamer wot should 'ave brought vittles
　　was more than nine weeks overdue.
For days we'd been living on biscuits—they was all
　　as there was left to eat.

205

On Sundays we fried 'em in lamp-oil, we did it by
  way of a treat.
But that give out arter a bit, sir, so we 'as to partake
  of 'em "rore."
Still the lamp was the wust of the bisness, we
  couldn't light up any more.
We'd only one small box o' matches and I took 'em above
  in the lamp,
And 'eld 'em afore the reflector, till my arm fairly
  ached with the cramp.
They didn't make much of a flare, sir, well, I 'ardly
  expected they would,
But I had this 'ere great consolation as I'd done all
  as any man could.
I soon finished up all the matches—there was nuffing
  more left I could do,
So I turns in my 'ammick being sleepy and was off
  in a minute or two.
Soon I dreamt that I sat at a banquet with some nobs
  in a West End hotel,
They was 'anding round liver and bacon, fried fish,
  tripe and onions as well.
A waiter asked me if I'd 'ave some, and I'd just stuck
  my fork in a lump,
When I almost fell out of my 'ammick for there
  come a most 'orrible bump!
I knew what it was in a moment, I could tell pretty
  well by the force,
It was one o' them big ocean liners wot 'ad got a
  bit out of 'er course.
There was dozens more come after that, sir, they
  cannoned us all thro' the night,
I tell yer I wasn't arf glad, sir, when I see it
  begin to get light.
I thought p'r'aps as some very likely might keep up
  the game all the day,
So I 'ung out a board with "Wet paint" on, which
  I fancied might keep 'em away.
Being woke up all night by them vessels was enough
  to make anyone mad,
And the langwidge the crews used was 'orrid,
  and the skipper's was ten times as bad.

So I calls to my mate what was dozing and tells 'im
      some oil must be got,
"There's a shop arf a mile off" 'e answers, "shall
      yer swim there or fly there or what?"
"I shall fly there!" I says, "or I'll try to, just
      'ark while I tell you my plan,
You must fasten me on to a rocket and aim it as
      straight as you can.
I must take one as well to come back with, for they
      mightn't p'r'aps 'ave one on land,
But them ships knockin' bits off our lighthouse is
      a thing as I'm hanged if I'll stand."
So he fastens me on very careful, I'd a can in my 'and
      for the oil,
And the wind was a 'owlin' and screamin' and the
      water was all of a boil.
Now remember, I says afore startin', I'm a-risking my
      life I'll admit,
But a Briton ne'er shrinks from his duty and that
      lamp there tonight must be lit!
Them words was scarce out of my mouth, sir, when I
      'ears a loud kind of whizz,
And away thro' the air I was soarin', and a rummy
      sensation it is!
My mate 'e 'ad once been a gunner, and 'is aim was
      surprisingly true,
I missed the shop-door I'll admit sir, but bang
      thro' the window I flew.
But the face of the man wot was serving was the thing
      as you ought to have seen,
When I landed full length on the counter and arskes
      for some best paraffin.
He took me at first for a h'angel till 'e saw as I
      'adn't no wings,
And noticed a 'am disappearing with a loaf and
      some pickles and things.
To bring a long tale to a h'end sir, I returned the
      same way as I came,
'Twas a coastguard as touched off the rocket and I
      can't say a lot for 'is aim.
But my mate who was up in the tower sees me coming
      and 'eld out 'is net,

I'd 'ave missed by a yard if 'e 'adn't and might
a got 'orribly wet.
And talking o' wet, sir, reminds me as I'm dry
enough now thro' and thro',
Wot's that you says, "Will I join yer" Well,
thankee, don't mind if I do.
Good 'ealth sir, it's lucky I met you for there's
men 'ere by dozens as tries
To get gents to stand 'em a drink, sir, by
tellin' 'em 'orrible lies.

THE LITTLE BOTTOM DRAWER

BY VALENTINE and CHARLES CORY   *1921*

It's a dainty little bedroom,
    And it's draped in white and blue,
There are easy chairs in plenty,
    And a cosy corner too.
There are all the little knick-knacks,
    And the things that girls adore,
But the most important of them all
    Is the little bottom drawer.
Girls, you'd just go into raptures
    If you had a chance to see
All its pretty little treasures
    Folded up so carefully,
A man, maybe would hardly know
    What half of them were for,
Still I don't think he'd mind
    Looking in that little bottom drawer.
There are little bits of hankies,
    There are dainty blouses too,
And the sweetest things in nighties
    With the ribbons threaded through.

And a host of pretty treasures
    That had very nearly gone.
But by real hard work were rescued
    When the great white sales were on.
Just unfold that tissue paper
    There are things inside you'll see
Little tiny precious somethings,
    Much too small for you or me.
Touch them lightly for they whisper
    Of a day that is no more
But they bring a touch of heaven
    To that little bottom drawer.
I can see her as she stood there
    In the charm of girlish grace,
With the light of God's own glory
    As it shone from out her face
I can hear the prayer she murmured
    For some golden day in store,
That would crown the longings centred
    Round that little bottom drawer.
Put them back—the dream is over,
    For the Finger moving on,
Leaves behind it but a shadow
    Of love that's past and gone.
Just a sigh for what has vanish'd,
    Just a sob for what is o'er.
And the key is turned for ever
    In that little bottom drawer.

A LITTLE BRASS BUTTON

BY FRANCIS R. BARNETT and HAROLD RAMSEY   *1940*

Only a little brass button,
    One of a million such,
A relic so petty in value,
    But to her it means so much.

There's a rusty satin behind it,
   And a crown is stamp'd before,
And it used to shine on a soldier's breast
   In the old dead days of yore.
Only a little brass button
   That shone on a soldier's breast.
The one little salve for an aching heart
   That tells her God knows best.
In dreams she pictur'd his proud return
   Thro' the flag-deck'd streets of the town.
But all that came back was a button,
   And on it was a crown.
Only a little brass button,
   But it tells her how he died
Saving a wounded comrade
   Who had fallen by his side.
His strong arms bore him gently,
   Just one more step to go
But the spirit of pity was blind and deaf,
   And a bullet laid him low.
Only a little brass button,
   Sent by a friendly hand
In a letter that told of his splendid death,
   And knew she'd understand
In dreams she pictur'd his proud return
   With glory and great renown,
But all that returned was a button
   And on it was a crown.
Almighty God of Battles
   When Thou bidst the strife to cease,
When the cause of Justice triumphs
   And clarion bells ring Peace.
When the boys come back with their trophies,
   And the Nations are all astir
All she's gained is just a button
   But it's all the world to her.
Only a little brass button,
   That shone in the sun like gold,
Flashing above a soldier's heart
   While the battle thunder rolled.
In dreams she pictur'd his soul at rest,
   The burden of life laid down

And she is wearing his button,
But he is wearing a crown.

A LITTLE GUTTERSNIPE

BY VALENTINE and T. C. STERNDALE-BENNETT   *1916*

It is quite a simple story of an ordinary type
   And the hero of it's only just a little gutter-snipe
There's not very much about it that's particularly
      new
   But he told it me exactly as I'm going to tell
      it to you.
I fancy it is quite a year or more since it took place
   But it's left behind a memory that nothing can
      efface.
And I know that he'll remember it when years have
      passed away
   How the Fresh Air Fund once took him to the country
      for a day.
"Blimey Guv'nor I remember it, it was a 'eavenly day
   We went down to Eppin' Forest in the country
      miles away
The trees they was in 'undreds, my word they was a
      sight.
   All growin' thick like coppers dahn our street
      on Sunday night!
There was birds, they weren't in cages, they just
      flew about on wings
   And butterflies and bumblebees, sort o'
      coloured flies wot stings
There was little sheep wiv wooly coats a-'oppin'
      round and round
   Wot 'ad got no labels stuck on 'em at one and four
      a pound.
But the flowers 'swelp me, guv'nor, they fairly giv me
      fits

211

The colours, why they beat me muvver's Sunday 'at
    to bits.
They let me pick 'em, decent o' the owner I must say
    But p'r'aps he knew I doesn't get an outin' ev'ry
    day.
Would I like to go down there again—why guvnor, if
    I could
    I'd sell papers for a solid week for nuffin'— that
    I would.
I'd promise to pick no flowers at all, for I
    eggspect
    If we did it sort o' regular the owner might
    object
I'd even walk there all the way, I wouldn't want no
    train
    If I only thought them Fresh Air blokes would take
    me there again!"
One little shilling does it—and I think you'd be content
    To hand it over gladly if you know just what it
    meant
For if you could see the joy that it can make or it
    has made
    Well I reckon you would think yourself a thousand
    times repaid.
It only means a drink or a cigar to you perhaps
    But it means a touch of Heaven to these little
    ragged chaps
Just an hour or two of brightness in their misery
    and strife
    Just a glimpse of God's own sunshine in some
    little East End life.

LITTLE JEAN

BY RUPERT HAZELL and JAN HURST   *1917*

Introduction: Ladies and Gentlemen. At a point on the Western front, where the British and French lines meet, an English soldier was exchanging confidences with one of our gallant allies. The Englishman happened to mention that he was quite familiar with the Frenchman's native village. The Frenchman grew reminiscent and eventually got on to his favourite topic—his little son.

You do not know my leetle son?
  Zen life for you 'af not begun.
'E is the sweetest leetle t'ing
  Zat evaire make ze 'eart to sing
'E 'af zc sort of 'appy smile
  Zat make ze summaire all ze while.
Ze sun out of 'is eyes does shine
  'Is name? Ah oui, ze same as mine.
We call 'im "Jean."
  An imp of mischief say you? so
Was you and me some time ago
  Mon cher, now do not say zose t'ings,
When you was young you not 'af wings.
  I know 'e shout and make a noise,
But 'ow you say "Boys will be boys."
  I will not 'af 'im cry all day,
I soonaire 'ear 'im shout and play,
  My little Jean.
He fight? Ah oui, I know 'e fight
  But always mind you for ze right
And if 'e lose 'e nevaire cry
  Sometimes 'e get ze-er-blue eye.
And if 'e beat 'im in the end
  Zat boy is always 'is best friend.
'E fight? ah oui, and so 'e may
  I will not 'af 'im run away
My little Jean.
  And when at last I 'af to go
And leave the boy 'e seem to know

213

I do not say I go to war
I do not say my 'eart is sore
But when I come to say good-bye
I see ze sadness in 'is eye
But 'e look at me so brafe and true
And say "Some day I fight for you."
My little Jean.
And so I'm very happy 'ere
I always feel zat he is near
And sometimes when I'm all alone
I feel 'is face close to my own.
So when ze time come to advance
If it shall be I fall for France
E'll 'elp 'is muzzaire to be brafe
I know she always will be safe
Wiz little Jean, My little Jean.

LIZETTE, QUEEN OF THE APACHES

BY PERCY EDGAR, LESLIE PAGET and CYRIL CARLTON   *1924*

Oft as I sit alone at night and gaze in the embers'
    glow,
    A wistful face comes back to me from out of the long
    ago.
Lizette, Queen of the Apaches!
    'Twas over in Paris first we met in those Quartier
    Latin days,
Ah, those happy days of struggle and fun,
    It was jolly companions every one.
Even now there's a mist before my gaze,
    When I think of those dear old student days;
She crept to my door a tragic mite,
    One eve when the snow lay deep and white,
She seemed all big eyes and golden head,
    'Some bread to eat' was what she said.
My first impulse was to ring my bell

For the police, but I loved them none too well.
Then those pleading eyes brought me 'neath their sway,
   And she crept in my home and my heart to stay.
They were happy years we together knew,
   Till unnoticed, the child to a woman grew.
She was mixture of mother, sister, child,
   With a touch of the tigress too when wild.
And a love that I was too blind to see,
   Yet it had its beginning and its end in me.
To me she was comrade, nothing more,
   The woman in her I hardly saw
Till a blackguard sneer struck the jarring note
   And I chocked back the lie in the coward throat.
Too late! A curse on that hated word,
   For I knew next morning she'd overheard.
She left me a note but all it said, was
   "Adieu mon ami." LIZETTE HAD FLED.
THREE YEARS PASSED ON and I found myself
   With a dare-devil English chum,
We were seeing life in the underworld,
   In a low Parisian slum.
'Twas a spice of danger tempted us,
   For grim death was always nigh,
And for strangers who sought Apacheland
   Discovery meant to DIE.
Twas a Cabaret called "The Café of Death."
   Well named if there's ever one been.
By some she-desperado kept, we'd heard,
   Tho' the Apaches, they called her QUEEN.
Danté himself could scarce describe
   The frequenters of that place.
Every nameless crime of the human kind
   Was stamped on each vicious face,
The room was hot, or the wine was drugged,
   For Heaven alone knows why—
         Suddenly Hell itself broke loose—
And they pointed at me whilst *"Spy!*
   Spy!" burst from every throat!
Standing back to back were we.
   It was death to us both remaining there
And death to us both to flee.
   Came a sudden stir in the ring of knives

And a woman reached my side,
  In the gruff *patois* of Apacheland.
"Stand back you dogs" she cried!
  She was supple and lithe as a panther,
I saw two bright eyes gleam
  Through the mask she wore, and that silver voice,
Was I mad, or in a dream?
  "Stand back, Canaille, your Queen commands!"
See! At me a knife-thrust sped,
  But a woman throws herself between,
And she caught the blow instead!
  The police break in, of course too late,
Mad with grief I hold her head,
  "Bon soir, mon ami, you know me, Yes?"
Then a sigh—and *Lizette was dead!*
  La Reine des Apaches, La Reine des Apaches
Save a wealth of love to myself bequeathed,
  With sin and crime is her memory wreathed,
But a woman, if ever a woman breathed—
  Was Lizette, La Reine des Apaches.

LOR! LUMME! YOU'D NEVER BELIEVE IT

BY H. M. BURNABY and HERBERT TOWNSEND   *1938*

'Ow do-ev'ry one—Missis Crowe is the name.
  A respectable woman, I 'opes you're the same;
Now my old man retired from 'is bizness last year,
  So I goes out charin' yerss, that's why I'm 'ere.
I've a regular round, *and* the things as I've seen,
  Take the people I *do* for, at Number Sixteen!
All this 'ere central 'eatin', armchairs made o' steel.
  Lor lumme! you'd never believe it!
They sleeps in twin beds, they're a swindle I'd say;
  Ain't no twin in the family—yet—anyway,
They've a son, drives a motor, it goes whizzin' by,

All covered with mottoes, fair catches yer eye,
There's one on the front of it, sez "Jump or die!"
  Lor lumme! you'd never believe it!
Yerss! an' wots more, they're noodist, they've ladies
      an' gents,
  In their bit o' back garden, no clothes, no pretence,
I know, 'cos I once had a garp through the fence
  Lor lumme! you'd never believe it!
There's them couple o' corfdrops, wot's took "Mon
      Repos"
  They only moved in there a few days ago,
Now *she* went out charin' one time, same as me;
  While *'e* used to be a bricklayer, yer see,
Touched lucky, they did, which you don't as a rule,
  'Avin' got 'em all right in a big football pool.
They sits down to breakfast, in full h'evening dress.
  Lor lumme! you'd never believe it!
Big six course dinners, she puts on at night;
  'E kicks, 'cos there ain't tripe and onions, that's
      right.
She dresses 'im up, like a posh country squire,
  An' keeps talkin' of tutors she's goin' to 'ire;
'Cos 'e *will* drop 'is haitches, and spit in the fire.
  Lor lumme! you'd never believe it!
Card parties! such luck you'd never conceive,
  Ev'ry thing that they touch turns to gold I believe,
And it will, while 'er old man's an ace up 'is sleeve.
  Lor lumme! you'd never believe it!
Now old Mother Finch, where I goes, at 'The Firs'
  She's a packet, and so is that daughter of 'ers,
When the two of 'em starts, they fair makes the place
      buzz,
  Wot one doesn't think of, the other one does,
'Arf-a-crown *and* me dinner I gets, if yer please,
  And last Thursday I clicks, for some nice bread
      and cheese.
All 'oity toity', as poor as church mice.
  Lor lumme! you'd never believe it!
They've bin lookin' so 'ard for a 'usbind for years,
  That they've both gorn and sent theirselves
      crosseyed, poor dears,
'Ere! she giv' me a 'at once, a 'at's, wot she said,

It was more like a 'ouse, and as 'eavy as lead,
Like a blinkin' great bee-hive stuck upon me 'ead,
   Lor lumme! you'd never believe it!
And one day she sez, with 'er eyes, all aglow
   "Ere's lingerie *you'll* find it useful I know,"
And there's me, give up red flannelette, years ago.
   Lor lumme! you'd never believe it!
Now the ol' Missus 'Obson, at flat number three,
   Between me and you, she's a nice cup o' tea,
Lor! the things she ain't bin, and the things she
         ain't done,
   From wot I can see, that old girl *is* a 'one,'
She's a bit of a mystery, no shadder o' doubt,
   Where 'er money comes from, I can't just make out.
Ev'rything's posh like, an' all up to date.
   Lor lumme! you'd never believe it!
Yet if anyone knocks at the door of the flat,
   She goes all 'ot an' bothered, and yells out
         "Oo's that?"
There's orniments, all 'idden up, more or less,
   Knives, forks, an' spoons, well you can't 'elp
         but guess,
'Cos some is marked Lyons and some L.M.S.
   Lor lumme! you'd never believe it!
She gits watched by the Tecs at the big stores in town
   "I'm just pickin' up bargains," she'll say with
         a frown.
They say "We'll pick *you* up, if you don't put
         'em down."
   Lor lumme! you'd never believe it!
But, I knows a backroom, where the sun's peepin' through
   Up three flights o' stairs, the address, is West
         Two,
One o' my Reg'lars, she's just eightyfour,
   Yerss, I've known 'er for years, so I *knocks* on
         the door,
And I 'ears a "Come in", in a voice soft an' low,
   And an old lady's step, as is falterin' an' slow.
All alone with 'er mem'ries, of days past an' gorn.
   Lor lumme! you'd never believe it!
Yerss, *she* give me my first job, as maid, at the
         Hall

I've the picture in front o' me, 'angs on the wall,
There's 'er 'usbind, the General, 'e won a V.C.
There's the 'orses, an' 'ounds, 'neath the old chestnut
tree,
And then came the smash up, then Napoo, Fi*nee.*
Lor lumme! you'd never believe it!
But I'd trudge up them stairs if they measured a mile,
Just so me and My Lady can chat for a while,
And me payment is 'andsome, just 'er *thanks,* and
'er *smile.*
That's right though you'd never believe it!

THE LOUNGER

BY CHARLES J. WINTER   *1914*

Performed by Bransby Williams

I've 'ad a shock this last few years what's nearly
·turned me white.
I mean the shutting up of pubs for 'arf the day
and night.
Wy wot's the use of leavin' bed to try an' earn a bob
By leaning 'gainst a empty 'ouse, when workin'
at my job?
The pub is shut till 12, so there's no customers
d'yer see,
That makes my bloomin' spirits fall to thirty five U.P.
I've been supportin' of this 'ouse for fifteen year
or more,
And as for drink,—I've 'ad enough to float a man
o' war.
I'm such a reg'lar landmark, and I keep so still yer see,
That people often come along and tie their
'orse to me!
Now no one comes till 12, and then they walks, or
comes by car;
And I get all the *smell* outside while they
taste at the bar.
I reely don't know 'ow I'd live by workin' of this
pub,

But the missis goes out charrin' just to git me a
    bit o' grub.
I've told 'er she must put in for a rise and get more
    tin,
    Or a hextra job as night nurse just to bring more
    money in.
We've 'ad to give up something, Now we 'ave no
    Sunday's jint,
    For they've put the people's food up, yuss to
    fivepence 'arf a pint!
And when you get it, wot's it like? It's bad, and it
    ain't cheap,
    With not sufficient biff in it to promote a 'ealthy
    sleep.
You git a chance to drink from six till ten I will agree,
    And if you can't get canned by then—well you
    ain't a-tryin' see!
It's just the same with *all* our food, we works
    for every crust,
    Yuss, *works* for it, and swallers it, but
    'as to chew it fust!
Then look at the unfairness—take the bloke wot sweeps
    the road
    'E's gettin' nigh four quid a week to 'elp 'im with
    'is load;
And take the case of bricklayers at about a quid a day,
    It's fair if they 'ave only twenty bricks an 'our
    to lay;
I often 'as to nod my 'ead, and sometimes 'as to shout,
    And from my pocket take my 'and to point a buildin'
    out,
Each day I'm workin' at my job for quite three hours
    or more,
    With only—p'raps six drinks, and yet they say
    "we won the war!"
And then there's Joe what works the pitch outside the
    private bar,
    I've chucked 'im, 'e's got uppish and 'e don't know
    where 'e are.
Today 'e finds some baccy, and 'e's gettin' such a dude,
    'E wouldn't put it in 'is pipe because it 'ad been
    chewed!

And then last week 'e washed 'is 'ands at the 'old
  road-mender's tank!
  I dropped 'im after that, what O! I can*not* stand
  sich swank.
I never wash *my* 'ands and I am dirtier than 'im
  I told 'im so: and 'e says *"well, you're three
  year older Jim!"*
There's work agoin' up the street at very decent pay,
  But I ain't takin' none myself; I've done enough
  today.
I starts my job at ten o'clock as usual feelin' grand,
  I 'ad a drink inside, and filled my match-box
  at the stand,
I gets a clay pipe while I stands to 'ave my mornin' sup.
  (I likes a clay 'cause if it falls you needn't
  pick it up)
And then I 'as a think about what job I'd tackle first.
  I drink much better when I think, it 'elps to bring
  a thirst.
Some say that beer kills more smart men than bullets
  in a war,
  If *I'm* to 'ave a skinful—I prefer the beer by far.
Well, fust I 'eld a 'orse leastways I watched 'e
  didn't fall,
  And twice I carried parcels when I seed that they
  was small,
I fetched the guv'nor's dog 'is meat and got a nasty
  sneer,
  The bloke says "shall I wrap it up, or will you
  eat it 'ere!!"
And then I minds some kiddies while their mother 'ad a
  drink,
  She'll git me on that job again *for tuppence*
  I *don't* think!
It's arf past two, the missis will be 'ome now with
  'er pay,
  So I'll be knockin' off too as it's early closin'
  day.
'Old 'ard! they say there's work down there for them
  that want a bit,
  What an escape! I might 'a gone *and run right
  into it!*

221

LOVE AND ARITHMETIC

BY CUTHBERT ROSE and WINIFRED FAIRLIE   *1919*

A tutor went one day to teach
  A rich man's lovely daughter
The four rules of arithmetic,
  And this is how he taught her.
The first rule was a simple one,
  He showed by love's tuition,
He kissed her once, he kissed her twice,
  And said, "Now that's *Addition*."
And so he added kiss to kiss,
  In joyful satisfaction,
And then he took a few, from her,
  And said, "Now that's *Subtraction*."
And so they sat there side by side
  In mututal admiration,
He said, whilst paying back tenfold,
  "This is *Multiplication*."
But papa thought he heard one day
  The sounds of osculation.
He asked his daughter what it meant,
  By mild expostulation.
And when he learnt the truth from her
  He shouted in derision,
He kicked the tutor from the door
  And said, "That's *Long Division!*"

LOYALTY

BY GLORIA STORM, NOSMO KING and ERNEST LONGSTAFFE
        1937

Never believe the worst of a man
  When once you have seen his best,
Of any loyalty worth the name

This is the surest test.
Gossip is ready at every turn,
   Your faith and trust to slay,
But the loyal soul is deaf to doubt,
   Whatever the world may say.
Whatever you hear on others' lips,
   Don't let it soil your own;
Let your faith still stronger be,
   While the seed of slander's sown:
Keep the image before your eyes,
   Of the friend who's a friend to you:
And stand by that friend through thick and thin
   Whatever the world may do.
Never believe the worst of a man,
   When your own soul sees the best;
All that matters is what *you* know
   Not what the others have *guessed*
And if all that *you* know is straight and fine
   And has brought you friendship's joys.
Be proud to treasure the truth that's yours,
   Whatever the world destroys.

THE MADMAN'S WILL

BY PETER CHEYNEY and HAROLD ARPTHORP   *1925*

Performed by Albert Whelan

In a work-house ward that was cold and bare,
   The doctor sat on a creaking chair,
By the side of a dying madman's bed.
   "He can't last much longer," the doctor said.
But nobody cares if a pauper lives,
   And nobody cares when a pauper's dead.
The old man sighed, the doctor rose.
   And bent his head o'er the ricketty bed,
To catch the weak words one by one—
   To smile—as the dying madman said:—
"Beneath my pillow when I am gone—

Search—hidden there you will find it still!"
"Find what, old madman?" the doctor asked,
    And the old man said, as he died, "My *WILL.*"
How they all laughed at the splendid jest—
    A pauper madman to leave a will.
And they straightened him out for his final rest,
    In the lonely graveyard over the hill,
And the doctor searched for the paper and found
    The red taped parchment—untied it with zest,
Whilst the others laughingly gathered round
    To hear the cream of the madman's jest.
Then the doctor with mocking solemnity said,
    "Silence, my friends," and the Will he read.
"I leave to the children the green fields,
    The fresh country lanes for their play,
The stories of fairies and dragons,
    The sweet smell of heather and hay.
I leave to young maidens romantic
    The dreaming which all maidens do.
And the wish that some day in the future
    Their happiest dreams will come true.
To youth I leave all youth's ambition,
    Desire, love, impetuous hate.
And to youth with years I leave wisdom,
    And the hope that it comes not too late.
I leave to the lovers the gloaming,
    The time when all troubles are old,
When true love, hand in hand, goes aroaming
    To the heart of the sunset of gold
To the mother I leave children's voices
    And curly heads close on her breast,
The soft whispered prayer that rejoices
    Her heart as she puts them to rest.
I leave to old people sweet memories,
    And smiles that endure to the last,
With never a fear for the future,
    And not a regret for the past.
I die without earthly possessions,
    Without the last word of a friend,
To you all I leave good cheer and friendship
    That lasts through all time to the end.
I leave to the wide world my blessing

In the hope that the long years will find
That my wishes shall grow like a flower,
And bring God's good peace to mankind".
The ward doctor laid down the parchment,
His smile had gone—turned into pain.
The faces around laughed no longer,
But grew grave with regret that was vain.
No wonder that he looks so happy,
Whilst we who derided are sad,
For the things he has left are the best things in life
"I wonder if he *was* mad?"

THE MAN WHO KILLED THE DAISIES

BY ADA LEONORA HARRIS and HENRY E. PETHER   *1929*

Performed by Suzette Tarri

Though once I used to like the gardener very much
    indeed.
    (I loved to watch him at his work and often helped
    him weed).
I do not like him any more, because you see, he's been
    And cut down all the daisies with his horrid old
    machine.
If he'd cut the grass round each one, as I wanted him
    to do,
    Though it might have taken time and been a little
    trouble, too,
They'd all of them been living now as happy as could
    be,
    But though I begged him very hard, he only
    laughed at me.
They looked so pretty growing in the grass—I cannot
    think,
    How anyone *could* hurt a little daisy tipped
    with pink.

Before the gardener cut them down I used to call
    him "Jim",
Now "The Man who killed the daisies" is the
    name I've given him.

THE MAN WHO NEVER FORGAVE

BY E. A. SEARSON and HERBERT TOWNSEND   *1925*

There are natures we meet with both callous and cruel,
    There are some too soft-hearted to live,
But the nature I pity and sorrow for most
    Is the one that can never forgive.
Such a nature had one whom I knew in the past,
    I'll call him "John Smith"—that will do;
He was "one of the best," in the cant of the day,
    As a pal he was steadfast and true.
But he made it no secret, he couldn't forgive,
    And he'd boast if he injury met
That called for requital, his vengeance he'd have,
    If it took him a life-time to get.
Well, for years he'd a life quite unruffled and calm,
    Then the blow Fate arranged for him fell,
The "Other Man" dastard-like, fled with his mate,
    And his soul held the blackness of Hell.
The man had a start, but he tracked him to France,
    Thence to Italy, Switzerland, Spain;
Over mountains he traversed, he battled with streams
    That were swollen by tempest and rain,
But ever his vengeance was first in his mind,
    And he tired not, but ever sped on,
Thro' forests he struggled,.the deserts he crossed,
    Until nigh twenty-five years had gone.
Then in a mean street off the Whitechapel Road,
    On a day of tempestuous wind,
They met face to face, and no other was near
    But John Smith and the man who had sinned.

With a laugh fiends might envy, John Smith struck his
    blow,
    His soul with his vengeance a-thirst,
But I'm sorry to say that his blow didn't land,
    For the other man put one in first.
He biffed poor John Smith with a horrible biff,
    He'd a fist like a bundle of wood,
Then he landed his left upon Smith's off-side eye,
    And it closed up that organ for good;
He got a right hook on the side of his ear,
    Then he got in a big, hefty punch
Right bang on the diaphragm, just half an hour
    After Smith had had steak-pie for lunch;
A kidney punch followed, and right from that time
    The issue was never in doubt,
A tap on the jaw put poor Johnny to sleep
    And his enemy counted him out.
In a spot that's half hidden from curious eyes,
    There's a modest and neat little grave,
Displaying the legend, "Below lies John Smith,
    The party who never forgave."

THE MAN WITH SINGLE HAIR

BY ROBERT GANTHONY and ARTHUR H. WOOD   *1902*

He was not bald: for on his shining cranium
    Remained one hair, it's colour pink geranium.
Oh, how he idolized that single hair
    That, last of loved ones, grew luxuriant there.
He counted it each morning: fondly viewed it
    This way and that way: carefully shampooed it.
Brushed it, combed it, scented it, and oiled it,
    Dared scarcely put his hat on lest he spoiled it.
In evening dress, arrayed for swell society,
    He'd part it in the middle for variety.
Often he'd curl it, train it o'er his brow

227

In navy fashion, as our middies now.
Omitting nothing, with devoted care,
   He'd pet his hirsute pride, his single hair.
But sad to tell!
   Ah bitter was the blow!
There came a day—
   A day of direst woe—
When in his soup it fell! He quickly spied it,
   Then rescued it, and on his napkin dried it,
His only hair. His pet, his flowing tress,
   Chill was his forehead, deep his heart's distress.
"I'm bald at last" he wailed, in bitter grief,
   "My only hair has fallen like a leaf.
What ho! A taxidermist," shouted he,
   "I'll have it stuffed, for all mankind to see.
And when, within its case of glass installed,
   The world shall see I was not *always* bald."

THE MAN WHO STAYED AT HOME

BY F. RAYMOND COULSON and GEORGE WELLS   *1914*

Mister Brown, of Turnham Green,
   View'd all bikes with baleful glare,
He was never, never seen
   Scorching off to anywhere.
"Oft a fall upon the head
   Dislocates the vertebrae,
So I'll ride no bike," he said.
   "Home's the safest place for me!"
Mister Brown of Turnham Green,
   Never motor'd out of town,
Flashing through the sylvan scene,
   Cutting laggard chickens down;
Never went to hunt the deer,
   Never after grouse would roam.
"No," he cried, "I'm safest here,

So I'd rather stay at home."
Mister Brown of Turnham Green,
    Never in the summer took
Tourist trips; he'd never been
    "On the Continong" with Cook.
"Fogs and rocks and tempests grim
    Menace ships that cross the foam,
And," he cried "I cannot swim,
    So I'm better off at home!"
Mister Brown, of Turnham Green,
    Didn't care for sport at all;
Knew a fellow who had been
    Crippled by a cricket ball.
Knew a man who, catching trout,
    Caught a cold, and—R.I.P.
"Ah," said Brown, "beyond a doubt
    Home, sweet home's the place for me!"
So from home at Turnham Green
    Brown was never coax'd away;
Never in a train was seen,
    Off to spend a happy day.
Shunning risk in ev'ry shape,
    There he sipp'd his quiet cup.
But, alas! a gas escape
    One bright morning blew him up.

THE MAN WITH THE SWOLLEN HEAD

BY ALEC KENDAL and CUTHBERT CLARKE   *1931*

It takes all sorts to make a world.
    And it's full of all sorts no doubt.
There are men *and men* but of all the men
    There's one we can well do without.
The man with the swollen head, that's him,
    With that satisfied atmosphere,
Full of himself and inwardly thinks
229

The world's all right, *I'm here.*
You know the man, you've seen the type,
    As a rule his own praises he sings.
Put him on horseback he'll ride to hell,
    When he feels the strength of his wings.
You needn't look far to find him,
    You can soon pick him out from the rest,
He thinks all the pavement and part of the street
    Are essential to show off his chest.
The man with the swollen head,
    The fellow who *will* put on airs,
Face made of brass, full of bombast and gas,
    Born lucky and vacant upstairs.
He's a world in himself so he thinks,
    Right off the beaten track
His hat goes on with a shoehorn,
    And his shirt buttons up at the back.
He likes to hear himself talking,
    What *he* did and what *he* can do,
Admits the world was made in *six* days,
    But *he* could have made it in *two.*
He and himself, alone they stand,
    Aloof midst the mighty throng.
How was the world made without him?
    When he dies, will it all go wrong?
The man with the swollen head,
    A cheap picture lavishly framed.
Sympathize with him, poor devil,
    He's more to be pitied than blamed.
It isn't his fault—it's his parents.
    It's with them we should feel annoyed.
They should have drowned *him* not the *others,*
    He's the one they should have destroyed!
Still, we all have our faults, why worry.
    We each have our lives to live.
Here below, there's few of us *perfect.*
    So it's best to forget and forgive.
We pass this way but once, that's all:
    What does it matter who's who?
Jack'll be as good as his master
    When we stand in the final queue.
And when Gabriel sounds his trumpet

And the names of the good ones are read,
Let's hope there'll be room for us as well *AS THE*
MAN WITH THE SWOLLEN HEAD.

ME AND MY PIPE

CLIFFORD GREY, BERT LEE and ERNEST LONGSTAFFE   1940

We sit by the fireside in my easy chair,
  Just watching the shadows that play here and there.
We've only a cottage upon the hill side,
  But it's home and it's shelter so we're satisfied.
Me and my pipe, my pipe and me,
  Old pals together content as can be,
Some sigh for wealth, some want a name,
  But my ounce of 'Baccy' is worth all your fame.
When others start nagging and cannot agree,
  I smile at my pipe and my pipe smiles at me.
Easily pleased with a pipe you say.
  Maybe I am but I'm built that way,
For he comforts me with his soothing weed,
  Tho' my old pal costs a bit more to feed,
I've got to pay, and I gladly do.
  It takes more than a Budget to part us two.
Folks tell me mine is a lonely life,
  Instead of a pipe, I need a wife,
For a pipe goes out, I say with a grin,
  Well so do wives you can't keep em in.
Folks shake their heads, and they often say
  "He doesn't like girls, he's not built that way."
That's what they think, but they don't know,
  There was someone once in the long ago
As fair as a summer rose was she:
  And one brief summer she bloomed for me.
The golden sunshine lit love's flame,
  But she droop'd and died when winter came.

Me and my pipe, my pipe and me,
Old pals together content as can be,
Some sigh for wealth, some want a name,
But my ounce of 'Baccy' is worth all your fame.
When others start nagging and cannot agree,
I smile at my pipe, and my pipe smiles at me.
Spoken
And now, as I sit in my lonely den
Through the hazy smoke-clouds once again,
I see my rose of the long ago,
And she smiles at me, for she seems to know
That I've found a pal who is staunch and true,
Who'll comfort me when the day is through,
And that's why my pipe is a pal to me,
He brings back a fragrant memory.
Repeat Refrain.

MEBBE SO-I DUNNO

BY J. MILTON HAYES and R. FENTON GOWER 1913

Well! I dunno—can't explain it—
It's the weather I suppose.
Feel like—dunno *what* I feel like—
Sorter wanter dream an' doze.
Feel I wanter think o' nuthin'—
Jes' ter lounge about an' doze.
It's the weather—I suppose.
Mebbe so—I dunno.
Well! I dunno—can't eat nuthin'—
Indigestion I suppose.
P'r'aps it's—no it can't be smokin'
Don't smoke many goodness knows—
P'r'aps a dozen—mebbe twenty—
Ain't no smoker goodness knows.
Indigestion I suppose.
Mebbe so—I dunno.

Well! I dunno—always yawnin'—
Over-workin'—I suppose.
Business?—well it *is* a worry—
What with draughts and dominoes.
An' they're sure to say I'm wanted
When I'm playin' dominoes
Over-workin' I suppose.
Mebbe so—I dunno.
Well! I dunno—feel so lonely—
Oughter marry I suppose.
Prospec's—nuthin' *much* to speak of—
Might get snubbed if I propose.
Then again—she seems to like me—
Might say "yes" if I propose.
Do I love her?—Do I—Well!
I should say—*rather!*

MEMORIES

BY PETER CHEYNEY and LAURI EDWARD   1926

Love, Life and Laughter, Walk for a way,
    Sun—then rain after, Night follows day.
Sadness and gladness, Joy and regret,
    Weaving together Life's golden net.
A net of fine memories kept ever fresh,
    Whilst Fate goes on spinning Mesh upon mesh.
Gold strands for joy, Drab strands of grey,
    Sun—then rain after Night, Dawn and Day.
And in the evening when the shadows fall,
    When twilight spells the passing of the day,
Comes Fancy's kingdom—sweetest time of all,
    The quiet that follows every busy day.
Crowded with memories stealing fast or slow,
    A smile of sadness flung from out the years,
A ghost of happiness of long ago,
    A flash of laughter or a wrath of tears.
"Do you remember?" Joy lives in those words,

Some scene that lingers still within your brain.
Perhaps a sunset gladdened by the birds,
    Some joy remembered—lost, and found again.
A word of yours—some sentence left unspoken,
    A fleeting smile that brought you gladness then,
A picture born of happiness long past,
    Dead with the years—in memory born again.
Now in this peaceful hour old friends return,
    In fancy's garden talk with you awhile
Of all the long-sped things for which you yearn,
    Greet you with joy, and leave you with a smile.
And, as they pass before you one by one,
    Bringing new gifts and leavening ancient pain,
You smile 'a-dieu' still knowing as they go,
    That with each evening they'll return again.
Soft in the quietness comes the hand of truth,
    Pointing the way from out an old mistake,
Healing some bitterness that lived in youth,
    Showing some hand that friendship bids you take.
The shadows in the sunlight's dying rays
    Are like the memories of our little life,
Sombre and gold—the story of our days,
    Remembered gladness and forgotten strife.
Love, Life and Laughter, Be with you yet,
    Sun, then rain after, Joy and regret.
Maybe life's smiling, Maybe it's sad,
    Meet it with courage, Laugh—good or bad.
Smile at the rough road, Keep smiling yet.
    Cherish your memories, Never forget.
And in life's evening, When all things are old,
    Walk from the drab days into the gold.

MEMORIES OF WATERLOO

BY CYRIL PERCIVAL and CUTHBERT CLARKE   *1930*

What's that you called me? "Old Timer"—
  I'm not goin' to say it ain't true—
Don't mind if I do 'ave a pint sir,
  Though it ain't like the old time brew.
'Ere's my best respects for yer 'ealth, sir,
  I always drops in 'ere for two—
'Cause this 'ere pub's called "Dook o' Wellington",
  Which reminds me of Waterloo.
Do I remember it? Not arf!
  I don't see no call for surprise—
I may be just going on ninety,
  My 'ead's clear when memories do rise.
I served with the Dook from the start, sir,
  A youngster just bursting with pride,
I can see it as clear as today, sir,
  When the Dook and I took our first ride.
'Ow the guards envied me on that day, sir,
  Down the line standing by the Dook's side—
And they all tried 'ard to be chosen
  For behind the Dook to ride.
Together we faced many dangers,
  But always we won our way through,
I remember that charge through the snowdrift
  On the journey to Waterloo.
We've been through 'ail and fog, sir,
  And nights dark enough for a spook,
With the guard behind acheering
  For my pluck and the Iron Dook.
We've dashed down the line at a run, sir,
  Without any fear for the worst,
And sometimes we worked at such pressure
  The Dook 'as been fit to burst.
We fought many battles together,
  But nothing we ever went through
Could compare with the records we made, sir,
  From the coast to Waterloo.

235

Times 'ave changed since them days, sir,
  With aeroplanes, motors, and so
When the old dook was finished, it broke my 'eart
  And they told me that I'd have to go.
There's a new dook about so they tell me,
  Just an idea to keep up the name—
They can say what they like 'bout the new 'un,
  But believe me, the old dook was game!
What's that, sir, where are me medals?
  Don't chip in—the story you'll spoil,
I was just going to say that they're thinking
  Of runnin' the new dook on oil!
'Oo's a liar?—I never said soldier!—
  I've a pension—I'm not kiddin' you—
The old "Iron Dook" was my engine
  What I drove to and from Waterloo!!

MERCHANDISE

BY MILTON HAYES and ELSIE APRIL   *1920*

Dedicated, by gracious permission,
to H.R.H. THE PRINCE OF WALES.

Merchandise! Merchandise! Tortoise-shell, spices,
  Carpets and Indigo—sent o'er the high-seas;
Mother-o'-Pearl from the Solomon Isles—
  Brought by a brigantine ten thousand miles.
Rubber from Zanzibar, Tea from Nang-Po,
  Copra from Hayti, and wine from Bordeaux;
Ships, with top-gallants and royals unfurled,
  Are bringing in freights from the ends of the world—
Crazy old windjammers, manned by Malays,
  With ratridden bulk-heads and creaking old stays,
Reeking of bilge and of paint and of pitch—
  That's how these ocean-girt islands grew rich:
And tramps, heavy laden, and liners untold
  Will lease a new life to a nation grown old.
236

Merchandise! Merchandise! England was made
By her Men and her Ships and her OVERSEAS TRADE.
Widen your harbours, your docks, and your quays,
Hazard your wares on the seven wide seas,
Run out your railways and hew out your coal,
For only by trade can a country keep whole.
Feed up your furnaces, fashion your steel,
Stick to your bargains and pay on the deal; ·
Rich is your birthright, and well you'll be paid.
If you keep in good faith with your Overseas Trade.
Learn up geography, work out your sums,
Build up your commerce, and pull down your slums;
Sail on a Plimsoll that marks a full hold:
Your Overseas Trade means a harvest of gold.
Bring in the palmoil and pepper you've bought,
But send out ten times the amount you import:
Trade your inventions, your labour, and sweat:
Your Overseas Traffic will keep ye from debt.
Hark to the song of the shuttle and loom,
"Keep up your commerce or crawl to your tomb!"
Study new methods and open new lines,
Quicken your factories, foundries and mines,
Think of what Drake did, and Raleigh and Howe,
And waste not their labours by slacking it now:
Work is life's currency—earn what you're worth,
And *send out your ships to the ends of the earth.*
Deepbosomed mothers with widefashioned hips
Will bear ye good sons for the building of ships:
Good sons for your ships and good ships for your trade—
That's how the Peace of the World will be made!
So send out your strong to the forests untrod,
Work for yourselves and your neighbours and God,
Keep this good England the home of the free,
With Merchandise, Men and good Ships on the Sea.
Merchandise! Merchandise! Good honest Merchandise!
Merchandise, Men and Good Ships on the Sea.

THE MERCANTILE MARINE

BY SAM WALSH and DAISY Mc.GEOCH   *1918*

I think perhaps 'tis possible that some of us forget
   In reckoning up the gratitude we owe
That there's another fighting fellow to whom we owe
     a debt,
   A gentleman that's not so much on show.
He's dressed in Navy Blue, and he wears a badge, 'tis
     true,
   But a gold lace decoration isn't seen.
But he'll go it "hell for leather" in the dirtiest
     kind of weather,
   In the service of the Mercantile Marine!
His aim is sure and steady and his eye alert and keen,
   On the periscope that chases in his wake.
He'll thrash across the ocean past the skulking submarine,
   Through mine-strewn fields of terror, for our sake.
He's the goods train of the ocean, he's the Santa
     Claus of war,
   He's the arm on which we nationally lean.
He's the best part of a sportsman, of a soldier, of
     a tar,
   He's the Service of the Mercantile Marine.
So shout the songs of allies, the battle-hymn of France,
   America, Belgium and Japan.
Britain and her Colonies and all the other chaps
   Heroes and sportsmen to a man.
And when the glory of the war and the history of its
     fame,
   Is written plain for all men to be seen.
Not the least who shall be honoured for upholding
     Britain's name,
   Is the Laddie of the Mercantile Marine.

MERCHANT NAVY

BY V. F. STEVENS and S. BROWN   1943

Charlie's said good-bye to Nell,
  Jim's got his seaboots to pack,
Shorty and Pete stroll down the street,
  Arm in arm with Jack,
They've finished their spell of shore leave
  They've had their round of sport,
And the sea blue glint in their fearless squint
  Tells that their ship's leaving port.
No braid adorns their reefer, no flash, no stripes,
    no pips
  But a tiny "M.N." denotes they're the men who
    go down to the sea in ships.
Out where the convoys muster on the wide eternal blue
  'Midst mine, torpedo, bomb, and shell, they've
    got a job to do,
A job for nerves of tempered steel, and hearts that
    ne'er will slack,
  For where they're bound no peace is found, either
    going or coming back.
Oh it's peep thru' those glasses Shorty, and mark well
    what I say,
  Up there, in the heavens J.U.87's and blimey
    they're headed this way.
So get Charlie out o' the galley, tell the doctor
    he'd better stand by,
  Clamp down your tin hat, you're bound to need
    that, especially when stuff starts to fly
There goes Action stations for Merchant Navy Man
    too,
  And the heliograph's ray from the battleships say,
    The convoy must get through
With the escort's guns a spewing and the carrier's
    brood in flight,
  Scorched by the breath of sudden death, these
    men know how to fight.
Fight thru' the hell of battle on the seas o'er
    which they ride,

And the U Boats spoil is a patch of oil left on the
place where they died.
Gentlemen! Here is a toast and keep their memory
green.
Up on your feet, and drink it neat!
The Mercantile Marine!

THE MISSING PIECE

BY E. A. VASEY and CUTHBERT CLARKE   *1933*

Life is just a jigsaw puzzle,
    With pieces odd and quaint,
Some marked with fine strong outlines,
    Other pieces very faint.
And it seems to be peculiar
    That the pieces don't quite fit,
That the puzzle's always incomplete,
    It lacks one little bit.
There is a piece called Innocence,
    Or Ignorance by some.
Virtue, Vice; not much between them;
    There's Experience to come.
There's a brilliant piece called Honour,
    A flag nailed unto a mast,
Of all the pieces this the one
    We'd keep until the last.
There's a bit that's known as Tolerance—
    A gift great people own;
There's also Pity, Charity, Friendship,
    Fear of things unknown;
There's a bitter piece called Hatred—
    A piece filthsoiled and black!
Near it one called Vengeance,
    The art of paying back.
And of course there's Music, Laughter,
    Grace and Beauty too,
Also Perseverance,
    As well as Work to do.

A piece that shines, called Kindness,
  One much larger, Love its name—
A piece of many colours
  Love that's proud—or hides with shame.
Ambition, Fame and Glory,
  Achievement, Pride as well,
Misery and Sorrow,
  Pieces shaped in Hell.
We start, we get these pieces,
  Many others too we take,
And we think we'll solve the puzzle,
  The scene complete will make.
And we fit them in their places,
  As best the fates allow,
And struggling on look back and think,
  "I've got the picture now".
And you think you've solved the puzzle
  When you see—and catch your breath—
You cannot solve Life's puzzle,
  Till you've got the piece called *DEATH.*

MISS WILLIAMS

BY NOSMO KING and ERNEST LONGSTAFFE   *1939*

If you wander through the village,
  And cross the village green,
You'll see an old world cottage,
  Very neat and clean;
If you go into the garden,
  You're almost sure to find,
A charming old world lady,
  Beautiful and kind.
All the village know her,
  She's lived there from her birth,
All the village love her;
  And realise her worth,

241

And if you ask them who she is—
    This lady sweet and staid,
They'll say "Oh that's Miss Williams,
    Just a poor old maid."
Poor? Well, perhaps,
    In what some consider wealth,
But the power of gold is limited,
    It cannot bring us health;
It cannot bring true happiness
    Or help us to forget;
It cannot dry our bitter tears,
    When our eyes are wet.
I asked this sweet lady once—
    Why she had never wed,
She smiled at me so sadly
    And gently shook her head
And gazed into the dying fire,
    Wistfully—and cried,
As tho' her heart were breaking
    Then bravely she replied.
"I had a lover years ago—
    His voice has long been stilled,
In the early dawn of our wedding morn
    He was thrown from his horse and killed;
He was only twenty-seven, I but twenty-one,
    So you see my life was ended, before it had begun.
Now I've nothing but my dreams,
    Dreams from which I cannot wake,
Dreams of many lovely years—
    Lived for rememberance sake."
Softly then I left her,
    In the dying firelight's glow,
To live again in memory those days of long ago.
    And should you ever pass that way
And wander by the square,
    You'll see the little churchyard,
And if you walk in there
    You'll find a little marble cross
That for years has been arrayed,
    With flowers, from the garden,
Of *"A poor old maid."*

MUD!

BY MALCOLM BROOKE   *1949*

Just think what romance has owed to mud—
    A splatter of mud on the coat of a girl,
The petulant toss of her rain swept curl
    But it's due to the mud that boy met girl—
Just mud!
    It's stickily strewed thro' history's pages
It's altered the trend of men's lives thro' the ages
    When the flood was upon us it lay by the mile
And just think what was found on the banks of the Nile
    In the mud!
When Raleigh's broad cloak was spread o'er it's face,
    A great Queen of England was saved from disgrace,
And Raleigh was set in a much lighter place
    By the mud,
Poets have sung of the joys of the spring
    Of the woods in the autumn and birds on the wing
But mud? Well it's hardly worth writing a thing
    About mud!
But, sometimes, I think when the river's in flood
    And the valley is left with its coating of mud,
That it's rather like man when he's up at the top,
    When he's swollen with pride and there's nothing
        to stop
His ego, his power, he's master of all,
    And he can't see that one day the floodtide will fall,
And he'll find himself lowly, just like you and I,
    And the world, like the river, will soon pass
        him by,
To leave him alone without friends, without hope—
    In the mud!
The power that he wielded has gone like a dream,
    The lip service paid him is now a has been,
And all that is left from the what might have been—
    Is mud!
Remember this, won't you when fortune's your friend
    And good luck seems likely to stay to the end,

The kindly word spoken today means a lot,
  When Jade fortune departs and you find that
    you've not,
Quite as good friends as you once thought you had,
  And the luck that was good has now chang'd into bad,
Leave the mud to be slung in a scandalous phrase,
  To the rest of the world, and you'll find that it
    pays,
For mud has a habit of sticking like glue
  So beware in the throwing that none sticks to you!

MY ENGLAND

BY ARTHUR VICTOR and ERNEST LONGSTAFFE   *1941*

Old England is a country of fields an' 'edges green,
  Of little streams an' little woods, the prettiest
    you've seen.
It's a tanner to the country on the bus outside
    your door
  You, the missus and the kids what could a bloke
    ask more?
An' I want to keep it Just like *that!*
  Yes, I want to keep it Just like *that!*
Old England ain't a country what's ruled by Gestapos.
  By blokes dressed up in uniforms and goodness
    only knows.
You sees a copper now an' then but if you ain't on
    the twist,
  They treats you matey an' polite there ain't
    no mailed fist
An' I want to keep it Just like *that!*
  Yes, I want to keep it Just like *that!*
Old England ain't a country of Heils and raise
    yer arm
  An' you can 'ave a pint at night and never do
    no 'arm,

An' if you 'as a drop too much an' runs the
    guv'ment down,
There ain't no concentration camps around an
    English town,
An I'm going to keep it Just Like *that!*
Yes I'm going to keep it Just Like *that!*
This England's full of freedom for blokes like me an'
    you,
Make no mistake we treasure it an' are fighting
    for it too.
I don't allow nobody for to dictate fings to me,
    Excepting p'raps the missus—still that's 'ow it
    ort to be,
An' I mean to keep it Just Like *that!*
Yes I *mean to keep it Just Like That!*

MY LEETLE ROSA

BY ERNEST LONGSTAFFE   *1927*

Yesterday I went into the Flower shop and I ask-a
    the man
    "How mooch you want for-a one red-a rose in da
    window?"
The flower-a man, he look-a and he say "Two-a
    shilling each."
    Then I say "I canna pay-a so mooch, mak' a
    leetle cheap."
The flower-a man he say, "No cheaper—they're Two-a
    shilling each."
    I go outside and look-a in da window at the nice-a
    red-a rose,
And pretty soon a young-a lady come (a beautiful
    young-a lady)
    And she say-a "Oh the pretty red-a-rose—How
    mooch?"
The flower-a man he smile and say-a "Six-a pence each."
    The lady she buy-a one-a red-a rose, and she go away.
I go-a once-a more to da flower-man, I say "Scusa
    me—Signor,

How mooch you want for one-a red-a rose in da
    window?"
The flower-a-man, he say "I tell you before, they're
    Two-a shilling each."
    I say "Mak' a little cheaper of me Signor, mak'
    a leetle cheap?"
The flower-a-man he say "No cheaper—Two-a shilling
    each.
    What-a for you want-a red a red-a rose?"
I say "I tell-a you what for I want-a the red-a
    red-a rose.
    I had a leetle girl-a once, and she was just
    like-a dis (so high)
And because she look-a like dis-a flower, we call-a
    her "Rosa".
    We were so happy together—me,—da mamma and-a
    da leetle Rosa.
But one day-a da mamma she die, Signor.
    I bury her quite away in da country and-a leetle
    Rosa and-a me were left alone.
How I love-a that child, She was such a sweet leetle-a
    child
    And every night when I come-a home from da work
I go da hill-a top, And I say-a "Hello Rosa"
    And she say-a from da window up-a high "Hello
    Papa"
And-a every night Signor, I go that-a way.
    But one night just-a like-a always I say "Hello
    Rosa."
But there was no "Hello Papa."
    She was-a no-a there Signor—she was dead.
I bury my leetle Rosa by da mamma
    And I have been all alone.
Signor, I just-a want-a red-a red-a rose
    To put on da grave of my leetle-a Rosa.
That is all—Signor that is all.
    Scusa me, Signor to take-a so mooch of your time.
Scusa me, Signor, What you say?
    The whole bunch-a for nothing?
The whole bunch-a for me for nothing?
    Thank-a you (Gratzia) Thank-a you (Gratzia)
    Signor thank-a you."

MY LOVE AFFAIRS

BY GREATREX NEWMAN and WOLSELEY CHARLES   *1921*

Performed by Bransby Williams

Through falling in love I've had lots of surprises
  I've flirted with girls of all sorts, shapes and sizes;
My first love affair was a bad one I'm told,
  I think at the time I was eighteen *months* old—
And *she* was the baby next door, such a pet,
  We went out each day,—in the same bassinette,
Till one Sunday morning when down in the park,
  She sucked all the paint off my new Noah's Ark,—
So then, very coldly, I bade her adieu,
  And took back my presents,—and some of hers too.
The years rolled along, but I stayed fancy free,
  Until I met Rose, it was down by the sea,—
Her beauty ensnared me, and swift as a flash,
  I formed for that maiden a wonderful "pash."
I think I was just over eight, or p'raps nine,
  And scorning all warning of women and wine
I spent all my savings, while she led me on,
  Until all my fourpence was squandered and gone;—
Then quickly she left me, that false, fickle jade,
  And stole both my heart and my bucket and spade.
The next one concerned was a damsel named Kate,
  At last, now I thought, I have met my true mate,
'Twas no boy and girl sort of friendship I mean,
  For when I met Kate I was nearly—*thirteen.*
The course of true love though can never run smooth,
  Her mother soon showed that *she* did not approve.
And though Kate had sworn that to me she would cling,
  Well,—*back came my solid gold nine-penny ring!*
Next Daisy enslaved me, that girl I adored—
  Until my affections were captured by Maud,
And Maud had two sisters, named Elsie and Claire,
  I couldn't choose which,—so I courted the pair;
All these, and lots more, I attempted to win,
  Both tall ones, and short ones, and thick ones, and
    thin,—
I worshipped them all and would gladly have wed,
  But each chose some *other* young bounder instead.

I went to their weddings, then screwed up my pluck,
  And sent just a clock or a cruet, for luck.
Ah well, such is life, and left out in the cold,
  I soon settled down as a bachelor bold,—
Till one day *she* came, and in blissful content
  I then started learning what love really meant.—
We planned for our wedding, how happy those hours,
  The birds gaily sang to the trees and the flowers,
The breeze whispered joy, but that never came,
  I found I'd a rival, and he made a claim.
The days turned to night, and made Winter of Spring,
  The flowers drooped their heads, and the birds ceased
    to sing,—
The breeze said "good-bye" with its tenderest breath—
  My rival had won, and his name—it was—Death.

MY OLD FOOTBALL

BY MILTON HAYES and CUTHBERT CLARKE   *1920*

You can keep your antique silver and your statuettes
    of bronze,
  Your curios and tapestries so fine,
But of all your treasures rare there is nothing to
      compare
  With this patched up, worn-out Football Pal 'o mine.
Just a patched-up worn-out football, yet how it clings!
  I live again my happier days in thoughts that
      football brings.
It's got a mouth, it's got a tongue,
  And oft when we're alone I fancy that it speaks
To me of golden youth that's flown.
  It calls to mind our meeting,
  'Twas a present from the Dad.
  I kicked it yet I worshipped it,

How strange a priest it had!
   And yet it jumped with pleasure
When I punched it might and main:
   And when it had the dumps
It got blown up and punched again.
   It's lived its life;
It's played the game;
   It's had its rise and fall,
There's history in the wrinkles of
   That worn-out football.
Caresses rarely came its way—
   In baby-hood 'twas tanned.
It's been well oiled, and yet it's quite tee-total,
      understand.
   It's gone the pace, and sometimes it's been
      absolutely bust,
And yet 'twas always full of bounce,
   No matter how 'twas cussed.
He's broken many rules and oft has wandered
      out of bounds,
   He's joined in shooting parties
Over other people's grounds.
   Misunderstood by women,
He was never thought a catch,
   Yet he was never happier
Than when bringing off a match.
   He's often been in danger—
Caught in nets that foes have spread,
   He's even come to life again
When all have called him dead.
   Started on the centre,
And he's acted on the square,
   To all parts of the compass
He's been bullied everywhere.
   His aims and his ambitions
Were opposed by one and all,
   And yet he somehow reached his goal—
That plucky old football.
   When schooling days were ended
I forgot him altogether,
   And 'midst the dusty years
He lay a crumpled lump of leather.

Then came the threat'ning voice of War,
And games had little chance,
My brother went to do his bit—
Out there somewhere in France.
And when my brother wrote he said,
"Of all a Tommy's joys,
There's none compares with football.
Will you send one for the boys?"
I sent not one but many,
And my old one with the rest,
I thought that football's finished now,
But no—he stood the test.
Behind the lines they kicked him
As he'd never been kicked before.
Till they busted him and sent him back—
A keep-sake of the war.
My brother lies out there in France,
Beneath a simple cross,
And I seem to feel my football knows my grief,
And shares my loss.
He tells me of that splendid charge,
And then my brother's fall.
In life he loved our mutual chum—
That worn-out old football.
Oh, you can keep your antique silver
And your statuettes of bronze,
Your curios and tapestries so fine,
But of all your treasures rare
There is nothing to compare
With that patched-up worn-out football—
Pal o' mine.

MY SHIP

BY *WARREN HASTINGS and HERBERTE JORDAN*   *1942*

I sent my ship a sailing across the rolling sea,
  All laden with a cargo of dreams for you and me.
Of happiness that might have been of things we meant
      to do,
    Until the brutal drums of war crashed out
      their dread tattoo.
With you so far away, my dear,
    With all my heart I pray,
That God will, of His mercy,
    Speed the coming of the Day
When Peace shall come with Victory,
    And all the world be free,
And then my ship will find you dear,
    And bring you back to me.

NAPOLEON'S LAST DREAM

BY *ALBERT CHEVALIER and ALFRED H. WEST*   *1914*

I dreamed last night of ev'ry fight
    Where in my might I conqu'ring led.
Of battle cries; of lung-pierced sighs;
    Of glazing eyes; of all my dead!
For I had killed and stormed and stilled,
    As I had willed, in ruthless fray.
I knew—too late— relentless fate
    Had marked a date— had fixed—a Day!
There stood revealed, that hated field
    Where doomed to yield, I bowed the knee.
My bravest slain; my courage vain!
    A cup to drain Grief filled for me.
Once more, in trance, I saw my France a prey to chance,
    A conquered land— and 'ere surprise
Had stunned my eyes

251

Beheld her rise erect and grand!
And at her side there stood, allied,
A Pow'r world-wide, my conqu'ring foe!
The brave all came,
And loud their claim
In freedom's name
To lay Lust low—
The lust of greed, of braggart breed;
Of War Lord's lead 'gainst Peace, grown bold.
True friends in need, in word and deed,
Close bound they bleed
Their faith to hold.
Their faith—in PEACE.
In earth's increase,
When war shall cease—when Caesars die!
For this they fight in all their might,
And they are right, *I* say it—I!
For good or ill my iron will, unrivalled still,
Can know no peer. Stern fate will see who copies me,
Shall bow the knee in abject fear.
I know when Peace the whole world seeks,
When Peace, on War, grim vengeance wreaks,
The Dawn is near—Napoleon speaks:
God sends—The Day!

NA-POO!

BY F. C. HENNEQUIN and JOHN WEAVER   1917

When you first comes out there's lots of things
    You'll find you never knew,
And if you're wise you'll start at once
    To learn to parley voo.
It's nice to swank along the *Rues*
    And show your *savvy faire,*
By saying to them bearded blokes
    Voila cheveux! There's 'air!

And when they charge you through the nose
   You're in the *potage* quick
If you can't say *Pas bong! trop cher,*
   That means a bit too thick.
It's fine to say Well 'ow's the game?
   That's *comment allez vous*
And when you wants to say "Not 'arf,"
   You simply says *Na-poo!*
We'll say you've been and bought some eggs,
   The French for them is "oeufs,"
And when you starts to crack the lid
   It's more like bully *boeuf!*
You says *"Bong Dieu! abominable"*–
   That's French for poison gas–
And takes them back and says "Mounseer,
   These eggs is *mauvais cas."*
'E ses *"comment"* and *"kes-ker-say"*
   Which means "what's wrong with you?"
You puts them *oeufs* beneath his nose
   And says to him *"Na-poo!"*
Or p'r'aps you feel you'd like a drink,
   Vous avez soif, Oui oui!
You goes to an *estaminet*
   That's French for pub you see.
There's lots of drinks,
   Ving or dinaire, Ving blanc and Eau de Vie,
And most of 'em will give you gripes,
   You take a tip from me.
But once I sampled, Oh! *mong Dieu!*
   The stuff they say is beer,
But what it's brewed from I don't know,
   It isn't 'ops, no fear!
I think it must be dandelions
   Or sea-weed, oh! *par bleu!*
It isn't beer, it's medicine!
   No, not for me–*"Na-poo."*
The girls out there is extry "bong"
   Tres jolie filles "What ho!"
But you can take and keep the lot
   For one old dame I know.
Somewhere back of Armenteers,
   She tends a plot of ground
253

Where chums of mine who travelled "West"
　　Are sleeping deep and sound.
She's well nigh four score years of age
　　And bent and white and spare,
But every little mound and cross
　　Is safe within her care.
She calls 'em all 'er *"chere enfants,"*
　　And treats them like it too.
She's part of France I can't forget,
　　Gawd bless her heart *"Na-poo!"*
There's times the chaps gets fair fed up
　　Tres fatiguee pas bong!
They say this blooming muddy War's
　　A *sacre* sight too long.
But if sometimes they grouse a bit,
　　They're stickers to a man,
And while they know all's well at home,
　　They do the best they can.
Just let them feel their wives and kids
　　Will never want for bread,
They'll laugh through hell and back again,
　　And do it on their head.
And if it lasts a hundred years
　　They'll say the same to you,
We ain't down-hearted are we mates?
　　Na blooming likely *-poo!*

NECKTIES

BY HARRY ROWLAND and CHAS. ELSTREE　　　　　*1922*

In the depths of an old-world secret drawer,
　　Concealed from prying eyes.
There has lain undisturbed for many a year,
　　This bundle of worn-out ties.
And in thought you picture the hand that hid them
　　Carefully and so well.

And fancy embroiders a history round
　　The tales those fragments tell.
This knitted tie of rainbow hue,
　　With its fragrance of lavender left,
Speaks it a token of love from *Her,*
　　Who worked it with fingers deft.
And *he* you are sure adored her too,
　　From her shoe to the crown of her hat.
For a man must be deep! *deep! deep* in love,
　　If he'll wear a tie like *that!*
Then this crumpled strip of cambric
　　Tells of some long forgotten ball,
He'd ask for a dance,
　　She'd give him her card,
And he'd greedily bag them all.
　　Then they'd quarrel, as young fools often do,
Though Lord knows what about,
　　Then he'd drown his cares,
For the state of the tie,
　　Tells the tale of a wild night out.
This silken scarf of lavender grey,
　　Brings the echo of wedding bells.
And this satin, well it's simply a stain of wine,
　　Of the toast to the happy pair tells.
And in fancy again this frayed edge speaks
　　Of much later, you'll understand.
The pranks with Daddy's necktie played,
　　By a baby's tiny hand.
And last this cravat of simple black,
　　Tells of the eyes that wept.
And of her who had been his manhood's star,
　　Gone to eternal sleep.
And fancy again a solace finds,
　　To ease a sad heart's pain,
In the dear dead memories brought to life,
　　By these old ties once again.

THE NEED

BY EDGAR A. GUEST and ERNEST LONGSTAFFE   1936

We were sittin' there,
  and smokin' of our pipes, discussin' things
Like taxes, votes for wimmin'
  An' the totterin' thrones of kings.
When he ups an' strokes his whiskers
  With his hand an' says to me:
Changin' laws an' legislatures ain't,
  As fur as I can see,
Goin' to make this world much better,
  Unless somehow we can
Find a way to make a better,
  An' a finer type of man.
The trouble ain't with statutes or with systems,
      not at all;
  It's with humans jus' like we ar an' their petty
      ways an' small.
We could stop our writin' law-books an' our regulatin'
      rules
  If a better sort of manhood was the product of our
      schools,
For the things that we ar needin' isn't writin'
      from a pen
  Or bigger guns to shoot with, but a bigger type
      of men.
I reckon all these problems ar jest ornery like
      the weeds,
  They grow in soil that oughta nourish only decent
      deeds,
An' they waste our time an' fret us when,
  If we were thinkin' straight
An' livin' right,
  They wouldn't be so terrible and great.
A good horse needs no snaffle
  And a good man, I opine,
Doesn't need a law to check him
  Or to force him into line.

256

If we ever start in teachin'
    To our children, year by year,
How to live with one another,
    There'll be less o' trouble here.
If we teach 'em how to neighbor
    An' to walk in honor's ways,
We could settle every problem
    That the mind of man can raise,
What we're needin' isn't systems
    Or some regulatin' plan
But a *bigger* an' a *finer*
    An' a *truer* type of man.

NELL

BY GEORGE ARTHURS and CUTHBERT CLARKE   *1939*

Nell was my friend at college,
    The best friend I ever had,
We shared each other's secrets,
    She laughed when I was sad;
And I did the same with Nellie,
    We were a loyal pair,
And we vowed that ever after
    All things in life we'd share.
We parted, met, then once more
    We parted for a while,
But yesterday we met again,
    She kissed me, with a smile,
Then murmured, "Phyllis! Dearest!
    Oh, aren't you looking well!
I do believe you're slimmer!"
    A darling girl is Nell!
We asked the usual questions,
    You know how women chat,
"Do say who made that gown, dear?"
    And "Oh, that lovely hat?"
Then in a tiny tearoom,
    Exchanging hopes and fears,
257

We talked of what had happened
   Within the last few years.
And when at last she left me,
   It was to say good-bye,
A tear fell when she kissed me,
   I–I had to cry;
With sympathetic glances,
   We each arranged our furs,
When she went back to *MY* husband,
   And I went back to *HER'S!*

NINE O'CLOCK

BY MARGARET HODGKINSON, NOSMO KING
and ERNEST LONGSTAFFE 1941

Throughout the long, long day, its heat and burden,
   There is no time, no time to think or pray;
Work on! Fight on! That is the Nation's watchword.
   And Britain, stripped, goes to it grim or gay.
Throughout the night unwearied and unceasing,
   With heart and hand we serve the common cause,
Our tears and toil, our blood and sweat we offer
   Except for that one moment when we pause.
Voice of Big Ben, What does he say?
   Lift up your hearts, Pause, think and pray.
'Neath burning skies of far off Afric desert,
   Where sons of Britain stand with unsheathed sword;
Round this beloved Isle where steel-clad sea-dogs
   Are keeping their eternal watch and ward.
In humble cottage home, in stately mansion,
   In field and factory, office, shop and mine,
Throughout the land we stand with hearts united
   When old Big Ben chimes out the hour of nine.
Voice of Big Ben, Doubtings dispel
   What does he say? Keep faith All's well.
Though London's suffered wanton devastation,
   Though land marks that we loved have passed away,
Though hearts are filled with righteous indignation

Clamouring that the guilty shall repay.
The Voice of Big Ben sounds above the tumult
In every land and corner of the Earth,
Lifting up the hearts of all our people
With music from the cradle of their birth.
Sweetly it calls, Your heart and mine,
Come let us meet in the silence at nine.
No matter what of triumph or disaster
The day may bring, our hearts to cheer or quell,
Each eventide those chimes send forth their message
Around the listening world that all is well.
O God, we dedicate this hour of vigil
With humble hearts to Country, King and Thee
And then go forth refreshed, to meet the morrow,
With sober courage and serenity.
Voice of Big Ben, What does he say?
Lift up your hearts, Pause, think and Pray.

NOT UNDERSTOOD

BY THOMAS BRACKEN and D'AUVERGNE BARNARD   *1904*

Not understood! We move along asunder,
    Our path grows wider as the seasons creep
Along the years; we marvel and we wonder
    Why life is life, and then we fall asleep,
Not understood. Not understood.
    We gather false impressions,
And hug them closer as the years go by;
    Till virtues often seem to us transgressions,
And thus, men rise and fall and live and die,
    Not understood. Not understood.
Poor souls with stunted vision
    Oft measure giants by their narrow guage,
The poisoned shafts of falsehood and derision
    Are oft impelled 'gainst those who mould the age,
Not understood. Not understood.
    The secret springs of action
Which lie beneath the surface and the show,

Are disregarded; with self-satisfaction
We judge our neighbours and they often go,
    Not understood. Not understood.—
How trifles often change us!
    The thoughtless sentence or the fancied slight
Destroy long years of friendship and estrange us,
    And on our souls there falls a freezing blight,
Not understood. Not understood.
    How many breasts are aching
For lack of sympathy! Ah! day by day,
    How many cheerless, lonely hearts are breaking!
How many noble spirits pass away
    Not understood. Not understood.
O God! that men would see a little clearer
    Or judge less harshly where they cannot see!
O God! that men would draw a little nearer
    To one another they'd be nearer Thee,
And understood.

NUTSHELL NOVELS

BY HERBERT HARRADEN   *1902*

My literary qualities are very, very great.
    I'm not a Novel-Writer, but the plots I perpetrate.
I have a scale of prices,
    And of course, it's understood,
The charge is low for what is bad,
    But high for what is good.
My lowest is a *pound*
    For which I give you at the most,
One stolen Will they never find,
    One murder, and one ghost.
For twice that sum, two stolen Wills—
    Both found again, remark!
Two ghosts, one murder when it's light,
    And one that's in the dark.
For *three pounds, three,* I open with the pastime
        of Ping-Pong,

260

At which a Vicar's daughter and a Curate go it strong.
The Vicar and Vicar's wife
   Look on with inward glee.
The Curate (who has private means)
   Is asked to stop to tea.
The Vicar's daughter and the Curate
   Often take a walk;
And here's the chance for chapters
   Full of wishy-washy talk.
Their marriage ought to form
   The closing phrases of the book,
But no! the Curate marries—
   A surprise! the Vicar's Cook!
For *five pounds, five* (it's worth much more)
   I give a missing heir,
Of whose existence only one, (the Villain—) is aware.
   The Villain (who's a Lawyer—)
Wants the hand and heart to win
   Of the missing heir's tenth cousin,
Who's, of course, the next of kin.
   He pleads his suit.
She spurns his love. He threatens! She defies!
   He drags her to a deep, dark pool that in the forest
      lies.
She shrieks for help!
   The missing heir a willow tree descends—
They struggle—
   And you know the way this kind of story ends!
For *eight pounds, eight,*
   I let you have a gang of Gipsies bold,
Who carry off a female babe,
   Who wears a cross of gold.
Years pass. Inside St. James' Hall
   There sits a Gipsy Queen,
So sadly gazing on the man
   Who holds the tambourine.
She listens spell-bound when he plays.
   What means this strange delight!
He sees she wears a cross of gold
   That gleams and glitters bright.
Regardless of the burnt-cork marks
   He leaves upon her face,

The father clasps his long-lost child
   Within his black embrace.
For *tenpounds, ten,*
   My scenes amidst the highest Life I place.
My hero is a Duke of ev'ry virtue,
   Ev'ry grace.
Although adored by six proud maids,
   (All daughters of an Earl)
His heart he has bestowed
   Upon a first-row *Ballet*-Girl.
One evening, at the Pantomime,
 ˙Her dress is set on fire!
Who gave the bribe to do the deed
   It's needless to enquire!
Before his eyes, upon the Stage,
   A roasted heap she falls,
And then a madman strangles
   Six proud ladies in the Stalls!

OF ONE HEART

BY MARGARET HODGKINSON, NOSMO KING
                                   and CUTHBERT CLARKE1942

We did not lightly draw the sword,
   But ways of peace and reason sought instead,
Till brute aggression reared its ugly head
   Till "one man's" thieving hands with blood were
      red;
And then—with hearts and minds in one accord,
   We drew the sword!
And now we stand with naked blade,
   Facing the Evil thing with dismay:
With many comrades fallen by the way,
   Britain still stands, unconquered in the fray:
Unflinching, resolute, and unafraid

She stands with naked blade.
The glorious people of our land
    Into the very front line have been hurled,
Their deeds of courage, echo thro' the world
    Where 'ere the flags of freedom are unfurled;
Our enemies can never understand
    The people of our land.
Though death may hurtle from the skies.
    And home and life and limb may be at stake,
And loved ones' peril our hearts to ache,
    Nothing shall daunt us, nor our spirit break;
Britain in all her splendour will arise,
    And conquer in the Skies.
We shall not lightly sheathe the sword,
    With grim resolve and steadfast hearts, we wait
To meet the onslaught of the "Powers of Hate:"
    To God and King, our cause we dedicate,
Till freedom, right, and justice be restored,
    We *will not* sheathe the Sword!

THE OIL AND THE FEATHER

BY F. E. WHITE and EVA FLOYER   *1933*

A little drop of oil and a feather will make
    A mighty engine work with ease.
The oil will penetrate its inmost workings
    While the feather all the outward parts will grease
Just a little drop of oil and a feather
    Will make the wheels run smoothly, all together.
So a lesson we may glean from this marvellous machine
    And the little drop of oil and the feather.
Now every day we all need lubrication,
    The oil we need is sympathy, a smile
Applied with tact which represents the feather,
    You will find this true so try it for a while
Just a little drop of oil and a feather

Will make the wheels of life run well together
If you have a touchy friend, I would strongly recommend
Just that little drop of oil and a feather.

A word to married ladies.

For his club perhaps your husband has a weakness
While in solitude you darn his socks at home
To you I would impart this little secret
When your lord and master seems inclined to roam
Try that little drop of oil and the feather
Then you'll spend your evenings both together
Should his temper ever rust
You may place implicit trust
In that little drop of oil and the feather.

A word to married men.

Now in married life one sometimes hears of friction
'Tis said such things will happen now and then
Of course the fault is never with the ladies
And it absolutely couldn't be the men!
Well a little drop of oil upon a feather
Might help a man and wife to pull together
So you never need despair if your wife should lose
        her hair
Try a little hair restorer on the feather.

AN OLD BACHELOR

BY ALBERT CHEVALIER and ALFRED H. WEST   *1904*

They call me an old bachelor, I'm known as poor old
        bachelor.
    Although I'm really rich in what this world
        considers wealth.
But money can't buy everything, No! money is not
        everything,
    It cannot bring you happiness, it cannot
        purchase health.
I'm hale and very hearty too,

Play "poker" and écarté too,
To pass the time away at home—
My only home the Club!
The boys all know my Christian name!
They call me by my Christian name!
And if they're running short of cash, and want a
    modest sub—
They know I've more than I can spend,
    I may say that I will not lend,
But still they get it in the end,
    From a poor old bachelor.
I've heard I save my money up—
    I scrape and hoard my money up,
Why don't I have a trifle on a gee gee now and then.
    A modest little flutter,
Yes, it's called, I think, a flutter,
    By some of my acquaintances who think they're
        sporting-men.
You're old, they say, and out-of-date,
    A trifle slow, at any rate.
I tell them they're so go ahead and p'r'aps I've lived
    too long.
    I only back the winners—And I do pick the
        winners—
Although before the race they always tell me that I'm
    wrong.
    They envy me my luck, they say,
And I?—Well I can only pray
    That know my luck they never may. A poor old
        bachelor.
I've been advised to settle down,
    To choose a wife and settle down,
To find some homely body who is sensible and good.
    A tempting combination. An unusual combination.
I only smile and say I wouldn't marry if I could.
    They little guess when chaffingly
They question me and laughingly
    I answer how each thoughtless word recalls
        a dream of youth.
A dream from which I cannot wake,
    Of life lived for remembrance' sake,

They call me woman-hater! If they only knew the truth!
  But way out where the flowers are seen,
A white cross marks the place I mean,
  Who keeps a little grave so green? A poor
    old bachelor!

THE OLD BARNSTORMER

BY FRANK WOOD and CUTHBERT CLARKE   *1933*

Don't wake me up, for I'm dreaming to-night
  Of the good old days long since taken flight.
We were either play-acting or running a booth
  With animals, freaks, and our motto—"The Truth!"
Walk up! Walk up! Walk up and see
  The horse's head where his tail ought to be.
Yes, that was the old Barnstormers' cry
  In the good old days long since gone by.
The unselfish days when each of us shared
  The good with the bad and nobody cared.
When luck was out and little to eat,
  The ground for a bed, the sky for a sheet.
Walk up! Walk up! Walk up and see
  The Horse's head where his tail ought to be.
How the people laughed when his "rudder" they saw
  In the manger while there was his head on
    the floor.
Walk up and see the Giddy Giraffe,
  With a neck ten foot long that'll make you 'laff',
And all that he lives on is one meal a day,
  'Cos a little with him goes a blooming long
    way.
Walk up! and see the famous freak,
  "The Bearded Lady" from Cripple Creek.
There's only two nights to gaze on this freak,
  He's got to go back to his wife next week.
The Human Ostrich, a funny galloot,

Swallowed swords and chewed glass like a
  kid eating fruit.
Then he had to lay off, for the silly great goat
  Had some kippers and got a bone stuck in
    his throat.
Jugo, the Juggler, who juggled with knives,
  And scared all the audience out of their lives.
His wife on the stage, and he in the pit,
  While ev'ryone marvelled why she wasn't hit.
He'd throw at her head and he once got so near,
  By the eighth of an inch a big knife grazed
    her ear.
And a navvy somewhere in the back seats roared
  "I'm blowed if 'e ain't gone and missed 'er,
    the fraud!"
Walk up! Walk up and take a good view
  Of the old spotted leopard from Wongapaloo!
He can change all his spots and without any bother,
  When he's tired of one spot he sits on another.
Here walk up and see the performing flea,
  He was born in Brighton in seventy-three.
To the people what went there to spend a week-end,
  He was known to the crowd as a bosom friend.
I shall never forget our old play-acting crowd,
  We'd tramped fifty miles and though poor we
    were proud.
We arrived at a village and there we could see
  The sun in the distance as bright as could be;
I cried "Cheer up, laddies, and on with the show,
  Yon sunset provides us a welcoming glow."
Then a yokel cried "That be no sunset, ole Squire,
  Vor that be the bloomin *theatre* on fire."
Walk up! Walk up! what glorious times—
  No velvet curtains with headlights and limes—
None of your talkies and music that's canned
  A drum and a whistle that did for a band.
When the curtain falls and a voice calls me
  To a place be it colder or warmer
I hope I shall hear Walk up and see
  THE LAST OF AN OLD BARNSTORMER!

OLD FLAMES

BY W. S. FRANK and FRANK S. WILCOCK 1924

N.B. *During the introduction* the artist pulls a handful of photo's from his pocket and refers to them as required by the monologue.

Of photos I've here quite a charming collection
    Of girls I have loved with a passing affection.
Full many a maid in my time I have kissed,
    For things that are sweet I could never resist,
And many a maiden of bashful fifteen,
    I've thought quite divine till another I've
        seen.
My darling Babette I shall never forget,
    She wept on my shirt front and made it all wet.
Quite charming was Grace all excepting her face,
    And her nose which kept 'Roman' all over the place.
And then there was Kitty whose teeth were so pretty,
    She used so much Odol her kisses were gritty.
While darling Pandora with hair like Aurora,
    Spent a small fortune on Boots' Hair Restorer.
And beautiful Betty I kissed on the jetty,
    Nose like a radish and hair like spaghetti.
I leave Isabella to some other fellow,
    Her ribs stick out just like a broken
        umbrella.
Amelia, Ophelia, and haughty Cordelia,
    To some might appeal but they didn't
        appeal 'ere. (Help!)
And here's darling Lulu, I might have wed you Lou,
    But when I met you Lou we hadn't a sou Lou!
And Eleanor who lived just next door,
    Her face was her fortune, but oh! she was poor.
There's sweet little Minnie who hails from New Guinea,
    I called her banana for she was so skinny.
In her garden so green I met charming Eileen,
    She'd scores of cucumbers but never a bean.
Bewitching Vanessa, so pretty, God bless her,
    She broke it all off when she fell off the dresser.

And here is the last of this charming collection
  Of girls I have loved with a passing affection,
The best of the bunch, well now who can it be?
  That tip-tilted nose seems familiar to me;
Those cherry-like lips, now I'll swear on my life,
  I'll give 'em a kiss, and why not?
      She's my wife!

AN OLD MEMORY

BY HICKMAN SMITH and ERNEST LONGSTAFFE   *1940*

In an old and musty cupboard, that lies underneath
  the stair:
  I was turning over litter when I came quite
    unaware
Upon a little oddment, a small relic of the past:
  That set me idly dreaming of the years gone
    by too fast.
Just an old torn sheet of music, soiled and worn
    beyond repair,
  But it brought back vivid memories of life—
    once young and fair.
A dream of what once might have been, if love had run
  its course:
  A dream of long lost happiness, of sadness
    and remorse.
A dim lit room, I seem to see: an old piano there,
  A vision of a beauteous girl up on a quaint
    old chair.
A sudden hush, as fingers struck a cord that made me
  start,
  A silvery voice that trilled a song that
    touched me to the heart.
I wonder if she's thinking of those days of long ago,
  Of the song she sang that evening when the
    lights were dim and low

For 'twas "Just a song at twilight" the most perfect
    song of all,
  That bound our hearts together in love's sweet
    entrancing thrall.
"Just a song at twilight" what fond memories it
    weaves,
  And "When the lights are low" what
    remorselessness it leaves
In a heart that's lost its feeling for the lovely
    things of life,
  And has looked upon a world that's filled
    with bitterness and strife.
And yet how memory once again brings back to me,
    it seems,
  All the things I meant to do in my fairyland
    of dreams.
The happiness we both would seek—the heights we meant
    to climb
  In the new found world of romance—that will
    live as long as time.
But alas, our dream was broken, and how bitter was
    the pain,
  When I heard the fateful words "We must
    never meet again."
How I begged and how I pleaded that my life must surely
    end,
  If she could not hope to love me, Would she
    be to me a friend?
But vain was all my pleading—I must never see her more,
  I must never even write to her—which hurt
    me to the core.
So I left her broken hearted—vowing through the world
    I'd roam,
  But you see I had no option *Her Husband
    had come home.*

270

OLD PIERROT

BY SIVORI LEVEY   1922

Old Pierrot he sit by the fire,
  Watching the flame burn higher and higher;
Watching the flame burn down so low,—
  Old Pierrot, he know, he know.
What are the visions he can see
  Of what has been, and what yet will be?
Past and future there in the glow,—
  Old Pierrot, he know he know!
Young Pierrot think he is asleep,—
  Towards the door he start to creep,
While father's head is bent so low,—
  But old Pierrot, he know, he know.
Young Pierrot he cross the floor,—
  Quick, he's out through the quiet door
To meet Pierrette with her eyes aglow,—
  But old Pierrot, he know, he know!
Did he not once woo sweet Phrynette,
  Just as his boy woos fair Pierrette?
Young Pierrot come; Phrynette she go
  Old Pierrot, he know, he know.
Grief and gladness, sorrow and joy,
  So Life will be for his only boy;
But Love that will last will its blessings bestow,—
  Old Pierrot, he know, he know!

OLD SKIPPER BOB

BY LYELL JOHNSTON and HARVEY LINTON   1912

Thanks all the same I'd rather not,
  I've chucked the beer and gin.
You laugh; You knew me as I was,
  Not as I might 'a been.

271

The very same old skipper Bob;
  A crock as used to be
The hardest drinkin' trawler boss;
  As e'er dropped nets at sea.
Beg pardon! What! You've been abroad?
  Then 'course you haven't heard
About the wreck and how we lost,
  Our ketch the "Saucy Bird."
A gruesome tale! Repeat it?
  Well I don't know as I should,
And yet to young 'uns such as you,
  Perhaps 'tmight do ye good.
Four of us there were all told
  A roughish, hardened crew,
As didn't care a tinker's cuss
  For anyone we knew—
We lived afloat for wives and girls
  We left to youngish tars
We fished to earn the kind o' food
  We stocked in gallon jars.
Back to my yarn—Midnight it was,
  From land a league or more,
Our craft adrift, Her crew chock full
  O' grog all blessed four.
"Muddled?" Aye I must 'a been
  But wakened with a shock!
The ketch's keel a-scrunchin' as
  She scraped across the rock
Then quick as knife I realized
  We'd drifted into shore—
I yelled "Ahoy!" But *no* reply,
  Except a drunken snore:-
It wasn't dark: No, black as pitch
  Or Hell—or nigger's bleed,
A wind that howled—a sea that ran
  Like naught I'd heard or see'd.
I hadn't heart to pray just then
  But thanked God for the light
That came down from a single star
  That flickered clear and bright
For just a second pointing out
  The way I'd got to steer

To strike a cleft a'twixt two rocks
   The danger safe to clear.
Alas! Too late! The drink had won,
   I'd lost my nerve and spleen—
A giddy ride abreast a wave
   Then *crash* and *smithereens.*
They tell as how four lumps o' wreck
   Were found at break o' morn;
Four relics of the "Saucy Bird"
   All battered, scratched and torn,
Three of 'em beyond all use
   For work on land or sea,
And one alive, *a miracle*
   Well least-ways here I be.
The parsons say that folks wot's good
   Called Angels work at night,
And earn their bed and board above
   By keeping stars alight.
To qualify they say "Be good,"
   And now so 'elp me Bob,
The bit o' life that's left in me's
   Apprenticed to *That* Job!

O MEMORY

BY J. HICKORY WOOD and LESLIE HARRIS   *1903*

When I was a youngster I loved a nice girl,
   Who prepared her hair just to keep it in curl.
I nearly went mad for I loved the girl so.
   I love her more fondly, the older I grow.
Her dear name was—um—well I really don't know.
   Oh Memory! Oh Memory!!
Her nose was—now what *was* the shape of her nose?
   When she smiled you could see all her teeth
      in two rows—
Her eyes were delightful—so brilliant in hue—

A beautfiul grey—no they weren't—they were
   blue
Or else black—*I* don't know—Anyhow she had two.
Oh Memory! Oh Memory!!
Her hair fell in silky luxuriant locks,
   She gave me a tress which I kept in a box,
'Twas lovely dark brown—no—it wasn't 'twas light.
   At least, it was—something between black
   and white—
It *can't* have been red! Still, I don't know, it
   might—
Oh Memory! Oh Memory!!
Well, well, after all, she married another—
   A fellow named Jack—no *that* was his brother.
But when I enquired how he liked being wed,
   He replied—"Go to"—*No*—That can't be
   what he said—
Oh! *now* I remember he "wished he was dead!"
Oh Memory! Oh Memory!!

OPEN SPACES

BY H.M. BURNABY and HAROLD ARPTHORP   1926

Performed by Bransby Williams

I'm the voice of open spaces, calling—calling—ever
   calling
To you workers of the city—of the country—
   of the town.
Come and share my many riches—let me tell you wondrous
   secrets
'Neath the vault of God's high Heaven, 'neath
   the good sun streaming down.
Workers! Workers! I am needing all your sinew, bone
   and muscle.
Bring me strong wills, bring me stout hearts,
   from your homes across the sea.
I am ready—I am waiting—for your pick and shovels
   mating.

274

'Tis the voice of open spaces, calling—calling—
  come to me!
Come and delve into my vitals; score my body with
  your plough-shares,
  Seeds within my bosom planting—let me nurture
  them awhile.
Bring your energy and spirit—there'll be glory in the
  conquest,
  While you work your will upon me I shall bless
  you with my smile.
Smiling! Smiling! Proudly yielding, crops of yellow
  grain in summer,
  Let me feed you—clothe you—house you,
  gladly will I pay your due,
I am Earth! and I am Mother! let us live for one another,
  'Tis the voice of open spaces calling—calling
  now—to you!
Voice of virgin open spaces calling—calling—ever
  calling.
  Not for you! you wastrels, shiftless men of
  straw—Beware!
Better that you starve at home—than take the toll I'll
  be exacting,
  I can only break your hearts and crush you,
  crush you to despair.
Stalwarts! Stalwarts! Send me stalwarts men to fight
  and wrestle with me,
  Men of blood and iron and courage, mansion
  born or from the slum,
I am Land! I am lonely! Send me Workers!—Workers only!
  'Tis the voice of open spaces calling—calling—
  will you come?

ORANGE BLOSSOM

BY SAX ROHMER   *1921*

Note:- Where costume is not worn, it may be desirable to
announce that "Orange Blossom" is "A story of Chinese

revenge; the lines are supposed to be spoken by a cultured
Chinaman."

My little Orange Blossom—light of my life
    Sleep on, tender flower—sleep on!
Hist!—Wu Chang!—Greetings! greetings!
    Ha! Wu Chang, long have I waited.
But that my friend would answer to my call
    I had not fear. See, old friend, the tea awaits,
It is the famous Pekoe!
    Sit!! My friend, Wu Chang, Wu Chang, my friend!
I love you for your heart of gold.
    Alas! Wu Chang, much water's flown from Honan
To the Yellow Sea since you and I were playmates—
    Playmates in the valley where the opium
        poppies grow.
The tea is to your liking? Then we smoke.
    You gaze 'round for my wife?
Ah! The little Orange Blossom. I know you loved her
        well
For my sake? Yes, Wu Chang, my friend!
Have Courage! Courage! Heart of gold!
    It is the incense that you smell—
The little Orange Blossom's dead!
    You start! 'Twas sudden? Yes!
She died at dawn. But let us smoke.
    At dawn she lived, Tonight her soul is free.
Her body lies in yonder.
    Come! Come! Wu Chang and kiss her. No?
Her red lips smile, her eyes are kind.
    So slender is the thread of life, that even I,
Or you, Wu Chang, might die to-night! How pale you grow!
    The tea is to your liking? Is the incense
        so oppressive?
Well, the flowers are fresh. For she, too, was a
        flower, Wu Chang,
    A lily, slender white—so frail a flower—my
        wife.
My journeys left her much alone.
    But when I placed her in your care,
My old and trusted friend Wu Chang,

I deemed her safe, But see!
Your tea grows cold. Drink up!
   Her lips were red, her heart was young
How fair she was! and I so far away!
   You shudder yet, your brow is wet, nor do
      you smoke.
Your face is grey, and how you twitch and clutch with
      clammy fingers.
   You thought me safe in far Honan! Yes!
So did the little Orange Blossom!—
   Sit!!—Look well into your empty cup—
The same from which your mistress drank at dawn,
   Wu Chang—her last! Your whispered vows,
      each stolen kiss,
All reached my ears!
   I heard, I saw, my friend, Wu Chang!
In yonder room, the room where now our little Orange
      Blossom lies—
   I lay, concealed!
No, no! You have no strength to raise your knife!
   The poison cup has done its work.
Her lips were sweet? Her arms were soft?
   You writhe, and why, your eyes are glazed!
'Twas so with her, at dawn, as 'tis with you to-night
   Go sleep in hell—in HELL! my friend, Wu Chang!

ORANGE PEEL

BY MILTON HAYES and CUTHBERT CLARKE   *1920*

   The Colonel stopped, and glared around,
      Then, pointing sternly to the ground,
   "What *does* this mean?" demanded he,
      "A piece of orange peel I see!"
   The Major called the Captain then,
      And said, "By Gad! Your fault again!
   Now what the blazes do you mean
      By letting all this filth be seen?"

The Captain sniffed, but took the snub,
    Then, calling to the Junior Sub.,
Observed, "Look here, what's all this mess?
    It's fit for pigs, sir, nothing less!"
The Junior Sub. blushed crimson red,
    Then, to the Sergeant-major, said,
"I'm quite fed up, and all that rot!
    I mean to say—a pig-sty! What?"
The Sergeant-major, filled with rage,
    Attacked the Sergeant at this stage,
"You careless swab! Jump to it smart.
    Oh strewth! You break my blinkin 'eart!"
The Sergeant, starting in to cuss,
    Apostrophized the Corporal, thus,
"You lazy, lumberin', boss-eyed lout!
    Who chucked this crimson fruit about?"
The Corporal frowned, and turned his eye
    On Private Atkins passing by;
"Hi! you! Come 'ere, you slobberin' sweep,
    Just shift this festerin' rubbish 'eap!"
And Private Atkins, filled with gloom,
    Applied himself with spade and broom:
"They talk a ruddy lot," quoth he,
    "But 'oo does all the work? *Why me!* "

OUR DEBT OF HONOUR

BY ROBERT LEFTWICH AND VERNON LEFTWICH   1914

The booming of cannon resounds through the world,
    The searchlights are scanning the sky,
The armour is sheening the flags are unfurled,
    And troops marching millions. And why?
Because of a fiend in the shape of a man
    Regardless of honour and worth,
Who holds himself built on Napoleon's plan
    And decreed to be Lord of the earth.

With battleships, cruisers, torpedoes and guns,
   And Britain the chief of his foes,
He little expected that Great Britain's sons
   Would be *greater* when trouble arose.
He thought the disruption in Ireland his chance,
   Our Colonies passive and cool,
Insulted by thinking us traitors to France,
   That Belguim would act as his tool.
But Belguim unmoved by temptation or threat,
   Held firm to the promise she made,
Defied the invader and honoured her debt
   To the nations who've come to her aid.
All glory to her and the courage she's shown,
   How she's ready to suffer and bleed,
She kept *him* at bay and she did it *alone,*
   And the world stands amazed at the deed.
And the allies, united in justice and right,
   Are weaving the funeral pall
That is closing around o'er the armed bully's might
   With faith in *their* cause and *his* fall.
It *shall* come, and the march of the tyrant shall
     cease,
   And fair fields shall rise where he trod,
Where a massacre raged and the fiend who cried *peace*
   Shall render account to his *God.*

OUR GRANDPARENT'S YARNS

BY LEONARD POUNDS and CUTHBERT CLARKE   *1921*

Now our grandparents sit in their easy chairs,
   With wrinkled-up brows 'neath their silver
     hairs
Comparing our latter-day ways with theirs
   And shaking their heads the while.
Their assertions will all of them go to show
   How pure were the people of long ago.
We're told that their standard we're far below;

That mankind then knew no guile.
The yarns that our grandparents spin!
    In their day it seems the world was free of
        sin!
Boys all loved to go to school,
    Where they never broke a rule,
Or inserted in the master's chair a pin!
    It appears that all young men,
Never stayed out after ten,
    And no maiden bared her shoulders at the play!
They possessed no vice or taints—
    Just a crowd of earthly saints
Were the folks of our grandparents' day!
    Hear our grannies avow, with a wry grimace,
That slang on their tongues never found a place,
    And never a maid would her lips disgrace
By cigarette held between.
    In quarrels all men a soft answer chose,
Instead of proceeding by violent blows,
    To alter the contour of someone's nose,
To vent a revengeful spleen!
    The yarns that our grandparents spin!
In their day it seems the world was free of sin!
    Ev'ry lawyer just would be,
And would ne'er accept a fee
    If a client's case perchance he failed to win!
Calves and ankles were not shown;
    Tittle-tattle wasn't known;
And from church umbrellas never went astray.
    This conclusion we derive—
All too good to be alive
    Were the folks of our grandparents' day.
Our credulity strains at its leashes tight
    When we gather that cabmen were all polite;
That every post office pen would write:
    And that little boys all said "please."
To his elders each junior raised his hat,
    No person played billiards, or games like that!
One doubts if a dog ever chased a cat,
    Or a mouse ever stole the cheese!
The yarns that our grandparents spin!
    In their day it seems the world was free of sin!

They will laud up to the sky
   Deeds performed in days gone by,
But decry our own with supercilious grin.
Though we smile at tales like these.
We grow older, by degrees,
   And grandparents *we* may be some future day:
And when we're toothless, bent, and lame,
   We shall say the very same
Things as all of our grandparents say.

OUT AT MONS

BY *WARREN HASTINGS* and *HERBERT JORDAN*   *1916*

There's a simple kind of cross
   Out at Mons,
Stuck in a heap of stones,
   Out at Mons.
It's there to mark the bones
   Of Private William Jones,
Just a little heap of stones,
   Out at Mons.
That cross is just a British Tommy's gun,
   With the business end a-pointin' to the sun.
With a bayonet 'cross the top,
   As a cross it ain't much cop,
But it's planted there to stop,
   That Tommy's gun.
There ain't no pretty flowers
   On that grave.
'Tain't always marble tomb-stones
   For the brave.
He chucked his life away,
   With his thirteen pence a day;
Saved his captain, so they say,
   And found a grave.

There's a pale faced little girl
   Over here.
Works hard to earn a living,
   Over here.
She's no Venus in the face,
   She don't tog in frills and lace,
But her heart's right in its place,
   Never fear.
She was walkin' out with Bill
   'Fore the war
She was all the world to Bill,
   That was sure.
And now buried 'neath the stones,
   With Private William Jones,
Her soul lies with his bones,
   Ever more.

THE 'OXTON 'ERO

BY RUPERT HAZELL and JAN HURST.   *1917*

'Ere 'eard the latest? I'm a hero just because I
   strafed some Huns
  And they're goin' to D.C.M. me 'cause they
   say I saved some guns.
Yus and I'm a noble patriot so the Colonel says—it's
   right,
  Patriot why I joined the Army cos I loves to
   have a fight.
'Ere it's a rummy sort of feeling this 'ere 'ero
   business is,
  Why they treats me like a Baron and they
   fusses rahnd my Liz.
It's a funny world, now ain't it, I remember fightin'
   once
  Fifteen policemen down at 'Oxton an' all I
   got was eighteen months.

Yus and now I'm paid to fight like and I puts eight
    Germans out,
    Gets' a bullet in me shoulder and me features
        knocked about.
Ladies comes into my ward and brings me fags and
    'ugs me wife,
    Asks me if I'll sign their albums Oh! my
        uncle what a life.
Yus, an' as soon as I gets better, up they comes wiv
    motor-cars,
    Brings me sweets and brings me 'bacca, yus
        an fifteen-inch cigars.
An' they spreads me out on cushions wiv a big fur rug
    on top,
    Me on cushions like a necklace in a Bond
        Street jew'ler's shop.
Why they fights to take me out to tea and dinner
    every day,
    So I 'as a little bit wiv each, it's easier
        that way.
And once when I gets back and couldn't eat nurse says
    "You must!"
    And she tempted me wiv rabbit-pie—well I 'ad
        to 'ide the crust.
But there's only one thing spoils it and upsets me
    'appy life,
    Between ourselves—it's like this 'ere I've
        got a jealous wife.
There's a gal wot's allus 'angin rahnd, (of course I
    knows it's wrong)
    And Liz says when she says good-bye she 'olds
        me 'and too long.
I think she's rather gorn on me, they calls her
    'Lady Rose',
    'Cos just before she gets to me she powders
        up her nose.
But the missus needn't care about this little bit
    of fluff,
    I'll bet old Liz could give her points at
        makin' currant duff.
Well, I suppose I'd better get along, there's quite
    a big affair

At arf-past five at our Tahn 'all I've got
   to meet the Mayor,
They're givin' me a watch and chain, and after that
   I goes
To 'ave a bit of dinner (mum's the word) with
   LADY ROSE.

PADDIN' ALONG

BY H. M. BURNABY and HARRY STOGDEN   *1951*

I've combed your coat till it looks like silk
   And your ears where they touch the ground;
And in half-an-hour they'll be all mussed up
   'Cos we're off for a mooch around—
There's a pond—an' the feller that's throw-in' the
   sticks
Is me!—so I can't go wrong,—
   Little brown spaniel c'm-on—let's go—just
Pad-pad-paddin' along.
   What do you think of this cock-eyed world
With the noise—its clamour—and dust?
   Or maybe your world's just the one to whom
You've given your faith and trust.
   Yes! I guess you'd be satisfied with that
Just the feelin' that you belong,
   Nothin' to gain—no axe to grind,
Pad-pad-paddin' along.
   Sloppy old So-an'-so—that's what you are!
But where did you get those eyes?
   All soft—an' dewy—an' wistful like,
Pensive an' sad an' wise.
   If a dog could talk he'd have much to say:
Would his language be mild—or strong?
   Nobody knows—'cos he's just content,
To go, Pad-pad-paddin' along.
   Snuggle up closer old brown pal

We've had such a busy day,
   Scampers an' barks an' shakes an' rolls
An' sniffs—all along your way.
   Supper time son! then away to bed
While the birds sing their even song,
   Don't tell me—I know what your dreams 'll be
Pad-pad-paddin' along.

PADDY

BY H. M. BURNABY and CUTHBERT CLARKE   *1922*

He was just a happy youngster, and the school was
    breaking up,
  For the summer holidays were drawing near.
And that day someone had given him a tiny mongrel pup,
  Like most small boys his love for dogs was
    queer.
'Twas a quaint and ugly rascal—little Paddy was its
    name,
  And as dogs go he was quite outside the pale;
He possessed ancestors somewhere—tho' to trace 'em
    was a game,
  But Johnnie loved that wagging stump of tail
Now they went off to the seaside and a broken-hearted
    boy
  Sat shedding bitter tears that seemed to
    blind him,
The thing in life he loved the best, that pup—his
    only joy,
  Of course he had to kiss—and leave behind him,
So on the beach—despondent—played a melancholy kid,
  While the dog remained at home in charge of
    daddy;
The world was such a dull place, and he wanted oh!—he
    did
  That little mongrel puppy known as Paddy.

Now Johnnie never could forget that ever-wagging tail,
  His holiday was spoiled he grumbled sadly;
And got fed up completely with his little spade and
      pail,
  The absence of that "pup" he felt so badly.
He went right off his feed—at ev'rything he made a fuss,
  And then misfortune came to crown his sorrows;
They told him that his daddy'd been run over by a 'bus,
  Badly injured, and they must return tomorrow.
His sad-eyed mother's counsel was—that he must be a man;
  For now 'twas up to him to play the hero.
He said "I'll try to brave it just as bravely as I can!"
  Though at the time his spirits were at zero.
The journey home accomplished, Johnnie heard his
      mother say
  "Now darling, just you come and see poor Daddy".
And then surprise lit up his face, he shouted "Hip hooray
  Why! I thought you said the 'bus' runned over Paddy!"

PENNY FOR DA MONK

BY MARTYN HERBERT and LOUISE MacBEAN   1929

Ain't got no fader, ain't got no moder.
  Ain't got a friend in da world, no sister
      or broder.
Dat's why I'm lonesome, dat's why I'm blue
  Only da monkey to love me, dat's why I say
      to you:
Give-a me a penny for da monk'. you make-a me 'appy,
  'Cos da monk' he verra beeg-a friend of mine.
Ain't got any money for an organ for to play,
  Only got-a da leetle monk', so dat is why
      I say:
Give-a me a penny for da monk; he verra hungry,
  An' he's all I got, you see.

S'pose you feelin' sorry an' you give-a da monk' a
    penny,
Den da monk', he give-a da penny back to me.
He make-a me 'appy, he make-a me smile,
    He make-a me angry as well, just once in a
        while.
He see da banana, he pinch dem an' run.
    I scold him an' den I forgiven him,
Cos da monkey he give me one.
(As though speaking to monkey inside coat)
Oh ho, Pietro, you ready for show-a da treeck?
    Oh you feel-a da cold?
Il poverino, he verra cold he verra hungry
    An I no getta da money for to buy-a da banana.
Both my broder, dey make-a da money.
    Antonio, he play-a da organ.
Giovanni, he make-a da ice-cream,
    Make-a da hokey-pokey, verra nice.
Ride-a da tricycle, ring-a da bell,
    'Stop me an' buy one.'
Me, I only got-a da leetle monk .
    Never mind,
Amico da mio, you show-a da treeck,
    Make-a da smile, make-a da money.
Den one day, may-be,
    We take-a da beeg ship back to Italie,
Caro Napoli, where da sun shine,
    An' da skies are blue all-a da time.
Give-a me a penny for da monk', you make-a me 'appy,
    'Cos da monk', he verra beeg-a friend of mine.
Ain't got any money for an organ for to play.
    Only got da leetle monk', so dat is why I say:
"Give-a me a penny for da monk'; he verra hungry,
    An' he's all I got, you see.
S'pose you feelin' sorry, an' you give-a da monk'
        a penny,
    Den da monk', he give-a da penny back to me."

PERIODICALS

BY GREATREX NEWMAN, GRAHAM SQUIERS and FRED CECIL 1916

Have you noticed what parts *Periodicals* play
 In these *Times?*
A sweet girl, for instance, can't keep long away
 From the *Mirror,*—
She owns the *Wide World* as along she will sail,
 Her best frock,—the *Pink 'Un,*—turns
  other girls pale,
Of course she is hoping that her *Daily Mail*
 Will *Observer.*
Now the *Modern Man* sometimes will ask her to say—
 "Yes" or *"No;"*
If she *Answers* "Yes,"—and he *Windsor,* next day—
 Financial News;
But the *Bystander* notices after a year,
 He gets tired of *Home Chat,* and his club
  is his *Sphere,*
He *Telegraphs* home—"I am working late dear,"—
 The Storyteller!
Of course later on, there will doubtless appear:
 Little Folks.
His boasting is *Graphic,* and all who are near
 Get the *P.I.P.*
And at night there's a *War Cry,* papa you will guess,
 Looking just like a—*Sketch* in his—
  well—evening dress,
Walks round the room trying in vain to suppress
 Home Notes.
Later on their ambition in life is to be
 In the *Smart Set,* and you'll often hear
  New of the Worlds that they see
From the *Tatler;* But the *Truth* is, these
 Tit Bits soon fade right away,
Such *Ideas* have vanished, their *Cassells* decay,
 They leave all *Town Topics,* and end up
  their day
In *Country Life.*

PHIL BLOOD'S LEAP

BY ROBERT BUCHANAN and CUTHBERT CLARKE   *1918*

We were seeking gold in the Texan hold, and we'd
    had a blaze of luck,
    More rich and rare the stuff ran there at
      every foot we struck;
Like men gone wild we t'ild and t'ild and never seemed
    to tire,
    The hot sun beamed and our faces streamed
      with the sweat of mad desire.
I was Captain then of the mining men, and I had a
    precious life,
    For a wilder set I never met at derringer
      and knife;
Nigh every day there was some new fray, a bullet in
    some one's brain,
    And the cussedest brute to stab and to shoot
      was an Imp of sin from Maine:
Phil Blood, well, he was six foot three, with a squint
    to make you skeer'd,
    Sour as the drink in Bitter Chink, with
      carroty hair and beard.
With anything white he'd drink or he'd fight in fair
    or open fray,
    But to murder and kill was his wicked will,
      If an Injun came his way.
We'd just struck our bit of luck, and were wild as
    raving men,
    When who should stray to our camp one day but
      Black Panther, the Cheyenne.
So I took the Panther into camp and the critter
    was well content,
    And off with him, on the hunting tramp, ere long
      our hunters went.
    And I reckon that day and the next, we didn't
    want for food:
    And only one in the camp look vext—that Imp of Sin—
    Phil Blood.

Well, one fine day we a-resting lay at noontide
    by the creek,
The red sun blazed, and we felt half dazed, too
    tired to stir or speak.
When, back just then came our hunting men, with
    the Panther at their head.
Full of his fun was everyone, and the Panther's eyes were red,
    And he skipped about with a grin and a shout,
    for he'd had a drop that day.
And he twisted and twirled, and squeal'd and shirl'd
    in the foolish Injun way.
With an ugly glare, Phil Blood lay there, with
    only his knife in his belt,
And I saw his bloodshot eyeballs stare, and I knew
    how fierce he felt!
When the Indian dances with grinning glances
    around Phil as he lies,
With his painted skin and his monkey grin—
    and leers into his eyes.
And before I knew what I should do, Phil Blood
    was on his feet,
And the Injun could trace the hate in his face, and his
    heart began to beat.
And "Git out o' the way," he heard them say
    "for he means to have your life."
But before he could fly at the warning cry, he saw the
    flash of the knife.
"Run Panther, run!" cried everyone, and the
    Panther turned his back,
With a wicked glare like a wounded hare,
    Phil Blood sprang on his track.
Now the spot of ground where our luck was found was
    a queerish place, you'll mark,
Jest under the jags of the mountain crags and the
    precipices dark;
Far up on high, close to the sky, the two crags
    leant together,
Leaving a gap, like an open trap, with a gleam of golden
    weather.
If a man should pop in that trap on the top he'd
    never rest arm or leg,

Till neck and crop to bottom he'd drop and
    smash on the stones like an egg!
"Come back, you cuss! come back to us, and let
    the Injun be!"
I called aloud, while the men in a crowd stood gazing
    at them and me.

But up they went, and my shots were spent, and
    at last they disappeared,
One minute more, and we gave a roar, for the Injun
    had leapt, and cleared!
For breath at the brink—but—a white man shrink,
    when a red had passed so neat?
I knew Phil Blood too well to think he'd turn his back
    dead beat!

He takes one run, leaps up in the sun, and bounds
    from the slippery ledge,
And he clears the hole, but—God help his soul!—
    just touches the t'other edge!
The edge he touches, then sinks, and clutches
    the rock—our eyes grow dim—
I turn away—what's that they say?—He's hanging on to
    the brim!
And as soon as a man could run, I ran the way I'd
    seen them flee,

And I came mad-eyed to the chasm's side, and
    what do you think I see?
I saw him glare, and dangle in air, for the
    empty hole he trod,
Help'd by a pair of hands up there—the Injun's, yes, by God!
I held my breath so nigh to death, Phil Blood
    swung hand and limb,
And it seemed to us all that down he'd fall, with the
    Panther after him;
But the Injun at length put out his strength and
    another minute past,
Then safe and sound to the solid ground he drew Phil
    Blood at last!
What did Phil do? Well, I watched the two, and
    I saw Phil Blood turn back,
Bend over the brink and take a blink right down the
    chasm black,

Then stooping low for a moment or so, having
    drawn his bowie bright,
He chucked it down the gulf with a frown, then whistled
    and slunk from sight.
And after that day he changed his play,
    and kept a civiler tongue,
And whenever an Injun came that way, his contrairy head
    he hung;
But whenever he heard the lying word "It's a
    lie!" Phil Blood would groan;
"A snake is a snake make no mistake! But an Injun's
    flesh and bone!"

PHILOSOPHY

BY V.F. STEVENS and S. BROWN   1941

The front door's proper wonky, the bottom 'inge is gorn,
    And the curtins in the passage is all mucked
        up and torn;
The banisters to the kitchen ain't there no bloomin'
        more,
And you ought to see the great big 'ole wot's in the
        parlour floor.
    We've 'ad no gas sin Lord knows when, but the
        missus she still grins,
She says we'll 'ave ter do our best wiv 'cold stuff'
        out o' tins.
    It's a licker 'ow she sticks it, she keeps
        cheerful night and day,
But *did* she lose 'er temper when the bomb fell 'cross
        the way?
    Well, the blinkin' fireplace went in two an' a 'ole
        came in the wall,
Wallop! went the dresser Yus! and that ain't all,
    O' course, she doesn't mind a bit what 'appens
        to herself,

But to 'Blitz' the photer of the kids wot stood up on
  that shelf—
  That prop'ly got 'er paddy up and ooooh! the fings
  she said—
Spesh'ly when she found she'd got a gash acrorst 'er
  ead,
  They put four stitches in it in the Aid Post dahn
  the street,
They're smart people there, they are! They patched 'er
  up a treat.
  We've 'ad 'er roof all mended now and she's back
  again wiv us,
And we carries on just usual-like wivout the slightest
  fuss.
  'ERE! I don't know why I'm tellin' you all this,
  'cos I can see,
There must be fahs-ends of us in the same boat just like
  me,
  Nah don't fink I'm complainin' 'cos that ain't
  in my line,
But fancy droppin' bombs at night on a little 'ouse
  like mine,
  I'll git me bloomin' own back, tho' I ain't got
  much cash,
I've bought some chalk, an' I'll wear it out? wiv free
  dots and a dash,
  They say that means we're goin' to win an' we
  mustn't be downhearted,
But blimey! I could a' told 'em that the very day it
  started,
  WIN!!! why, course we're goin' to win, the blokes
  ain't yet bin born,
Wot can pull 'airs out o' the lion's tail, an' 'old 'im
  up to scorn,
  He tried to drive us underground like a lot o'
  bloomin' ants,
Huh! took it on the chin we did but he'll get it in
  the pants.
  What's 'at? You're on Fire watch ternight and
  can't afford ter tarry?
O.K. China, so am I!!! I'll see yer later, 'Arry.

293

PHOTYGRAFS

BY H. M. BURNABY and HERBERT TOWNSEND.   *1947*

I've been out playin' . . . all day long, As busy as
    can be . . .
    I've only stopped since breakfus' . . . For my
    dinner . . . and my tea,
And when I've got through supper . . .
    An' . . . been put in my barf,
Tomorrow . . . Mummie says that she . . .
    Will take my . . . pho-ty-graf.
She's always takin' photygrafs, I cannot make out why?
    She's got a great big bundle now, They must
    stand quite . . . that high!
You'd fink she'd get so tired of it and never take no
    more . . .
    I asked her why . . . but mummie laughs, I wish
    I knew what for.
There's pictures of me . . . sittin' down an' standin'
    up . . . as well,
    I'm sure there must be fahsands more as near as
    I can tell.
She took me on a sheepskin rug wiv-out my clothes . . .
    all bare!
    And now . . . she wants annuver one, it really
    isn't fair.
I've asked my Daddy . . . and he smiles an' gives my
    ear a squeeze,
    Says . . . "parents when they're very old is . . .
    fond of memories."
Jus' like they say our old dog dreams of when he was
    a pup . . .
    That's why my mum . . . takes photygrafs . . .
    Cos . . . photo's . . . don't grow up!

THE PIGTAIL OF LI FANG FU

BY SAX ROHMER

TRANSCRIPTION FOR PIANO BY T. W. THURBAN.   *1919*

Performed by Bransby Williams

They speak of a deadman's vengeance; they whisper a
    deed of hell
'Neath the Mosque of Mohammed Ali.
    And this is the thing they tell.
In a deep and a midnight gully, by the street where the
    goldsmiths are,
'Neath the Mosque of Mohammed Ali, at the back
    of the Scent Bazaar,
Was the House of a Hundred Raptures, the tomb of a
    thousand sighs;
Where the sleepers lay in that living death which
    the opium-smoker dies.
At the House of a Hundred Raptures, where the reek of the
    joss-stick rose
From the knees of the golden idol to the
    tip of his gilded nose,
Through the billowing oily vapour, the smoke of the black
    chandu,
There a lantern green cast a serpent sheen on
    the pigtail of Li-Fang-Fu.
There was Ramsa Lal of Bhiwâni, who could smoke more
    than any three,
A pair of Kashmîri dancing girls and Ameer
    Khân Môtee;
And there was a grey-haired soldier too, the wreck
    of a splendid man;
When the place was still I've heard mounted
    drill being muttered by "Captain Dan."
Then, one night as I lay a-dreaming, there was
    shuddering, frenzied screams;
But the smoke had a spell upon me; I was
    chained to that couch of dreams.
All my strength, all my will had left me, because
    of the black *chandu,*
And upon the floor, by the close-barred door,
    lay the daughter of Li-Fang-Fu.

295

'Twas the first time I ever saw her, but often I
    dream of her now;
For she was as sweet as a lotus, with the
    grace of a willow bough.
The daintiest ivory maiden that ever a man called called fair,
    And I saw blood drip where Li-Fang-Fu's whip
    had tattered her shoulders bare!
I fought for the power to curse him—and never a
    word would come!
To reach him— to kill him!—but opium had
    stricken me helpless—dumb.
He lashed her again and again, until she uttered a
    moaning prayer,
    And as he whipped so the red blood dripped
    from those ivory shoulders bare.
When crash! went the window behind me, and in leapt
    a greyhaired man,
    As he tore the whip from that devil's grip,
    I knew him: 'twas Captain Dan!
Ne'er a word spoke he, but remorseless, grim, his
    brow with anger black.
    He lashed and lashed till the shirt was slashed
    from the Chinaman's writhing back.
And when in his grasp the whip broke short, he cut
    with a long keen knife.
    The pigtail, for which a Chinaman would barter
    his gold, his life—
He cut the pig-tail from Li-Fang-Fu. And this is the thing they tell.
    By the Mosque of Mohammed Ali—for it led to a deed of hell.
In his terrible icy passion, Captain Dan that pig-tail
    plied,
    And with it he thrashed the Chinaman, until
    any but he had died—
Until Li-Fang-Fu dropped limply down too feeble,
    it seemed, to stand.
    But swift to arise, with death in his eyes—
    and the long keen knife in his hand!
Like friends of an opium vision they closed in a
    fight for life,
    And nearer the breast of the Captain crept
    the blade of the gleaming knife.

Then a shot! a groan—and a wisp of smoke. I swooned
    and knew no more—
Save that Li-Fang-Fu lay silent and still
    in a red pool near the door.
But never shall I remember how that curtain of
    sleep was drawn
And I woke, 'mid a deathly silence, in the
    darkness before the dawn.
There was blood on the golden idol! My God! that
    dream was true!
For there, like a slumbering serpent, lay the
    pigtail of Li-Fang-Fu.
From the House of a Hundred Raptures I crept ere
    the news should spread
That the Devil's due had claimed Li-Fang-Fu,
    and that Li-Fang-Fu was dead.
'Twas the end of that Indian summer, when Fate—or
    the ancient ties—
Drew my steps again to the gully, to the
    Tomb of a Thousand sighs;
And the door of the house was open! All the blood
    in my heart grew cold.
For within sat the golden idol, and he leered
    as he leered of old!
And I thought that his eyes were moving in a sinister
    vile grimace
When suddenly, there at his feet I saw a
    staring and well-known face!
With the shriek of a soul in torment, I turned like
    a frenzied man,
Falling back from the spot where the moonlight
    poured down upon "Captain Dan!"
He was dead, and in death was fearful; with features
    of ghastly hue—
And snakelike around his throat was wound
    the pigtail of Li-Fang-Fu!

THE PILLAR BOX

BY GLADYS EVA KITCHEN and PAULINE WILTON   *1928*

It's silly to be frightened, but I hate to go to post,
And Nannie says when I come back, "Why child,
you're like a ghost."
Whenever I have letters and they send me down our
street,
"Just post this for me, darling," I get shaky
on my feet.
You can see it from our window, you can see it oh
so plain,
And I wish I could see it from the corner of our lane.
Each time I have to pass it by I get electric
shocks,
It's silly to be frightened but I hate our pillar
box.
It's silly to be frightened, but its mouth's so
very wide,
And though I can't look down it, I know its
dark inside.
It's like a big red giant, and on me it seems to grin,
And say, "Be quick, be quick my child, and push
those letters in.
Come, come, don't keep me waiting, I'm so hungry,
can't you see?
If I'm not given letters little girls are nice
for tea."
It's an ogre, I feel certain, at me it jeers and
mocks;
It's silly to be frightened, but I hate our pillar
box.
It's silly to be frightened, but it is so stiff and
round,
I wonder if it's got big feet the part that's
underground.
Maybe it was a dragon so perhaps it has a tail,
The fairies must have frozed it there, one night
of snow or hail.

It cannot move about, nor even bend to eat the grass,
   I wish it wasn't frozen in the place I have to pass.
Of course I haven't told a soul, they'd laugh, but
   my heart knocks.
   It's silly to be frightened, but I hate our pillar
   box.
It's silly to be frightened, and that is why I try
   To face that horrid pillar box and look it in the
   eye,
'Cause p'r'aps if I'm too frightened why the spell
   might come undone,
   And if it ever came unfroze I'd have to run and
   run.
I simply won't be frightened, when a girl's as big
   as me,
   She oughtn't to be frightened by a thing that cannot
   see.
I'll soon be wearing stockings now instead of baby
   socks,
   I'll just stop being frightened, but I hate our
   pillar box!

PINCHER D.C.M.

BY F. C. HENNEQUIN and CUTHBERT CLARKE   1916

The British soldier 'as 'is faults, 'e's 'uman like
   the rest,
   'E 'as the little weaknesses that's common to the
   best.
   'E's 'asty in 'is language, but you wouldn't call
   'im mean.
   'E's fairly open-'anded and I think you'd say 'e's
   clean.
'E's respectful to the women folk, wherever 'e may roam
   And 'e don't 'urt little children 'e's too fond of
   'em at 'ome.

299

'E likes 'is bit of grousing, but 'e's straight and
    'e can shoot,
  And there's one thing you can bet on, 'e doesn't
    burn or loot.
Now of course there *is* exceptions, there's
    bound to be you know,
  When you come to take an army of a million
    men or so.
I know one who's got a medal, and 'e well deserves
    it too.
  Tho' 'is principles was rotten, but I leaves 'is case
    to you.
'E 'adn't got no shame at all, 'e ses "What o! the
    loot!
  Bits and things dropped in a 'urry, we shall find
    when we're en route."
So we tried 'ard to convince 'im and 'e 'ad three
    scraps that night
  Because we named 'im 'Pincher' and it
    suited 'im all right.
When we got on active service, oh 'e 'ad a
    shocking blow
  For the orders about looting was most plainly N O,
    no
And 'e couldn't eat his 'bully' when he passed things
    on the road
  For 'e got the 'ump with thinking of the things
    'e might 'ave stowed.
But at Mons 'e turned quite cheerful, and I 'eard the
    blighter say—
  "There's no 'arm now in looting, where the
    folks have gone away.
For you see it stands to reason all the things
    they leave behind
  Will be collared by the Germans without asking
    Do you mind?"
But 'e didn't get much looting, we was moving night
    and day
  With 'ardly time to eat or sleep and fighting all
    the way.
Till one evening spent and weary, we 'ad a spell of
    rest.

In a village called Le—something—and then Pincher
did 'is best.
First 'e started on a chateau, just to see what 'e
could find
And 'e found most every blessed thing the
owner'd left behind.
When 'e 'ad to leave the chandelier it nearly
broke 'is 'eart.
And 'e'd a took the grand pianner if 'e'd 'ad an
'orse and cart!
You ought to 'ave seen 'im loaded with what ever 'e
could bring,
'E was full of clocks and vases all tied up with
bits of string.
'E got a marble statue of a girl without her clothes,
And a bust of Julius Caesar that 'e'd dropped and
broke its nose.
There was spoons in ev'ry pocket all mixed up with
bric-a-brac,
And half a dozen 'earthrugs, rolled up careful
on 'is back.
When 'e come into the café, we was looting on our
plan
I ses "Love a duck, its Pickford been and lost
'is bloomin' van."
We was just agoing to ask 'im where the dickens 'e
'ad been,
When a coal-box 'it us sudden, and the roof came
tumbling in.
All the bottles fell on Pincher, and it fairly
made 'im squint
When the lady with no clothes on 'ad a bath in
cream de mint.
Then a bullet knocked me over, and I couldn't laugh
no more,
When 'e dropped 'is precious 'earthrugs just to
lift me from the floor.
For tho' 'e knew 'e'd lose the lot, 'e stuck to me
like glue
An' when 'e got me in the lines, so 'elp me bob,
it's true,

301

'E'd got three bullets in 'im, 'e could 'ardly stand
    or see,
And the only loot left on 'im was 'is trousers,
    shirt and me!

PITY THE BOY
WHO'S GROWN OUT OF HIS CLOTHES

BY HARRY HEMSLEY   *1943*

Pity the boy who's grown out of his clothes,
    My clothes do not fit me at all
I was once very small, now I'm well in the cart
    'Cos I've started to grow very tall.
My elbows commence to stick out of my sleeves
    And my shoes they are pinching my toes
My pants shrink above me and nobody loves me
    I'm the boy who's grown out of his clothes.
It's jolly rough luck I think you'll agree
    To have to wear clothes not intended for me,
Such as Aunty's pyjamas, pulled in at the waist,
    Without any turnups, she says "It's bad taste"
And all just because I am growing so fast,
    And suits that once fitted they somehow don't last
And new suits need coupons, and then there's the tax
    So now I am wearing my Grandma's old slacks.
Grandma's not Grandad's, as wide as a sack
    Too tight in the front and too big at the back,
And feeling a draught every time the wind blows
    Pity the boy who's grown out of his clothes.

THE PLUMBER

BY *HARRY KENNETH WYNNE* and *CUTHBERT CLARKE*   1916

Performed by Bransby Williams

I'm a plumber, I ham, an' I'm proud o' me trade,
　　An' I tells yer I can't hunder-stand
Why Kiplin' should talk o' 'is soldiers and squads
　　When there's 'eroes like me in the land.
I was once called from bed on a cold, frosty morn
　　Fer ter go to the 'ouse of a toff,
Jest ter look at the tap in the scullery sink,
　　What they seys as they couldn't turn hoff.
Well, I shoves on me clothes, an' I puts on me 'at,
　　An I goes ter the 'ouse right away.
Ter hinspect this 'ere job, an' ter see if the case
　　His has bad has they'd sent round ter say.
They shows me this tap as they couldn't turn hoff,
　　They was right, 'cos I tried hit ter see,
Then I studies hit like, an' I scratches me 'ead,
　　An' I asks what they wanted wiv me.
The toff 'e explains as 'e wanted hit stopp'd,
　　So I asks for some hink an' a pen,
An' I makes hout a list o' the tools I shall want,
　　And I shoves 'em hall down, there an' then.
Then I goes ter the shop fer ter fetch 'em along,
　　But me wife, she was fryin' a chop,
An' there was me breakfast, hall tasty an' nice.
　　An' the smell of it tempts me ter stop.
I gets thro' me grub an' I puts on me pipe,
　　An' I sits down to wait fer me mate,
'E's a feller what fancies 'ome comforts, like me,
　　An' 'e never gets hup afore height.
When hat larst 'e arrives we goes round ter the place,
　　An' we starts on the job in a trice,
While the boys of the tradesmen, what call'd ter the
　　　　'ouse,
　　Stands hadmirin' an' givin' hadvice.
First we tries fer ter plug up the tap wiv a cork,
　　But the water squirts hall round the place,
An the toff, what was jest comin' hin hat the door,
　　Gets a gallon or two in his face.

'E dances about hin a terrible rage, An' 'e treads
    hon the kitten's 'ind legs,
  An' the cook 'ears hit squeal, an' she faints hin
    ⸱ han 'eap,
An falls 'flop' hin a basket hof heggs.
  By this time the water was hup to our knees,
An' the tables an' chairs was afloat,
  So the toff 'e yells hout, "Save the women an' <u>kids</u>,"
An' 'runs hoff ter borrow a boat.
  Then the greengrocer's boy, what was watchin' the
    scene,
Comes a-pokin 'is nose hin again,
  An' the himpudent feller seys, "Take my hadvice,
An' jest turn it hoff at the main!"

THE PORTRAIT

BY OWEN MEREDITH and ERIC MAREO   *1911*
Performed by Bransby Williams

Midnight passed! not a sound of aught thro' the silent
    house, but the wind at his prayers.
  I sat by the dying fire and thought of the dear
    dead woman upstairs.
A night of tears for the gusty rain had ceased but
    the eaves were dripping yet;
  And the moon looked forth, as tho' in pain, with
    her face all white and wet.
Nobody with me, my watch to keep but the friend of
    my bosom, the man I love;
  And grief had sent him fast asleep in the chamber
    up above.
Nobody else in the country place all round, that knew
    of my loss beside,
  But the good young priest with the Raphael-face, who
    confessed her when she died.
That good young priest is of gentle nerve and my grief
    had moved him beyond control.

For his lips grew white, as I could observe, when he
speeded her parting soul.
I sat by the dreary hearth alone; I thought of the
pleasant days of yore.
I said "The staff of my life is gone; the woman
I loved is no more.
On her cold dead bosom my portrait lies, which next
to her heart she used to wear.
Haunting it o'er with her tender eyes, when my own
face was not there.
It is set all round with rubies red and pearls which
a Peri might have kept,
For each ruby there my heart hath bled, for each
pearl my eyes have wept."
And I said "The thing is precious to me, they will
bury her soon in the church yard clay.
It lies on her heart and lost must be, if I do not
take it away."
I lighted my lamp at the dying flame and crept up the
stairs that creaked for fright.
Till into the chamber of Death I came, where she
lay all in white.
The moon shone over her winding sheet, there stark
she lay on her carven bed,
Seven burning tapers about her feet and seven about
her head.
As I stretched my hand I held my breath I turned as I
drew the curtains apart.
I dared not look on the face of Death: I knew where
to find her heart.
I thought at first, as my touch fell there, it had
warmed that heart to life with love;
For the thing I touched was warm, I swear, and I
could feel it move.
'Twas the hand of a man, that was moving slow o'er the
heart of the dead from the other side,
And at once the sweat broke over my brow, "Who is
robbing the corpse?" I cried.
Opposite me, by the taper's light, the friend of my bosom,
the man I loved.
Stood over the corpse, and all as white, and neither
of us moved.

"What do you here, my friend?" The man looked first at
    me and then at the dead.—
"There is a portrait here"— he began. "There is.
    It is mine." I said.
Said the friend of my bosom "Yours, no doubt, the
    portrait was till a month ago,
When this suffering angel took that out, and placed
    mine there, I know."
"This woman loved me well" said I. "A month ago,"
    said my friend to me
"And in your throat," I groaned "You lie!" He
    answered "Let us see."
"Enough!" I returned "Let the dead decide, and
    whosoever the portrait prove,
His shall it be, when the cause is tried, where
    death is arraigned by Love."
We found the portrait in its place: we opened it by the
    taper's shine.
The gems were all unchanged: the face was—neither
    his or mine.
"One nail drives out another, at least! The face of
    the portrait there" I cried,
"Is our friends, the Raphael-faced young priest,
    who confessed her when she died."
The setting is all of rubies red and pearls which a
    Peri might have kept.
For each ruby there my heart hath bled: For each
    pearl my eyes have wept.

A PRAYER OF EMPIRE

BY A. HICKMAN-SMITH and ERNEST LONGSTAFFE   *1940*

O God, our help in ages past, once more we seek
    Thy aid

To give us courage in the strife our enemies have
     made,
To help us in our direst need, so when the war shall
     cease
We stand again before the world symbolical of Peace.
We seek not aid to do a wrong or dedicate our might,
     Our mission in the present cause is Justice and
     the Right,
Protection for the weaker ones, against the greed
     and lust
Of those who would all treaties break and trample
     in the dust.
The whole wide world of Christendom while sleeping
     in its bed,
     Was awakened by the mad career of those who saw
     blood red,
     Whose greed for gain and despot sway ran riot in the
     night,
     And peace on earth will reign no more unless we curb
     their might.
So grant to all right thinking lands wheree'er
     Thou holdest sway
     A measure of Thy kindly aid throughout the toilsome
     day,
So when one day with peace proclaimed triumphant at
     the last,
     All tongues will offer thanks to Thee, Our Help
     in ages past.

PRISONERS OF WAR

MARGARET HODGKINSON, NOSMO KING and
ERNEST LONGSTAFFE   *1941*

We cry "God Bless our glorious fighting forces"
     Whose exploits echo through the watching world:
     Whose deeds of deathless valour stir the pulses

Where ere the flags of freedom are unfurled.
We honour too, our great civilian army,
The men and women of the Home Front ranks,
Whose splendid deeds midst carnage and destruction
    Have earned the nation's proud and grateful thanks.
Our Merchant Navy too we sing their praises:
    Stout fellows of the bulldog breed are these;
Despite the U. Boat, mine or bombing aircraft,
    They're still the masters of the seven seas.
But while to these we give our grateful homage,
    And willingly admit the Nation's debt,
There is another host of noble heroes,
    Whom we salute tonight lest we forget.
Lest we forget their great renunciation
    Of all the things a Britisher holds dear,
Home, friends, and freedom, these and more they offered
    And went with head held high to exile drear.
Midst alien faces, far from home and kindred,
    With hopeful hearts they wait the dawn of peace,
The weary hours crawl past with leaden footsteps
    Each day is one day nearer to release.
And all of them have left behind their dear ones,
    Who patiently with splendid courage wait
With anxious hearts for news of all their loved ones,
    Daily wond'ring what may be their fate.
None but themselves can tell just what they suffer,
    And though their bitter tears must often flow,
Bravely they smile when fondly thinking of them
    Proudly they face the world. Because they know.
They gave their liberty for King and Country,
    They made their sacrifice for you and me,
Bereft of all their hopes of fame and glory,
    They gave their freedom that we might be free.
So when you're offering your thanks and praises
    To those whose deeds will live for evermore,
Just spare a passing thought for many thousand
    Brave Britons who are Prisoners of War.

PRIVATE BROWN

BY ALEC KENDAL and HERBERT TOWNSEND   1941

When you talk of your heroes and such like,
  Have you ever heard tell of "Jim Brown?"
He was known in the words of the classics
  As the toughest tough guy in the town.
Dirty Dick and Dick Turpin were big shots,
  Sweeney Todd, you've heard all about him;
But I reckon them Sunday School teachers
  When you put them alongside of Jim.
He was called all the names you could think of,
  I could mention a few if I chose;
Names a chap wouldn't call his own missus,
  And you can't think of much worse than those.
He was one mass of swank, brawn and muscle,
  In his boots he stood round six foot one;
I don't know what he stood with socks off
  'Cos he never had any socks on.
His one pal was his own blessed shadow;
  It stuck to him all round the town,
But sometimes even that doublecrossed him,
  When the sun disappeared and went down.
There was only one thing in his favour,
  And I'd give him a medal for that;
No one ever saw Jim strike a lady
  Never once, without raising his hat.
When the war came and things went all khaki
  All the boys had joined up barring him;
Then the finger of scorn began pointing,
  And he fair got the wind up, did Jim.
Then a letter came for him one morning,
  But Anonymous it had been sent;
And inside was a tiny white feather,
  He had no need to ask what that meant.
From then no one seems to have seen him,
  Jim had vanished clean into thin air;
Half the folks never knew where he'd blown to;
  And the other half didn't much care.
There were all kinds of rumours about him,

309

And I heard a few rude remarks too;
Till someone said "P'raps he's enlisted"
That's the last thing they thought he would do.
But sometimes truth is stranger than fiction;
    I was reading the war news one day,
And right there, 'mongst the missing I noticed
    A Jim Brown had been killed in the fray.
There was nothing to say how it happened;
    Just the usual few lines that's all,
Saying Jim had gone out like a hero
    And had answered the last bugle call.
There's a grave in No-man's land somewhere;
    Where red poppies are growing all round,
And Jim Brown is the name that's inscribed there
    On a wooden cross stuck in the ground.
In my eyes Jim was never an angel;
    And he never intended to be,
But if angels wear wings up in heaven,
    He'll be wearing a pair I can see.
And whatever he was, there is one thing;
    Yes! in histr'y his name'll go down,
There'll be clicking of heels and saluting
    When they mention the name "PRIVATE BROWN."

PROVIDENCE

BY ERNEST R. HEALE, NOSMO KING and
ERNEST LONGSTAFFE   1938

Have you ever been broke, just to the wide
    With just what you stand up in, and nothing beside?
Living on scraps for best part of a week,
    When you can't get 'em and know where to seek.
I've been like that on a cold winter's night
    When the streets were deserted with nothing in sight
But a slow moving Bobby, whose job is to see
    That the public's protected from fellows like me.
Who get put inside to answer the Court
    Why they're wandering round with no means of support.

It always strikes me as a queer sort of joke,
   To pick on a man just because he is broke.
Do they think he enjoys wand'ring round in the rain.
   Soaked thro' to the skin with a dull aching pain,
Thro' his stomach forgetting its last decent meal,
   Just praying for the time when its too numb to feel.
Life isn't worth much when you get to that state
   Of just waiting to die with nowhere to wait—
I remember the time, its a long while ago,
   When I stood on a bridge, with the river below.
The last food I'd had was two days before
   And I never expected I'd need any more—
That night was the worst that ever I've known,
   With a dirty wet fog that chilled to the bone.
I set my teeth hard, and I set down my heel,
   On the rail that my hands were too perish'd to feel,
When a snivelling pup came out of the fog
   And whimpered at me—just a scrap of a dog.
Bedraggled and dirty like me, just a wreck, ,
   With a sad little face on his poor scraggy neck.
A few seconds more and I would have died
   But he just licked my hand and I sat down and cried.
And I covered the poor little chap with my coat
   And I carried him off, with a lump in my throat.
I took him along to the one place I knew
   Where they'd give him a bed and a biscuit or two.
They didn't feel keen on taking him in
   But the sergeant in charge gave a bit of a grin
When I told him the dog could do with a meal
   "I'll fix *him* up, but how do *you* feel?"
It may be, perhaps, that the Sergeant had seen
   The state I was in, I wasn't too clean,
The hunger and cold that I'd suffered all day
   Exhausted my limits—I fainted away.
Well, they fed me and slept me, and gave me two bob,
   And the following day they found me a job.
I've worked ever since and put a bit by,
   I'm comfortable now and I don't want to die.
I've a nice little house in a quiet little street,
   With a decent sized garden that's always kept neat,
I've worked there a lot when I've had time to spare,
   And I'm so proud of one little corner that's there.

With the pick of the flowers round a little old stone
  That stands in a corner, all on its own.
It bears an inscription—not very grand—
  The letters are crooked, but you'll understand—
That I wasn't too steady, I couldn't quite see
  At the time that I carved it—quite recently
Here are the words that I carved on the stone:
  "Here lies my friend—When I was alone,
Hopeless and friendless, just lost in a fog,
  God saved my life—with the help of a dog."

PUSHFUL JIM

BY THEODORE CURZON and KATE FLINN   *1917*

He wasn't much to look at was our Jim,
  But people thought a mighty lot of him.
He'd push along his barrer with his vegetable marrer,
  And potatoes and other useful things.
He'd had the same old pitch for many a year,
  And was known as "Pushful Jim" both near and fur,
When Jim Smith started bawlin', you'd have thought
        the roof was fallin',
  Tho' it's I who knows how gently he can purr.
He never pushes barrers now since he went out to France,
  He's done with spuds and cabbages, he's taking
        of his chance.
But when it comes to fighting you can bet your
        Shepherd's Bush,
  That "Pushful Jim" will be there when they make
        that final push.
Before Jim went I bought a handkerchief,
  All silky red, he said he'd always keep
And he'd use it as a banner, presented by his Anna,
  His regimental mascot so to speak.
He wore it, as he wrote, when on parade,
  And a lot of kind remarks the sergeant made,

When the sergeant cursed and strafed, why Jim he only
   laughed,
And he wrote to say that C. B. he'd been made.
"What's that," the acting sergeant said, "tied up around
   your face?
Attention! Private Smith, Advance Step forward
   from your place."
So Jim he strides out spick and span, My! how the boys
   did laugh,
As pointing to his red bandana, Jim said, "Oh,
   Sergeant,—Staff!"
One day they mentioned Jim in a dispatch,
   Ten German scouts, and Jim he bagged the batch,
In a somewhat startling manner, for he simply took
   his banner
   Which to his bayonet point he did attach.
Then he flings himself from off the parapet,
   In a way the C. O. says he shan't forget,
And they watched that flag awavin' till the whole
   durned crew they gave in,
   Oh Pushful Jim was in it you can bet.
He didn't write a lot to me, he didn't make much guns,
   He merely said "I've been across the lines to see
   the Huns,
And I showed them all that handkerchief, they hadn't
   much to say,
   In fact they really didn't speak, it took their
   breath away."
It's quiet there up in the market place,
   Without a sight of Jim's old honest face,
And I miss his dandy barrer with the vegetable marrer,
   Though the marks of where it stood you can still
   trace.
But we keep the spot still sacred where it stood.
   No one wants his pitch, wouldn't have it if they could.
How I miss his cheerful bawling, now he's out there in
   the brawling,
   But I pray that God will keep him safe and good.
We've got a Roll of Honour there, right in the market
   square,
   And Jim Smith's name is at the top in letters
   large and clear,

So I sit and dream of Jim in France, and I see him in
   my sleep,
And I pray one day he'll bring me back that red
   silk handkerchief.

QUESTIONS

BY ARTHUR DU SOIR and ARTHUR STROUD   *1936*

> *What curious questions children ask*
>   *The If?—and How?—and Why?—*
> *To answer them is difficult*
>   *However hard we try.*
>   *Arthur Du Soir.*

Oh, won't you tell me why, mummie?
   I wish you'd tell me, do!
Why soldiers' coats are red or brown,
   And sailors' always blue.
Why does the sun most always shine
   In daytime, when it's light:
And only just the moon and stars,
   And 'lectric lamps at night?
And where does daddy go all day,
   And not come home till dark?
Why can't he stop and play with me,
   Or take us in the park?
What should we do for food and things,
   If nobody keeped a shop?
Where should we go to in a lift
   That didn't ever stop?
Why don't kittens 'woof' like dogs?
   Or puppies 'miauw' like cats?
And why does auntie always wear
   Such funny lookin' hats?
If I woked up tomorrow,
   Like daddy, big and strong,

Would daddy be a little boy
Like me, 'fore very long?
There's lots of things I want to know
I've lost 'em in my head
'Cause I'se so sleepy, now mummie,
And want to go to bed!"
You say, "God bless my curly nob,
Just go to sleep"—but oh!
There's lots o' things you grown up folk
Will never, never know!

"RAKE" WINDERMERE

BY LEONARD POUNDS and HERBERT TOWNSEND   *1914*
Performed by Bransby Williams

Disgrace he'd brought on an ancient name;
    A smirch on an honoured crest.
He'd blotted the page of glorious fame
    That his family once possessed.
Eton he'd left beneath a cloud,
    And left in the greatest haste.
He'd proceeded whilst there in revels loud,
    Life's choicest hours to waste.
Sent down from Oxford next was he,
    The result of orgies wild.
He'd filled the cup of vice with glee,
    And a noble stock defiled
A nickname he'd earned by his acts of shame,
    'Mong comrades of many a bout.
From the broken shell of his own true name
    "Rake" Windermere stepped out.
As a fitting end to an angry scene,
    He had quitted the family home
With a tearless eye and a smile serene,
    He had started the world to roam.
Still lower he'd sunk than e'er before,
    And never a vice he'd shun,

Till even his roystering friends of yore
   Forsook him one by one.
He'd drifted at length with a tourist band
   To the land of the war-like Moor.
And there on the dreary desert sand
   Had disaster attacked the tour.
Approached by a tribe of bandit brand,
   The party had turned and fled;
But first a shot, fired by some foolish hand,
   Had pierced a Moorish head.
Besieged for a week on a mound of stone,
   And with water getting low,
The bandit chief had appeared alone
   And said "Thou art free to go,
If thou first deliverest up to me
   Of thy number any one,
So that True Believer's blood may be
   Avenged ere to-morrow's sun."
Each looked at each as he rode away.
   Grim silence reigned supreme.
The sun went down, and the moon held sway,
   Flooding all with silver stream.
Then a muffled form crept down the mound,
   With a wistful glance about.
Then with head erect but without a sound,
   "Rake" Windermere stepped out.

THE REFLECTIONS OF A PENNY

BY VALENTINE and T. C. STERNDALE BENNETT   *1916*

I was sitting in my armchair in my room the other
   day,
And I drew from out my pocket, casually,
'Mid a handful of loose silver—a penny old and worn
And it seemed to catch my eye immediately.

316

It was only just a penny, slightly battered, slightly
    bent,
And the date on it was almost worn away,
But I dreamed that as I gazed at it, it spoke its
    history,
And this is what it seemed to me to say:
"What do you know of this world for all your thirty
    years of life?
What do you know of its trials or its tears?
Why, I've seen full ten times more of life in just one
    single day,
Than you have seen in all your thirty years!
I have wakened 'mid a crowd of gold and silver in
    Park Lane,
At one, I've help'd to buy some typist's grub,
I've been thrown out to a news-boy for the special
    four o'clock
And spent the night down in an East-End pub!
I've carried folks for twice their proper distance
    on a 'bus,
Through me, couples spoon for hours in the park,
I've been dropped sometimes in streets and held the
    traffic up for hours,
And been mistaken for a half-crown after dark!
I've been thankfully accepted by a West-End flower-girl.
    I've been hugged by little urchins in the street,
I've been given to a chauffeur as a tip—and then I've
    heard
Language that I couldn't well repeat!
Some people say I should be proud, but yet, you know.
    I'm not!
I often hear some beggar make request,
And although my owner's got his pocket stuffed quite
    full of cash,
He chooses *me* in preference to the rest.
If ever I'm in church, and they are passing the plate,
    It's *I* who am dropped in immediately
While Scotchmen I have known have often shed a silent
    tear
At the moment they have had to part with me!
On some cold and bitter day outside an East-End
    pastry-cook's,

317

I have often known just what it means to stand,
While my tiny ragged owner gazes in with wistful eyes.
Clutching me within his little grimy hand.
P'r'aps I don't feel proud to know I only mean one
    small meat pie,
Or a sticky jammy tart maybe—but when
I see his little hungry face just lighten up with joy,
Well—I'm rather glad that I'm a penny then!
Yes! I'm only just a penny in my suit of dingy brown,
    But my colour doesn't fret me in the least,
And it never troubles me, although they laugh at me
    up West,
    For I guess I've got some real good pals down East.
And one reflection comforts me as through the world
    I roam
    That although a humble penny I may be,
I can say what some of your banknotes and quids can
    never say,
    That all the world has shaken hands with me!"

REWARD OF THE GREAT

BY F. RAYMOND COULSON and ROBERT M. ANGUS   *1913*

You in obscurity thirsting for fame,
    Think of the bitters the famous have quaffed.
Mighty Napoleon in exile and shame,
    Plato, the wise man, who never once laughed.
Wolsey brought down for base scullions to mock,
    Chatterton under the suicide's pall.
For Charles, the great King, and brave Raleigh—the
    block,
    And Calvary Cross for the greatest of all!
The axe of the heads-man for Mary, the Queen,
    For Joan of Arc martyrdom—flames raging hot,
For Antoinette's beauty the red guillotine,
    For Lincoln and Garfield the murderer's shot.

For Coriolanus the villainous thrust—
    Death's dagger stained black with ingratitude's gall.
St. John by base treachery laid in the dust,
    And Calvary Cross for the greatest of all!
Citizens lowly who yearn to be great,
    Glory, the goddess, has dust on her wings.
Pause in your bitter arraignment of fate,
    Gaze on the guerdons of Captains and Kings.
The rack for Galileo—torture and strife,
    For Cranmer the stake, cruel death for St. Paul,
For Socrates hemlock, for Caesar the knife,
    And Calvary Cross for the greatest of all!

THE ROAD OF THE 10,000 CROSSES

BY MILTON HAYES and H. NEIL VERNON   *1923*

These are the orders—orders divisional—
    Send to the Traffic and the M. P. too:
Clear all the roads for the stop-press batteries—
    Four and twenty guns, and they MUST get through.
Four and twenty guns coming up from Dickebusch,
    Bash 'em up to Passchendaele! The staff are in a
        stew,
Clear all the traffic for the stop-press batteries—
    Coming Hell for leather, and they must get through.
What's to be done? Limber, lorry, ambulance,
    Three days blocked—and the rations overdue.
Turn 'em off at Mill Cot. Chuck 'em on the roadside
    Anything so long as the guns get through.
Guns—Guns—creeping up at Vlamertinghe.
    Who gave the order? God knows who!
Roads like porridge, and they're shelling like the devil,
    But the stop-press batteries must get through.
East of Wipers—battered to a shambles!
    One-way road, and we're using it for two.
Mud—Blood—and the rain on top of it.

Clear up the traffic, let the guns get through.
Guns—Guns—passing the gasometer,
  Night—Black—and the mud like glue.
Couple up a caterpillar—ditch that lorry,
  Only twenty minutes till the guns come through.
Roads—roads—patch 'em up with anything:
  Horses—mules—yes—and dead men too.
Five minutes more! Tell the sappers for the love of God
  The guns will be here and they MUST get through.
Hark—now—through the thunder of the shelling—
  Comes the rattle and the thudding of the stop-press
    crew.
Four and twenty field guns clattering to Passchendaele—
  God work a miracle—They MUST get through.
Blast—that—driver with the ambulance.
  Park it on the run-round. Men, stand to!
The ragtime scallywags acantering to Passchendaele—
  Roads all clear, sir!—Guns go through.
Those were the orders—orders divisional,
  From somebody or other who had never seen the front.
Four and twenty field guns—ten thousand Lancashires,
  All gone to glory for a damfool stunt.
Twenty thousand Lancashires pushing into Passchendaele,
  Following the orders of the Lord—knows—who—
Ten thousand Lancashires slaughtered up at Passchendaele!
  Ten thousand crosses where the guns went through!
For the Guns—the guns—that galloped up to Passchendaele
  Never fired a shot,— but they went right through!
And who was the lunatic—the muddle-headed lunatic—
  Who sent them up to Passchendaele? No one ever knew.
But the "Traffic" got the order,
  "Roads" got the order, and the "Guns" got the
    order,
So the guns—went through.

THE ROADS

BY PETER CHEYNEY   *1926*

Life is a Road—a Road of Fate,
  To fashion as we will,
A glad or sad or broken road,
  To walk for good or ill.
A road beset with bitter tears
  Or lightened by a smile.
Luck gives a lift to happy ones,
  Misfortune adds a mile.
There's the road the children toddle,
  Leading to the realms of Youth.
A way still free from falsehood,
  A crystal path of truth.
There's the golden road of happiness,
  The road of Life's sunbeams
That hopeful road which lovers walk,
  A road of happy dreams.
There's the road that runs across the sea,
  The road of storm and spray,
The path of ships and sailor-men,
  Of ventures grave and gay.
There's the long, white country highway,
  Swept by the cool clean air,
A road of fragrant flowers,
  Ending in a sunset rare.
There's the road be-decked with roses,
  Where we do not see the briers
That hedge the way with bitterness,
  The scarlet path of liars.
There's the purple path of easy wealth,
  The tortuous road of pain,
The hard road of endeavour,
  And the road that's just a stain.
There's the road of glittering baubles,
  Turning drab skies into blue,
A road that's old as Hades,
  Where we search for something new.

There's the highway of ambition,
And the weary road of years,
Where we stumble slowly onward,
Gazing—hoping—through our tears.
All our roads must finish some day,
And when our sun has set,
And we look back on Life's highway
At the folk we've passed and met.
Then, perhaps, some happy memory,
, A word—may-be a smile,
Will wipe out the bitterness
And make our road worth while.

THE ROAD TO LA BASSEE

BY BERNARD NEWMAN and HAROLD ARPTHORP   *1934*

I went across to France again, and walked about the
        line,
    The trenches have been all filled in—the country's
        looking fine.
The folks gave me a welcome, and lots to eat and
        drink,
    Saying "'Allo, Tommee, back again? 'Ow do you?
        In ze pink?"
And then I walked about again, and mooched about the
        line;
    You'd never think there'd been a war the country's
        looking fine.
But the one thing that amazed me most shocked me,
        I should say
    *There's buses running now from Bethune to
        La Bassée!*
I sat at Shrapnel Corner and I tried to take it in,
    It all seemed much too quiet, I missed the war-time
        din.

I felt inclined to bob down quick—Jerry sniper in
      that trench!
A minnie coming over! God what a hellish stench!
Then I pulled myself together, and walked on to
      La Folette—
And the cows were calmly grazing on the front line
      parapet.
And the kids were playing marbles by the old
      Estaminet—
   Fancy kiddies playing marbles on the road to
      La Bassée!
You'd never think there'd been a war, the country's
      looking fine—
   I had a job in places picking out the old front line.
You'd never think there'd been a war—ah, yet you would,
      I know,
   You can't forget those rows of headstones every
      mile or so.
But down by Tunnel Trench I saw a sight that made me
      start,
   For there, at Tourbieres crossroads—a gaudy ice-
      cream cart!
It was hot, and I was dusty, but somehow I couldn't
      stay—
   Ices didn't seem quite decent on the road to
      La Bassée.
Some of the sights seemed more than strange as I kept
      marching on.
   The Somme's a blooming garden, *and there are houses
      in Peronne.*
The sight of dear old Arras almost made me give three
      cheers;
   And there's kiddies now in Plugstreet, and *mamselles*
      in Armentiers.
But nothing that I saw out there so seemed to beat the
      band
   As those buses running smoothly over what was No
      Man's Land.
You'd just as soon expect them from the Bank to Mandalay
   As to see those buses running from Bethune to
      La Bassée.

Then I got into a bus myself, and rode for all the
    way,
  Yes, I rode inside a bus from Bethune to
    La Bassée.
Through Beuvry and through Annequin, and then by
    Cambrin Tower—
  The journey used to take four years, but now it's
    half and hour.
Four years to half an hour—the best speedup I've met.
  Four years? Aye, longer still for some—they haven't
    got there yet.
Then up came the conductor chap, *"Vos billets
    s'il vous plait."*
  Fancy asking for your tickets on the road to
    La Bassée.
And I wondered what *they'd* think of it—those mates
    of mine who died—
  They never got to La Bassée, though God knows how
    they tried.
I thought back to the moments when their number came
    around,
  And now those buses rattling over sacred, holy ground.
Yes, I wondered what *they'd* think of it, those
    mates of mine who died.
  Of those buses rattling over the old pave close
    beside.
"Carry on! That's *why* we died!" I could
    almost hear them say,
  "To keep those buses *always* running from
    Bethune to La Bassée!"

RUMINATIN'

BY A. LESTER BEADLES and HARRY HUDSON   *1940*

I've tended this old garden now,
  Nigh three score year an' ten,

324

For I started as a tiny lad,
   Squire's granfer owned it then,
An' now the squire be gettin' grey
   So quick the years do pass.
While ruminatin', ruminatin'
   Cuttin' of the Grass.
I ruminates on men an' things
   Long dead an' gorn they say,
But I can tell 'ee different
   I sees 'em ev'ry day.
P'raps they're ghosts why 'oo can tell?
   They're plain to me I know.
While ruminatin', ruminatin'
   Leanin' on me hoe.
They come into the garden
   The gents and ladies too,
They've all a word for gard'ner Joe
   Wot's close on eighty-two.
But 'ale an' 'arty—God be thanked,
   An' still obeyin' orders
While ruminatin', ruminatin'
   Clearin' up the borders.
So when me last long path is swept,
   An' Joe is laid to sleep,
I 'opes they'll put me 'andy like
   So as I still can keep,
Me eye on these 'ere flowers o' mine
   Though I be lost to sight,
Still ruminatin', ruminatin'
   Around these walks at night.

SALLY'S UPS AND DOWNS

BY CHARLES J. WINTER   *1923*

I met a dear old friend of mine today,
   A chap I hadn't run across for ages:

Of course we talked about the good old times
　　And all that had occurred at different stages.
I asked about his mother and his dad,
　　And all his friends with whom I had been pally,
And then I said "one thing I'd like to know
　　If you can tell what's happened to dear old Sally?"
He laughed, then shrugged his shoulders, then he sighed
　　And said "I'm sure I don't remember quite all,
She's had so many curious ups and downs,
　　But still, I'll try to give a full recital.
Well, first you must know that her old uncle died,
　　He was fond of her, that you can tell,
For he left her a good sum of cash at the bank,
　　And he left her the business as well."
Said I "Well that was a good thing!"
　　"Oh not *very* good, for the business went wrong,
Till of all her wealth she was bereft;
　　And when she'd paid up and got everything square,
She just had *one* sovereign left."
　　"Oh dear," said I "that was too bad."
"Oh not *very* bad, for this sovereign I'm told,
　　She'd invested with great enterprise
In a lottery ticket, and heard later on
　　That this ticket had won first prize."
Said I "What a slice of good luck!"
　　"No, it wasn't a slice of *good luck*," said
　　　　my friend,
"It turned out an unfortunate job;
　　For being hard up, this same ticket she'd sold
Just a few days before—*for five bob.*"
　　"Well," said I, "that was bad luck indeed."
"Well not *quite* so bad, for the man who had won,
　　Out of sympathy so it was said—
Came to see her, got chummy, and then fell in love,
　　And after a time they got wed."
"Come" said I "that was good after all."
　　"Well not quite *so good* for this fellow it seems
Led a terrible dissolute life.
　　He spent all the money, then started to drink,
And came home and browbeat his wife."
　　Said I "Well that was rotten luck!"
"Oh not *quite* so bad for he died in a month,
326

And although all his cash he'd got through
He wasn't quite broke, for he left her the house,
  All crammed with old furniture too."
"Come, come, that was not bad," said I.
  "Oh well it *was* bad in the end," said my pal,
With a curious kind of grin,
  "For a thunderstorm came and the house it got struck,
And the whole of the roof fell right in."
  "Great Scott," said I "that was bad luck."
"Oh not *very* bad, for an old chest got smashed,
  And lay all in bits on the ground.
And there in a secret drawer open to view
  Were bank-notes quite ten thousand pound."
Said I "well her luck turned at last!"
  "I'm not sure" said he, "but she banked all the
      cash,
For somehow she felt that she must.
  And I'm wondering what's going to be the next move,
For I've just heard the bank has gone *bust.*"

SAM'S GUGGLE BOX

BY STAN MASTERS and HARRY STOGDEN   *1951*
        Performed by Stanley Holloway

Once upon a time there lived a man wi't name o' Sam,
  Thee mought 'ave 'eard that name afore,—maybe.
One day 'e got t'notion, that e'd like to sail on't
      ocean.
  So 'e went away an' listed, in 't King's Navee;
'E went to the recruitin' place, one mornin' on 'is
      bike,
  An' said—"Ah've coom t' join, wi' Drake, an' Nelson,
      an' the like."
Chap looked at Sam, an' said "You've got ambition,
      I can see.

327

But afore y' gets t' Admiral, y' starts 'ere, as
    A.B.
Now, what's yer name"—'e says, like that—as sharp
    as any knife,
    "An' what's yer occupation?—that's yer job, in
        Civvy life."
Sam looked quite 'urt at bein' spoke to curt, as you
    might say,
    But 'e stood 'is ground to show 'e weren't
        afeared in any way,
"Sam 'Awkins is the name" 'e says—as 'aughty as
    'e could,
    "An' me job is makin' "GUGGLE BOXES" out o' bits
        o' wood."
Bloke look'd at Sam from wheer 'e sat at desk, an'
    raised 'is eyes.
    An' on 'is face is what you'd call a look o' pained
        surprise,
"So you makes 'GUGGLE BOXES' eh!" says 'e "Ah've 'eard
    them tales afore
    Now what exac'ly would they be, an' what d'you make
        'em for?"
"Thou's got me theer," says Sam at last, wi' puzzled
    look in eye,
    "Ah must a' made some thousands, but they never
        towd me why,
Ah made 'em just six inches wide, an' just six inches
    tall,
    An' just six—why, they'd be six inches overall;
Reet in t' top Ah used t' put an' 'ole two inches wide,
    An' tho' Ah tried, Ah never could quite get me 'and
        inside."
Bloke says, "This GUGGLE BOX sounds a funny tale to
    me,
    So Ah'll put thee down as Carpenter"—an' so Sam
        went to sea.
One neet, a great big storm coom up, An' battered Sam's
    poor boat—
    An' officer nex' mornin' says "Ah! well,—we're still
        afloat,
There'll be some Carpent'rin', an' what not—to be done."

An' 'e looks at list o' names an' says "Sam 'Awkins
    'e's the one,"
'E sent for Sam, an' when Sam coom 'e looked 'im thro'
    an' thro',
'E says, "So you're a Carpenter—Ah've got a job
    for you."
"Nay lad," says Sam—"I ain't no Carpenter,—not me,
    Ah ne'er made nowt but GUGGLE BOXES 'fore Ah
    coom to Sea."
'E looked at Sam, as tho' poor Sam were talkin' thro'
    'is 'at,
    "A GUGGLE BOX! by gum, owd lad,—now what the 'eck
    is that?
"Thou's got me theer," says Sam wi' puzzled look in
    eye,
    "Ah must a' made thousands, but they never towd me
    why;
Ah made 'em just six inches wide—an' just six inches
    tall—
    An' just six—why—they'd be six inches overall;
Reet in t' top Ah used t' put an 'ole two inches wide,
    An' though Ah tried Ah never could quite get me
    'and inside."
Officer—'e glared at Sam, quite nasty, you could see,
    "Ah'll take thee oop t' Captain, 'e'll know 'ow
    t' deal with thee."
So oop in front o' Captain, Sam were taken right away,
    An' Officer explained what Sam 'ad said that very
    day.
T' Captain wi' a puzzled frown, were plainly very vexed,
    "GUGGLE BOXES!—ummm," says 'e—"what will tha'
    think o' next?"
'E turned to Sam, an' said, "Now look in all me life
    at sea,
    Ah ne'er did coom across one. Now then, what's it
    s'posed t' be?"
" 'E lad, you've got me theer," says Sam, wi' puzzled
    look in eye,
    "Ah must a' made some thousands, but they never towd
    me why.
Ah made 'em just six inches wide, an' just six inches tall

An' just six—why, they'd be six inches overall;
Reet in t' top Ah used t' put an 'ole two inches wide,
    An' though Ah tried, Ah never could quite get me
        'and inside."
The Captain takes a look at Sam,—"Ah'll tell thee
        what, says 'e,
    Thee go an' get a GUGGLE BOX, an' bring it 'ere to me."
So Sam gets leave to go ashore, to fetch a GUGGLE BOX,
    An' later on 'e coom's reet back to t' Captain's
        door an' knocks.
"Ah've browt thee one," 'e says, an' places box in
        Captain's 'and,
    An' Captain looks at it an' says, "This beats t'
        bloomin' band,
It is about six inches wide,—an' just six inches tall,—
    An' just six,—why,—it's just six
        inches overall.
    An' in the top theer *is* an 'ole, about two inches
        wide,—
An' blowed if *I* can get me blinkin' 'and to go inside."
    'E turns it round an' round, an' puts the 'ole up
        to 'is eyes
Like Nelson did afore 'im, wi' 'is telescope,—an'
        sighs,
    An' then 'e lost 'is temper,—"Drat the bloomin' thing,"
        says 'e,
"I can't see what it's for,—an' then 'e kicks it,—
        in the sea.
    Sam looks at Captain,—then at Sea, they both rush
        o'er t' t' side
An' look at box, that's floatin' on t' gently ebbin'
        tide,
    An' then as box drew water,—an' it sank wi'out a
        struggle,
They both distinctly 'eard it,—GUGGLE GUGGLE—GUGGLE
        GUGGLE.

SAM'S PARROT

BY V. F. STEVENS and LAURI BOWEN   *1934*

Optional introduction: Ladies and Gentlemen, I'm sure quite a lot of you must have heard about Sam Small, and of his various escapades. He is represented as being a very wide awake person, but in reality he is just as open to being 'caught' as anyone else, and this little monologue deals with an occasion on which 'Owd Sam' was anything but wide awake.

Na tha's 'eard of owd Sam, well, that very same chap
    Were out walking one day for a stroll
'E were padding down t' high street just casual like,
    On his way to sign on for the dole.
After passing three tripe shops 'e 'appened to come
    To a place 'e'd not noticed afore,
'Twere a shop where they sold diff'rent live stock and
       pets—
A kind of menagerie store.
'E stood garping in th' window at pups, slugs and birds,
    All int'rested like as could be,
When a voice near at 'and seemed to shriek in his ear
    "EEH LAD, AH KNAWS SUMMAT 'BOUT THEE."
'E were that surprised, an t' shopman inside,
Having noticed how Sam had turned pale,
    Come outside to see if owd Sam wanted owt,
'E were keen like on making a sale.
Sam said "No lad, there's nowt theer that I want
    to buy."
And then went as red as a carrot,
    "But that theer thing's champion—by gum, I'd like 'e."
And the shopkeeper yelled "WHAT! THAT PARROT?
    But no lad, tha reely could not afford 'e
Unless tha can spare fifteen quid,
    An' even at that price I'd lose on the deal,
She cost more'n that, that she did."
    Owd Sam were crestfallen, but then an idea
Must have entered the shopkeeper's head.
    "Theer's only one thing tha can do, lad, says 'e,

Take two of 'er eggs 'ome instead.
They're two bob apiece, an' all tha's to do,
Is to just shove 'em under a hen,
An' tha'll 'ave a parrot like *that* in a month,
Aye they're bound to be 'atched out by then."
Well, Sam dubs up brass and goes 'ome with th' eggs.
As pleased wi' 'imself as could be
And the Parrot's last words seemed to ring in his
ears
"EEH LAD AH KNOWS SUMMAT ABOUT THEE."
Now it must 'ave been fully six months after that,
When Sam went down t' High Street once more.
An' 'appening to pass by that very same shop,
'E 'eard someone calling from t'door
"EEH LAD", said the voice, "BUT AH KNOWS ABOUT
THEE."
Said Sam, "Aye, but tha's out of *LUCK!*
'Cos Ah knows summat 'bout *THEE* too, owd lass,
THY BLOOMIN' USBAND'S A *DUCK!*"

SANCTUARY

BY GWEN GIBBONS and NOSMO KING   *1948*

When you're working in a city does the longing come
to you
To wander in the country beneath the boundless blue,
Away from tears and turmoil where troubles never cease
And find yourself surrounded by an overwhelming
peace?
When sorrow overtook *me* I found I was alone;
Friends had shared my every pleasure but my sorrows
were my own!
So I wandered from the city, I walked for hours and
hours
Till suddenly I found myself amid the trees and
flowers.

The trees so tall and stately the flowers all
    smelling sweet,
As I walked my steps grew lighter and the grass
    caressed my feet.
I lay me down in wonder and thanked God for this kind
    of peace.
I knew I'd found a haven! My trouble here—would
    cease!
To those who seek wild friendships, mad days to shut
    out thought,
I pass to them this wisdom from a heart once over-
    wrought;
Go ye to the country and thank God on your knees,
    That, while men make heart-break cities, *He*
    sends us flowers and trees.

SCHEMES

BY GEORGE ELLIS and DAISY HILL   *1944*
I think you will agree that Army Orders nowadays, no matter
how important they may be are, in the end, always carried
out by the soldiers—well here's a little study in Army ranks
which I think bears me out.

The Brigadier held a pow-wow,
    "Gentlemen you see that hill—
Good for guns if we can make it,
    But first the infantry must take it;
So fourteenth foot-sloggers—Colonel brass hat-will
    occupy that hill—hmmmm."
The Colonel said to his company officers
"Please observe that hill or ridge,
    The Brigadier's in some dilemma,
So tomorrow, sharp at five Ack Emma,
    Captain cocktail with K— company will occupy that
    ridge!"
The Captain said to the platoon commanders

"On your maps, please note that rise,
The C.O., (stout old prewar soldier) has a notion
  As I've told you, that we, the cream of the whole
    battalion,
Should occupy that rise!"
  The subaltern said to the sergeant-major "I say—
    you see that thingummy-what-you-may-call
    it-how d'you-do-you-know-what-I mean-
    thingummy over there-that MOUND-well
Just parade a storming party,
  Give 'em sandbags—make it hearty,
And let our gallant lipstick eaters occupy that mound!"
  The sergeant said to corporal lead swing
"See that excrescence—mound—or knob,
  I dunno why the 'ell or wherefore—
All I know it's *orders* therefore,
  Take your lousy fourale wallahs And sit down on
    that knob!"
The corporal said to private pull thro'
  "Ere you—see that hill up top there?
Well now's your chance to flirt wiv' death,
  And *don't say 'Horlicks' under your breath.*
But shift your ruddy carcase up that ruddy hill—and
  stop there!"

THE SCOT'S LAMENT

BY KITTY KENNEDY ALLEN and KENNEDY ALLEN   *1929*
Performed by Will Fyffe

I'm Scotch and I'm married, two things I can't help,
  I'm married—but I have no wife—
For she bolted and left me—but that's nothing new,
  It happens sa often in life.
So I journeyed ta London, for that's where she'd gone
  With her lover to hide her disgrace.
And though London's a big town I swore I'd not rest
  Till I'd searched every street in the place.

And I tramped—how I tramped—weary mile upon mile,
Till exhausted and ready ta drop.
I would not give in, so I climbed on a bus,
And took a front seat on the top.
We came to a halt in a brightly lit square
To my joy, there ma lassie I spied,
Looking weary and worn, but thank heaven—ALONE—
From my heart—"Maggie—Maggie" I cried.
She gasped with delight as I rose from ma seat,
But a harrowing thought made me wince,
I couldna get off—for I'd just paid ma fare,
AND I'VE NEVER CAUGHT SIGHT OF HER SINCE.

THE ACCIDENT

BY KITTY KENNEDY ALLEN and KENNEDY ALLEN   *1929*

I may say, though I'm not proud, that I do not like a crowd,
I do not like a crowd—though I'm not proud:
To be ONE man in a thousand is a compliment,
    I know,
But *that's* a crowd and should not be allowed.
Now standing in the street and watching other people
        work,
    Or an accident, or something of that kind,
Just shows some nosey-parkers have got nothing else
        to do,
    And a crowd like that is foolish—to MY mind.
Now yesterday I saw a crowd assemble, and I thought
    What a lot of time some people have to spare,
But I felt it might be interesting, so *I* had a look,
    To see what made the silly fools stand there.
A poor man lay upon the ground, and moaned
            and moaned, and moaned,
    And a Scotch policeman took the case in hand,
And as he shook the injured man he groaned and
            groaned and groaned,

335

And fell down again when he was made to stand.
And the p'liceman said "Hi! VER-R-Y drunk—
　　Now then, pass along."
But a kindly coster very bravely spoke,
And said "'Ere guvnor, 'ave a 'eart, don't run the poor
　　bloke in,
　　Naw can't you see 'is blinkin' leg is broke?"
Then the constable took out his book and made a
　　note of that,
　　(Did he try to get an ambulance? not he.)
And a thrill of indignation ran amongst us as he said
　　"Pick up your leg and come along with me."
The poor man tried in vain to rise up once again,
　　We could not help, we would not be allowed.
This is a land of liberty, but NEVER interfere,
　　For the LAW will stand no nonsense from a crowd.
Then he sucked his pencil, and he said "Your name
　　and your address—
　　Oh, that's just round the corner—stir your peg,
And a man of your age should know better on a
　　frosty night
　　Than go sliding when he's got a wooden leg.
Sa just tuck your leg safely under your arm,
　　And in future avoid sloppy weather,
Ye tak' the dry road and I'll do the same,
　　And we'll hop—skip—and jump hame together."

THE SCRAPPER AND THE NUT

BY F. CHATTERTON HENNEQUIN and PHYLLIS NORMAN PARKER 1915

By his Christian name the "Scrapper," you may very
　　fairly guess
　　He was a most unholy terror and a bully more or
　　less,

336

In the neighbourhood of Hoxton where he lived but did
    not work,
    Things that were clean and decent he much preferred
      to shirk.
But hidden in his brutal mind, *was* something that
    was good,
    For when his country needed him, he did as all men
      should;
And though he'd never learned to work, he tried his
    awkward best,
    Until the Sergeant counted him a soldier with the
      rest.
Now the "Nut" in nowise differed from the others
    of his kind,
    For his socks and ties were perfect and his manners
      most refined,
His silk neckwear was immaculate, by dainty pins
    secured,
    His mother called him "Cecil," and his nails were
      manicured.
And underneath his wellbrushed hair, perhaps he owned
    a brain,
    Though he hated mental exercise, and thinking
      gave him pain.
He was fairly hot at tennis, and at most sports you
    could name,
    So when he too was needed, well, he had to play
      the game.
Now, call it chance or what you like, I hold it something
    more,
    These two enlisted side by side, and loathed each
      other sore,
For 'East is East and West is West', as Kipling truly
    says,
    And Hoxton and Belgravia, are different in their
      ways.
So it happened in the canteen, Cecil's temper to
    annoy,
    The "Scrapper" called him "Lizzie" and his
      "mother's only joy,"
Then the "Nut" put down his paper, as he languidly
    arose.

And smote the astonished "Scrapper" most
    severely on the nose.
The "Scrapper," give him credit, could have killed
    him on the spot,
And knowing what he might have done, he waited and
    did not.
For something woke inside him, as he scratched his
    puzzled head,
And "Love-a-duck I'll take it back" was all the
    Scrapper said.
And from that time, these opposites have seldom
    disagreed,
But try to help each other, in their ever present
    need.
For death close by their elbow, in the slaughter pen of
    strife,
Has taught them both the meaning of the riddle we
    call "life."
Day after day they struggle, while the "Scrapper"
    laughs at fate,
And the "Nut" is keen as mustard in his very
    muddy state,
And when each grim day's work is done, they lie down
    side by side,
And not yet is the bullet cast, that can these
    two divide.
Oh Private "East" and Private "West," may both
    come home again,
But if you live or if you die, the debt will
    still remain,
For 'tis of you and such of you, in days beyond
    your ken,
Our children's children will repeat; *you, both
of you, were men!*

SEEIN' THINGS

BY EUGENE FIELD   1922

I ain't afraid of snakes or toads, or bugs, or worms
    or mice,
  An' things 'at girls are skeered of, I think are
    awful nice.
I'm pretty brave, I guess, an' yet I hate to go to
    bed
  For when I'm tucked up warm an' snug, an' when my
    prayers are said,
Mother tells me "Happy Dreams," an' takes away the
    light
  An' leaves me lyin' all alone, an' seein' things at
    night.
Sometimes they're in the corner, sometimes they're
    by the door
  Sometimes they're all a-standin' in the middle
    of the floor
Sometimes they're a-sittin' down, sometimes they're
    walkin' round,
  So softly and so creepy like they never make a
    sound.
Sometimes they're as black as ink, and other times
    they're white
  But the colour makes no difference when you're
    seein' things at night.
Once, when I licked a feller 'at had just moved on
    our street,
  An' Father sent me up to bed without a thing to
    eat,
I woke up in the dark, an' saw things standin' in a
    row,
  A-lookin' at me cross-eyed, and pointing at me so!
Oh my I was so scared that night, I never slept a wink
  It's almost alluz when I'm bad that I see things
    at night.
Lucky thing I ain't a girl, or I'd be skeered to death,
  Bein' a boy I duck my head, an' hold my breath.

An' I am oh so sorry I'm a naughty boy an' then
   I promise to be better, an' I say my prayers again.
Gran'ma tells me that's the only way to make it right
   When a feller has been wicked and sees things at
      night.
An' so when other naughty boys would coax me into sin,
   I try to skwush the Tempter's voice 'at urges me
      within.
An' when there's pie for supper, or cakes 'at's big
      an' nice
   I want to but I do not pass my plate for them things
      twice.
No I rather let starvation wipe me slowly out of sight
   Than I should keep a-living on and seein' things
      at night.

A SENSE OF HUMOUR

BY E. H. ORGAN and NOSMO KING   *1949*

When spite is rife, and malice, with flickering,
      venomed tongue,
   When love and truth are crowded out and hymns of
      hate are sung,
When mankind is divided up and class made into faction
   And the deadly sin of envy is the spur of ev'ry
      action,
When healing wounds are opened by the poisoned spear
      of rumour—
   Then is the times we need, my friends, a little
      sense of humour!
A little joke, a bit of fun will shed a bright, clear
      ray
   Of sunshine just to brighten up our dreary lives
      to-day.
We had this gift in days gone by to meet all ills
      and danger,

We even smiled at death himself—God knows he was
    no stranger!
We're surrounded now by little men, such very little
    folk—
The self-important, fussy ones, who cannot take a
    joke;
How frail the structure of their souls, imposing though
    they seem;
When a little shaft of humour shatters all their
    self-esteem!
We loved the great ones of the past, we saw that they
    were big—
They laughed with us, at little faults, exposed
    by humour's dig!
Let's not get sour and humourless, that's not the
    British way,
    Let's give a joke and take a joke, good humour
    have its way;
And clear the spiteful murmurings the rancour that
    comes after
    With the cleansing blast of a roaring gust of
    good old British laughter!

THE SERMON

BY NOSMO KING and RACHAEL FILEWOOD   *1938*

In his study one night by the fading light
    Sat the vicar tired and worn,
Trying to dream of a novel theme
    For his sermon on Sunday morn.
He could think of none, for his little son
    Was playing around with his toys,
With laughter shrill as children will,
    He was making a terrible noise.
To meditate and concentrate,
    The vicar tried in vain,

If he could only find the key,
    Some peace and quiet to gain;
Just then he noticed a map of the world,
    And an idea entered his head,
"By a simple ruse, my son I'll amuse
    While I finish my sermon," he said.
"Take this map of the world
    To the nursery my boy,
Cut it up into little bits,
    Then try to piece it together again,
Till every particle fits."
    With a sigh of content,
As the youngster went,
    His longing to write increased,
And he knew the boy'd be well employed,
    For over an hour at least.
So he took up his pen and paper and then
    Beginning his task once more,
He'd scarcely written a single page
    When a knock was heard at the door,
With a confident grin the boy walked in
    His map of the world complete,
"How did you do it so quickly my son
    It's correct and so perfectly neat,"
"On the back of the map," said the little chap
    "Is the picture of a man,
And I thought if I only got *him* straight
    I must get the world to plan."
"You're right" said the vicar
    "My sermon I've learnt
You've made it so wonderfully plain,
    It's by getting men's hearts the right way turned,
That the world will come straight again."

THE SEVEN AGES BOTTLED

BY NOEL PHERNS 1931

Foreword:—Ladies and gentlemen, doubtless you are all familiar with Shakespeare's "Seven ages of man": now I should like to give my version of it—bottled.

Of infant cares you bear the brunt,
   You're mother's latest hope;
Well powdered down the back and front
   And ears all full of soap;
Then you gurgle, gasp and blink
   And you learn the way to drink . . .
From a *BABY'S BOTTLE*.
   You go to school and learn to write;
You're lanky, lorn and lean;
   They make you bath on Friday night
And yet you're never clean.
   But you quickly learn the knack
How to make your collar black . . .
   From an *INK BOTTLE*.
Well, perchance, you find a job
   And learn to 'push a pen';
You earn a wage of thirty bob
   And hobnob with the men
You assume a waggish mood
   And you learn to take your food
From a *BEER BOTTLE*.
   Anon, you find the youthful snags
When love holds you in check:
   Beneath the bed you press your 'bags'
And start to wash your neck!
   Then your hair's all nicely groomed
And your handkerchief perfumed
   From a *SCENT BOTTLE*.
There's furrows now upon your brow,
   You're going bald from care,
But aren't you pleased with wifey now
   She's given you an heir?

And you feel a real live wire
   As new 'spirit' you acquire . . .
From a *WHISKY BOTTLE.*
   Then comes a time when you feel old
And life is nearly through;
   'Tis then that fairy tales are told
Of what you used to do.
   Now you're getting rather stout
And a martyr to the gout . . .
   From a *PORT BOTTLE.*
And now, at last, you're on the shelf,
   A nuisance, be it said,
You haven't strength to dress yourself,
   It's time that you were dead.
For you've got no strength to eat,
   And you warm your poor old feet
On a *HOT WATER BOTTLE.*
   And to finish my rythme,
Just you think of the time
   When you can't draw your breath through your
      throttle;
At the foot of the mound,
   When you're put under ground,
There's a bunch of flowers
   STUCK IN A BOTTLE!

SHE

BY FRED GIBSON   *1913*

She is all I have to love,
   Quite divine is she.
Placing with a silent faith
   All her trust on me!
Through the cosy winter hours,
   By the fireside glow,
Oft I wonder if she loves me—

Yet can never know.
Steadfast eyes of palest blue,
Locks like silky down,
Touch as light as osprey tips
By faintest zephyr blown.
As I stroke her little head—
I fall beneath the spell,
She nestles closer to my side,
But love—ah! who can tell?
Though her mouth is small and shapely,
Something cattish there I see;
Just the old eternal woman
Peeping surreptitiously—
Nose—well, some might say retroussé,
But it gives her piquance rare,
Innocent her face of powder,
Beauty unadorned is there.
Though her wants are few and simple,
Money her most distant thought—
Oft her voice, with plaintive pleading,
Asks—and I refuse her nought.
Introduce you? Why, with pleasure!
Tho' she may not care for that,
"She" is rather shy of strangers,
She's my blue-eyed Persian cat!

SHELL SHOCK

BY NELSON JACKSON   *1920*

At Victoria Station a soldier I met,
The night it was dark and night it was wet.
His wrist had a sort of a twist and a jerk,
Which seemed as if uncontrolled nerves were at work.
I said, "Dear old bean, could you do with a drink?"
And he answered me kindly, "Well, what do *you*
think?"

"Two beers" was the order, and "Cheero," said I,—
"Cheero" he answered, and drained his glass dry.
"Could you do with another?" "Why, search me,"
    said he—
And his wrist still was twitching, 'twas painful to
    see.
"Cheero," again said he, "Cheero," said I,—
And he set down his glass, and again it was dry.
"Couldn't manage another I s'pose" I beguiled—
And "'s only a rumour" he said, and he smiled.
We filled up again and got on with the work
    With his wrist all the time on the twitch and the
    jerk.
"Now tell me," I said, "Just before I depart,—
    What's the matter, old son, is it shell-shock, or
    heart?"
And the poor fellow answered, his language was free—
"My gal has presented a wrist watch to me;
And if I don't jerk it and twitch it just so,
    I'll be blanked if I *can* get the dam' thing
    to go."

THE SHOOTING OF DAN McGREW

BY ROBERT SERVICE and CUTHBERT CLARKE   *1917*
Performed by Bransby Williams

A bunch of the boys were whooping it up in the
    Malamute Saloon,
    The kid that handles the music box was hitting a
    jag-time tune;
Back of the bar, in a solo game, sat Dangerous Dan
    McGrew,
    And watching his luck was his light o' love, the
    lady that's known as Lou.
When out of the night, which was fifty below, and into
    the din and the glare,

There stumbled a miner fresh from the creeks,
  dog-dirty and loaded for bear.
He looked like a man with a foot in the grave, and
  scarcely the strength of a louse.
Yet he tilted a poke of dust on the bar, and he
  called for drinks for the house.
There was none could place the stranger's face
  though we searched ourselves for a clue:
But we drank his health, and the last to drink was
  Dangerous Dan McGrew.
There's men that somehow just grip your eyes, and hold
  them hard like a spell,
And such was he, and he looked at me like a man who
  had lived in hell;
With a face most hair, and the dreary stare of a dog
  whose day is done,
As he watered the green stuff in his glass, and
  the drops fell one by one.
Then I got to figgering who he was, and wondering
  what he'd do,
And I turned my head and there watching him was
  the lady that's known as Lou.
His eyes went rubbering round the room, and he
  seemed in a kind of daze
Till at last that old piano fell in the way of his
  wandering gaze
The rag-time kid was having a drink, there was no one
  else on the stool,
So the stranger stumbled across the room, and flops
  down there like a fool.
In a buckskin shirt that was glazed with dirt he sat,
  and I saw him sway.
Then he clutched the keys with his talon hands—my
  God but that man could play!
Were you ever out in the Great Alone, when the moon
  was awful clear
And the icy mountains hemmed you in with a silence
  you 'most could hear;
With only the howl of the timber wolf, and you camped
  there in the cold,
A half-dead thing in a stark dead world, clean mad
  for the muck called gold.

While high overhead, green, yellow and red the North
    lights swept in bars.
Then you've a hunch what the music meant, hunger
    and night and the stars.
Then on a sudden the music changed, so soft that you
    scarce could hear,
But you felt that your life had been looted clean
    of all that it once held dear.
That some one had stolen the woman you loved, that her
    love was a devil's lie;
That your guts were gone, and the best for you was
    to crawl away and die.
'Twas the crowning cry of a heart's despair, and it
    thrilled you thro' and thro'.
And it found its goal in the blackened soul of the
    lady that's known as Lou.
Then the stranger turned and his eyes they burned in
    a most peculiar way,
In a buckskin shirt that was glazed with dirt he sat,
    and I saw him sway.
Then his lips went in, in a kind of grin, and he spoke
    and his voice was calm,
And "Boys," says he, "you don't know me, and
    none of you care a damn,
But I want to state, and my words are straight and I'll
    bet my poke they're true,
That one of you here is a hound of hell and that
    one is Dan McGrew".
Then I ducked my head, and the lights went out and two
    guns blazed in the dark
And a woman screamed, and the lights went up, and
    two men lay stiff and stark:
Pitched on his head, and pumped full of lead was
    Dangerous Dan McGrew
While the man from the creeks lay clutched to
    the breast of the lady that's known as Lou.

SHOULD A WOMAN TELL?

BY WILLIAM WALLACE   1921

I want you to picture a drawing-room scene
    In a snug little house in Mayfair.
Where the shaded light fell on the face of a man,
    Who was sitting asleep in his chair.
He was careworn and tired, with the strain of life
    In which others were "setting the pace,"
But the troubles and worries had gone for the day,
    And a smile hovered over his face.
The clock in the hall chimed a quarter to twelve,
    When he suddenly woke with a start,
To find at his feet shrinking back from his gaze,
    His idol—the wife of his heart.
He pushed back the beautiful curls from her brow,
    "My darling—why shrink from me so?"
"Oh, George,—I've got something to tell you,
    Something I think you should know.
I've waited so long for this moment,
    I've wanted to hear what you'd say,
But somehow . . . it's dreadfully hard dear,
    When one's said one would love and obey."
He rose from his chair like a man in a dream,
    His handsome face clouded with wrath,
And casting her from him like poison,
    In scathing indictment burst forth.
"So this is the end of my beautiful dream,
    So this is your secret, alas,
To think that the very foundations of love,
    Should fall in this shattering mass.
My future, my hopes—and ambitions,
    Lie in ruins—this bolt from the blue,
Has shakened my faith in the stoutest of friends,
    And all through the frailty of YOU!"
His twitching hands clutched at her lily white throat,
    The veins on his forehead nigh burst,
"False Woman," he cried, "speak your secret,
    And tell me—yes—tell me the worst."

349

She rose from the floor, and upon both her cheeks,
  Two patches of colour flamed red,
She looked at her judge with the utmost contempt,
  And these are the words that she said.
"Oh George—I've got something to tell you,
  It is you who should be "on the mat,"
A lady called round here this morning and said,
  You had left your cigars *at her flat!!*"

SHUT UP!

BY TED LYMBERY   *1919*

If you want to succeed, there's one thing to do—
  Shut up!
You'll find that your mouth is most useful to you—
  Shut up!
Just listen whilst wiser men have their say,
  You can practise to-morrow what they preach to-day,
For it's better to learn, than talk, anyway, so
  Shut up!
We're told speech is silver, but silence is gold, so—
  Shut up!
And a secret let loose is everywhere told, so
  Shut up!
You'll be far more respected, and I'll bet a pound
  That people will class you uncommon profound,
And a "very wise bird," if you just hang around and
  Shut up!
But when you're at home, and business is done—
  Speak up!
For a home that is tomb-like is very poor fun, So—
  Speak up!
Talk to your kiddies like most parents do,
  If you can squeeze in edgeways just one word, or two
But, when the wife's speaking, between me and you,
  ——————————!!!

SINGING LIZZIE

BY MAB DAVIS 1936

I'm a charwoman by birth, and me name is Missus Worth!
　Though the people round 'ere allus calls me Lizzie.
I ain't afraid of work I was never one to shirk,
　And you'll allus 'ear me singing when I'm busy!
Now I listens in a lot on a wireless wot I've got,
　Tho' I don't get much o' wot you might call 'leisure'—
But I thinks as music's *grand!* I jes' loves to
　　　'ear the band
　It reelly is me only bit o' pleasure!
You can 'ave them blokes wot spout. ('Evin knows wot
　　　it's *about!*)
　To let it orf on us! It isn't sporting!
And that poitry they read, well! *I* can't see the
　　　need
　To 'owl it out like some ole cat wot's courtin'—
Last night I 'ears a gel wot could play, *and* sing
　　　as well!
　"Songs at the pianner" so they told me!
'Ow she done it I can't think most o' mine are "At
　　　the *sink*—"
　And once I gets agoing you can't 'old me!
When I'm working for the folks wot's alivin' at the
　　　"Oaks,"
　It's "Red sails in the Sunset" while I'm scrubbin'!
And it's "Onward Christian Soldiers" tho' it do go
　　　up so *high!*
　While the brasses and the silver I'm a rubbin'.
"Jes' a song at twilight's" a favou*rite* with me.
　It helps me clean the grate and sift the cinders!
But the "Grey home in the West" is the one I likes
　　　the best,
　I busts meself on that when cleanin' winders!
I've another repetory and it's quite a different story!
　When I'm workin' for that lot up at the "Lilocks"
She makes sich a "ter-do" if I breaks a thing or
　　　two

MEAN! they are a reg'lar lot of Shy-locks!
Once, I upsets me pail, an' I sings "The Long, long
    trail"
An' me lady tells me orf My! She was frorsty!
I let 'er 'ave 'er say then I sez to 'er "Good-day"
An' I treats 'er to a little bit of Tosti!
When Missus Jones was bad 'Twas pewmonier she 'ad!
    I jes' pops in a song or two to give 'er—
I sings 'er "Poor ole Joe" And "We fink you oughter
    go!"
And finishes with "Gather at the River."
She seemed a bit depressed, still I felt I'd done me
    best—
    There's nothing like a song or two to *cheer!*
So when you're over busy, why not send for "Singing
    Lizzie?"
'Arf a crown a morning! AN' me beer!

SIXPENCE

BY F. RAYMOND COULSON   *1913*

When you and I were little boys,
    (Or little girls) with little toys,
What was the crown of all our joys?
    Sixpence!
O childhood! O lost happy land
    Where we in ecstacy would stand,
On getting, from some kindly hand,
    Sixpence!
But when, by grim parental power,
    Coerced, we viewed with tearful glower
The moneybox that swallowed our
    Sixpence!
And now, arrived at man's estate,
    We still discern its worth and weight,

352

Though less we may appreciate
   Sixpence!
What sends a wire to cause a stir?
What makes inferiors defer?
What makes the waiter call you "sir?"
   Sixpence
O little coin, a tender spot
   For you I keep. I grieve a lot
To think the income tax is not,
   Sixpence.
In fact sometimes, amid my mirth,
   I think that nothing on this earth—
Not even life itself is worth
   Sixpence.
And so its praises I shall shout,
   And so I say, with soul devout,
Friends, may we never be without,
   Sixpence.

SMILE!

BY MILTON HAYES   *1920*

I've searched the world's philosophies,
   And found much good in most of 'em,
Experience has taught me sense the while,
   And I've come to this decision:
That, thro' life, man's noblest mission
   Is to show the other fellow how to smile.
The man who smiles is ever young,
   For age can't make him old;
He greets the grey old work-a-day
   And turns it into gold.
His eyes are wise, like summer skies,
   He steals the sun's fair beams,
And when the world seems wrapt in gloom,
   And life a dismal, darkened room,
He opens up his wondrous store,

And brings the sunshine back once more;
And, when he smiles, it only seems
Our fears were naught but foolish dreams.
Smile when you lose. Smile when you win,
  Fate cannot conquer the man who can grin.
'Tis the armour of wisdom that naught can defile,
  So smile, and, in smiling, make other folk smile.
I've tried my philosophy, proved that it's true
  In love and in war, and it's sound thro' and thro',
And I'll back it right on to the very last smile,
  You'll get these where you want, if you know how to smile.
And when I'm a ghost, from vanities freed,
  You'll find I'll be still advocating this creed,
I'd be proud of an epitaph couched in this style—
  He lived.—loved—and tried—and he died *with a smile.*"

THE SNOB

BY WISH WYNNE   *1939*

It's sickening straight it is and every day it's just
      the same,
  When I come 'ome from school my mother she
Says yer needn't take yer 'at off take these boots 'ome
      and be sharp,
  'Cos until yer get the money there's no tea.
Me father 'e's a snob yer know 'e mends boots, father
      does,
  'E says 'e's always on is uppers too.
But they never 'as no money nor no nothing doesn't
      snobs.
  I wish 'e adn't been a snob I do.
I wish me father could 'ave been a policeman,
  I'd set 'im on a boy wots on ter me.
Or else the driver of a 'lectric tramcar.
  Then I could ride on it and not pay nothing see.

A girl wots in our class at school she is a stuck
    up cat.
She's got the measles now and a good job.
She's always swanking just because 'er father is a
    postman.
Yer can't swank when your father is a snob.
There's the blooming school-bell ringing I'll be late
    again you see,
And tomorrow's our examination day.
I bet yer what yer like I fail again I always do,
    And it's not my fault I don't care what yer say.
Oh! I do 'ate to stay at 'ome, I like our school yer
    know.
They learn us French they do, and Latin too.
A dandelion it ain't a dandelion at all it ain't,
    It's a liontedongterraxecum, it's true.
And now we're 'aving cooking classes,
    We cook such lovely cakes and pies as well.
I like the cooking classes best of all things
    But I get so starving 'ungry with the smell.
I asked me mother yesterday why she don't make us
    cakes,
    She says she can't afford to with us mob,
She says she dunno 'ow it manages to run to bread
    and dripping.
    Look at me boots! Now you'll know me dad's a snob.
Young Lily Smith, the ugly cat, that lives next door
    to us,
    Says she's going on the pictures when she's big.
If they 'ave 'er in a picture I shall never go and see it,
    'Cos 'er face is just the image of a pig.
'Er father is a 'shuvver, yes 'e drives a motor car,
    And now she is as lucky as yer like,
'Cos 'e ran into a girl today and 'it 'er in the boro,
    And after that 'e run over a tyke.
I'm sick of running errands if I tell yer,
    I'm sick of lots of things as well as that.
I'm sick of minding babies and I'm sick of washing
    pots up
    And I'm sick of Gladys Palmer, too, the cat.
When I grow up a woman and get married, if I do,
    There's three things I won't do I bet a bob.

I'll never live in our street, and I'll never 'ave
   no children.
And I'll never 'ave a 'usband wot's a SNOB.

A SOLDIER'S REMINISCENCES

BY BERT LEE and ERNEST HASTINGS   *1915*

I am an old Soldier with hair iron grey,
   My mem'ry's not bad tho' I'm sixty today;
Or else sixty-two; I can't be sixty-four,
   Well, maybe I am, but I'm not a day more.
I can reckon it out, I was born in—dear me!
   Why at that rate I must be turned seventy-three.
Dear me, this confusion it makes me upset,
   Why I'm eighty I think—I forget— I forget!
Only loved once, 'twas a girl called Elaine,
   Elaine or Priscilla, no! perhaps it was Jane—
However, one evening my brain in a whirl,
   I went to her father and asked for the girl.
Said he "Which girl is it? for I possess three,"
   I said "Gladys Maud is the best girl for me."
Now did he consent in a tone of regret,
   Or say "Take the three?"—I forget— I forget!
I first joined the Army in seventeen ten,
   No, that can't be right for I wasn't born then,
'Twas eighteen six three, wrong again, it was not,
   No, that's somebody's telephone number I've got.
They asked me what regiment I'd like to choose,
   Would I join the Hussars? I said "No, the Who's Who's."
'Twas with General Buller we captured De Wet,
   Or did he catch us? I forget, I forget!
Ah! well! I suppose that I get very old,
   And I'm not so much use in the Army I'm told,
So I just jog along as the days come and go,
   And wait for the call that is coming I know,

When the final halt comes, and I hear the last call,
    That comes from the Greatest Commander of all,
Then whatever there is in the past to regret,
    I shall hand up my sword and just hope He'll forget.

THE SOLILOQUY OF AN OLD PIANO

BY LESLIE HARRIS

I'm only a poor old wornout thing,
    With many a broken and rusty string;
And I'm wond'ring what will they do with me now?
    'Tis a subject that worries me greatly, I vow.
Will they chop me up to make firewood of,
    Or keep me, unused, for the sake of old love,
Or seeing that the music within me is dead,
    Will they make me into a bookcase instead?
Taking away all my poor old inside,
    And leave me standing, a piano that's died.
I once had a pow'rful and brilliant tone,
    And a strength of vibration entirely my own.
But now, all I have is a tinkling sound,
    And you'll find, by the way, if you turn me around,
That my back is all torn and my sound-board is split,
    And I'm not like a decent piano a bit.
And tho' with art-muslin my frame they may deck,
    Inside I am still but a useless old wreck.
I've thundered out fugues by Sebastian Bach,
    Till I thought ev'ry board in my body would crack.
I've murmured sweet Mendelssohn's Lieder ohne Worte
    And music, Ah me!, of a diff'rent sort.
Chubby fingers have thumped me in innocent glee,
    Little recking the pain they were causing to me.
Love's fingers have strayed o'er my ivory keys,
    And I've echoed back music I well knew would please.
For I seemed to be speaking the love of true hearts
    Ay! I've had to play many and various parts.

357

I've sounded forth love, and I've sounded forth strife.
  And all the emotions of frail human life.
And it's hard for a poor old piano like me,
  To be in this doubt as to what I shall be.
For a new one is coming I hear them all say,
  So I, now, of course, must get out of the way.
So I'm wondering what they will do with me now.
  'Tis a subject that worries me greatly, I vow.
Will they chop me up to make firewood of,
  Or keep me unused for the sake of old love—
Or, seeing that the music within me is dead,
  Will they make me into a book-case instead?
Taking away all my poor old inside,
  And leave me standing, a piano that's died.

SOLILOQUY OF A TRAMP

BY GERALD MORRISON   *1932*
Performed by Chesney Allen

Why am I sittin' on this 'ere seat,
  Feelin' so discontent?
'Cos I'm 'ungry and weary, and fed up with life—
  I'm broke—yus—I ain't got a cent.
I've walked and I've walked, till me boots is wore out,
  With no breakfast, no dinner nor tea.
And 'atred and bitterness fills me w'ole soul,
  Why the 'ell do they stare at me?
Yus, I'm fed up with life, and wish I wos dead,
  But nobody seems to take 'eed.
Why, I'd barter me soul, and swear black was white,
  If I could sit down to a FEED!
Just look at them swells in their fine motey cars—
  'undreds in every street,
They chokes you with dust, or they splash you with
      mud,
  From the top of yer 'ead to yer feet.
They never goes 'ungry—they wastes enough food
  To feed dozens of kids ev'ry day.

358

If they had to work for their bit o' grub—
    Well, God 'elp 'em, that's wot *I* say.
And you bows and you scrapes and you takes off yer 'at
    To the Duchess, the Duke and the h'Earl.
Then you reads all about their carryings on,
    In the papers all over the world!
They're always in some kind o' trouble or mess,
    Or else their digestion is gorn,
I've never been troubled in that kind o' way,
    No, never—not since I was born!
Still, when all's said and done, they carn't have it
        all,
    There's something that we all can share,
The right to live in this funny old world,
    And to breathe the Almighty's fresh air.
I've 'ealth and I've strength, and I goes where I
        likes,
    And I don't want no h'ancestral 'alls.
So between you and me, this funny old life
    Ain't quite so bad, after all!
Keep joggin' along with a jolly old song,
    You carn't do much 'arm, and you carn't go far
        wrong.
When we've finished with life, and we've passed
        through death's door—
    Well, we're all the *same* then both the rich
        and the poor!

SOLILOQUY OF THE FIRE

BY VALENTINE   *1917*

You, all of you, have known me since the day that
    I was born,
    You leave me reluctantly each night, you welcome
        me each morn.
In the summer I'll acknowledge that you don't see me
    a lot,

359

But in winter you'll confess that I'm the best pal
    you have got.
You always make a fuss of me when I am bright and hot,
    But there's no language bad enough for me if I am
    not.
And even when I'm dying you don't send in to enquire
    You let me die and go to bed that's how you treat
    your fire.
I find that as a rule young couples love me best at
    night,
    For I'm always such a good excuse for turning out
    the light.
She'll start to tell him fairy tales as maidens often do,
    Then they gradually get closer and he tells her one
    or two.
Till her head rests on his shoulder and she gazes in
    his eyes
    And the love that lies within them, well it lies,
    and lies, and lies.
One big armchair is generally all that they require
    And you'd think the very last thing that they needed
    was a fire!
In railway station waiting-rooms I'm a puzzle without
    doubt,
    For when you hope to find me in, you always find me
    out.
In some homes that I know, wives treat me like their
    husbands quite,
    For they find they've got to watch us or we both go
    out at night.
It's wonderful the pow'rs I have if I am not
    controlled,
    People insure against me in enormous sums I'm
    told.
And though I ruin some, yet I help others to retire,
    Yes I know lots who bless the chap who first invented
    fire.
But though now I mayn't mean much to you there'll
    come a time I'm sure,
    When you'll cherish me far closer than you've ever
    done before.

When you're getting old and feeble and your hair is
    turning grey
And you sit beside me in your chair three-quarters
    of the day.
Then I'll conjure up before you mem'ries of the long
    ago.
And I'll bring back sweet dream-visions of the days
    you used to know,
Faces you have loved and lost, regrets, hope, joy,
    desire
    It is only I can bring them back to you, just I,
        your fire!

SOMEONE

BY V. F. STEVENS   1945

Someone threw a shower of black confetti in the air.
    It was a flock of swallows and they floated
        everywhere.
Someone took a big black cloud and squeezed with might
    and main.
    Then draped it all around the sun and let it drip
        with rain.
Someone took a box of paints and spread across the
    sky
    An arc of rainbow colours and left it there to dry.
Someone tucks the autumn sun behind the old church
    spire
    And makes the highway and the trees appear to be on
        fire.
Someone lays in winter a carpet soft and white,
    Then rolls it up again in Spring to make it fade
        from sight.
Someone on a Summer eve will dust the flowers with
    dew.
    Do you know who that someone is? Why certainly
        you do!!

THE SPARROW

BY WILLIAM H. DAWES and NOSMO KING   *1948*

A stealthy step, an opening door, a pencil beam of
    light;
    A grasping hand—and Jim the Rat was gone into the
      night
The Rat! All London knew that name, though none had
    seen his face;
    Grim stories of his evil deeds were told from place
      to place,
And ev'ry lawful citizen had but one thought in
    mind:—
    "The Rat must come to justice—he's a menace to
      mankind!"
O, passing strange, though mercy's cup is ours with God
    to share,
    Pardon and pity for a fellow creature is so rare!
Love shall grow where love is sown—but Jim the Rat
    knew none,
    And just as he was hated so he hated everyone.
And yet the basest of us has some hidden spark within,
    Some secret touch of the Divine, tho' blackened
      o'er with sin;
And, as through alley ways and dark back streets his
    way he'd wend,
    His lone, embittered spirit sought—and sought in
      vain—a friend.
A little bird fell from its nest one windy day in
    Spring,
    And lay upon the carriage-way with tiny broken wing;
The passing crowd, they saw it there, helpless and
    frightened eyed.
    They saw it there—and yet pass'd by upon the other
    side.
Yet one there was who noticed it—a lonely, outcast
    man;
    He picks it up—the bird has found its Good
    Samaritan.

They, who ignored the sparrow, had ignored the outcast
    too.
The common bond between them gave him grace, Christ's
    work to do.
Skillfully, yet tenderly the broken wing was set,
    And 'neath his ragged coat he gently placed his
    new-found pet.
He took it home with him; he calmed its fears and
    eased its pain,
    And nursed his little feathered pal to health and
    strength again.
At length, one Sunday eve, it ventured on a trial
    flight,
    With Jimmy following close behind and keeping it
    in sight.
It flew a little way, then fell—beside an open door
    Of a little church that Jim the Rat had never seen
    before.
He peered within. With throbbing heart, he listened
    to the sound
    Of music and of words that held him rooted to the
    ground.
They echoed in the arches and through the rafters
    rang—
    A choir of children's voices—and this is what they
    sang:
"He sees the little sparrow fall, it meets His tender
    view,
    If He so loves the little birds, I know He loves
    me too."
Then could it be (it seem'd so from the message of
    those words)
    That there was One who cared, like Jim, for little
    broken birds?
And could such love and tenderness be for the likes
    of him?
    With wistful hope he shyly crept within the precincts
    dim,
Just as he was—a man unclean in body and in soul,
    Seeking that unkown Friend whose pitying love might
    make him whole.

And ere the Evensong was ended, Jimmy knew in part
  That here was found a salve divine to heal his sinful
    heart.
God moves in a mysterious way, His wonders to proclaim,
  He is His own interpreter, and He makes all things
    plain.
And in that church unto this day the oft-told tale is
    heard,
  How Jim the Rat was brought to God—by a little
    broken bird.

THE SPHINX AND THE WOMAN

BY LESLIE T. CROSSLEY and PERCY WATSON   *1915*

Under the sand 'neath the shade of the Sphinx
  Where the desert and Cairo part
Lies a dark eyed Arab girl
  Who died of a broken heart.
She lived in the city of White and Gold
  With its palm-trees and ever blue sky
And no one in Egypt knows the truth
  But the Sphinx who stands on high.
She sold perfumes in an old Bazaar
  Where the travellers rest awhile.
And many men brought her Mena scent
  For the sake of an Arab girl's smile.
But one stayed longer than the rest
  He came from a far-off land
And her lonely heart beat wild with joy
  When he bent and kissed her hand.
Love comes but once to the Eastern race
  So strong that it cannot die
And many a story of passion's greed
  Might be told by the Sphinx on high.

She gave her soul to this Englishman
  While he swore by his God above
She was his all, his guiding star
  And nothing would kill his love.
Alone in the desert of silence
  Wrapped in the spell of the East
With only the Sphinx as a witness
  They revelled in love's own feast.
But little she knew of the Western World
  Or the price she would have to pay
Till his ship went gliding down the Nile
  Gliding gliding away.
In a West End club he tells his friends
  The romance he had in the East
His story causes many a laugh
  While never a man says "beast"
The woman's version none shall hear
  Only the Sphinx on high.
No one is there to curse mankind
  When the desert hears her cry.
The man is petted and loved by all
  He lives in Society's whirl
Where little is known of his callous heart
  Or the truth of that Arab girl.
Slowly she creeps from the old Bazaar
  Down the winding Cairo street
Shunned, disgraced a fallen soul
  Afraid her race to meet.
Leaving the city of White and Gold
  In the desert she seeks her rest
And never a sound is heard from the girl
  Or the babe that clings to her breast.
Under the sand neath the shade of the Sphinx
  Where the desert and Cairo part
Lies a dark eyed Arab girl
  Who died of a broken heart.

SPITFIRE STORY

BY JACK BRITTAIN and HERBERT TOWNSEND   1944

Ain't feeling quite so good to-day—I'm even off my
    beer;
  Altho' they've given me ten days leave—I still feel
    kinda queer,
I've had a nasty shock you see—I've lost my biggest chum;
  It happened just a week ago—and better men don't
    come.
My pal! a famous fighter ace—D.S.O. and D.F.C.
  His score of Jerry busses had just reached twenty-
    three.
Squadron Leader Tony Brand, the finest bloke I've met,
  Him and me was really pals—that makes you smile I'll
    bet.
Him a proper English gent—Public School and Oxford
    Blue
  And me—a common cockney bloke—just an A. C. 2.
A Spitfire Fighter Pilot and his rigger—that was us,
  The bloke wot did the scrapping, and me what did
    his bus.
A "fighting team" he said we were—altho' he'd got
    three rings,
  "Jimmy you're all right" he said—altho' he'd got
    the wings
"You're the bloke that I depend on when I'm up there
    in a fight,
  I can't shoot 'em down unless you fix my Spitfire
    right."
He was always kind and thoughtful—when my missus had a
    kid;
  He sent a wire—a bunch of flowers, as well as fifteen
    quid,
I told him we was grateful—said I'd make it up to him;
  He gave a crooked smile and said "You owe me nothing
    Jim,

I've got a pair of silver wings, two medals on my chest
My names been in the papers, there's promotion,
and the rest.
I've got twenty-three swastikas painted on my petrol
tank,
For all these things its blokes like you I've really
got to thank."
The day he'd been to see the King to get his D.S.O.,
They 'ad a lovely party—all his friends—and the
C.O.,
But he got away for just a while to buy us drinks all
round,
"You can't win medals in the sky with dud blokes on
the ground"
"Killer" Brand they called him the pilots of no Wing,
What a name to give a bloke who'd never harm a thing
Except when he was chasing Huns, Blimey then he'd
fight!
You see he'd lost his sister when Jerry came one
night.
The girls were crazy after him, they chased him near
and far
Made his life a misery—just like a Movie Star.
Wouldn't have no truck with 'em—perhaps they thought
him dumb,
If they did, he didn't worry—his best girl was
his mum.
A week ago last Monday—I won't forget that day,
It was cold, wet and dreary, all the sky was grey.
They took off them twelve Spitfires on an early morning
sweep,
Just like a hundred other days, I waved and said
"God keep."
I couldn't seem to settle down the time they was away
I seemed to have a feeling this was going to be
His day.
I waited on the airfield till I sighted them—and then
One, two, three, four, five, six, seven, eight, nine,
ten
I quickly checked them over—but his crate wasn't there,
I asked the other pilots if they'd seen him bale—
and where?

They'd seem him crashing down in flames "Tony's gone
   we fear,"
I ain't feeling quite so good to-day—I'm even off
   my beer!

"SPOT"

BY MARTYN HERBERT and HERBERTE JORDAN   *1923*

Little mongrel, name o' Spot,
   Can't talk, but 'e thinks a lot, You see.
Wags 'is tail, an' licks my 'and,
   Tries to make me understand,
Thinks as 'ow it must be grand to be,
   Big an' 'an'some, reg'ler swell,
'Stead o' just a ne'er-do-well, like me.
   'E'd take no prizes in a show,
Got no pedigree, you know. Great Scott!
   'E's terrier's ears, an' spaniel paws,
Touch o' bulldog round the jaws
   Couldn't call him class, because 'e's not!
T'tell the truth, it seems to me
   'E's too much bloomin' pedigree, 'as Spot.
Isn't much as 'e won't eat,
   Biscuits, bones, an' bits o' meat. Look 'ere,
I've seen the little blighter chew,
   A pair o' trousers almost new,
It beats me where 'e puts 'em to. It's queer.
   I s'pose it's what 'e fancies, see?
The missus says it's same as me, wiv beer.
   Liza 'ad 'im well weighed up,
Time when 'e was just a pup. Says she,
   "You an' 'im you're just a pair."
But underneath 'er stony stare,
   I sees a little twinkle there. An' Gee!
Although at times we catch it 'ot,
   She thinks the world of me,—an' Spot.
An' though 'e's what they call a cur,
   Old Spot, 'e'd give 'is life for 'er,—like me.

368

SPRING IN FRANCE

A war epic written on the Ramparts at Ypres 1915

BY KENNETH HEATHER and ERNEST LONGSTAFFE   *1915*

Spring in France in all its glorious splendour;
   The leafy trees, the sweet fresh air, the budding
      bush, the blossoms rare,
The pansy and forget-me-not, the tulip tall and
      slender.
   I see them all as I've seen before,
In sweet Springtime in days of yore,
   God's glorious works, so beautiful, so marvellously
      tender.
Shall I yet see another Spring? I wonder! I wonder!
   Spring in France amid the murd'rous strife.
The leafless trees; the sulphurous air:
   The blighted bush, naught blossoms there:
In poison gas, midst Hell's devices rife.
   Big guns boom and shells shriek o'er
Dealing death in seething gore,
   Depriving man of God's most precious gift, his life.
Is this God's will? I wonder! I wonder!
   Spring in France where battle tumults passed awhile
Lie little mounds where poppies bloom:
   Each marks the place of a hero's tomb
Strong men pass half conscious of a spectres smile
   The shade of death each strong man knows
Will hover near where e're he goes
   Then reason asks is this hell's delight worth
      while?
Oh what on earth can it avail? I wonder! I wonder!
   Spring in France aye Spring o'er every land and sea
The Spring of peace a perfect peace
   When wars must once for ever cease
The victory won, from military bondage men set free.
   It can be ours without a doubt
If rulers will but reason out.
   Their differences with common sense and equity
Upon the knee all nations raise their hands to thee

369

Rememb'ring those beneath the sod,
They pray to thee Almighty God,
That peace may reign from now through all
    eternity
Shall we yet behold God's glorious peace?
I wonder! I wonder!

SQUARE DEAL SANDERSON

BY FRANK A. TERRY   *1925*

They called him Square-deal Sanderson, down Fallen
    River way,
    A poker face, with eyes of steel, and when he
    made gun-play,
His draw was just like lightning, that made men catch
    their breath,
    And fall, or leap back out of range beyond that
    belching death.
He didn't always shoot to kill: he'd give his gun a
    twist,
    And ere you'd touched your trigger he'd got you
    through the wrist.
You never saw him stunting; but off the trail one day
    I heard some shots, and, peeping through saw
    Sanderson at play.
He'd been firing at a tree-trunk on which he'd cut a
    knot;
    And by the look of things I guess he'd got it ev'ry
    shot.
He'd call round once or twice a year, then hit the
    trail again;
    From North to South, from East to West, his tracks
    were ever plain.
He never picked a quarrel; he never owed a sou;

Square-deal was his name, and he was square deal
through and through.
Animals adored him: a man once kicked a dog;
Sanderson's left arm shot out and felled him like
a log.
I shan't forget the night in Jackson's Poker Dive,
And the look upon his face when he saw Bully Deane
arrive.
Now, Bully was a "two gun" man, a killer, real
darned bad;
He'd cheat at cards and cheat you at the "draw"
if you'd be had.
Well, Square-deal flashed a roll of notes, and Bully
saw the pile,
And said, "Say, stranger, what d'yer say to poker
for a while?"
They played, and Bully lost at first—it always was
the same,
Until the stakes grew higher, then he played
another game.
Square-deal said, "Well, I'll play these", and Deane
discarded one,
Then as he dealt another, like a shot out of a gun
Square-deal knifed his hand and card right through
the table-top.
His gun flashed out: "You cur", he said, "You
see I've got the drop:
You've got three aces in your hand; the joker's at
the back;
The other card my knife's gone through was dealt
beneath the pack.
I've waited for you, Bully Deane, and got you fixed
at last:
And now we'll have a little chat about your dirty
past:
About the girl you lured from home, from a husband
clean and white,
Who left her unprotected while he went to France
to fight.
You told her lies about him, until at last she fell.
She fled with you one night, and then you made her
life a hell.

371

You clubbed her, kicked her, starved her, you played
    the Devil's game.
  Her husband found her dying, and learnt about her
    shame.
And when he followed after you you waited in his track,
  You didn't fight him like a man, you shot him in the
    back.
That youngster was my brother, the woman was his wife.
  I've waited now for three long years, and sworn to
    have your life.
I ought to shoot you like a dog, I guess I've got the
    right,
  But you're going to get a square deal from Sanderson
    to-night.
Now keep your left hand on the board, I'm going to
    sheathe my gun,
  And then you're going to start for yours the minute
    I say "one"!
Square-deal drew his hand back slow, and let his iron
    drop,
  Then brought it back to touch the bully's; 'cross
    the table top.
Then quickly changing hands he got the knife into his
    right,
  "That makes us both left-handed, and the fairest
    way to fight.
And, furthermore, you're going to get a start in case
    you whine,
  I'll give you to the table edge before I start
    for mine.
Now draw your hand back slowly, then dive quick for your
    gun."
  The Bully's hand went slowly back, and Square-deal
    shouted "One".
Then like a flash of lightning that rends the clouds
    apart
  Square-deal's hand swept back and shot the bully
    through the heart.
His head fell on the table; his left hand hit the floor;
  His gun was in its holster—he hadn't time to draw.
Then Square-deal lifted up his eyes towards the
    ceiling there,

And murmured: "Brother, Sonny Boy, I reckon that's
      all square".

OPTIONAL FINISH
Then standing up, he sheathed his iron, not looking
      left or right,
With head erect and shoulders squared he walked
      into the night.

THE STAKE

BY NOSMO KING, ANDREW SPILLER and ERNEST LONGSTAFFE1941

The seas are swept by a mighty fleet
      All Europe echoes with marching feet,
Skies fill with the drone of the swift war plane—
      And Britain's youth goes forth again.
Goes forth again to do and dare
      Risking death on land, on sea, in air—
And while our children pay the price
      We too must make *our* sacrifice.
If we're over age to march or shoot
      We can still join up, we can still recruit,
In the army that marches behind the guns
      Providing the shells for our soldier sons.
For the bombs that burst, and the planes that fly,
      Are sinews of war that we've got to buy,
And the tanks that roll, and the shells that crash,
      Have got to be paid for in solid cash.
Each Dreadnought, each cruiser, each submarine—
      Each bolt and each screw of the war machine—
Each used, each worn and yes, each lost,
      We've got to supply and forget the cost.
We're out of line and we've got safe jobs
      We're not so short that we'll miss the "bobs,"
Which will help to swell, in their humble way

The ten million pounds that it costs each day.
But how shall we do it? I'll tell you how!
Cut luxury spending! Start saving *now.*
That surplus, which might have done good to your own,
Will do far greater good as a government loan.
Defence Bonds and Savings Certificates wait
To gather your savings, and so dedicate
Your efforts, your strivings, the fruits of your toil
To the victory which comes to the faithful and loyal.
For we're fighting a foe that we daren't underrate
Who enters the ring with equal weight!
In an all-in scrap where the fouls are rife;
So, put up the stake: for the stake is *LIFE!*

THE STEAM ROLLER MAN'S STORY

HARRY J. ROWLAND and GEORGE HAY   *1914*

(Spoken) The road in which I live is *up* as usual and we
have a steam-roller endeavouring to put it *down.* Yesterday I
chanced to pause for a moment to look at it. The gentleman
in charge of the roller seized the opportunity for a few
minutes rest and conversation. Carefully checking his iron
steed in its wild career, he leisurely climbed down and
addressed me thusly:—

"G' morning—'blige with a match, sir?
    Thanks! Mind if I take a few more?
It's always a bit of a job, sir,
    To get this 'ere bacca to draw.
I can tell by the smell of your pipe, sir,
    As you knows the right sort to smoke.
Thank y', sir,—I should smoke this myself sir,
    If I wasn't so 'orrible broke.
Engineering jobs ain't what they was, sir,
    In the days—but I ain't goin' to brag,
When in front of me roller I'd always
    A man, sir, to carry a flag.

That reminds me of something wot 'appened
    To a flag-man, the name o' Jeff.
Careless bloke, sir, but 'ard working,
    And all right except 'e was deaf.
One day we wos working as usual,
    When I 'eard, sir, a sort of a grunt.
Then we jolted a bit and I looks, sir,
    But I couldn't see old Jeff in front.
Then I thought of his being deaf, sir,
    And I trembled just like a leaf,
For I guessed, sir, 'e'd been extra careless
    And somehow 'ad got under-neaf.
He lay in the road—I thought dead, sir,
    But 'e moved,—I was thankful for that.
But bless you, sir, I was a-staggered
    When I see as I'd rolled him out flat.
Yes, sir, flattened him out like a pan-cake,
    All thin like you understand.
As broad as a dozen like you sir,
    But only as thick as your hand.
At first, sir 'e seemed a bit stunned like,
    And 'e laid in the road there and grinned,
So I helped him up, then started home, sir,
    Lor'! I did 'ave a job with the wind.
For the breeze kept a-catching him broad-side,
    And taking him up like a kite,
And I 'ad to 'old on like grim death, sir,
    To stop him from taking flight.
His family at 'ome they was knocked, sir,
    And you should 'ave 'eard his wife,
Said she'd sooner go 'ome to her mother
    Than live with a freak all her life.
But they took him, sir, into the parlour
    And propped 'im against the wall,
An' they wanted to put 'im to bed, sir,
    But they couldn't think how to at all.
Then I thought of folding him up, sir,
    I 'ad to think everything out,
And next morning we got a hot iron, sir,
    And ironed his creases out.
And we watched him get thinner for months, sir,
    As each evening around him we sat.

You see, sir, 'e lived on flat fish sir,
  And even his voice was flat.
Well, I worried myself wot to do, sir,
  But it wasn't no good to talk,
At last, sir, an idea it struck me
  And next day I takes Jeff for a walk.
And we walks down the road to the yard, sir,
  Where the roller had always stood,
And Jeff props himself up on his thin end, sir,
  And stays like it as well as 'e could.
We knew it was kill or cure, sir,
  So I shakes 'ands, sir, and says good-bye,
And as I climbed on to the engine
  I wiped, sir, a tear from my eye.
Then I starts her right over Jeff, sir,
  And the very next thing I see
Was the roller 'ad rolled out Jeff, sir,
  To the shape as 'e used to be.
Pleased? I should just think 'e wos, sir,
  Tho' some of our blokes was annoyed.
Jeff sir? 'E's carryin' a flag, sir,
  Along o' the unemployed.
He got the sack when they stopped our flags,
  But 'e's well as 'e's ever bin,
You can take my word that it's true, sir,
  The word, sir, of Truthful Jim."

THE STREET WATCHMAN'S STORY

BY CHARLES J. WINTER   *1910*
        Performed by Bransby Williams

Some chaps gets the fat, and some gets the lean,
    when they start on their journey thro' life,
Some makes pots o' money by being M.P.'s and some
    gets it by taking a wife.

Some learns a good trade such as dustman or sweep,
 which the same I'd have done if I'd
 knowed,
But the special profession I've drifted to now is
 "minding a 'ole in the road."
As a rule it's a nice quiet comfortable job, but there's
 times when I've hated the work.
For instance, I once had to go Christmas Day on a
 job which I'd tried hard to shirk.
I minded that 'ole sir, the whole blessed day, till my
 dinner and teatime had gone,
And *my* Christmas dinner (if any was left) I
 should have when relieved later on.
At home we'd some friends and we'd got a big goose,
 and I'd ordered a half ton of coal,
Yet here was I sitting at seven P. hem a shivering
 in front o' my 'ole.
And I thought of them all making merry at home, stuffed
 with goose from their heads to their
 toes,
They'd just about leave me a cut off the beak or the
 end of the parson's nose.
And I sat quite despondent and dozed half asleep, I was
 feeling quite humpy and sore,
When from one of the big houses just on my right
 a swell flunkey stepped out through
 the door.
He came straight to me and he said with a bow, which
 made his gold lace gleam and shine,
"The Countess's compliments as you're alone she'll
 be pleased if you'll step in and dine."
Well I very near dropped to the ground with surprise,
 for it wasn't a safe thing to do
What if thieves came and pinched a great heap of them
 stones or 'opped off with a drain-pipe
 or two?
Then I thought of the Countess's kindness of 'eart
 how she'd thought of me lonely outside
So I scraped the clay off of my boots with a spade
 and I follered the flunkey inside.
And there sat the Countess all merry and bright, with
 diamonds and jewels all aglow,

377

In a silk dress which must have cost nigh twenty
    pound, though there wasn't much of it,
    you know.
Her husband the *Viscount* was there at her side,
    while the waiters flew round with a whizz,
And in half a jiff I was seated with them a-eating
    and shifting the fizz.
The *Viscount* he drank to my jolly good health as he took
    from his wineglass a pull.
I only jest nodded—I couldn't say much—for my mouth,
    like my heart, was too full.
When we'd finished, us gents, all puts on a cigar and the
    perfume was simply sublime,
By the bands that was on 'em why I'll guarantee they
    must have cost fourpence a time.
Then the ladies they starts playing "Kiss-in-the-ring,"
    and the Countess enjoyed the game too,
When she gets in the ring she just turns straight to
    me, and she says "Mr. Nobbs, I'll have you."
Oh, I didn't know which was my 'ead or my 'eels it was
    like being in fairy land
But I threw down my smoke and I wiped my moustache,
    just like this with the back of my 'and.
She put up her lips looking saucy and sweet, and I
    blush'd as towards her I stole,
I bent forward and then—I woke up just in time, or
    I might have fell clean down the 'ole.

THE STUDENT

BY JOHN EDWARDS   *1908*

Performed by Bransby Williams

At a certain University not many years ago
    There lived a student, learned, wise and slow.
From flighty feelings he was quite exempt.
    And all frivolity held in contempt.
In fact for knowledge he was widely noted

And as a model was oft-times quoted.
One fatal day, on serious thoughts intent,
  Our hero o'er a ponderous tome was bent,
Extracting wisdom from its musty pages,
  For knowledge is not gained by easy stages.
When a light foot-fall at his door he hears,
  And in his room a fair damsel appears.
"What, Sister Madge," cried he with unfeigned glee,
  "Sit down my dear, We'll have some tea."
They whiled away the hours with pleasant chat
  Of plays, pictures, and her last new hat.
When suddenly at the door there came a loud rat-tat.
  Brother and sister both exclaimed "Tut tut.
    What's that?"
"Oh," said the youth, with reassuring look,
  'Twill be some fellow student for a book.
You get behind those curtains there—just so
  And in a moment I'll make him go."
Then turning to the door which he opened wide,
  There a grey wizened old man espied.
"Excuse me, sir," the ancient one began,
  "I occupied these rooms some fifty years ago,
And thought I'd like to see them once again before
    I died."
  "With pleasure sir, just step inside and look around.
You'll find them interesting, I'll be bound."
  "Ah me! the same old place I see once more,
The same old ceiling and the same old floor.
  The same old grate where I have often sat till very,
    very late.
The same old window and the same old view."
  Then he the curtains wide apart withdrew,
His quick eye resting on the dame, He chuckled,
  "Aye, aye, aye, and the same old game."
"Excuse me, sir," said the youth, hurt at the slur,
  "This lady is my sister sir!"
The old man smiled and quick to make reply
  Said, "I beg your pardon, Sister? Oh!
Aye, aye, aye and the same old lie!"

THE SUFFERER

BY L. E. BAGGALEY and EDWIN JOHN   *1934*

Now hospitals aren't cheerful places,
  Not even the best, you'll agree:
But the one that fair gives you the horrors
  Is that at St. Earaches-on-Sea.
It says o'er the gate "English Martyrs,"
  A name that inspires a doubt,
It's appropriate, though, because many go in,
  But very few live to come out.
A cousin of mine, name of Arnold,
  Who went there for treatment last year,
Says the bloomin' place very nigh killed him,
  And it all came about like this 'ere.
He lay there one day in a dark dreary ward,
  Its name was the "Angel of Death."
They'd all got such names, nice and sociable like,
  When you saw 'em you fair caught yer breath.
Now Arnold was not feeling robust,
  His face was a nice shade of green,
He'd a mouth like a dustbin, and felt a bit raw
  Around where his appendix had been.
A sour-faced Sister then entered
  And said "You're to come right away,
Operation it's got to be done o'er again."
  The patient looked up and said "Eh?"
She retorted "It's no good being stupid,
  Them forceps has got to be found,
They must be inside you, so Doctor Scull says,
  And that's where they are, I'll be bound."
Our Arnold was always obliging,
  'Twas a way that he'd had all his life.
So he pulled on his slippers and followed her out,
  And was shortly put under the knife.
The next day a towel and bandage were missed,
  And Arnold was opened once more.
By then he began to get slightly annoyed,
  Life for him seemed to be one big bore.

The staff of "The Martyrs" all laughed and agreed
   That the series of mishaps was rummy
The Matron remarked "When we slit him again,
   We'd best fit a 'zip' on his tummy."
The climax arrived on a Tuesday
   When they all gathered round him to gloat
And Matron said "Come on, you're wanted,
   For Doctor Shroud's lost his white coat."
At that Arnold's patience fair failed him,
   "Oh has he," said he, "where's my hat?
I don't mind a bandage or forceps and such,
   But a jacket—I'm not wearing that.
An instrument-shelf and a cupboard I've been
   Since I came in but three days ago.
But at being a cloakroom gratuitous like
   I'm drawing the line—cheerio!"

SUICIDE

ROY CLEGG and HAROLD CLEGG-WALKER   *1931*

Now I am a fellow who's lived—
   I've lived and I've loved and I've lost,
I loved a fair damsel who didn't love me,
   So my fate to the winds must be tossed.
She laughed when I tried to be serious,
   Her pretty heels trampled my heart,
The future means nothing, so now I must die,
   But the question is—how do I start?
To jump in a river and drown
   Is a good plan, or so I've been told.
But if some poor simpleton does fish you out,
   You get such a terrible cold.
To turn on the gas and be smothered
   Is one way, but you never can tell
If someone will biff in and spoil the whole thing,
   And just curse you for making a smell.

To hang by the neck on one's braces
  Is sometimes considered the thing,
But I fear mine would hardly stand up to the strain,
  For already they're tied up with string.
I like the idea of revolvers,
  I'd prefer to be shot than to hang,
But ever since childhood I've always been scared
  Of things that go off with a bang.
I once had a vague sort of notion
  Of leaping beneath an express,
But one has to consider one's fellows, you know,
  The chappies who clear up the mess.
Still the Underground might offer scope,
  One could sit down upon a live rail,
But that involves trespassing—what a disgrace
  If the corpse had to serve time in jail.
Now Keatings kills bugs, moths and beetles,
  In that case it ought to kill me.
The butler must make me some sandwiches. James!
  No. Dash it! he's gone out to tea.
Never mind though, there must be some way,
  Such as hurling yourself from a cliff,
Even then you might find that you'd only been stunned,
  And you'd wake up most frightfully stiff.
I've given up thinking of razors,
  I've tried and I'm wondering yet
How these fellows who do it can cut their own throats,
  It's a thing that's beyond my Gillette.
No, really, I'm finding that this sort of thing's
  Not as easily done as it's said.
So I think I'll pop off for the week-end or so—
  And perhaps shoot some rabbits instead.

SUPPLANTED (Child Imitation)

BY IRIS POTTER and CUTHBERT CLARKE   *1923*

We've got a nasty ickle baby come to live with us,
  I fink it really isn't fair the way they make a fuss
About a fing what's got no sense and hardly any hair,
  And isn't half so pretty as my ickle Teddy Bear.
What is the use of baby? Well! I really cannot see,
  But mummie finks it's awful nice and loves it better'n
    me.
I've been so very lonely since that nasty baby came,
  I'm sure that fings will never, never, never be
    the same.
Why! When it cries they always run to cuddle it and
    see
  If anyfink's the matter, or perhaps it wants its
    tea!
They spoil it somefink awful and don't care 'bout me
    at all,
  I'd like to frow dat baby right across our garden
    wall.
The uvver day I stuck a pin in baby's arm to see
  If sawdust twickled out of it, but baby squealed
    at me!
It never lets me play with it just like my dollies
    do,
  And when it sleeps I have to be so quiet and sleeping
    too!
I mustn't shout or make a noise, or play upon the stair,
  I'd like to punch that baby—if I only dare!
My nursie says that baby's put my nose all out of joint!
  It doesn't feel no different, though it's wobbly
    at the point,
But den my nose was always small and rather hard to
    blow,
  I cannot see what baby's done until it starts to
    grow.
And if it grows all crooked I'll just tell you what I'll do
  I'll pray to God for baby's nose to grow all crooked too!

'T'AINT YER KNOW!

BY H. M. BURNABY and HARRY STOGDEN

'As it ever struck yer, as yer poodle along,
    That the things wot you think is orlright, is orl
        wrong?
'Ave yer argued the toss, Yerse! and bin pulled up
    dead,
    While some nosey bloke's interrupted and said—
"'T'ain't yer know!"
    Nah! a bloke 'as a pal wot's got on, and made
        good,
An' 'e sez to 'isself "Cunnin' barsket 'e would!—
    Why should 'e 'ave it all? look at me! proper
        stuck.
Falls into 'is lap it do—Nothink but—luck."
    'T'ain't yer know!
Orf yer goes to the races, well britched as to
        tin,
    Yer knows the game backwards, and wot's goin'
        ter win.
Then up comes an' 'orse, on this 'orse goes yer shirt,
You've bin told for a fact, it's a stone blinkin' cert!
    'T'ain't yer know!
Take yer fav'rite film star, of whom you're a fan,
    'E's persued by the villain; a bad wicked man,
In the distance 'e clouts this 'ere 'ero a sock,
    P'r'aps yer think it's yer star wots bin poked in
        the clock.
'T'ain't yer know!
    For a bit of a change to the local you'll go,
Just to knock back an 'arf pint of wallop or so.
    Then someone gets excited and starts actin' queer,
And says "Blimey! I've just found an' 'op in me beer!"
    'T'ain't yer know!
'Ave yer seen these 'ere sweater girls? Yerse! I've no
    doubt,
    You'll 'ave noticed the way they goes in, and comes
        out?

In the street you'll say, "'ere comes a nice little
    lot,
Wot a picture, cor strewf! wot a figure she's got!"
'T'ain't yer know!
    Climbin' over some other bloke's back to success,
Laughin' at failures—ignorin' distress.
    Shovin' tears in the eyes of yer 'trouble and
        strife'
D'yer reckon that's gettin' the best out of life?
    'T'ain't yer know!
Coshes!—revolvers—shop-breakin' by kids,
    'Ome life gone west, they're just wheels with no
        skids,
Sparin' the rod. Yerse! and spoilin' the child.
    'Oo's fault? Is it theirs, when you've let 'em
        run wild?
'T'ain't yer know!
    And so we go in this dizzy mad world,
You'll find us wherever the flag is unfurled,
    Yerse! 'ard up and 'appy, still second to none—
Listen—don't let 'em kid yer, this old country's
        done,
    'T'ain't yer know!

TALE OF ACKMED KURD

BY CEDRIC FORBES and MINNIE G. CRISPIN   1925

Down in the bazaar of the Cobblers
    Where the stitcher of shoes doth lie,
Was the Haschish den of Kaleef,
    A dog with an evil eye.
His body was round and fattened
    Like a sow that had taken its fill
His eyes were full and watery,
    With hands that could grasp and kill.
'Twas at the hour of sunset
    While the Faithful were at prayer,

385

To the Haschish hell of Kaleef,
    Came a stranger and entered there.
He was young by the grace of Allah
    Tho' his hair was touched with grey,
And his frame so bent and shaken,
    Told the curse of the smoke held sway.
Kaleef had seen him enter,
    And knew him for easy prey,
Then he bade one dark-eyed houri
    Place a stem in his teeth straightway.
The stranger sat for a moment
    And sucked as a babe at play,
Then his bloodlit eyes rolled upwards
    And he cursed like a beast at bay!
Give me more you dark-eyed she-cat!
    He cried to the houri by,
For the vision and peace are departed,
    Give me more,—more,—or I die!
Now Kaleef had taken a maiden
    Whose skin was as white as the snow,
And forced her to stay in his hell-house,
    Though she pleaded in vain to go.
He forced her to dance for his pleasure,
    And henna'd her fingers and toes,
Then when she would not he lashed her
    With cruel unmerciful blows!
Now on this night in his smoke den,
    While the music and scents arose,
He commanded the maid to strip naked,
    And dance for his friends and his foes.
She would not, and then in a moment
    Her clothes from her body he tore;
And cast her with one brutal movement
    In the lantern's glare on the floor.
She fell with a cry of anguish,
    And then as she did not rise,
He lashed with a brutal thong-whip
    A blow in the maiden's eyes.
Then down came the lash and blood spattered
    From the breast of the white-skinned maid!
At which Kaleef laughed like a mad-man,
    As another cut he made.

At that laugh something seemed to kindle
  In the breast of the stranger there,
With a bound like a maddened panther,
  He bit, like a fiend, at the air,
Straight at the throat of Kaleef,
  He sprang with a devilish curse,
And bore him down and held him
  Till the veins in his hands seemed to burst.
They fought like fiends in a hell-pit,
  Rolling over the blood-stained floor,
And swayed like a roaring torrent,
  Till they reached the curtained door:
Then, in the heat of deathly throes,
  Was heard a sudden crack!
And Kaleef lay both prone and still,
  Dead,—with a broken back.
Black-faced and picked by vultures' claws,
  Lies Kaleef in desert waste;
While safe within the stranger's land
  Dwells the white skinned maiden chaste!

A TATTOO TRAGEDY

BY CLIFFORD GREY, GREATREX NEWMAN and FRED CECIL 1933

Her name was Ermyntrude,
  In a circus she tattooed,—
A girl who had designs on ev'ry man;
  Until she traced a heart
On the arm of Joseph Smart,
  She won him—and they furnished her plain van.
Of course she left the show
  The day she married Joe,
The tattoo needle she would 'need' no more,
  But Joseph, foolish youth,
Soon learned the dreadful truth,

The 'Bearded Lady' was his MA-IN-LAW!
All day about the place
    He could see that hairy face,
He couldn't dodge it even in the street.
    It made him use an oath
To see that stringy growth,
    That harvest festival of shredded wheat!
Each day he longed to get
    A present from Gillette,
And hand it to the mother of his bride.
    'Twas obvious of course
She'd swallowed some poor horse,
    And left the tail to dangle just outside.
Joe's bearded MA-IN-LAW
    Out-whiskered Bernard Shaw,
And sometimes drove poor Joseph on the 'binge';
    He staggered home one night
At four *A. M.*—quite 'tight',—
    So Ermyntrude, his wife, planned her re*v*enge.
Up to his side she crept
    And while he soundly slept
Undid his coat and shirt in manner weird.
    Then when his chest was nude
Upon it she tattooed
    Her Mother's face, the Lady avec Beard!
Joe woke at halfpast nine
    And saw the dread design,
It stared out through his little Aertex vest.
    A horrible surprise,
Could he believe his eyes?
    The face he hated, grinning from his chest!
He straightway signed the pledge
    And lived on fruit and veg',
He thought that he was 'seeing things,' poor youth.
    But even when T.T.
That fungus'd face he'd see,
    Until at last there dawned the tattooed truth!
He left his wife, of course,
    And sued for a divorce,
And as the neighbours kept asking why?
    He roamed from Shepherd's Bush
To Ashby-de-la-*Zush*,

From far-off Peckham Vale to Maida Rye.
In deep despair at last
    He bought a mustard plast',
And plonked it on his chest without delay.
That plaster burned and burned.
To tear it off he yearned,
    But hoped it would singe the beard away.
The mustard was so strong
    He left in on too long.
And while he peeled it off, his chest was sore.
    So blistered was the skin,
It made a *double chin,*
    The beard looked *twice the size it was before!*
Poor Joe went raving mad,
    His end came swift and sad,
That tattooed picture must remain he knew;
    Resigned, he softly sighed.
Then whispered as he died:
    "Thank Heav'n it's not a TALKING Picture too!"

THANKS JOHNNY

BY BEECHER STEVENS and HARRY STOGDEN   *1951*

Performed by Jack Watson

I was feeling pretty low one day—
    A really miserable cuss.
You know—when you've nothing to say
    And everything's a fuss.
I'd scoffed at my breafast with my head in the news
    And grunted out answers to all my wife's views.
I'd banged the doors as I busied about
    And finally banged myself out
I got to the gate—without looking back
    And then was greeted with "GOOD MORNING,
        UNCLE JACK!"
'N' there all beaming and large as life

Was JOHNNY, the ORPHAN KID, with a large pocket
    knife.
"JOHNNY! I snapp'd—what have you got there?"
And I fixed poor JOHNNY with an awful stare.
"I've got a sword—and it's a beauty—
I'm looking after Auntie—while you go on duty"—
You know—that kid, with his great big smile
Just knocked the bottom out of me for a while,
Why? Well—here was a kid with no mum or dad,
    And nothing, really, to make him glad.
Yet, there he was all happy and gay—
    (Quite frankly, I was about to turn him away.)
I stopp'd in my tracks and turned my head
    But suddenly, I smiled instead.
The first that morning—in fact for many a day
    To think young Johnny had shown me the way.
I looked at him and he continued to grin,
    Why—not to smile now seemed a sin
So—soothingly I said—"Johnny—Take care with that knife"
    Then I looked back home, waved—and smiled to my wife
I went on my way feeling full of joy
    Why the heck can't we always be like that boy?
Carefree—yet thoughtful most of the while—
    THANK'S JOHNNY for making me smile.

THANK YOU!

BY MARGARET HODGKINSON, NOSMO KING and
                    HERBERT TOWNSEND 1946

In this glorious hour of victory, when the world at
    last is free,
    Free for ever from the shackles of a hateful
        tyranny;
When the long, dark night of anguish and of dread has
    passed away

And there dawns the radiant promise of a new and
    better day;
In the midst of our rejoicing, let us pause awhile,
    and think
Of those to whom we owe so much, who brought us from
    the brink
Of disaster and destruction to the final shining goal,
    Who saved this land from conquest—aye, saved its
    very soul,
Let us think of them today, and of our overwhelming
    debt,
    And say a simple "thank you" lest we all too soon
    forget!
First then, THANK YOU, Royal Navy, for the service
    that is yours,
    Of keeping safe, inviolate, our sacred British shores;
We thank you for Tarranto, Matapan and Narvik Bay,
    For the conquest of the U-boat,—for the Bismark
    the Graf Spee
And we THANK YOU Merchant Seamen, you of finest mettle
    bred,
    For your superhuman task in keeping Britain armed
    and fed,
We THANK YOU British Army, for your grand immortal
    work,
    From that hour of tragic glory on the beaches of
    Dunkirk,
Till the day when, four years later, with your allies
    you were hurled
To storm a fortress continent and liberate the
    world.
We THANK YOU Royal Air Force—who can count our debt
    to you?
    From that "finest hour" when we were saved by your
    immortal "few"
Until as lords and conquerors of the air, we saw you
    rise
    And sweep your way to overwhelming victory in
    the skies.
We THANK YOU "Monty," Eisenhower, McArthur and the
    rest,

Our leaders in the field, whose names fill ev'ry
    British chest
And over all, for ever shining in undying fame.
    We THANK YOU Winston Churchill—blest for ever be
    your name!
Our brothers of the Commonwealth, who loyal proved
    and true,
    Who gave your all to serve the Mother-land—we
    THANK YOU, too;
We THANK YOU, gallant Allies, who have striven at our
    side,
    Whose sons, with ours, have won the day, with
    our sons fought—and died
We THANK the Women of this land, with heartfelt
    proud "well done!"
    The factory lass, farm hand, the nurse, the girl
    behind the gun,
We THANK those brave civilians, who, thro' terror,
    loss and grief,
    Endured unto the end with fortitude beyond belief,
And let us now remember too; with mingled pride
    and pain,
    In silent grateful homage, the unnumbered
    thousands slain!
They died for us that we might see this day—their
    blood was shed;
    Sorrowfully, yet proudly, we salute our honoured
    dead,
And in their ranks one dear loved name stands forth
    for ever blest,
    Son of a brave and mighty race, the noblest and the
    best;
Through all these years, deep shrined in ev'ry
    British heart he's dwelt,
    With grateful hearts we bless and thank him
    Franklin Roosevelt.
But more than all, with humble hearts, we cry on bended
    knee,
    Thanks be to Thee, Almighty God, Who gave us
    Victory!

THE 11.69 EXPRESS

BY RONALD BAGNALL and WILLIAM S. ROBINSON   *1906*

You want a railway story while you wait for the
    London train,
It's a story I've never told yet, so I'll tell it
    to you again.
I was only a guard at the time, sir, on the London
    and Smash'em Line
But I shan't forget the mishap to the eleven sixty
    nine.
'Twas a terrible foggy night, sir, and a day I shan't
    forget
The fog was a kind of Scotch mist, sir, and the train
    it was somehow wet!
The train ran upon the line, sir, and the line ran along
    the ground
The engine was full of steam, sir, and the wheels
    were going round;
What *made* the wheels go round and round it's more
    than I can say,
But the signal was dead against us, so we went the
    other way.
We were going a mile a minute, when I stepped out on to
    the line,
And the driver said we were due, sir, at eleven
    sixty-nine.
So I got back into the van, sir, and swallowed a bottle
    of Bass;
While we waited two hours, or more, sir, for luggage
    train to pass.
When all of a sudden I heard, sir, the sound of a mighty
    crash
We could hear the shrieks of survivors, and I thought
    of their ready cash.
So after I'd finished my pipe, sir, I strolled out on
    to the line.
And gazed on the wretched wreckage of the eleven
    sixty-nine.

For the coaches were all in a heap, sir, though why—
    I cannot tell.
  And the passengers lying around us, were none of
    'em looking well.
They slept their last sleep on the sleepers, we
    could hear the sleepers snore.
  It's a sight I've never seen, sir, and shall never
    see—before
For the line was a mass of hats, sir, and blouses all
    over the place
  Whilst one of the passenger's noses was in the middle
    of his face
We could hear the hiss of the engine and the moans of
    the living souls;
  I thought of the missus at home, sir, and collared
    some of the coals!
I shall *never* forget the sight, sir, though I
    can't remember it now.
  But with my tattered banner, I wiped a tear from
    my brow.
I picked my way through the wreckage and got to the
    heart of the smash,
  I busied myself with the injured, and helped myself
    to the cash.
For I wanted the money badly, 'cos my rent was in
    arrears,
  And mother-in-law had come, sir, on a visit for
    sixty years.
Then I saw a sweet young lady in a mashed potato state,
  And her final words were "Doctor is my hat on
    straight?"
We stumbled across the stoker, and I thought that he
    was dead:
  For his body and legs were missing and we couldn't
    find his head;
I forget what happened next, sir, I remember it all
    quite well.
  The crashing of heavy timber all a-tumbling as
    it fell.
The doctors and the looters were round us by the
    score,

394

And the police were an hour late, sir, as they've
   often been before.
Then two of us lifted the engine and placed it upon
   the line
But here's your down train up, sir, the eleven
   sixty-nine.

THERE IS EVER A SONG SOMEWHERE

BY JAMES WHITCOMB RILEY and HARRIET KENDALL   *1920*

There is ever a song somewhere my dear,
   There is ever a something sings alway,
There's the song of the lark when the skies are clear
   And the song of the thrush when the skies are grey.
The sunshine showers across the grain,
   And the bluebird trills in the orchard tree,
And in and out when the eaves drop rain,
   The swallows twitter ceaselessly.
There is ever a song somewhere my dear,
   Be the skies above dark or fair,
There is ever a song that our hearts may hear.
   That our hearts, our hearts may hear.
There is ever a song somewhere my dear,
   In the midnight black or the midday blue,
The robin pipes when the sun is here,
   And the cricket chirrups the whole night
      through,
The buds may blow and the fruit may grow,
   And the autumn leaves drop crisp and sere;
But whether the sun, or the rain, or the snow,
   There is ever a song, There is ever a song,
Somewhere, somewhere, my dear.

THEY ARE COMING

BY J. R. STEBBINGS, NOSMO KING and ERNEST LONGSTAFFE1943

They are coming from the Rockies; from the hills and
    from the plain,
  From beneath the great sky-scrapers; from Kentucky
    up to Maine,
And they have but one objective; these gallant men and
    true;
  Just think of it, Herr Hitler, they are coming after
    you.
They march along the highway; they crouch inside the
    tanks,
  The youths from city offices, the men who run the
    banks,
And Garge who did the ploughing's got another
    job to do,
  They're all together Hitler and they're coming after
    you.
They roar through dotted cloudland; they race beneath
    the stars,
  They kiss the dawn in splendour; they ride the road
    to Mars,
Young bloods of many countries; a really desperate
    crew,
  With *one aim* Mister Hitler they are coming after
    you.
They did not seek this battle; they longed to love and
    live,
  To be just human beings, to smile, to help, to give,
But you've changed their happy outlook and the devil
    will get his due,
  And it won't be very long because they're coming after
    you.
Their crosses dot the landscape; their mother's tears
    fall fast,
  Somewhere 'neath the grim Atlantic a lone son sleeps
    his last,

396

But other sons are waiting as your crimes mount up
    anew,
    Your days are numbered Hitler, they're coming after
    you.
Old Joe out there in Russia, just sighs a bit and grins,
    He's got it all weighed up for you, you'll pay for
    all your sins.
And all the conquered countries—*they're* waiting
    for you too,
    There's no escaping Hitler they're all coming
    after you.
Life is sweet, great Mister Hitler, and but *once*
    we pass this way—
    To cheer, to love, to cherish, not to rape, to
    burn, to slay;
And the ghosts of murdered millions, they're going to
    haunt you too,
    In your hours of darkness Hitler—They'll be coming
    after you.
They are coming Mister Hitler across the great
    wide seas,
    Their ships go out, their ships come in,
    with, or without a breeze,
And they'll *get* you, Mister Hitler no matter
    where you run,
    And they'll *hang* you Mister Hitler, for the
    bloody things you've done.

THINGS THAT ISN'T TRUE

BY MARTYN HERBERT and HERBERTE JORDAN   *1929*

The priest was after meeting little Micky yesterday,
    An' started askin' questions just to see what he would
    say.
He asked him what we mean by "Faith", an' what did
    Micky do.

But says "Sure it's just believin' Sir, in things
    that isn't true."
The priest he came and tould me wid a twinkle in his
    eye,
    I says "Yer Riv'rence, it's myself that's shamed
    for his reply."
He says, "Ah now, be aisy, 'twill be hard for me
    an' you,
    Whin we have to stop believin' in the things that
    isn't true."
We'll be losin' all our childish dreams of happiness
    or fame,
    They never seem to come true, but we dream them
    all the same,
An' all our happy memories of days of long ago,
    They're coloured by our fancy, an' 'tis maybe,
    better so.
Ah, 'tis youth that has the golden dreams, the olden
    dreams, still new,
    Of love and joy and laughter, an' the things we're
    going to do.
And when we're old and weary, an' the race is nearly
    run,
    We just sit by the fire and dream of what we might
    have done.
Sure our dreams are like the fairies that they tell
    us don't exist,
    They cover all the ugly things of life wid rosy
    mist.
They paint their fairy pictures for the folk wid eyes
    to see,
    An' show us things, not as they are, but as we'd have
    'em be.
They make the sunshine brighter an' the sky a deeper
    blue,
    So God help us keep believin' in the things that
    isn't true."

THRILLING STORIES

BY HERBERT TOWNSEND and REUBEN MORE　　　　*1920*

I'll relate some thrilling stories,
　　Told down at the Old Ship Inn,
By a sea-dog who has travelled,
　　By the name of Mack'rel Jim.
"Once," said he, "on board the Eggshell,
　　We were wrecked off Monkey Brand,
Sinking fast, but from the funnel,
　　I jump'd ten miles on to land.
Then I heard the shouts of "Save me, save, oh
　　　　save me from the wreck."
Let those women perish, never!
Back I jump'd upon the deck.
　　One by one I safely fired them from our cannon to
　　　　the shore,
Crowds were cheering, but I told them that there would
　　　　be no encore.
　　People gave me watches, money, with excitement most
　　　　intense,
Talk of wealth, well altogether, two bob short of eighteen
　　　　pence."
　　Landlord, just fill up Jim's tankard, (this you'll
　　　　nightly overhear)
Want another yarn, says Jimmy, "Right you are," then
　　　　drinks his beer.
　　"Once upon a desert island, I was stationed for a
　　　　time,
Stationed,—tho' there was no station,—
　　Picking chloride out of lime.
Animals, you ask? Well rather, snakes of all kinds in
　　　　your bed,
　　Tigers there with double bodies,—some with only
　　　　just a head.
One dark night (it made me shudder) came a most
　　　　unearthly growl.
　　Looking up I saw a lion, out upon its nightly
　　　　prowl.

399

Then it sprang and soon devoured me,—
But my senses did not roam,
With a knife I ripped it open—
Had it stuffed and brought it home.
Hand my mug Bill; "Here's good health boys" 'nother?
thanks, I'll try a beer.
How's the clock? It wants five minutes—time for one
more yarn to hear.
I shall ne'er forget the night boys, up at Jarrow on the Tyne.
From the railway station platform,—fell a woman
on the line.
On the track I in a moment—sprang as people shrieked
with fright,
Round the bend the Scotch Express was dashing madly
into sight.
Quickly then I knelt beside her,—to the metals holding fast,
The train it rattled o'er my body,—like a switchback
thundering past.
The girl was saved,—but that reminds me, once I heard
the cry of "Fire,"
A New York building "sixty stories" flames were
leaping "liar"—higher—
A child up at the attic window,—cried for help, each
heart stood still.
Fiendish flames in all directions,—who will risk
their life?—"I will."
Through the blinding smoke I mounted,—upward with
determined face—
Seized the child, then from the window—sprang midst
yells into space,
At blinding speed we dashed to earth, ten miles a second
I suppose,
The awful rate gave me a chill, I stopped midway
to blow my nose.
Then the child screamed out—"where's mamma? left behind
to burn—to die!"
"No," said I, "She shall not perish!—I'll return
my child, don't cry."
Back I went and left the infant—floating on the fiery breeze—
Saved the mother,—bet your life—what?" "Come along
now—Time, gents, please!"

TIMMY MY OLD TABBY CAT

BY ERNEST LONGSTAFFE   *1940*

There are lovers of horses and lovers of dogs
   And no one can quarrel with that,
But don't think it's absurd if I say a good word
   About Timmy my old tabby cat.
Folks say cats don't care, but when I've been away
   He makes such a terrible fuss,
For he's so glad to meet, he gets all round my feet
   And purrs like an old motor bus.
Him on the hearth-rug, me in my chair,
   Often for hours we've sat,
I thinks of the time that so far away seems,
   He thinks he's a kitten and chases sunbeams,
So no wonder we're pals, for we both have our dreams,
   A lonely old man and his cat.
How he looks at me sometimes with great saucer eyes
   And seems to say "Thank you for home—
For I'm not like those poor little cats out of doors
   Who've been turned in to cold streets to roam."
He wonders does Timmy and I wonder too,
   How people can be so unkind
As to pack up their homes when they seek safety zones
   And leave the old puss cat behind.
Him on the hearth-rug, me in my chair,
   Often for hours we've sat,
The grandfather clock ticks the minutes away,
   I'm too tired to work and he's too tired to play,
We're just two old fellows who've each had his day,
   A lonely old man and his cat.

TIMMY'S SACRIFICE

Wm. H. DAWES, NOSMO KING and HERBERT TOWNSEND   1946

One evening ev'ry year the local Mayor was wont to
    meet
  The children of the city at their annual Christmas
    treat;
And so that none should hunger at this season of Good
    Will,
  The board was spread with Yuletide fare that all might
    eat their fill.
A mighty Christmas tree was placed at one end of the
    hall,
  It's glitt'ring branches laden down with lovely gifts
    for all.
"But with so many guests to satisfy," His Worship
    smiled,
  "There can be but one gift—and only one—for every
    child."
So one by one each childish heart was fill'd with happy
    joy,
  And sounds of "Ooh!" and "Ah!" were heard as
    each received his toy.
One little chap called Tim seemed dazed at this
    display;
  'Twas plain to see that presents very rarely came
    his way.
His clothes, tho' tidy, bore the mark of many a
    patched up tear,
  Sign of a loving widowed mother's never-failing
    care.
'Tis now his turn to take a gift—O, what a glad surprise!
  A box of soldiers! Timmy's joy was written in his
    eyes.
He stretched his hands out eagerly—and then, we saw him
    pause;
  One wistful look, and then he spoke—and oh, the loud
    guffaws
That echoed round the room as, shyly, timidly, he said,

"Please, sir, I'd like a dolly for a little girl,
   instead."
The jeering sniggers of the rest made Timmy blush with
   shame;
"He wants a dolly!" someone sneered, another:
   "What's her name?"
The kindly Mayor said, "Oh, but why a doll, my little
   son?
The soldiers for a lad like you are surely much more
   fun?"
"It's for my little sister, sir, she's ill, and—oh,
   I know
She's longing for a little doll because she told me so.
You said one present for each child, and so I'd raver,
   sir,
Give back the sojers and I'll take a doll instead—
   for her."
As Timmy finished speaking, not a single sound was heard,
   Glances were averted and many eyes were blurred.
Sarcastic sneers and sniggers—faded in a trice,
   For Timmy's story told a tale of great self-sacrifice.
And when the children, homeward bound, went filing thro'
   the door,
   A lovely doll—and soldiers, too—young Timmy proudly
   bore.

'TISN'T WORTH IT

BY MARTYN HERBERT and FRANK S. WILCOCK   1925

You're frettin', kiddie, 'cos you've broke your doll.
   Well, never mind, there's other things to love.
An' they'll get broken too, that's life all over.
   Lovin' an' losin'; why Good Heavens above!
No matter what you love or what you lose,
   You'll always find there's something better yet,

Until you find the thing that's best of all,
    And even if you lose that, well, don't fret.
'Tisn't worth it.
    You're troubled, sonny, 'cos they've been unkind,
And said hard things about you, course they do.
    Just play the game an' never mind 'em lad.
They've said hard things of better men than you.
    You try for big things, and the little folk
Can't understand the sort of stuff that's in you.
    Never you mind 'em lad, go straight ahead,
Don't worry, not if all the world's agin' you.
    'Tisn't worth it.
You're grievin' mother, 'cos you've lost your boy?
    You haven't lost him, he's become a man.
He's gone to face the world, an' you're alone.
    It always was so, since the world began.
Pack up his baby clothes an' bits o' toys
    His boy will maybe want 'em later on.
Think of the man you've given to the world,
    An' don't be grievin' for the child that's gone.
He's had his childish troubles an' you've seen him
        through 'em all,
    But you know you can't be always there to catch
        him should he fall.
You'll have to watch him climbing, an' you'll have to
        stay behind.
    You'll see him gettin' farther out of reach, but never
        mind.
It's you that he'll come back to with his triumphs or
        his failures.
    An' you'll know it has been worth while after all.

TOMMY OUT EAST

BY ALAN SANDERS and HENRY GEEHL   *1932*

    I am baked and I am thirsty, in this blarsted
        burnin' sun,

For the sand's got in my system, and it's damned
    near spoilt my gun.
But our blue-eyed baby captain, who is learnin' 'ard
    to swear,
Says we're 'oldin' up the Empire, though we're far
    from Leicester Square.
I believes him when 'e says it, but at times I wish
    I knew
That a little 'ome I thinks of, in the Dials—where
    I grew,
Were just a trifle nearer, so that I could go and see
What my mother is a-doin'—if she's thinkin' 'long 'o me.
For it's marchin', and it's fightin.' and it's 'ard I
    give my word
To keep yer face a-smilin' when they've given yer
    'the bird',
But when murky day is over, and we gets the 'LIGHTS
    OUT' clear,
I can 'ear the call of London, and I dream I'm
    tastin' beer.
I've got a gal in Shoreditch—'ere's photo next me 'eart—
And Gawd, I wonder if she's gone and left me in the
    cart.
For this waitin' game don't suit 'er; she says all
    soldiers flirt,
Just as if she couldn't trust me with another
    bit o' skirt!
The rosy East ain't rosy like them writers 'ave you think.
And if you should 'ave a 'beano', well, they shoves
    yer into 'clink.'
With the Temples and Pagodas all a-roastin' in the sun,
You can 'ave the blinkin' blindin' East—give me
    'Apmstead 'Eath for fun!
Oh, we're 'oldin' up the Empire, though we're distant
    from the smoke,
And the sun beats down in glory, 'nuff to burn up
    any bloke.
But it's night-time when I feels as if I'd copped out
    unawares
'Cos my 'eart's in Seven Dials, in my 'ome up
    many stairs!

TORTOISES

BY H. M. BURNABY and HAROLD ARPTHORP   *1928*

Now I'm just an or'nery kind o' bloke, contented with
    my fate,
I lives my life—I does my work each day
A keeper at the Zoo is what I am—I'm proud to state—
And with h'animals I've got a kind o' way.
For sixty year I've worked among 'em—know 'em through
    and through—
Lions—tigers—camels—all the lot—
Halligators—heagles—'awks and harmadillos too—
Without me this 'ere place 'ud go to pot.
But now, I'm getting on like, and can't move about
    so fast,
At least, that's what our big committee sez.
They've been an' gone an' given me a job what's safe
    at last,
A-lookin' after these tortoises.
Now, a tortoise—'e's a hinseck, so they tells me,
    that may be,
'E's a lazy one, there ain't the slightest doubt.
'E'll live a hundred years or two—or sometimes even
    three,
So 'e's got time to think 'is problems out.
See that one there? That's 'Erbert—'e will have his
    little joke,
You should watch him if you've got an hour to spend.
You'd swear that part in front is where his head's
    agoin' to poke,
And then 'e shoves it out the other end.
There's Bill an 'im runs races—that's excitin if you
    like—
You ought to see 'em dashing on their way.
I don't know what ails Bill—I think he must 'a got
    the spike,
Jim's gained an 'arf an inch since yesterday.
I always think these tortoises has gone an' took their
    cue

From the government or some concern like that;
Or watched the blokes as mends the roads, an' noticed
 what they do,
An' tried to beat 'em an' they 'ave that's flat.
That reminds me—it's just time for Kate to take her
 morning stroll,
I shoves her on a chain—she looks a treat.
It keeps 'em fit—Oh! not but what they're 'ealthy
 on the whole,
Although at times they drag me orf me feet!
They say a bloke in time gets like the h'animals 'e
 feeds,
That sort o' cheers me up it does—not 'arf.
Why even now, I feels at times—the limit of my
 speed's
This 'ere slow motion cinematograph.
Lor! bless us! I'd a letter, when I come to work
 today—
Well blow me if this don't beat fairy-tales!
The Committee has decided to promote me straight
 away,
I commence my duties next week—WITH THE *SNAILS!*

THE TOUCH OF THE MASTER'S HAND

BY MYRA BROOKS WELCH and ERNEST LONGSTAFFE   1936

'Twas battered and scarred and the auctioneer
 Thought it scarcely worth his while,
To waste much time on the old violin
 But held it up with a smile.
"What am I bidden good folks" he cried,
 "Who'll start the bidding for me?
A guinea, a guinea, then two, only two?
 Two guineas, and who'll make it three?
Three guineas once, Three guineas twice,
 Going for three?" But NO!

From the room far back a grey haired man
    Came forward and picked up the bow,
Then wiping the dust from the old violin
    And tightening the loose strings.
He played a melody pure and sweet,
    As a carolling angel sings.
The music ceased and the auctioneer
    In a voice that was quiet and low,
Said "What am I bid for the old violin?"
    And then held it up with the bow.
"A thousand guineas, and who'll make it two,
    Two thousand, and who'll make it three?
Three thousand once, three thousand twice;
    And going and gone" said he.
The people cheered but some of them cried,
    "We do not quite understand
What changed it's worth?"
    Swift came the reply "The touch of a master's
        hand."
And many a man with life out of tune,
    And battered and scarred with sin,
Is auctioned cheap to a thoughtless crowd
    Much like the old violin.
A "mess of pottage," A glass of wine.
    A game, and he travels on.
He is "going once," he's "going twice,"
    He's "going" and almost "gone;"
But the Master comes and the foolish crowd
    Can never quite understand,
The worth of a soul and the change that's wrought,
    By the touch of the Master's hand.

THE TOY GUN

BY L. WALDRON and CUTHBERT CLARKE   1915

The babe was asleep in its wooden cot
    With a smile on its mouth from a dream begot

The mother was sobbing her grief to the night
For he who could never return from the fight.
But brave little Jacques with a throbbing heartache
Lay quiet on his pillow alert and awake
And wondered and pondered the cause of it all
Why soldiers should fight and how kingdoms should
fall
And wished with the innermost heart of his heart
Whatever the reason he might take a part
Like the father who'd left them with tender good-byes.
A smile on his lips and a mist in his eyes,—
But his grief was forgotten at dawning of day
When he *was* a soldier if only in play.
With a toy wooden gun on his shoulder so slim
And a cap on his curls with a bright painted
rim.
He was *ever* so strong if he was rather small
He could fight fifty Germans and slaughter them all.
The women need fear not nor children need run
When he was about with his fine wooden gun.
A beating of drums and a tramping of feet
A terror struck flying crowd rush down the street.
The Germans! dear God! they are here! they are here!
And Jacques with a shudder fights down his own fear
And sallies forth boldly his gun pointing straight
All heedless of warnings he runs thro' the gate.
He stands on defensive awaiting the foe
And wishes his limbs were not quivering so.
Here they come! what a roaring and rumbling of sound
A dustcloud is marking their flight o'er the ground.
With faces relentless and ruthless as death
They shriek and they jibe and they curse in a breath.
And the slight little figure of Jacques in the way
Stirs never an inch but still standing at bay
He quivers and orders to "halt" everyone
And dares them approach in the range of his gun.
Then a cowardly thing in a uniform fine
With a curse from his foul lips at courage divine
And a devil's own grin at the sight of a toy
Defends King and Country and murders a boy.
So Jacques with his curly head veiled with the dust
Died a victim to valour and cowardly lust.

They buried him quietly at setting of sun
And on his frail form rests his little toy gun.

A TRAGEDY IN ONE ACT

BY VICTOR MARSH and WALTER SHEPHARD   1904

The moon shone through the grimy window pane
    Athwart the dusk that gathered in the room.
The day was over, twilight on the wane
    And all seemed wrapped in dark and dismal gloom
Except within the gas light's flickery flare
    Which weakly shed its sickly radiance down
Upon a somewhat strange fantastic chair
    Where sat a beardless youth whose eyes so brown
Seemed starting from their sockets as in fear.
    He clutched the chair with hands both white and bony
With head thrown back with throat exposed and bare.
    His whole frame shook and quaked with agony.
Horror! Is this some dreaded den of torture where suffer
        those who sin against the State?
    Is this some youthful and rebellious courtier who
        now in pain his crimes must expiate?
I see the dreaded operator near
    As if to seize his victim in his wrath,
To glory in the agony of fear,
    That flecks the victim's lips and chin with froth.
I see the beads of sweat upon the brow,
    The mute appeal within that poor youth's eyes,
As his tormentor pounces on him now,
    For his escape no earthly chance now lies.
I see the glint of steel—a bright blade flash—
    Oh! horrid sight that makes my marrow freeze—
But stop! From out the chair he makes a dash,—
    Pays twopence for his first shave. Next please.

410

TRAMP PHILOSOPHY

BY R. G. BERRY and J. VAUGHAN BERRY   *1911*

I'm a wandering tramp, a happy old scamp, with never
    a thought or care;
For I live all day in the sunshine gay, my home is
    the sweet fresh air.
When the day is gone, and the night creeps on, I sleep
    'neath the starlit sky.
Do I covet a bed for my weary head? Not I.
Tho' my daily food may be rough and crude, (being
    what I can poach or snare).
I am satisfied, for the gods provide me with plenty
    to eat and to spare.
Then a measure cool from a stream or pool I quaff when
    my throat is dry.
Do I ever pine for a draught of wine? Not I.
You will doubtless guess, from the way I dress, that
    my wardrobe is somewhat bare.
One shoe, one boot, and an old patched suit, are all
    that I've got to wear.
But they're all I need for the life I lead, so why should
    I sit and sigh?
Should I gain anything were I dressed like a king? Not I.
My only wealth is my sovereign health, but that's
    quite enough for me.
Though I haven't a cent, I am quite content; what
    do I want with L. s. d.
To have cash in the bank I regard as "swank;" what
    good does it do laid by?
Do I ever crave for gold to save? Not I.
So if you would be content like me, the happiest tramp
    ever seen,
Don't worry and fret, and sigh with regret for the
    days of the "might-have-been."
Just play your part with a thankful heart till your
    time comes to say "good-bye,"
Then you'll say, with content, "Have I cause to
    repent?" Not I.

THE TREASURE OF THE TIGRIS

BY F. CHATTERTON HENNEQUIN *1921*

There's a simple tablet standing, where the ancient
    waters flow,
  And the minarets of old Baghdad reflect the sunset
    glow.
"Here lies a book" the inscription reads
  "Through all the years to come,
This book will lie for ever though the camel bells
    be dumb."
(Performer salaams)
  (Orchestra to sing) La-za il-al-la il-la Al-lah il-lal-la,
La-za-il-al-la il-la Al-lah il-lal-la
  La-za-il-al-la zah!
When they told us Mesopotamia, Toff says to Spike
    and me,
  "Of course you know that where we're bound's the
    land of mystery."
Spike says "I've 'eard it's full of smells, and dirt,
    and heat, and flies."
  "P'raps so", says Toff: "When *you* gets there;
    that won't cause no surprise.
But here's a book I've just picked up, it's called the
    Arabian Nights,
  Crammed full of facts about Baghdad, the City of
    Delights."
Enchanted 'orses, sacks of pearls.
  Aladdin's lamp, my son,
And a darned great bird they calls the Roc, whose eggs
    weighs fifteen ton!"
  Then 'e stopped for breath, and Spike says
"Garn! who wrote them shocking lies?"
  "You wait" says Toff "Till them Genises begin
    to put you wise.
When you resume your natural shape, and grunt around
    the sty—"
  That's all 'e said, for Spike rose up and punched 'im
    in the eye.
But somehow on the voyage out, that book made quite
    a hit,

And one by one the chaps on board began to borrow
    it,
And in a week, it's Gospel truth, the whole lot changed
    their names
To Ali, Hassan, Mustapha, in place of Bill or James.
But Baghdad put the lid on it, we all went up the pole,
    For the City of the Caliphs was a greasy smelly
    'ole,
For three whole days Toff wouldn't speak, and then
    'e brightened up,
    "I'm not so sure" 'e says to me
"We 'ave been sold a pup.
    There's vases in the Tigris, what's got Genises
    inside,
Was bottled up by Solomon and flung into the tide.
    They've laid there p'raps ten thousand years, an'
    if we lets one free
There's a hundred weight of emeralds for you, and
    Spike and me!"
    Well! we wanted some persuading, but at last 'e
    'ad 'is way,
So we hired a boat, likewise some nets, and got leave
    for the day,
    We dragged that blooming river, an' we found tin
    cans galore,
And boots, and dogs, and lots of mud, but never
    nothing more,
    When just as we was packing up, Toff gave a frightful
    "Ah!"
And from the mud inside the net, lugged out a kind of
    jar!
    Spike turned quite pale, I felt the same, we couldn't
    say a word,
But Toff says "Quick! the bloke inside is fluttering
    like a bird."
    When we reached the bank, we sat and stared, the jar
    was sealed all right,
It must 'ave laid there since the Flood, the lid was
    on so tight.
    First, Toff 'e tried 'is bayonet, till the edge got
    blunt and chipped,

Then Spike 'e used 'is clasp-knife, but the blade turned
    round and slipped.
And the things 'e said of Solomon and 'is wives and
    lady friends,
If that Geni could 'av 'eard 'im, would 'ave shook
    'im up all ends,
"Let's knock it off" I ses at last, and gives
    the top a crack,
Then the lid flew off with a shocking bang, and flung
    me on my back.
When I first looked up, them other two was fifty
    yards away,
Entrenched behind two lumps of rock and shouting
    "Bill! I say!
Go easy when 'e first appears." My 'air rose up—the jar!
    Then I gave one look, and I smelt one smell, and I
    left for fields afar,
Toff looked quite 'urt "Wot's up?" ses 'e,
    I ses "I think wot's wrong
Is the bloke inside that blooming jar's been bottled
    up too long."
So Toff puts on 'is poison mask and creeps back to the
    spot,
And we sees 'im take 'is bayonet, and probe inside the pot.
    Then 'e takes that jar, and 'e takes that lid, and
    'e 'urls em in the tide.
And comes back walkin' sad and slow, with a face like
    a pain inside,
    And at last 'e says in a strangled voice, that was
    'oarse with bitter tears,
"IT WAS PLUM AND APPLE JAM GONE BAD
FOR TWENTY THOUSAND YEARS!"
There's a simple tablet standing where the ancient
    waters flow,
    And the minarets of old Baghdad reflect the sunset glow,
"Here LIES a book" the inscription reads
    "Through all the years to come,
This book will *LIE* for ever, when the camel bells
    are dumb."

TRIFLES

BY CHARLES PLATT　　　　　　　　　　　　　　1933

What is it makes a man content,
　　A woman happy, a child all smiles?
We call it happiness, do we not?
　　Though nobody knows what it is beguiles.
It may be a trifle, the touch of a hand,
　　Or a friendly glance that we understand.
We call it happiness, do we not?
　　Though nobody knows what it is beguiles.
Most of us get through the days somehow,
　　We cross life's rivers, we climb life's stiles;
We seek for Happiness lurking ahead,
　　For nobody knows what it is beguiles.
We may find peace, or it may be strife,
　　For no one can tell what comes next in life.
All seek for happiness, seek and strive,
　　Yet few of us learn how a trifle beguiles.
Study those trifles so heedlessly missed.
　　Today is here, don't look ahead.
Each hour will bring so many things,
　　A kind word spoken, a tear unshed.
The touch of a hand makes love awake,
　　Or will ease some mourner's weary ache.
Trifles, no doubt, but in life's dull round.
　　That is where happiness will be found!

THE TRUTH

BY TED LYMBERY and HERBERT TOWNSEND　　　　1923

It's a habit.
　　And, like every other habit we have got,
It grows up on us with advancing years.

If started on in infancy and practised all through
    life
A name is made that everyone reveres
    And relies on.
For a man whose word has always been his bond
    Examples sets to every maid and youth—
"Trust so-and-so? Of course you can,
    He's never known to fail to speak the truth."
It's an asset.
    And, like every other asset always does,
It takes its place upon the credit side of character,
    And outweighs quite a lot of other things
That justify a little conscious pride and happiness.
    There comes a time when each of you must pay
For follies you committed during youth.
    But easy is the settlement,
If you have made a rule to speak the truth.
    It's a virtue.
And, like every other virtue, blesses all
    Who come within the radius of its power.
Where it abides is confidence—and confidence means trust—
    That gains in strength with every fleeting hour.
It's a maxim.
    And like every other maxim made for men,
It commends itself to every thinking youth.
    But if the wife asks questions you are anxious to
        evade, Well—*(Please your-self!!)*

THE TWIRP

BY ROBERT RUTHERFORD and NORMAN LONG   *1942*

Cuthbert, Clarendon, Chesney Chirp
    Said to his father "You're a TWIRP:
A TWIRP, that's what you are," said he.
    To which his dad replied, "I see
So I'm a TWIRP, and I conclude
    A TWIRP, my lad is something rude?"

416

"l don't know that," replied his son,
  "But whatever a TWIRP is, you are one!"
At which his father with a frown,
  Turned Cuthbert Clarendon's trousers down.
That evening in the pub. Jim Chirp
  Asked one and all, "What is a TWIRP?"
But all he learned, 'midst laughter hoarse
  Was, "You're a TWIRP yourself of course."
Next day the local librarian
  Was called on by an anxious man
Who said to him, "Can you tell me
  Just what a TWIRP'S supposed to be?"
The gent replied, "Stay where you are
  Whilst I consult Britannica"
And later came back with a grin
  And said, "l fear it isn't in;
But though the word is not defined
  I'm sure it cannot be refined."
Off to the British Museum Jim hied,
  And once again the question plied
"What is a TWIRP? You ought to know."
  The aged assistants in a row
Let out a howl that broke the gloom
  And echoed through the Mummy Room.
They turned up Hebrew, Latin, Greek
  But not of TWIRPS did any speak:
"The origin's obscure," said they
  "And obscene too Ha-ha Hey-hey!"
Said James, "It's very plain to me
  Whatever else a TWIRP may be
It's something that makes people laugh
  And laughter's what we want not half!"
So on the Music Halls went Chirp,
  And billed himself, "THE PERFECT TWIRP";
And packed with TWIRPS his patter runs,
  And everywhere he goes great guns;
Three hundred pounds a week earns Jim
  And that's not bad for a TWIRP like him.

THE TWO GOOD-BYES

"A TOMMY TO HIS GIRL"

BY DOROTHY SCULL and ALFRED H. WEST 1917

It's true, old girl, l'm goin',
 We're off tomorrow night—
An' all this bloomin' trainin's
 Made me ready for to fight
Fink of me old sporty,
 Wot's never 'ad no chance
Of ever seein' bloodshed,
 Agoin' off to France.
Why kiddo wot's the matter?
 Got somethin' in yer eye?
Aw, now don't you go an' tell me
 As 'ow you're goin' to cry.
Afraid I'll not be coming back,
 An' why can't you come too?
Aw—you bet there's someone somewhere,
 As is sure to see me through;
An' even if I do get "pipped"—
 An' there may be 'alf a chance,
There ain't no better way to die
 Than fighting out in France.
So Good-bye kid—Gawd bless yer,
 An' don't be down at 'eart,
Jest think that your bloke like the rest
 'As gone to do 'is part.

TWO MEN

BY GEORGE ARTHURS and CUTHBERT CLARKE 1928

I know a man who's bold and bad,
 His actions make his people sad.
But he's so tall and handsome, he

Can always get a smile from me.
But oh, he's bad, so people say,
  He turns the night-time into day,
But how he thrills me when he flirts,
  And kisses me until it hurts.
He's always chasing skirts!
  He drinks and smokes, tells risky jokes,
They say he's crooked, but, well, I don't know!
  He's devil-may-care, but I declare
He's got a voice that sets me all aglow.
  He gambles, too, I know it's true,
For what is love but just a game of chance?
  The things he's said make me turn red,
But oh, By Golly, how that man can dance!
  He's bad, they say, but all the same,
He's handsome, tall and slim.
  And I've got a happy feeling, 'cause
One day I mean to marry him!
  I know a man who's awful good,
He always does the things he should.
  He never smokes, he never swears,
But how he puffs when climbing stairs!
  He's always home at half-past eight,
For dinner he is never late,
  But he's so fat and looks so weird
Since he has grown a mottled beard,
  A thing I've always feared!
He loves to preach, and wants to teach
  All people how to eat and drink and live,
But he's out-size, has fishy eyes,
  Or that much I would probably forgive.
He flirts? Not he! He's fond of tea,
  We've never had a quarrel or a tiff,
His mind is strong, he's never wrong,
  But goodness me! That fellow bores me stiff!
He's good, they say, but all the same
  He's ugly, fat and grim.
Still I've got a happy feeling, 'cause
  Tomorrow I'm DIVORCING him!

419

UNCLE GEORGE

BY GREATREX NEWMAN and FRED. CECIL   1914

Performed by Bransby Williams

It's plain as I ain't a policeman,
   An' likewise I ain't a Boy Sprout,
I'm a Bailiff! Yes, that's my perfession,
   The bloke wot goes round chuckin' out.
Last Toosday I went to an'ouse to distrain,
   When the door was thrown open quite wide,
An' a woman, all smilin', takes old o' me 'and,
   An' ses *"Dear Uncle George come inside.*
We all was *so* pleased," 'er goes on, smilin' still
   "When we got yer last letter what say'd
As 'ow you was comin' back 'ome from Noo York,
   To retire now yer fortune yer'd made."
Then 'er 'usband *'e* 'eartily shakes both me 'ands,
   An' 'e gets a chair for me to sit:
"It's twenty long years since yer left us," ses 'e,
   "But lumme, *you ain't changed a bit!"*
O' course it was plain they was thinkin' as I
   Was their h'uncle jus' back from the States,
So thinks I to meself, this 'ere h'uncle's got brass
   So p'r'aps I shall "touch" if I waits.
So I sits meself down, an' I ses:— "Well me dears,
   I've come back at last from me roam;
Arter twenty long years in the wilds o' Noo York,
   I'm glad, once agen, to be 'ome."
Then the 'usband, 'e gets out 'is pipe, an' 'e ses:—
   "Me terbacca I've gone an' forgot:—
I'll try yours if yer like Huncle George?;"—An
   'e did!
   An' 'e very near took all I'd got.
Then 'e ses—"Now we'll all celebrate yer return
   By drinkin' yer jolly good 'ealth,—
*So lend us a bob;—*An' I couldn't refuse,
   Or else 'e'd a-doubted me wealth.
Well then it got late, Uncle George 'adn't come,
   But I thought 'e'd come next day all right,

So I ses: "My 'otel's a good distance from 'ere
  P'r'aps *you'd* put me up for the night?"
"We've jus' sent our h'only spare mattress away,
  To 'ave the springs cleaned" the wife said,
"But we've got some *old sacks* in the garret upstairs"–
  I ses: "Right, them'll do for a bed.
I've slep' on wus beds than sacks many a time,
  Yer should be in *Noo York,* that's the place,–
Why h'out there I've slep' *on the prairies for weeks,
  Wi' tigers a-lickin' me face!"*
"What a brave 'un you is h'uncle George to be sure,
  You're an 'ero," the bloke proudly said,
Then 'e touched me for fourpence;–'twas all as
      I'd got,
  So I left 'em and went up to bed.
When I got up next day, all the furniture'd gone!
  Exceptin' a rusty old fork,
An' a note, left beside it, said:
  "Dear Uncle George, *Good-bye, we're just off ter
    Noo York!"*

UNDEDICATED

BY HARRY WYNNE and WALTER DOWLING   *1912*

I'd dare indite a ditty to my lovely lady's eyes.
  I'd sing about them all day long, I'd praise them
      to the skies.
But then you see she squints and so perhaps it's hardly
      wise.
  I'd sing a simple sonnet to her ankle trim and neat,
That calls for such attention when she walks across
      the street.
  But tho' her ankle's rather small, she's got
      such whopping feet.
I'd make melodious music to the wonders of her face,
  And little trills and little runs I'd write to suit
      the case,

For to me her nose seems running all around the blooming
  place.
I'd pen a pensive poem to the colour of her hair,
But when I come to think of it, I'm rather baffled
  there,
  For the colour seems to alter with the dresses she
  may wear.
But oh my lilting lyric I had better not indite,
  For the lady who inspired it is in truth an awful
  fright.
And the whole thing's rather risky for she may be here
  tonight.
  And so my little ditty I shall never now begin,
For it might be most uncomfy for the lady's kith and
  kin,
  But they must feel very thankful that she wasn't
  born a twin.

UP AND DOWN THE STRAND

BY SAM WALSH   *1915*

Shove me off the pavement, push me in the dirt,
  Draw your dainty skirts away, fear they come to hurt.
Hurry past and leave me here, holding out my hand,
  Selling matches in the rain, up and down the Strand.
Lord, there isn't no romance, in a case like mine.
  I've had no inglorious fall through womenfolk or
  wine.
No bloomin' awful lurid past, no betrayin' of a trust,
  To make me stand here in the rain abeggin' of a crust.
I was simply born to this, same as thousands more,
  I am one of them what's called the underserving poor.
Selling matches in the Strand to anyone I can.
  Yet, God help me now and then I'd like to be a man.
In the Army shelter where I gets my dole
  Of bread and soup, by God, I'd like to smash the
  bloomin' bowl

And fling it in their faces and make a blazin' stir,
  And wake the manhood up in me. Yes, two a penny sir.
But I haven't got the brains, no, nor yet the heart.
  I have been, and always shall be, in the blooming
    cart.
Standing in the puddles, wond'ring what you'll give,
  Fearing very much to die, and loathing it to live.
Shove me off the pavement, push me in the dirt,
  Draw your dainty skirts away, fear they come to hurt.
Hurry past and leave me here, holding out my hand,
  Selling matches in the rain, up and down the Strand.

THE USHERETTE

BY V. F. STEVESN and JOE MURRELLS   *1945*

I'm an usher at the 'movies' that's wot I am.
  A utility 'commissionaire' no doubt,
I ushers people to their seats from half-past-twelve
    till 'free'
  And from 'free' till half-past-five I chucks 'em
    out.
I wear a luvly uniform:— sky-blue, maroon and gold;
  The fit is not so bad but then yer see!
The 'usherette' wot wore it long before I got the job,
  Was a girl about three times the size of me.
I don't stand any nonsense from those chaps wot come
    along
  An' try flirtin' wiv me while I mind the queues;
I watch 'em, see! and if they swank an' book for
    'arf-a-crown
  I promptly bungs 'em in the one-and-twos.
I always 'ave me torch wiv me in case there's any fuss,
  It's 'andy for the back rows where it's dark.
And since I've bin a usher—I've come to realize
  Spoonin's easier in the pictures than the park.
I've seen some sights I tell yer!

Enough to curl yer 'air,
Couples 'oldin' 'ands an' chewin' sweets;
   Women wiv big shoppin' bags an' kids wot cry an'
      scream
And leave their dirty bootmarks on the seats.
   The 'posh' seats are upstairs at 'three-an'-six' and
      'four-an'-nine'
But 'four-an'-nine' for pictures cuts no ice,
   Cos if just the same goes on up there, especially
      at the back,
Well at 'four-an-nine' I'll say it's worth the price.
   One night the batt'ry of me little torch ran out
I tell yer! I was in a proper state,
   I felt a strange 'and touch me and it didn't want a
      programme;
It was someone givin' me a "number eight."
   I 'ave a 'arf day orf each week,
I'm glad when that comes round;
   My boy-friend calls and takes me to the "Ritz"
It's such a change for me who is a usher by
      perfession
To 'ave someone come an' show me where I sits.
I love to see the news reels and those flashes wot
      they shows,
   Of diff'rent things an' wot they're all about,
But just as me an' Bert are gettin' matey someone says
   "That's the end of this performance—This way out!"

'V'

BY MARGARET HODGKINSON and NOSMO KING   *1942*

Thro' the wastes of darkest Europe, where the jungle
      law holds sway,
   Where the blood-soaked hosts of Evil gorge and fatten
      on their prey;
Where the infamous disciples of that madman, thrice-
      accurst

Bleed and torture countless millions to assuage
　　their master's thirst;
To the dark abomination of a continent in thrall,
　　From our own free island fortress comes a ringing
　　clarion call
A voice sounds forth a challenge to the peoples overseas,
　　Comrades, rise! Shake off your fetters! Rise and
　　sound your watchword V.
Can you hear it, Herr Kommandant, in the Cafe,
　　in the Street?
　　Guttural "achtungs" cannot drown it, nor the
　　tramp of marching feet;
And the Devil's Legions falter as they goose-step
　　on parade—
　　Laugh, mighty Jove! Laugh loud and long, the
　　swaggering bullies are afraid!
They understand the meaning—and the warning—of the
　　sign
　　They hear it gather volume, like the waters of
　　the Rhine;
They know, though chained and fettered, their victims'
　　souls are free,
　　And they hear their own death-sentence in the thunder
　　of the V.
Can you hear it, Dokter Goebbels? Can you hear it
　　swell and rise
　　Till it shatters the foundations of your rotten
　　house of lies!
Yes! you hear it, and in terror, in your sick,
　　distorted brain
　　You try to turn and twist it to your own pernicious
　　gain.
Fool! The whole world laughs to scorn, your feeble,
　　futile, frighten'd tale.
　　Of V for *German* Victory! Truth is great and
　　will prevail!
Your fellow gangsters tremble—one at least made haste
　　to flee
　　From the wrath to come, predicted by the tapping
　　of the V.
Can you hear it, Adolf Hitler, from the lands you made
　　a tomb?

Drawing nearer, ever nearer, like the rolling drums
   of Doom.
Does it beat into your frenzied brain and breast like
   two-edged swords?
Do you hear your death-knell, Führer, in Beethoven's
   mighty chords?
The Cross of Shame, the Swastika, is reeling to
   its fall.
Do you see it Hitler? Do you see the writing
   on the wall!
Your blood stained soul shall perish and Hell shall
   shriek with glee,
And slaughtered thousands be requited, in the
   vengeance of the V.
Can *you* hear it, tortured victims of the jack-boot
   and the whip?
Can you hear the stirring message, as it flies from
   lip to lip?
Lift your hearts up! Be of courage! Comrades of the
   V, unite!
The hearts of free men through the world are with
   you in the fight!
Let it swell up to a murmur, from a murmur to
   a roar—
Resounding and triumphant—Fate is knocking
   at the door!
Let the crashing chords proclaim it of the great
   V Symphony—
Till the whole world rings and echoes to the
   shout of VICTORY!

VALUES

BY NOSMO KING, E. H. ORGAN and ERNEST LONGSTAFFE 1948

The world is full of sons of discontent,
   Wealth without work their futile, feverish bent,

Fortune by lucky chance, the chains of toil to sever,
  Heedless of primal law—by sweet and stern endeavour.
The task takes second place, the pay is all that
        matters,
  The dream of easy cash their resolution scatters.
Less hours of work, more of uneasy leisure,
  Pursuing joylessly the costly myth of pleasure.
What part have I in all this restless quest,
  Where only that which costs the most is best,
Where values are in glitter and display,
  Where men are judged by what they have to pay?
There's so much more in life than this to me,
  So many precious gifts completely free;
God's bounty which He lavishly bestows –
  (Who really knows true wealth who only money knows?)
The rippling moonlight in a woodland pool;
  The dimpled, laughing infant at the school;
The long, cool shadows where the elm trees stand;
  The swelling bosom of this lovely land;
Cascading roses on a garden arch;
  An ancient wall that saw the legions march;
The smell of wood smoke in the evening breeze;
  The cawing rooks amongst the distant trees.
A handclasp with a comrade of the past,
  Renewing bonds that will forever last—
The song of birds at closing of the day,
  The fragrant perfume of the new mown hay,
The sweetness that the walls of home provide;
  Your children and a brave wife at your side;
The summer sun—the moon and stars that shine,
  What need have I of greater wealth, when all this
        wealth is mine?

VEILS

BY BRANSBY WILLIAMS and CUTHBERT CLARKE, Op. 86.   1923

The Veil of the Past is best undrawn,
   For the deeds that are done it is no use to mourn,
You know all the pleasures and pains that are there,
   You've seen them so oft they must need be threadbare!
Gladness may lie there but don't take a peep,
   Or you may rouse the sorrows you placed there to
      keep!
They are all in that cupboard, each on its own shelf,
   And guarded from view by Old Time himself;
Don't lay bare the storehouse of memory where
   Each hour is labelled, marked gladness or care,
Sigh not for glad days, for bad days don't mourn,
   There ne'er was a rose that had not a thorn
Just let the veil rest where it is till the last
   Don't let your hand draw the Veil of the Past!
The Veil of the Present I think spells deceit!
   Do you say what you mean to the friend that you
      meet?
Do you tell an untruth that may cause others pain?
   Or perchance do you tell it to bring self some
      gain?
Do you pose as a friend to someone you dislike?
   And greet with a kiss someone you would strike?
You may think it harmless this game of pretence!
   But it's really no good and it lacks common sense,
Come turn out the cupboard, sweep clear the shelf,
   If the linen is dirty then cleanse it yourself!
Tear the veil—tear it—to shreds and to tatters
   And just be your true self, then nothing else
      matters.
Be like the new moon a pure shining crescent,
   You've got no use for the Veil of the Present!
Veil of the Future the wise men have sought
   To pierce but the efforts have all come to naught.
With all the world's wisdom, and all the world's sin,
   Man has not drawn it or e'en peeped within

The cupboard that holds all the secrets of Fate.
   Is guarded by Time and for Him we must wait:
Man but presumes when he seeks to reveal
   The secrets of life that lie under the seal!
If the future we knew all mankind would go mad,
   All the gladness would go, we should always be,
      sad—
Don't seek to tempt Time He knows what is best,
   Just take what He gives and wait for the rest.
Behind that weird veil may lie gladness or sorrow
   Let Time draw the Veil of the Future tomorrow.

THE VILLAGE CONSTABLE

BY ALBERT CHEVALIER and ALFRED H. WEST   *1909*

Ah! wot a moighty wicked place our village it 'ud be,
   If 'twasn't vur the care Oi takes from crime to
      keep it free,
Oi've taught 'un to respect the law since Oi've been in
      the force,
   An' wot Oi sez, they 'as ter do, they 'as ter do,
      of course.
Oi can't 'ave that, Oi sez, Oi can't, Oi bean't agoin'
      to tell 'ee why,
   An' don' 'ee try no tricks on 'cos Oi'm moighty sharp
      and floy—
Oi can't 'ave that, Oi sez, Oi can't, Ah! you may
      stan' an' gi' Oi jaw,
   But when Oi sez a thing, Oi sez, the thing Oi sez
      be law.
They troies all koinds o' broibes wi' Oi, but Lor!
      Oi knows their game,
   There's nowt Oi can't see through at once, Oi puts
      un all to shame.
Oi be that quick they knows wi' Oi they don't stan
      arf a chance,

Oi be a reg'lar master-piece to see things at a
    glance.
Oi can't 'ave that, Oi sez, Oi can't, Oi bean't agoin'
    to tell 'ee why,
  An' don' 'ee try no tricks on 'cos Oi'm moighty
    sharp and floy—
Oi can't 'ave that, Oi sez, Oi can't, Ah! you may
    stan' an' gi' Oi jaw,
  But when Oi sez a thing, Oi sez, the thing Oi sez
    be law.
It's hard work tho', vor Muddleton's, a moighty busy
    place.
  There's foive-an'-forty people an' they loikes to
    go the pace.
But Lor! Oi've got un all inside the 'oller o' my 'and,
  They dursent call their souls their own, Oi tell 'ee
    as it's grand.
Oi can't 'ave that, Oi sez, Oi can't, Oi bean't agoin'
    to tell 'ee why,
  An' don' 'ee try no tricks on 'cos Oi'm mighty sharp
    and floy—
Oi can't 'ave that, Oi sez, Oi can't, Ah! you may stan'
    an' gi' Oi jaw,
  But when Oi sez a thing, Oi sez, the thing Oi sez
    be law.

A VOYAGE OF DISASTER

BY ARTHUR HELLIAR and CUTHBERT CLARKE   1909
Performed by Bransby Williams

Don't talk to me of the ocean!
  Don't talk to me of the sea.
I've done with the briny for ever!
  Dry land in the future for me.
But what brought things fair to a crisis,
  Was the luck as we 'ad the last trip.

From the moment we fust left the harbour,
 There was nuffink went right on the ship.
She was launched on a Friday to start with,
 But that ain't the wust, as you'll 'ear
The owner—'im being tee-total—'ad 'er christened
  with ginger beer.
 Stone ginger, a penny a bottle!
Not even with dry ginger ale,
 No wonder as luck was agen us!
It's surprisin' I'm telling the tale.
 From the fust things went reg'lar contrary—
As soon as the anchor was weighed.
 Tho' the tug was apullin' and strainin', not a hinch
  of the voyage she made.
O' course we all thought as she'd grounded,
 But the stoutest 'eart quailed when we found
Tho' she'd not move ahead or astern sir,
 She'd spin like a top round and round!
You'll 'ardly believe what 'ad 'appened!
 Why when they was fixing the mast,
They'd druv it right down thro' the keel, sir,
 And into the mud it had passed.
And there we was fixed on a pivot,
 As was sticking yards deep in the sludge,
So you'll own as it wasn't surprisin',
 As the tug couldn't get us to budge.
They fixed it agen right and proper,
 And we got down as far as the Nore,
Where the tug boat o' course went and left us
 And we fancied our troubles was o'er.
But that's where we made a slight error,
 For the skipper the crew loudly hails,
And tells 'em to jump and look lively
 And set to a-'oisting the sails.
"Aye, aye, sir!" says we, and the bo'sun
 And the mate up aloft took a gaze
And the langwidge they used I shall never forget
 If I live till the end o' my days.
Then *we* squints aloft, as was nat'ral,
 And wot d'yer think as we find
There wasn't no sails there to 'oist, sir,
 We'd been and we'd left 'em behind!

They'd all been took off don't yer see, sir,
　　At the time as the mast was unshipped,
And the fact as they 'adn't replaced 'em,
　　From ev'ryone's mind must ha' slipped
So we has to be towed back to London,
　　And *there* was our sails on the quay
And the captain 'e kept out o' sight sir,
　　Till once more we was off to the sea.
For a fortnight the weather kept misty, and the skies
　　　　was the colour o' lead.
　　Not a sight o' the sun to be 'ad, sir,
Not a glimpse o' the stars over-head.
　　Sou' west was the course by the compass,
But owin' d'yer see to the fog,
　　We was feeling our way very careful—
Dead reck'ning, it's called, with the log.
　　And the weather as should 'ave got milder,
Grew colder each day it was plain,
　　But we sighted some land tho' one mornin',
Wot the skipper 'e fancied was Spain.
　　He looked for a bit thro' 'is glasses,
And the mate took a squint at it too.
　　There was mountains all covered with snow, sir,
And h'ice as was plain to view.
　　"I never see Spain look like that, sir."
Says the mate "it's too snowy by far!
　　"We'd best send a boat to the 'arbour
And ask where the dickens we are"
　　The boat wasn't long in returning,
And the men were all grinning we saw,
　　Wot set our old man fairly raving—
As wasn't sweet tempered afore.
　　"Where the blazes" 'e yells "'ave we got to—
Is it Spain or Gibraltar, or what?"
　　"It's H'iceland" the mate says respectful
"That's the nearest to Spain as we've got!"
　　The old man—but I can't do fair justice
To the words wot come out of his mouth,
　　For a fortnight our course 'ad been North sir,
When it should ha' lain pretty near South.
　　But it wasn't 'is fault after all though,
For the sun soon ashining we found

As the man wot 'ad fixed up the compass,
'Ed shoved on the card wrong way round.
We'd several mishaps arter that sir,
But nuffink as mattered to *me.*
Though a thing as we found out at Melbourne,
Might have worried the owner maybe.
As soon as we took off the 'atches,
The bosun 'e says "Well I'm blowed"
Strike me pink! if the 'old wasn't empty—
The cargo 'ad never been stowed!

THE VOYAGE OF THE "SAUCY JANE"

BY VAL L. REGAN and HERBERTE JORDAN   *1941*

This is the tale of the "Saucy Jane,"
  Who sailed out to the lightship and then back again;
For years she had wallowed her way round the bay
  With trippers, and babies, and lovers each day.
Till a maggot, deep hid in a maniac's brain,
  Stirred; and lashed him to visions of lunatic gain.
Then the laughter was hushed as the war clouds drew
    near,
  And the "Saucy Jane" brooded alone at her pier.
Her sleek sides grew rusty, her paint drab and grey,
  Her engines stood silent as day after day,
The great ships of war; sisters under the skin
  Hurried past the backwater she lay rotting in.
While her skipper, as grizzled and old as was she,
  Fumed and groaned as he heard the guns thudding
    at sea.
Then a whisper was heard going round and around,
  Much too good to be true; yet the whisper gained
    ground,
Till the skipper climbed up on the bridge once again,
  And with tears in his voice said *"We're off,*
    Saucy Jane!"

Then the old ship moved off with a creak and a quiver,
  To join the strange fleet that had come down the river.
There were tug-boats and barges of curious smell,
  There were sleek motor-boats, paddle steamers as
    well,
River launches and wherries and sailing craft too,
  And each boat had an equally curious crew.
On that shore of the Channel where once had been
    France,
  Stood the men who had struggled thro' Death's
    crimson dance;
While the skies overhead rained a murderous hate
  And it seemed as though help would arrive much
    too late;
Till that curious fleet with the curious crew,
  Into sight and the bomb-spattered battle
    zone drew,
With the "Saucy Jane" puffing black smoke in a cloud
  While her skipper steered, cursing and swearing
    aloud.
By guess and by God, they were hoisted aboard,
  And the old "Saucy Jane" her defiance now roared,
While down in her vitals a strange stokehole gang
  Shovelled coal mixed with blood while they sweated
    and sang.
As the bullets whizzed round and the shrapnel fell fast
  Till a sickening crash robbed old "Jane" of
    her mast;
Then a wounded Jock shouted "Ah'll bet ye ma kilt
  That the auld girl will mak' it—*This tub was
    Clyde built!*"
The old ship floundered on in a last burst of pride;
  Then help was around her and boats at her side
But the old "Saucy Jane," with a strange kind of
    grace;
  Gave a sigh as she welcomed the sea's cold embrace;
Just as if she had known she was needed no more.
  She slid to her rest, on the soft ocean floor.
In the years still to come, when the story's complete,
  On the long scroll of honour, that curious fleet,
That ragtag and bob tail of vessels and crews,
  Will have earned a renown that *no* ship would refuse;

And more honour and glory no vessel will gain
Than that valiant lady *"The Old Saucy Jane!"*

THE WAGGY END

ADA LEONORA HARRIS and HENRY E. PETHER

A dog is called a quadruped,
    Which means he's got, of course,
A leg at ev'ry corner,
    Like a table or a horse.
The dog is called the friend of man,
    But I can tell you flat,
No matter what folks think or say,
    He's not the friend of cat.
Some dogs are rough and some are smooth,
    Some black, some brown and white,
And each dog has one end to wag,
    And one with which to bite.
But sometimes with a dog whose hair
    Is rather extra long,
You think you've got the waggy end,
    But find you've got the wrong!

THE WAIF'S PARADISE

BY FERRIS CARLTON and FRANK S. WILCOCK   1924

Why Sally I've been wondering where ever yer could be.
    I fort yer'd bin an' gorn ter sleep froo 'avin' too
        much tea.

435

That cake wos orlrite wasn't it, well that's wot Bill
      Jones sed.
  But I got mine in me pocket ter take 'ome ter
      little Ted.
If 'e 'adn't been so poorly 'e'd bin 'ere terday wiv
      us
  I shan't tell 'im 'ow grand it's bin, 'cos that might
      make 'im wuss.
Oo! Sal, ain't that a lovely bunch o' flowers in yer
      'and,
  Wot's that yer calls 'em? Dandy-liners? Lumme,
      ain't they grand.
'Ere! wot d'yer fink I see just now in that field
      over there?
  Why! some live sheeps 'eads wiv bodies on, they fairly
      made me stare.
An' some of 'em 'ad little pups, an' a gent sed they
      wos lambs,
  An' some wiv great big curly 'orns wos sheep, wot
      they calls rams.
'Ere Sally, I bin down a street, no 'ouses there at all,
  On'y grass an' lots o' trees, not even a brick wall,
Birds a-singin' wivout any cage, an' a rabbit wot lived
      in a 'ole,
  If I told farver wot I sore 'e'd say I was up the
      pole.
No boards wot says "Keep off the grass" yer could
      roll on it yer could.
  If it wasn't fer muvver an' Ted, I'd like ter stop
      down 'ere fer good.
I've seen some 'orses in a field wivout no 'arness on,
  An' a great big long-necked chicken in the water,
      called a swan.
They can't get 'ungry 'ere, cos their fields is full
      o' meat,
  Why! they lights their fires wi' faggots 'stead of
      usin' 'em to eat.
An' they can't 'ave busted water-pipes when winter
      time comes round,
  'Cos they keeps their water in a 'ole wot's dug
      down in the ground.

I see a man a-fishin', 'e wos in a little ship,
   'E got some string an' tied it on the end of a
      long whip,
Then 'e chucked it in the water an' I sees it bob
      about,
   An' 'e turned a little 'andle, an' 'e pulled a bloater
      out.
I wish I knowed where I could get one o' them 'ere
      whips
   'Cos then I'd catch the fish an' we should on'y
      buy the chips.
'Ark! Sally, there's the bell a-ringin', now we shall
      'ave ter go,
   There's a gen'l'man callin' us over there ter take
      us back yer know.
Why! Sally wot yer cryin' for? Yer wants ter stop
      down 'ere?
   Er course yer do, an' so do I, but we might come
      down nex' year.
An' then p'r'aps Ted'll be wiv us when we comes down
      again,
   So cheer up Sal, let's run an' be the fust ones in
      the train.

THE WASTER

BY F. CHATTERTON HENNEQUIN
and BLANCHE GASTON MURRAY   *1913*

I'm a thousand miles up country,
   And I'm frozen to the bone,
While my brothers sleep in London,
   And my very name disown.
It's a name that's simply rotten
   In the old land and the new,

Through the whole condemned Dominion,
   I'm a wrong 'un through and through.
A shoddy sort of failure,
   Eh? A Waster! Yes I know.
A kind of social leper
   So I'm rotting in the snow,
I'm not asking for your pity,
   You can save your little prayers,
I'm a brand beyond redemption,
   In a land where no one cares.
I was shipped without a blessing,
   In a hurry, so to speak,
And the things I left behind me
   Were forgotten in a week;
For the gods that built me crooked,
   Had a sense of humour left,
And the devil made me callous
   Of the good I was bereft.
In the gambling dens of 'Frisco,
   In the drinking halls of sin,
I've a sort of social entree
   That will always pass me in.
Oh they know me for a rotter,
   From the Yukon to the Clyde,
And many a friendly push I get,
   As down to Hell I slide.
Sometime inside this cursed cold,
   That grips me to the heart,
I'll pass my checks like some foul rat
   That dies his kin apart
And ne'er a soul will understand,
   The depth of my despair,
And never one within this land,
   Will either grieve or care.
But on my black and wasted years,
   Across the world's disdain,
I know of *ONE* whose tears will fall,
   With grief for me in vain.
And there you see my punishment,
   The shame that I must bear,
The love I never can escape,
   A crown of thorns to wear,

A shoddy sort of failure, Eh?
A Waster! Yes, I know.
A kind of social leper,
　So I'm rotting in the snow.
I'm not asking for your pity,
　You can save your little prayers,
I'm a brand beyond redemption,
　In a land where no one cares.

THE WATERLOO PUP

BY MABEL PAGDEN and GERALD MORRISON　　　　　　*1932*
Performed by Chesney Allen

The sweetest pup I know, had never seen a show,
　But he's quite the fastest thing I ever knew;
He was taken out and tried, and when he and
　　"Flea-Bag" tied,
　I knew I'd picked a winner good and true.
So the only thing to do was to buy a good shampoo
　And take him home and wash him with dispatch.
For though it was a bore: if we entered him before
　For any race we knew that he would scratch!
Well, when we got him back his coat was just like black,
　But when shampooed he turned as white as snow.
We called him "Tim" at once, but after sev'ral months,
　We found we had to change his name to "Flo".
We fed her oats and hay, till one fine summer's day
　We thought her fit to race upon the track.
For she'd won a race with case, against two Pekingese,
　From the dustbin to the garden gate and back!
We trained her very hard; made her skip in our back-
　　yard.
　And gave her jugg'd hare every day at four.
We tried to keep it dark, but the silly ass *would*
　　bark,

And reporters came around us by the score.
When the news was spread abroad what a victory
    she'd scored,
    The bookies got the "wind up" quite a bit.
Of course they tried to hedge, then rushed out and
    signed the pledge,
    And the poor old Tote it nearly threw a fit!
The betting was immense—enormous sums in pence.
    On every hand you heard them sing her praise—
Mr. Woolworth had a smack, and so had Ramsay Mac,
    And twenty Scotsmen shared a bob both ways!
The day dawned bright and clear—but "Flo" was looking
    queer
    As we saddled her and tied her girth beneath;
But altho' she wasn't well, we knew she'd run like—
    fury,
    When once she felt the bit between her teeth.
They're off! They're off! They've started, she's first
    upon my soul!
    She's given the hare a kick in the pants, and nearly
    scored a goal!
See! they're running down the straight: Flo's first,
    she'll win the race.
    Ah see, they're running tail to tail, Now look,
    they're face to face!
Flo is running like the wind, the hare she's nearly
    passed:
    She's leading all the other dogs: but now she's
    running last!
Aha! The pack has halted—the hare stands in the track,
    And in the twinkling of an eye Flo jumps upon his
    back!
They're rounding Tatt'nham Corner, they falter in
    their stride:
    The umpire blows the whistle, he's given Flo
    "Off-side".
They're off again like thunder, poor Flo is almost
    beat;
    Look look they're running neck and neck, and now
    they're feet to feet!
The race is nearly ended—they're coming down the
    straight;

440

The bookies pack their satchels up—they're edging
  near the gate.
Our Flo is running gamely, though she's missing
  on one lung:
Hurrah! She's started panting—Yes she's won by
  HALF A TONGUE!

THE WAXWORK WATCHMAN

BY W. S. FRANK and FRANK S. WILCOCK   *1926*
Performed by Bransby Williams

Watchman what of the night, d'ye say?
  Well b'lieve me tain't all honey
Bein' a night watchman. Though mind you 'e gets good
  money.
  I know what I'm a-saying of because I used to be
Night watchman at two swords waxworks what got
  burned down d'ye see.
  'Twas a gruesome sort o' job, an' it would fairly
  make you creep
If you had seen the sights I've see'd when you've
  been fast asleep.
The Watchman accepts an imaginary glass of beer,
nods his thanks, blows froth off, wipes his lips and
proceeds.
Watchman, what of the night, d'ye say, now wouldn't
  it make you stare
  To see them figures come to life and walk around
  you there.
Yes, Kings an' Queens an' Dukes an' Earls an' criminals
  an' all,
  A-hobnobbin' together like a Covent Garden Ball.
I see'd it with these optics, it ain't no fairy tale,
  It's gospel truth I'm tellin' you same as the
  Daily Mail.
'Twas Christmas Eve last Christmas, on December twenty-
  four,

441

An' I 'ad been on duty just about an hour or more,
I was gazin' on a bottle, wonderin' 'ow long it would
    last,
    When suddenly all down my spine I felt an icy blast,
An' then I 'eard a soulful sigh, an' then a mournful
    moan,
    An' when I looked the sight I saw, near turned me
    to a stone,
For there was Mary Queen o' Scots a-walking round the
    place,
    A-lookin' for Elizabeth—I thought now 'ere's a case.
But afore I 'ad a chance to move the other figures
    too,
    All came to life an' started makin' such a how-d'ye-do.
Lord Bacon and Will Shakespeare were having quite a
    tiff
    As to who wrote Willy Shakespeare's plays, says
    Bacon, with a sniff,
"Beshrew thee scurvy mounte-bank, you know I wrote
    the lot."
    Says Shakespeare, "Gertsher scurvy knave, don't
    talk such blinkin' rot."
And then I saw Richard the Third, they called him Dirty
    Dick,
    He roared "Ha ha! The Dook of York, off with his
    napper quick."
But Hall Caine only grinned and said, "Don't be a
    silly chump,
    It's no use getting waxy, just because you've got the
    hump."
Then Raleigh and Elizabeth they nearly came to blows,
    For Walter said that Lizzie had spoilt his Sunday
    clothes.
Said Raleigh "When I laid my cloak down in the muddy
    street,
    You made a nasty mess of it with your big plates
    of meat."
Then there was Henery the Eight a-sufferin' for his sins,
    For each of his six wives had got a pair of waxwork
    twins.
And Wolsey laughed until he cried and said,
    "Upon my word,

It serves you right you Mormon, for giving me the
   bird."
Then Henry started laughing too, till he was out of
   breath,
   And said, "Your Wolsey underwear just tickles me
   to death."
Then Charlie Peace strolled in and said, "I've just
   left Jack the Ripper,
   He's having quite a ripping time a-ripping up a
   kipper.
I'd like to murder someone too, it must be quite
   a time
   Since last I had the pleasure of committing
   of a crime."
His nasty eye then fell on me, my blood began to
   freeze,
   My breath came in short pants and I was shaking at
   the knees.
"It's time that you were dead," said he, "so someone
   fetch a chopper."
   But Joan of Arc then butted in, just like a female
   copper,
She said, "You'll hurt his feelings if you this crime
   commit,
   If you *must* murder someone, murder me, I'm used
   to it!"
But just then Charlie saw my nose, and that made him
   see red,
   With my wife's Christmas pudding then he bangs me
   on the head.
Eight savage blows he struck me on my poor blinkin'
   pate,
   And then I found 'twas day-light, and the clock
   was striking eight.
And when I found 'twas daylight, my courage rose once
   more,
   I punched old Charlie on the nose, and knocked him
   on the floor.
An' then I thought I'd 'ave a drink, an' looked round
   for my beer,
   But there was Crippen pinching it—I kicked 'im in
   the rear.

443

Then them waxworks made a set at me with murder on
    their faces,
  I fought 'em single-handed and I knocked 'em all to
    blazes.
Then I seized Napoleon, he met his Waterloo,
  I hit 'im with my bottle an' broke 'im clean in
    two.
My blood was fairly up an' so I set about those
    dummies,
  I chucked their arms an' legs about an' bashed
    in all their tummies.
What 'appened after that? Well, I don't exactly know,
  I must 'ave been unconscious for about an hour or
    so.
An' then I 'eard the guv'nor say, "To me it's very plain,
  We'll have to give old Bill the sack, 'e's had
    D.T's again!"

WHAT IS A GENTLEMAN?

BY Mrs. W. P. O'DONOGHUE and BOND ANDREWS   *1897*

What is a gentleman? Is it a thing
  Decked with a scarfpin, a chain and a ring?
Dressed in a suit of immaculate style,
  Sporting an eye-glass, a lisp, and a smile?
Talking of operas, concerts, and balls,
  Evening assemblies and afternoon calls?
Sunning himself at "At Homes" and Bazaars—
  Whistling Mazurkas and smoking cigars?
What is a gentleman? Say, is it one
  Boasting of conquests, and deeds he has done?
One who, unblushingly glories to speak
  Things that should call up a flush to his cheek.
One who, while railing at actions unjust,
  Robs some pure heart of its innocent trust.
Scorns to steal money, or jewels, or wealth,

Yet deems it no crime to take honour by stealth!
What is a gentleman? Is it not one
Knowing, instinctively, what he should shun?
Speaking no word that could injure or pain,
Spreading no scandal, and deep'ning no stain.
One who knows how to put each at his ease,
Striving consistently always to please.
One who can tell, by a glance at your cheek,
When to be silent, and when he should speak?
What is a gentleman? Is it not one
Working out all that is rightly begun
Living in uprightness, loving his God,
Leaving no stain on the path he has trod.
Caring not whether his coat may be old,
Prizing sincerity far above gold,
Recking not whether his hand may be hard,
Stretching it boldly to grasp its reward?
What is a gentleman? Say, is it birth
Makes a man noble, or adds to his worth?
Is there a family tree to be had
Shady enough to conceal what is bad?
Show me the man who has God for his guide,
Nothing to blush for and nothing to hide,
Be he a noble, or be he in trade—
He is the gentleman *Nature* has made!

WHAT'S IT FOR

BY MAB DAVIS   *1935*

The world seems crammed full, fit to BUST
With things I mustn't do!
I wonder they don't cage boys up,
Like lions at the Zoo.
And if they DID I shouldn't care,
If I was a lion I'd ROAR,

445

While, as it is, if I just SNIFF!
　　Well, what are noses FOR?
Yesterday I got so mad,
　　I *had* to tease our cat,
I pulled her tail, and made her squawk
　　Right out loud—like THAT!
And then they sent me straight to bed,
　　You bet I slammed the door
Well, anyway, the cat is mine,
　　And what are cat's tails FOR?
They said to me "Now, be quiet, do,
　　While grandpa has his doze,"
I never made a bit of noise,
　　But HE did—with his nose.
So I just splashed some ink at him,
　　To teach him NOT to snore!
So then there was *another* row,
　　Well, what are bald heads FOR?
I had a great big apple,
　　I bought it for a penny,
They said "Give little sister some,
　　Because she hasn't any"
And so I gave her all the pips,
　　The maggots and the core,
And then they said "You greedy boy!"
　　Well, what are sisters FOR?
I'm always asking questions,
　　The sort that start with "WHY?"
I want to know how hens lay eggs
　　And how the birds can fly?
I want to know 'bout 'BABIES'—
　　There's one called "twins" next door,
I b'lieve it's got a head both ends!
　　I wonder what that's FOR?
Oh dear! I dunno what to do—
　　I've scribbled on the wall,
I've been and let the hens all loose,
　　I've made holes in my ball.
I've turned on all the bathroom taps,
　　It's running on the floor,
And everybody's CROSS with me!
　　But—I *dunno* what *FOR!!*

446

WHAT WILL THE CHILD BECOME?

BY HARKER NICHOLLS 1912

The Child!
    What will he become? A serious matter truly
To a father of an only one, and perhaps but not unduly
    To one with children nine to ten, tho' in cases
        such you say,
Bright future's visions loom obscure thro' troubles
        of today.
    In a certain town a wise man dwelt, philosopher
        and sage,
Who told your future, read your past, just then
        Society's rage,
    Phrenology! Psychology! In these fertile fields
        of science—
He wandered plucking golden fruit, and incidentally
        his clients.
    To him went a parent fond, took with him his son.
Laid down a golden fee and said, "What may the child
        become?"
    The man of mystery took the coin, spun it in the
        air—
Bit it, put it in his vest, and motioned to a chair.
    He wandered round that youngster's head, paused on
        a monstrous bump
The father softly murmured—"The fender made that
        lump."
    The wise man frowned made no reply, but started off
        anew,
Till a piping voice said, "Daddy, must I have hair
        drill too?"
    At last the sage was satisfied and in manner most
        concise,
He took the parent on one side and gave him this advice:—
    "When even's sun is setting low, an hour before the
        gloom,
Place a bible and a sovereign and an apple in a room.
    Thither lead the child and leave him for an hour,

447

To see which potent agent has proved of greater power.
    For if he eat the apple it is a certain sign,
That comforts close at hand form his especial line.
    'Midst Nature's fruits he should be placed, coal,
        iron, corn or such.
As miller, miner, farmer, smith he may accomplish much.
    Should he read the bible, a scholar he should be.
Writer, teacher, poet, preacher, or Professor like
        me!
    But should he grasp the sovereign—beware, my friend
        for then—
He holds for weal or woe the power to rule his fellowmen.
    Financier or banker, buyer, seller he may be,
Or money-lender, with interest running to Eternity.
    For each can be of evil use—the sovereign most of
        all.
The Bible can be misapplied, and the apple caused our
        fall.
    Homeward went the parent—in the room he placed the
        youth
With a sovereign and an apple and the Book that stands
        for Truth.
    And in an hour that simple child, when father took
        a look—
Had eaten the apple, pocketed the gold and was sitting
        on the Book.
    And as the parent stood amazed, out spoke this precious
        kid.—
"I'd like another apple pa, also another quid!"'
    The child—What did he become? How fared this noble
        youth?
Who was filled with greed and avarice, and who sat
        upon the truth.
    The world alas! holds out rewards for such you must
        allow,
What did the child become?
    Well—he's a POOR-LAW GUARDIAN—now!

WHEELS

BY J. HARRINGTON WEEKS and HAROLD ARPTHORP   1926

All the world's a wheel!
And all the people in it always wheels.
They have their punctures and their pleasant times.
And in this life the wheel plays many parts.
There's first the infant riding in his pram
    With nurse attached, the pretty little lamb,
With joy he chortles or with temper squeals—
    On Wheels.
And then a child of six, a budding "sport!"
    His little scooter is his only thought;
He flies along—the utmost pleasure feels
    On Wheels.
When ten, or there-abouts he thinks it great,
    Upon one foot to fix a roller skate,
No other joy to him so much appeals—
    As Wheels.
Then pa buys him one of the best of bikes
    On it he goes—most anywhere he likes
And school he'll dodge—neglected are his meals
    For Wheels.
And then his motorbike with neat side-car next,
    It takes him swiftly, near and far,
With pretty flappers happy hours he steals,
    On Wheels.
Then a real car,—a bus that fast he drives,
    And poor pedestrians scared out of their lives,
Ducks, dogs and porkers take madly to their heels,—
    Some Wheels!
Perhaps he crashes in that self-same car
    And lying prone he sees, aye, many a star.
The ambulance arrives and with him deals,—
    More Wheels!
Years roll along, and grey-haired now is he;
    Gouty, and grown devoid of energy,
In bath-chair sat his form a rug conceals,
    Still Wheels.

A solemn silence falls, he sleeps that last long sleep,
    And round his bier the shadows creep,
Thro' the stilled air the sound of church bells steals,
    And to his rest he goes,
On Wheels.

WHEN I'M CROSS

BY MAB DAVIS   *1934*

My mother says when I am cross
    As I *am* now and then,
It's better not to talk at all,
    But count inside, to ten.
'Cos, if you do it slowly
    Just like this: ONE, TWO, THREE, FOUR!
By the time you've finished,
    You're not angry anymore!
It sounds all right, but then somehow,
    It doesn't work with me,
And when I've counted up to ten
    I'm CROSS as I can be.
And so I've found another way,
    I whisper very low,
And so that no one else can hear
    The RUDEST words I know:
Bother, bloomin', hang and drat,
    Female, blazes, beast and cat.
Golly, blinkin', pig and mug,
    Spit and stomach, bosh and slug.
When I've said all these I find
    I can feel quite good and kind.
Aunt Jane comes to stay with us,
    She's awfully tall and thin.
She always makes me very cross,
    As soon as she comes in.
Because she says "Now DON'T do that"

And "DON'T make such a noise"
She says, "Be seen and never heard's
     The rule for little boys."
She tells me not to slam the door,
     And not to tease the cat,
And "DON'T speak with your mouth full, child"
     And silly things like that.
I often feel I'd like to throw
     An inkpot at her head.
But then I'd get in such a row,
     And so I say instead: —
Bother, bloomin', hang and drat,
     Female, blazes, beast and cat,
Golly, blinkin', pig and mug,
     Spit and stomach, bosh and slug,
Then I say it all again,
     Out loud I say "Yes, Aunt Jane."
I know you won't believe it,
     But I've SEEN it, — and it's REAL!
My Mummy's bought a baby girl
     Imagine how I feel.
It's not a nice one, either,
     'Cos it's ugly, and it's bald.
It's not the leastest bit of good,
     It won't come when it's called.
If she'd only bought a puppy
     Well, that wouldn't be half bad!
But to go and waste her pennies
     On a BABY—makes me mad!
When I first heard about it
     I hid down in the shed
At the bottom of the garden,
     And right out loud I said: —
Bother, bloomin', hang and drat,
     Female, blazes, beast and cat,
Golly, blinkin', pig and mug,
     Spit and stomach, bosh and slug."
I said another one as well,
     I'd better spell this: H E L !

WHEN THE ROAD'S (H)UP IT'S (H)UP

BY ERNEST LONGSTAFFE   1926

Where ever there's a busy spot you'll find me,
   A-working in the middle of the street,
With traffic all around me and behind me.
   I marks a spot, then rails it nice and neat;
But first I lights a fire an' gets it glowin'
   To warm meself, an' cook a bit o' grub.
Then builds a hut for shelter when it's blowin',
   That's situated 'andy for the pub.
I digs an 'ole that goes down to Australia,
   Then mixes pints of earth with quarts of slops.
To try an' move me on would be failure,
   For 'ere I am, an' when I'm 'ere, I stops.
When the road's H'up, it's H'up;
   And the reason doesn't bother me:
True, the taxi-drivers swear,
   While policemen tear their 'air,
An' ask 'ow long I think I'm goin' to be?
   But *I* don't know, and *YOU* don't know:
So I ain't agoin' to tax me brain:
   For it's ten to one,
When the job is done,
   It'll all come up again (not arf)
It'll all come up again.
   I'd often longed to 'ave a bit of money
To rent a plot for cabbages and beans:
   With p'r'aps a hive of bees to give me 'oney,
Though never seemed to 'ave the private means.
   But *THESE* 'ere H'ope rations is H'extensive,
That means I'll h'occupy this spot for life,
   I think I'll make a will (though it's h'expensive)
An' see if I can leave it to the wife.
   I'm goin' to 'ave the wireless h'installated,
That's if I find I 'ear it thro' the din,
   Then in me leisure I'll get eddicated,
So don't disturb me when I'm list'ning in.
   When the road's H'up, it's H'up;

An' I'm goin' to live me life in peace.
When we've finished with the drains, There's
the gas an' water mains:
So it's just the same as 'avin' it on lease.
For *I* don't know, an' *YOU* don't know,
But the answer's pat an' plain,
That it's ten to one
If the job *GETS* done,
It'll *all* come H'up again, (Trust ME)
It'll *all* come H'up again.

WHEN YOU FIGGER IT OUT !

BY R. R. PECORINI and F. HARPER-SHOVE   *1921*

I do 'ave a time when you figger it out,
A-pushin' dead leaves and a-muckin' about
In the gutters and streets. Yus there isn't much
doubt,
I do 'ave a time when you figger it out.
I remember the days long ago when in luck,
There wasn't much need to be pushin' o' muck,
I didn't wear fusty old corduroy breeks,
An' I'd got some good colour in these poor
old cheeks.
I was straight, I was tall, an' I 'adn't a care,
An' I took such a pride in the clothes that
I'd wear.
Eh! many's the time why I'd shave ev'ry day,
And grease me old forelock the fash'nable way.
I'd put on swell duds, an' set out for the park,
A-bent on a-sparkin' by way of a lark.
I was "*IT*" I can tell you! Gals loved me some-how:
But lumme! who loves sich a poor old cuss now?
I married. Why, blow me! I'd nearly forgot,
It seems as 'twere back somewhere round the
year dot.

453

She's gone now, God bless her, she left me a boy.
　A cute little beggar, a bundle of joy.
He loved his old dad, too, Ah! bless him! 'Tis true:—
　You knows 'ow *your* boy thinks the world about you!
But he's gone too—My 'Arry, a-missin' they said,
　Then a-bout a year after, "Reported as dead."
Aye! he died, did my boy, an' he couldn't be found
　Tho' his mates, so they told me, searched all around
On the field where 'e fell when they made the attack.
　But one day they found 'im and carried 'im back.
Yus! He's up at the Abbey, and the great folk they say,
　Kneel and mourn for my 'ero while I work my way
Through the muck and the litter! They call 'im "Un-known,"
　But God let *me* know him—My 'Arry! My own!
I made my way up there a-dressed in my best,
　Just to see where my boy's been alaid out to rest,
An' it seems kind of helpin' me on with my job,
　Abrushin' an' pushin' to earn a few bob.
I do 'ave a time when you figger it out
　A-pushin' dead leaves and a-muckin' about
In the gutters and streets. Yus there isn't much doubt,
　I've 'ad a time when you figger it out.

THE WHITEST MAN I KNOW

BY J. MILTON HAYES and R. FENTON GOWER 　　　　*1914*

He's a'-cruisin' in a pearler with a dirty nigger
　　crew,
　A' buyin' pearls and copra for a stingy
　　Spanish Jew,
And his face is tann'd like leather 'neath a
　　blazin' tropic Sun,
　And he's workin' out a penance for the things
　　he hasn't done.
Round the Solomons he runs, tradin' beads and
　　cast-off guns,

Buyin' pearls from grinnin' niggers, loadin'
    copra by the ton;
And he'll bargain and he'll smile, but he's thinkin'
    all the while
    Of the penance that he's workin' out for sins
    he hasn't done.
We'd been round the Horn together, and I'd come to
    know his worth;
    The greatest friend I'd ever had, the whitest
    man on earth.
He'd pull'd me out of many a scrape, he'd risk'd
    his life for me,
    And side by side, for many a year, we'd rough'd
    it on the sea;
But a woman came between us; she was beautiful as
    Venus,
    And she set her cap at him until she hook'd
    him unawares:
And I sailed off on my own
    Leavin' him and her alone:
Sign'd aboard a tramp for 'Frisco, leavin' them in
    Bu'nos Ayres.
    When I met him in a twelvemonth he was goin'
    to the deuce,
For she's blacken'd all the good in him, she'd play'd
    him fast and loose,
    And she'd gone off with a Dago who was lettin'
    dollars fly,
And she'd left my mate to drink his precious soul
    away and die.
    Well, I talk'd and talk'd him over, and we
    sign'd aboard "The Rover."
It was just like good old times, until we shor'd at
    Rio Bay;
    Then the hand of Fate show'd pain—brought us
    face to face again
With the woman, and the Dago who had taken her away.
    We were sittin' in a cafe when the couple came
    along,
She simply smil'd and pass'd us by, then vanish'd
    in the throng.

My mate jump'd up to follow, but I wouldn't
    let him stir,
And later on a waiter brought a note that came from her:
    She pretended she regretted
What she'd done, and that she fretted
    For the wrong that she had done him, and she
        wanted to a-tone;
There was so much to explain,
    Would he meet her once again?
After midnight, in her garden—she would watch for him,
    alone.
    'Course he went, but unbeknown to him I
        follow'd on behind.
I watch'd, and saw the shadows of two figures on
    the blind—
    The woman—and the Dago—and I heard the Dago
        shout,
They quarrell'd, and the woman scream'd—and then a
    shot rang out.
    My mate dash'd thro' the curtain—
And I follow'd, makin' certain
    That my little gun was ready—case I had to
        make a stand:
There I saw the Dago—dead,
    With a bullet thro' his head,
And the woman standin' near him with a shooter in
    her hand.
    Before the Civil Guard came in my mate had
        snatch'd her gun,
And he ask'd them to arrest *him* for the *thing*
    he hadn't done.
    I tried madly to explain things, but they
        shook their heads at me,
And the woman let them take him, so that she might
    get off free.
    In the court I sat and heard her
Tell them all *he'd done the murder,*
    And I pray'd she might be stricken into some
        ungodly shape,
He was sentenc'd for his life—
    But out there corruption's rife,

456

And I brib'd and brib'd, until at last I manag'd his
    escape.
  Then I stow'd him on a hooker sailin' far from
    woman's wiles,
And he's workin' his salvation out amongst the
    South Sea Isles;
  And the woman's there at Rio, and she's weavin
    of her spell,
With a crowd of fools awaitin' her commands to burn
    in hell;
  Whilst the whitest man I know
Runs a Christy minstrel show,
  Buyin' pearls from dirty niggers—'neath a
    blazin tropic sun,
And he'll cuss 'em, and he'll smile—
  But he's thinkin' all the while—
Of the penance that he's workin' out for things he
    hasn't done.

WHY ?

BY MARGUERITE PARROT and HERBERTE JORDAN   *1929*

There's lot and lots of things I'd like to know
    about, and why,
  If I ask Nannie, she says "Mike, you'll know
    dear, by and by."
And Mummy, tho' I've always told her there's lots
    I want to know,
  Says "Yes dear, when you're older," or
    "Do not worry so."
If only they would just explain why night is dark
    not light,
  Why flow'rs come up, not down like rain, and
    why do puppies bite
And why my wooden soldier is wobbley 'stead of firm,
  And why I am a little boy, and not a wriggly
    worm.

But wait I've thought of someone else, I'm sure will
    soon explain,
So now I must know what I will do, I'll just
    fly back again
To heaven, on the great big stork who brought me
    on his wing,
And ask God, in a little talk, 'cos *HE*
    knows everything.

WILD BILL DRIVES THE STAGE

BY RIDGWELL CALLUM and CUTHBERT CLARKE   *1918*

Performed by Bransby Williams

It was Bill that bossed the outfit, and Job's Flat
    knew its man.
He'd throw a bluff, and back it, as only a live
    man can.
He was chock-full of hell inside, and as mean as a
    she coyote
For the feller who'd hurt a hoss, or a dog,
    or a kid, or a woman's repute
He'd "straddled" the fill of a jackpot when the
    news reached Minkey's Saloon
That a gang had held up the gold stage that
    very afternoon.
They'd robbed it for thousands of dollars in dust,
    the work of a week,
The keep of the women and kiddies and the boys
    of Suffering Creek.
He was raging mad as he pitched down his hand and
    quit the table dead,
But he gave no sign of the thoughts he had
    lying aback of his head,
Till the day came along when he handed it out,
    chalked on a slab of wood—
    "You can tote your dust on the stage today,
        Wild Bill's standing Good."

But even then there was none of 'em guessed the
    things about to begin,
    Till ten thousand dollars of horseflesh swept
        round from the barn—then their grin
Changed like a streak of lightning and the "hooch"
    drained out of their brains,
    For Bill was hunched in the teamster's seat,
        clawing the bunch of reins.
His eyes never quit those horses, and it made you
    wonder—well—
    He looked like an evil image on the trail of
        a red-hot hell.
He'd a halo of guns round his middle, and his eyes
    froze you through to the bone
    P'r'aps he was reck'ning the game out—the
        game he'd to play alone.
With careless jest they loaded the chest,
    Bill passed his horses the word,
They leapt at their bits, stark mad for the run,
    Their prairie blood full-stirred.
Across the flat to the hills beyond where the pine-trees
    rake the sky
    Bill raced his team with a master hand at a
        pace you'd hate to try.
Far in the hills the hold-up gang were waiting their
    golden haul—
    With merciless guns and coward hearts,
        blood-steeped beyond recall.
On came the thunder of racing hoofs—and each man
    held his breath—
    As Bill flung his team with fearless grip deep
        in the jaws of death.
Swift as a flash the scene was changed by a rain of
    speeding lead,
    The leaders swerved from the broken trail,
        and the "wheelers" pulled up dead.
Astride of the chest that held the gold of the folk
    he'd sworn to serve,
    Cold as a 'berg from a Polar flow Bill crouched
        with an iron nerve.
He hadn't a care for chances, tho' the odds were one to eight;

He was drunk with the scent of battle and the
    fire of a deadly hate.
A hail of lead swept down on the head of the man
    whose law was the gun.
His flesh was ripped and his lifeblood dripped
    as he shot 'em *one by one.*
The vicious yap of his barking guns ne'er ceased
    from their screech for blood
Till five stark bodies had yielded life there
    on the crimsoning mud.
Shot up in twenty places, bleeding and broken in limb,
    Hunched like a crouching panther, savage and
    ready to spring.
Like the swirl of a raging blizzard the bullets round
    him sang
Till he'd sent the last to his reckoning: the
    last of the hold-up gang.
He raised a hand to bloodblind eyes, and smeared
    'em clear with his sleeve,
His brain lived on while his body drained—
    holed like a human sieve.
Out of the silence there came a sound like the sigh
    of a soul that's lost;
A shuffle of desperate movement, with its tale
    of the awful cost;
Of a victory well and truly won, of a cruel wrong
    set right,
A half-dead thing, Bill clutched his seat—
    even with Death he'd fight.
With shaking hands he blindly groped in the box
    beneath his feet,
He sought a rawhide picket rope and lashed him
    to his seat.
The reins made fast to bloodstained wrists "By God!
    my hands shan't fail
To drive you home, my beauties." Again he hits
    the trail.
The miles flew by under speeding hoofs of a team
    that asks no rest.
The man they knew was behind them, helpless,
    and needing their best.

He lolled about—a broken thing—scarce life in his
    ghastly face
For Death was sitting beside him, and Death
    was making the pace.
The shades of night in the City were lit by the
    twinkling stars
The lamps on the wooded side-walks and the
    garish light of the bars.
When out of the far off distance came the rattle
    of speeding wheels
And the ghostly race of a team nigh spent,
    with terror lashing their heels.
Jolting and swaying behind them came the stage from
    Suffering Creak;
Pitched like a storm-tossed vessel it flashed
    thro' the town like a streak.
On to the barn beside the bank—how well they knew
    that place—
Right to the door—not a yard beyond—Bill's
    horses finished the race.
The boys rushed out with lanterns, and found Bill
    there in the seat
Held by the rawhide picket rope, the gold
    chest safe at his feet.
He'd fought his fight to a finish, No matter tho'
    riddled with lead,
He'd pledg'd his word—he'd kept it—
He'd driven for three hours *dead!*

THE WINDING LANE

BY BASIL HOWARD and GEOFFREY HENMAN   *1921*

Of all the walks that a child can go,
    A winding lane is the best you know,
For you always wonder what can be
    Round the end of the bend where you cannot see.

A dragon's cave or a fairy sprite?
  Or the shooting star that fell last night?
Or the snug little shop with the Dock-Leaf Porch
  Where the glow-worm buys his electric torch?
For things like this may always be
  Round the end of the bend—where you cannot see.
And when you're grown up, as a baby will,
  Oh the winding lane is winding still.
And you're still on pins as to what may be
  Round the end of the bend, where you cannot see.
Oh it may be wealth, and it may be fame,
  Or a stroke of luck—or a flush of shame.
And you round the bend with an eager thrill,
  And the windling lane keeps winding still!
And still you wonder what will be
  Round the end of the bend, where you cannot see.
Oh the winding lane is a weary grind,
  When you don't much care what it is you find—
But idly wonder what will be
  Round the end of the bend where you cannot see.
But the winding lane would wind no more,
  Could I find the thing that I'm looking for,
Which is parted lips—and eyes that shine,
  And a wee soft hand that is warm in mine!
So, perhaps one evening Love may be
  Round the end of the bend—
And then we'll see!

WISHES

BY H. M. BURNABY and HARRY STOGDEN   *1953*

Wishes!—Remember when you was a kid—
  And the things wot you wished you could be?
Like a swank engine driver—a Soldier—a Cop
  Or a Sailor—or p'r'haps a M.P.?
Dreams of yer childhood wot didn't come orf—

Wishes wot faded away.
Makes yer fink all them castles you built in the air
    Yerss! and look where they've got yer today.
If a kid dreams of flyin' a 'Plane,
    You can bet 'e's a coalminer when 'e's a man
Let him wish 'e's an actor—a film star—a spiv—
    'E'll be drivin' a vegetable van
Yerss! it all goes to show you can wish wot yer like
    If you don't let it go to your 'ead
Look at me! used to wish I was 'Enery the Eighth—
    Now I'm scared of me missus—instead!
And yet I recall—looking back, years ago
    There's me Mum, got me dahn in a chair
While she's pullin' and luggin' a comb through my
        locks—
    And me wishin' I 'adn't got 'air.
Cor! The times as I wished I'd got no 'air to lug—
    Now all I've got left is a few!
And I reckon one day, when I looks in the glass
    I shall find that me wish 'as come true.

WORDS

BY WARREN HASTINGS and HERBERTE JORDAN

The noonday sun was blazing with a grimly gruelling
        glare,
    The arid earth lay scorching in the torpid,
        torrid air.
When, seeking refuge from the heat, a haven I espied,
    And entered through the doorway to the cooling
        shades inside.
A lady there, with golden hair, a proud and haughty
        miss,
    Cried, "What Might You Be Wanting?" I
        answered her like this—
"My paramount ambition at the moment I confess,

Is to mitigate the craving, and ameliorate the
   stress.
Of symptoms hygroscopic that decidedly require,
   A nectarous libation to alleviate desire.
With amber-tinted body, and effervescent head,
   A perfect combination when all is done and
       said,
A modicum of beverage derived from hops and grain,
   To fortify the spirit, and stimulate the brain.
To flog the flagging faculties, and rapidly restore
   The enervated energies to function as before.
To titillate the tonsils with ambrosial delight,
   And treat the parching palate to a measure of
       respite.
In ultimate addition may I beg to specify
   A crystalline container pellucid to the eye.
But should this fail to make my meaning clear,
   to be concise—I WANT A GLASS OF BEER!"

WORK

BY MILTON HAYES and CUTHBERT CLARKE   *1920*

Everyone has work to do;
   Each one's task to each is known.
One may toil to till the soil
   Or carve a statue out of stone;
Each must follow his vocation,
   Working out his own salvation.
There's a task for me and you,
   And there's always work to do.
Everyone has work to do,
   Making bricks or writing plays;
You and I may each espy
   Some treasure veiled from others' gaze;
Speak the latent thought you cherish,
   Lest it fade away and perish;

Bring out all your best to view—
    That's the work you've got to do.
Everyone has work to do;
    Life is like a darkened room:
Yours the right to find the light,
    To shed its beams where now is gloom.
Genius in many cases
    Springs up in unlikely places;
Ever seeking treasures new,
    There is always work to do.
You and I have work to do!
    Do it now and do it here;
Learn to mould the thought you hold,
    And overcome the bonds of fear.
Wisdom—will—and understanding
    Fly to those who are demanding—
Happiness is there for you,
    Hidden in the work you do.

WOT VUR DO 'EE LUV OI?

BY ALBERT CHEVALIER and ALFRED H. WEST   *1905*

O'ive got a sweet'eart now Oi 'ave
    She be in love wi Oi,
Thought Oi should never 'ave the pluck
    Oi be that mortal shoy!
'Ay makin down at Varmer Giles
    Oi comes along side she,
An' Oi sez, to er Oi sez, sez Oi
    Wot's oop wi' you an' me?
Oi sez "Meg," Oi sez "Oi luv 'ee,"
    She sez "Garge Oi luv 'ee too!"
She sez "Wot vur do 'ee luv Oi?"
    Oi sez "Wot vur?—coz Oi *do!*"
Us walks vur moiles, an' moiles, an' moiles,
    She'll let Oi take a "buss"—

Soomtoimes she'll gi' Oi one as well,
    But Lard! she makes a fuss!
Us sets vur hours a 'oldin' 'ands,
    An' when'er gives a soigh,
Oi knows its toime to talk, and so
    Oi sez to 'er sez Oi:
Oi sez "Meg," Oi sez "Oi luv 'ee,"
    She sez "Garge Oi luv 'ee too!"
She sez "Wot vur do 'ee luv Oi?"
    Oi sez "Wot vur?—coz Oi *do!*"
Folks laugh at we, but us don't care!
    Sez Oi Oi'll tell 'ee wot,
"Us be in luv, sez Oi, us be,
    An' pities them that's not!
Don't take no notice—don' 'ee moind—"
    Oi tells 'er on the sloy.
"We'll make un jealous; then Oi sez
    To 'er, Oi sez, sez Oi;
Oi sez "Meg," Oi sez "Oi luv 'ee,"
    She sez "Garge Oi luv 'ee too!"
She sez "Wot vur do 'ee luv Oi?"
    Oi sez "Wot vur?—coz Oi *do!*"

THE WRECK OF THE "WHAT'S HER NAME"

BY RONALD BAGNALL and DENHAM HARRISON   1912

A little Recitation, Ladies and Gentlemen, which used to be inflicted on us by an old sea Captain during the winter evenings in the bar parlour of the "Dab and Flounder," Lobster-on-the-Lob.

It was all about the wreck of a ship but he had forgotten the name of the boat so he called it "The Wreck of the What's-'er-name" and after one or two *"what's-er-names,"* this is how the old gentleman muddled it up.

'Twas in '48 on a winter's night, on a broiling
    summer day,

The *What's-'er-name* sailed from port with
   a cargo of sherry and hay!
She'd seventy souls aboard 'er, dishonest, brave and
      true,
   But ninety of that seventy-five were nigh in
      Timbuctoo.
The crew it numbered sixty-eight, the Captain several
      more,
   The stokers numbered twenty-two and the brokers
      numbered four.
The first mate totalled thirty-one, the women numbered
      three
   The children sixty-five all told and the rest
      had passage free.
Gratis nothing free my lads Nothing, gratis, free.
   We'd been at sea for a year or more or nearly
      a month at sea.
Three days are long to feed a ship, when they all
      have passage frcc!
   'Twas a foggy night and the stars shone bright,
      while the watch kept a bad look-out.
When all at once and after a bit and all of a sudden
      a shout!!
   "Brokers ahead! d'ye hear the cry?" We all
      got on our stumps.
And thro' the fog we 'eard the Captain cry "What ho—
      she *does roll!*
   All hands on deck to clear the wreck, the
      wrecky deck to clear."
The men they called for smelling-salts, the women
      shrieked for beer!
   Good old glorious beer my lads, not arf,
      four alf beer!
'Twas a beautiful sight to 'ear 'em as they shivered
      in the heat
   To see the tramp of 'eavy 'ands the despairing
      clasp of feet.
Three cheers for the gallant Captain rang from a
      million throats
   The men they mann'd the lifebuoys, and the
      women mann'd the boats.

We sent up signal rockets as they fell upon the rocks.
   You might a' been at the Palace on a Thursday
         watching Brocks!
The Captain, brave and trembling was a block of the
         good old chip.
   He cross'd the bridge at midnight and was
         first to leave the ship.
A block of the old chip my lads, the first to leave
         the ship.
   The cabin-boy then took command to boss he
         was athirst.
"Women and children stand back there and let the
         men go first."
   The men poor frightened creatures soon were
         huddled in the boats.
While women filled by force their over-coats with
         Quaker oats.
   Ah! see there looming just ahead, astern, now
         what is that?
A snail! A sail! A ship to save? No only a matinee hat!
   "Just hand me a savage Woodbine", said a lady
         with a sigh.
The cabin boy he eyed his pipe and then he piped his eye.
   Eyed his meersham pipe m' lads and merely
         piped his eye.
Again another ship comes by, "Hullo there! Who are
         you?"
   "We're the *"What's-'er-name* and we're
         going down and you?" "We're
         the *Dunno-who!"*
The *Dunno-who* threw the *What's-'er-name* a
         yard of two-inch cord,
   And by a wireless aeroplane the Captain came aboard.
"Saved at last!" with a moan of joy they embraced
         the Captain bold.
   He blush'd a Labour Leader's blush and called
         for something cold.
And I talking of something *wet* sir? Well I think
         I'll have the same.
Did you ask me what I'll 'ave sir? I'll 'ave—well a
         "what's-er-name."

THE YANKEE IN LONDON

BY ALBERT CHEVALIER   *1900*

I've just arrived from New York, and I'm real glad
    that I came.
  This city's out of sight! Yes sir! It's worthy
    of its fame.
I've visited Chicago, Paris, Berlin, Cairo, Rome.
  But here I somehow kind of, sort of, feel that
    I'm at home.
America just owns the sun—you get it here in bits.
  We loan it—we're not selfish, we have more than
    we require,
Besides our hearts are warm enough to generate a fire.
  We're quicker on the other side, we can't
    afford to wait.
We always like to get in first, you bet, we're
    seldom late.
  There is, I know, some difference in
    Transatlantic time,
That may not p'r'aps explain it, but it helps me
    with a rhyme.
  Your busses and your cabs strike us Americans
    as slow.
Your theatres are O.K. when New York supplies the show.
  You can't say we're remiss, no sir, we send
    you of the best,
Why in your aristocracy we've been known to invest.
  We've many points in common with our cousins
    over here.
We come of good old stock, our sires were men who
    knew no fear.
  We may at times run England down, I'm sorry,
    but I know
That relatives will squabble, it's there priv'lege,
    that is so.
  The only real difference so far as I can see,
Is the language that you speak, which is not pure
    enough for me.

You have a horrid accent, you should hustle
    round and *git*
A genu*ine* New Yorker just to tone it down a bit
Great country sir, America, my own, I'm proud
    to state
And Britain is its 'mommer', so Great Britain's
    vurry great!

YOUNG 'ARRY

BY JOHN E. NESTER and CUTHBERT CLARKE   *1914*

This monologue should be rendered as a character study, and in working coster make up—Jacket suit, pockets to contain the following articles:- a broken clay pipe, empty "woodbine" packet, damaged watch, and on a table or box, a damaged bowler hat, and a cheap enlargement of a photo of a typical coster kid.

The various articles to be produced as mentioned in the course of the recital, which should be rendered in a semi-jocular manner emphasising the line "'E is a KID, no kid" more each time it occurs.

Produce the photo at the proper place and comment upon it so as to get the full effect of the paternal pride intended to be shown.

Now I wonder where that kid 'as gone, up to 'is games
    I s'pose
    A-sloshin' o' the other kids, and a-spoilin'
        of 'is clothes.
Lummy 'e's a "woolled 'un," o' that there's no
        mistake,
    An' at gettin' into mischief, 'e fairly takes
        the cake,
But 'is muvver thinks 'e can't do wrong, I'm not so
        sure o' that,

Well I'm blowed, I told yer so. 'E's done in
    my new 'at!!
'E is a *KID, no kid.*
    'E don't arf play some larks wiv me an' my
      old dutch,
Enough to send yer off yer dot, but o' course don't
    'urt yer much,
    An' arter yer gits over it, an' 'e's safely
      in 'is kip,
We soon fergits 'is 'ankin', an' as 'ow we 'ad the pip,
    But 'is muvver thinks 'e can't do wrong, an'
      when I gits the knock,
She says, "'E ain't done nothink, mate Why!!! 'E's
    busted up the clock!"
    'E is a *KID, no kid.*
You'd larf ter see 'im out wiv us, on Sunday, for a
    ride,
    Talk about the Lord Mayor's show!! 'E don't
      arf put on side,
An' the old moke seems to know as 'ow 'e's 'oldin'
    of the reins,
    An' pretens as 'e's a kerridge 'orse; the old
      'un's got some brains.
An' when we pulls up fer a drink, 'is 'Nibs' sits
    like a flunkey,
    A-foldin' of 'is arms like this, 'o 'e is a
      artful monkey.
But 'is muvver thinks 'e can't do wrong, acourse 'e's
    only six,
    Why, 'e's bin an' pinched me Woodbines now, an'
      left me 'ere wi' nix,
'E is a *KID no kid.*
    'E's only started school a week, an' talk about
      a 'ead:
'E asks 'is teacher questions wot makes 'er turn all
    red,
    An' when I counts me money up, 'e says as 'ow
      I'm wrong
At wot 'e calls arifmertick, my word 'e's going strong.
    'E starts ter tell 'is grannie off, wants me
      to sell the moke,

An' go in for a aireyplane!! Lor lummy, I'd be broke.
   Still 'is muvver vows 'e can't do wrong, I'm
      not so sure about it,
Where's me pipe? 'E's done that in, I'll 'ave ter do
      wivout it.
   'E is a *KID. no kid.*
But 'e's our only kid, well,—up to now, an' we
      sometimes wonders
   Wot we'd do if 'e was took, cos we nigh on
      lost 'im once,
When fever copped 'im, I thought the missus's 'eart
      'ud break,
   But she pulled 'im thro', an' now, if any time
      we 'as a shine,
Wot yer must 'ave, now an' then, to let yer know yer
      on the earth,
   She says to me, she says, "Now mate, wot's yer
      grousin' worth?"
An' then 'is Nibs chips in, an' straight, 'e pulls
      me round
   Like winkin', there's no denyin' 'im an' 'e
      knows it too,
And 'is muvver swears 'e can't do wrong,
   "Boys will be boys," o' course,
An' so I 'as ter give in to 'em,
   An' admire 'im for 'is sauce.
Lummy! 'E's a knock-out, 'e's a nugget, 'e's a lad,
      'ere's 'is . . . .
   Now don't 'e look a nut? Yuss, an' I'm 'is
      DAD!! *And 'e is a KID, no kid.*

INDEX OF FIRST LINES

473

476

479